D0934896

RENEGOTIATING COMMUNITY

Other volumes planned in the Globalization and Autonomy series:

Global Ordering: Institutions and Autonomy in a Changing World
Edited by Louis W. Pauly and William D. Coleman (2008)

Empires and Autonomy: Moments in the History of Globalization
Edited by Stephen Streeter, John C. Weaver, and William D. Coleman

Unsettled Legitimacy: Political Community, Power, and Authority in a Global Era
Edited by Steven F. Bernstein and William D. Coleman

Property Rights: Struggles over Autonomy in a Global Age
Edited by William D. Coleman and John C. Weaver

Deux Méditerranées: Les voies de la mondialisation et de l'autonomie
Edited by Yassine Essid and William D. Coleman

Indigenous Peoples and Autonomy: Insights for a Global Age
Edited by Mario E. Blaser, Ravindra de Costa, Deborah McGregor, and William D. Coleman

Cultural Autonomy: Frictions and Connections
Edited by Petra Rethmann, Imre Szeman, and William D. Coleman

Globalization and Autonomy: Conversing across Disciplines
Diana Brydon, William D. Coleman, Louis W. Pauly, and John C. Weaver

See also the *Globalization and Autonomy Online Compendium* at www.globalautonomy.ca.

 globalization + autonomy

RENEGOTIATING

Interdisciplinary Perspectives, Global Contexts

COMMUNITY

Edited by Diana Brydon and William D. Coleman

UBCPress · Vancouver · Toronto

17 16 15 14 13 12 11 10 09 08   5 4 3 2 1

Printed in Canada on ancient-forest-free paper (100% post-consumer recycled) that is processed chlorine- and acid-free, with vegetable-based inks.

Library and Archives Canada Cataloguing in Publication

Renegotiating community: interdisciplinary perspectives, global contexts / edited by Diana Brydon and William D. Coleman.

(Globalization and autonomy, ISSN 1913-7494)
Includes bibliographical references and index.
ISBN 978-0-7748-1506-2

1. Communities. 2. Globalization—Social aspects. 3. Autonomy. 4. Transnationalism. 5. Group identity. I. Brydon, Diana II. Coleman, William D. (William Donald), 1950- III. Series.

JZ1318.R46 2008   303.48'2   C2008-901771-4

Canadä

UBC Press gratefully acknowledges the financial support for our publishing program of the Government of Canada through the Book Publishing Industry Development Program (BPIDP), and of the Canada Council for the Arts, and the British Columbia Arts Council.

This book has been published with the help of a grant from the Canadian Federation for the Humanities and Social Sciences, through the Aid to Scholarly Publications Programme, using funds provided by the Social Sciences and Humanities Research Council of Canada. Research for the volume was supported by the Social Sciences and Humanities Research Council of Canada through its Major Collaborative Research Initiatives Program, Grant No. 412-2001-1000.

UBC Press
The University of British Columbia
2029 West Mall
Vancouver, BC V6T 1Z2
604-822-5959 / Fax: 604-822-6083
www.ubcpress.ca

Contents

Preface

The Globalization and Autonomy Series: Dialectical Relationships in the Contemporary World

THE VOLUMES IN THE Globalization and Autonomy series offer the results from an interdisciplinary Major Collaborative Research Initiative (MCRI) funded by the Social Sciences and Humanities Research Council of Canada (SSHRC). SSHRC set up the MCRI program to provide a vehicle to support larger projects with research objectives requiring collaboration among researchers from different universities and across a range of disciplines. The MCRI on Globalization and Autonomy began in April 2002. The research team involved forty co-investigators from twelve universities across Canada and another twenty academic contributors from outside Canada, including scholars from Australia, Brazil, China, Denmark, France, Germany, Slovenia, Taiwan, the United Kingdom, and the United States. Drawing on additional funding from the International Development Research Centre (IDRC), the project became affiliated with a separate interdisciplinary research team of twenty-eight scholars, the Groupe d'Études et de Recherches Interdisciplinaires sur la Méditerranée (GERIM). GERIM is based in Tunisia and includes members from France, Spain, Jordan, and Lebanon as well. Scholars from the following disciplines participated in the project: anthropology, comparative literature, cultural studies, economics, English literature, geography, history, music, philosophy, political science, and sociology.

The project was conceived, designed, and implemented to carry out interdisciplinary research. We endeavoured to put disciplinary-based theories and conceptual frameworks into dialogue with one another, with a view to developing new theories and understandings of human societies. Four conditions needed to be met if research were to be done in this way. First, we brought humanities and social science disciplines into a relationship of mutual influence, where perspectives were integrated without subordinating one to another. To achieve this integration, the team agreed on a set of core research objectives informed by existing writings on globalization and autonomy. Members developed a number of research questions designed to address these objectives, and a research plan that would permit them to address these questions in a focused, systematic way. Second, team members individually were encouraged to think inside disciplines other than their own and to respect differences across disciplines in terms of how the object of knowledge is constructed. Third, team members were selected to ensure that the research was carried out using multiple methodologies. Finally, faced with researching the complex relationships involved in globalization, an interdisciplinary approach meant that our work would be necessarily pluri-theoretical. We held to the view that theories would be most effective when, in addition to applying ideas rigorously, their proponents acknowledged the limitations of any particular theoretical perspective and consciously set out to cross boundaries and use other, sometimes seemingly incommensurable, perspectives.

To ensure intellectual integration from the start, team members agreed on this approach at the first full meeting of the project and committed to the following core objective: *to investigate the relationship between globalization and the processes of securing and building autonomy.* To this end, we sought to refine understanding of these concepts and of the historical evolution of the processes inherent in both of them, given the contested character of their content, meaning, and symbolic status.

Given that *globalization* is the term currently employed to describe the contemporary moment, we attempted to:

- determine the opportunities globalization might create and the constraints globalization might place on individuals and communities seeking to secure and build autonomy
- evaluate the extent to which individuals and communities might be able to exploit these opportunities and to overcome these constraints
- assess the opportunities for empowerment that globalization might create for individuals and communities seeking to secure and to build autonomy

- determine how the autonomy available to individuals and communities might permit them to contest, reshape, or engage globalization.

In seeking to address the core objectives for the project, we moved our research in three interrelated directions. First, we accepted that globalization and autonomy have deep historical roots. What is happening today in the world is in many ways continuous with what has taken place in the past. Thus, the burden of a contemporary examination of globalization and autonomy is to assess what is new and what has changed. Second, the dynamics of the relationship between globalization and autonomy are related to a series of important changes in the locations of power and authority. Finally, the globalization-autonomy dynamic plays out in the construction and reconstruction of identities, the nature and value of community, and the articulation of autonomy in and through cultures and discrete institutions. In each of these three areas, the team developed and agreed to answer core questions to provide clear direction for the research. The full text of the questions is available at http://globalization.mcmaster.ca/ga/ga81.htm.

Over successive annual meetings of the team, our research coalesced around the following themes: institutions and global ordering; democracy and legitimacy; continuity and rupture in the history of globalization and autonomy; history, property rights, and capitalism; community; culture; the situation and struggles of indigenous peoples; and the Mediterranean region as a microcosm of North-South relations. The researchers addressing these themes tended to be drawn from several disciplines, leading to interdisciplinary dialogue within each thematic group. The themes then crystallized into separate research problems, which came to be addressed by the volumes in the series. While these volumes were taking form, the project team also developed an online publication, the *Globalization and Autonomy Online Compendium* (see next page), which makes our findings available to the general public through research summaries; a glossary of key concepts, organizations, people, events, and places; and a comprehensive bibliography. The ultimate objective of all of these publications is to produce an integrated corpus of outstanding research that provides an in-depth study of the varying relationships between globalization and autonomy.

Globalization and Autonomy Online Compendium

Readers of this volume may also be interested in the *Globalization and Autonomy Online Compendium* (available at www.globalautonomy.ca). The *Compendium* is a collective publication by the team of Canadian and international scholars who have been part of the SSHRC Major Collaborative Research Initiative that gave rise to the volumes in the Globalization and Autonomy series. Through the *Compendium*, the team is making the results of their research available to a wide public audience. Team members have prepared a glossary of hundreds of short articles on relevant persons, places, organizations, events, and key concepts and have compiled an extensive searchable bibliographical database. Short summaries of the chapters in other volumes of the Globalization and Autonomy series can also be found in the *Compendium*, along with position papers and peer-reviewed research articles on globalization and autonomy issues.

Acknowledgments

THE EDITORS WOULD LIKE to express their immense gratitude to Nancy Johnson, the project editor for the MCRI on Globalization and Autonomy, for her excellent work, support, and committed professionalism. We are also grateful to Jennifer Clark, Sara Mayo, and Sonya Zikic for administrative support throughout the project. The editors acknowledge that the research for their contributions to the book was undertaken, in part, thanks to funding from the Canada Research Chairs Program. Finally, the editors and volume authors would like to thank the peer reviewers of this book for their helpful and insightful comments and suggestions.

Renegotiating Community

chapter 1

Globalization, Autonomy, and Community

Diana Brydon and William D. Coleman

> *These are things I know*
> *anonymity, autonomy*
> *freedom to self-define*
> *to forget*
> *to come out*
> *to escape*
> *sometimes there is (something I understand)*
> *no room to negotiate*
> — Shani Mootoo, "A Recognition,"
> *The Predicament of Or*[1]

THIS VOLUME DERIVES FROM an interdisciplinary research collaboration between the humanities and the social sciences. Our epigraph, a fragment from a poem by Canadian writer Shani Mootoo, reminds readers that understanding *how* a poem means is as important as determining *what* it means. Community, autonomy, and globalization are concepts that function emotively as well as analytically. This poetic fragment thus reminds readers that different interpretive communities bring different modes of thinking and arguing to the overarching team questions that have generated this volume and the series in which it participates. The poetic fragment shows how each community, to some extent, and always in a contingent fashion, generates its own modes of understanding out of the materials at hand. Reading this poem reminds readers of the relational and affective

I

dimensions of community, the contradictory emotions it may arouse, and the negotiations it requires around the pressures and satisfactions of belonging associated with community if there is to be room for individual autonomy within it. The poem reminds readers that community is less a given than a relation constantly under negotiation. Our study, like the poem, resists nostalgia for forms of ideal or mythic community that often seem to be revived in conditions of stress. The poem, however, does not consider what may be achieved beyond individual needs through engaging in collective action. In this volume, the affective and individual dimensions of community raised by the poem are placed in relation to the political, economic, and social aspirations of a variety of communities examined through a range of case studies. Our interest falls largely on the extent to which community autonomy may be achievable or even desirable under current conditions of globalization, where contemporary communication and information technologies and economic, social, and political relations are also changing how human beings understand their relations to others.

The poem dramatizes the ways in which claims to a shared community identity may be experienced as either limiting or expanding individual autonomy depending on the circumstances in which they occur. In this poem, the narrator tries to claim an affinity with a stranger based on a shared accent when both are far from the nation with which the accent is associated. But her claim to shared community on this basis is rejected. The narrator recognizes the irony in her desire to form a bond with this stranger in Canada when their paths would not likely have crossed back in Trinidad. Her "anonymity" in Canada, where she has escaped one community and not yet found another, it seems, is experienced as simultaneously alienating and liberating. The increased mobility associated with globalizing trends puts the imagined community of the nation under stress. When rebuffed by the stranger's terse rejection of her claim to recognition — "You're Trinidadian!" — with the words "I am Canadian" (Mootoo 2001, 84), the poetic persona produces the meditation that forms the epigraph cited above. The poem concludes with "Sometimes there is ... / no room to negotiate" (ibid., 85). Under contemporary conditions of diaspora, the poem implies, immigrants are likely to experience contradictory desires for communal belonging (to the nation left behind, to the diasporas in which they now live, and to the new country as a whole) that are not easily negotiated but not necessarily entirely exclusive either.

This book is dedicated to expanding the "room to negotiate" for individuals within communities and for communities within larger social structures. We locate our own investigations within the broad context of what Seyla Benhabib (1992, 70-1), following Jürgen Habermas, terms "communicative ethics," an understanding of community as formed, in part, through a process of reasoned argument sustained by a commitment to an ongoing moral conversation. Benhabib notes that Habermas often formulates his "insight concerning the intersubjective constitution of self-identity in the language of George Herbert Mead. The 'I' becomes an 'I' only among a 'we,' in a community of speech and action. Individuation does not precede association; rather it is the kinds of associations which we inhabit that define the kinds of individuals we will become" (ibid., 71).

In this book, we address particular instances of the contemporary rene-gotiations of community in response to various conflicts associated with globalization to interrogate received assumptions about community and autonomy in the hope of renewing their usefulness for changing times. A common thread is our concern with social justice and a view of com-munity as something dynamically created by the engagement of all par-ticipants, including those usually considered less powerful actors. Our aim is to take disciplinary specialists out of their silos and into broader scenes of intellectual and ethical belonging, encouraging further thinking about interdisciplinarity-as-community, a move that globalizing processes re-quire. Arjun Appadurai's sustained attention to what one of his essays terms "grassroots globalization and the research imagination" (2000) has proved an inspiration for our project. According to Appadurai, imagination "allows people to consider migration, resist state violence, seek social redress, and design new forms of civic association and collaboration, often across bound-aries" (ibid., 6). Our interest falls especially on the felt need to "design new forms of civic association and collaboration," often across previously estab-lished boundaries that mark physical and conceptual territories.

The poem addresses an individual's response to the conflicting demands and rewards of community, implicitly posing the dilemma described by Zygmunt Bauman in *Community: Seeking Safety in an Insecure World*. Bau-man argues that "there is a price to be paid for the privilege of 'being in a community,'" claiming that the "price is paid in the currency of freedom, variously called 'autonomy', 'right to self-assertion', 'right to be yourself'" (2001, 4). In claiming that diaspora provides little room to negotiate these contradictory pressures, described by Bauman as staged between "secur-ity and freedom" or "community and individuality" (ibid., 5), the poem illuminates what Mootoo terms, in the title of her collection, "the predica-ment of or." By recognizing the differences within her original national

3

community, based on class, gender, and sexual preference as well as race, Mootoo implicitly rejects any framing of the choices between community and individuality as a simple choice between "security and freedom" (2001, 5). Rather, she sees that any calls to community offer both security and freedom on a differential basis. Mootoo's poem and the collection in which it appears imply the necessity of moving beyond the limited choices framed by thinking within the established terms set for framing "the predicament of or."

Many of the chapters in this volume also move beyond conventional frames determining "the predicament of or" to investigate the ways in which communities can accommodate differences and operate productively on a variety of scales within changing conditions brought about by globalization. The choices facing individuals in communities need not necessarily be posed in such limited terms, though of course they often are. Some of our authors find alternative definitions of community as inherently or at least potentially based on reciprocity rather than homogeneity and on affiliation rather than identity. These alternative definitions challenge the assumptions about human personhood and autonomy that ground the idea that community can only be achieved at the expense of the individual. We also consider the challenges and limits to collective action faced by communities in situations where collective autonomy is threatened. It is widely accepted that community has emerged as an important concept in globalization studies, generating a range of responses that may be summarized as often "either celebratory or dismissive" (DeFilippis, Fisher, and Shragge 2006, 673). Recognizing the contributions of each of these streams, our contributors argue that community needs to be understood in more complex ways that challenge some of the assumptions behind each of these models. Our case studies demonstrate that community cannot be theorized without reference to the particular. Community cannot be isolated as a concept from either the market or the state. To this extent, our volume is in dialogue with other volumes in this series that address the roles of institutions, legitimacy, and property. Nor can community be considered as an unproblematized ideal without accounting for how it deals with internal and external differences. To this extent, our volume is in dialogue with the companion volumes that address the autonomy of culture and indigenous peoples within contexts of globalization.

Our volume, then, engages with community studies on a variety of fronts. We recognize, with Jan Fernback (2007, 52), that in many of its current usages community has become a diluted concept, in part because "the discourse about it tends to be totalizing," in many spheres it has become a "buzzword," and its use has been expanded to designate many different kinds of affiliation. We seek to reclaim community for more specific use by presenting case studies that locate our examination of community in interaction with the concept of autonomy. We interrogate definitions of community that depend on defining it solely in relation to a local place, as necessarily relying on relations based on sameness, and as requiring an intimacy of scale. Without idealizing or rejecting community, we ask how community functions within contemporary conditions that sometimes pose it as anachronistic and at other times require that it substitute in providing people with supports that were once provided by other institutions, especially the state. We question the extent to which community-based interventions, defined in such terms, may successfully modify the effects of neoliberal economics. A key issue for globalization scholars working on community remains that of determining in which direction globalizing processes seem to push: toward greater fragmentation of longer-standing communities or toward the formation of communities on a global scale. We see globalization operating on both fronts simultaneously. It may encourage greater diversity of communal identifications based on proliferating identities and identifications. It may also foster a broader awareness of shared circumstances that make the formation of global alliances and the recognition, on a transplanetary scale, of global community all the more urgent. At the same time, it can encourage a narrowing of community identifications based on the rejection of those perceived to be different. For us, these are not necessarily contradictory movements. Each may represent a response to the particular globalizing processes most urgent in a given situation.

Our case studies suggest that autonomy, the capacity for self-determination and the conditions enabling it, cannot be divorced from communal interactions. Communities remain important forms of collectivity for generating trust and feelings of belonging and for enabling humans to engage in collective action toward chosen goals. Furthermore, our studies suggest that communal autonomy remains a high priority for many individuals today. How that autonomy is exercised carries implications not only for the quality of life of an individual community but also for the larger human community brought into closer contact through forces of globalization. Sometimes the autonomy of one group will find itself in conflict with that of others. The autonomy of labour in relation to that of capital or of indigenous peoples in relation to that of their colonizers are relations of power where collective affiliations remain important, but they are not static. Rather than describe indigenous and labour communities as left behind by globalizing developments or as merely resistant to them, our chapters consider the ways in which they are adapting to such pressures and learning to use them for their own purposes.

Introducing Our Keywords

The discussion that follows arises from the interplay between our reading of the academic literature developed around globalization, autonomy, and community and the individual research that went into each case study. In undertaking this collaborative project, we have come to recognize that globalizing processes (perhaps especially those resulting from modernity and colonialism) have thrown universalist assumptions about the shared meaning of many central social concepts into question, with the idea of community among those most disputed. In the early years of the twenty-first century, theorists in several disciplines across the human and social sciences are approaching the variable meanings of community, autonomy, and globalization by seizing on the idea of the keyword, as introduced by the English cultural theorist Raymond Williams in an influential text first published in 1976 and revised by Williams in 1983 (published in 1985). In trying to understand the changing meanings attached to the word *culture* in the mid-twentieth century, Williams realized that, in addition to carrying histories of changing usages into their current employment, certain words assumed significance in clusters of relations. When examined in historical and cultural contexts, they might be understood to operate somewhat like keys to unlock the doors of perception. In other words, the available vocabulary constitutes a particular framework for seeing and thus understanding the world; it can also be used to open up issues or problems to new kinds of questions. With the rise of the Internet and search tools such as Google, the keyword assumes renewed importance in influencing and possibly determining how certain communal relations, framed through concepts such as globalization and autonomy, are perceived and hence how choices may be framed in the future.

Our first keyword is *globalization*. Like both autonomy and community, but in a more expansive and public way, this term has become part of daily life in the mass media and a common part of the discourse of politicians, corporate executives, social movements, and a wide range of non-governmental organizations (NGOs). Whether invoked publicly or privately, it carries a strong emotive content, signalling a position in major debates of the day, whether to liberalize trade further, to accept that environmental warming is real, to resist Western cultural influences, to give life to human rights for women, or to detect the legacies of colonialism and imperialism. Academics are participants in these debates and conflicts. They also observe these usages and try to understand their meanings and why they are being used in the ways they are. They also analyze the discourses involved to understand better what is being referenced and meant by globalization. Some look at political, cultural, economic, or other social processes through the lens of the global, questioning whether these processes are, in fact, globalizing ones. Others question any stark opposition between the local and the global, arguing instead that conventional borders are becoming blurred through globalizing processes. As Saskia Sassen argues, for example, subnational scalings may be viewed "*as* components of *global* processes, thereby destabilising older hierarchies of scale and conceptions of nested scalings" (2006a, 120). While Mulrennan's chapter in this volume shows how local communities may exploit such changes in nested scalings to enhance collective autonomy, Russell, Preston, and Nyers reinforce this point in order to caution that the local cannot be conceived of in any singular way: it may be constituted by competing versions of community and autonomy that complicate any simple conflation of the geospatial with the communal.

Community in its contemporary usage provides a good example of these blurrings of scale. It was once seen to designate a small social grouping operating on a local scale that often assumed face-to-face contact. This meaning has not disappeared but has been extended to designate imagined forms of relation within larger social structures. Theorists such as Benedict Anderson (1983) use it to designate the space of the nation. More recently, others have reinvented the term to describe transplanetary affiliations of people who share a sense of belonging, for whatever designated reason (professional, environmental, political), to a community that spans the globe. In this respect, these communities can go directly from the local to the global or vice versa. Sassen (2002, 371) observes that "today's re-scaling dynamics cut across institutional size and across the institutional encasements of territory produced by the formation of national states."

These various activities have led academic authors to ask the question what is globalization? As often occurs, however, we find that there are many answers. Still, the word *global* can be counterposed to "national," "regional," or "local" and given meaning in this way, even when, as Sassen (2006a) suggests, such boundaries may then require blurring. In this volume, Mulrennan shows how certain communities may operate in nested

7

fashion across these various scales without collapsing the distinctions among them. Jan Aart Scholte (2005) offers that the word *global* might be profitably understood as referring to phenomena that are "transplanetary." In this reading, globalization refers to processes, specifically the spread and growth of transplanetary connections between people (ibid., 59). This growth might take place in the economic, political, cultural, migration, military, or other realms. Clearly, this growth is uneven. As Arif Dirlik (2001, 16) writes, "not only are large parts of the world left out of those processes, but even in those parts of the world that are included in the processes, the processes appear as pathways in networks of one kind or another that leave untouched or even reduce to marginality significant surfaces of what is implied by the term *global*. The global therefore is something more than national or regional, but it is by no means descriptive of any whole." Chapters by O'Brien; Webb and Young; Cook; Schagerl; and Slemon make this point in particular ways, stressing the unevenness of what passes for the global in different contexts.

Nor is there anything inevitable or necessary about this growth. Transplanetary connections have been growing for centuries if not millennia. Even if we look back only a century, we note that the last half of the nineteenth century and the first fourteen years of the twentieth were characterized by accelerating growth in transplanetary connections, albeit connections mediated by nation-states and imperial powers, in most areas of social life. After the First World War, however, these connections shrank or were abruptly ended by economic, political, and other actors to the point that the levels of human migration and of economic interdependence at the end of the nineteenth century would not be seen again until the 1980s (Bairoch 2000; Bordo, Eichengreen, and Irwin 1999; Hirst and Thompson 1999). Similarly, more recent events such as the attacks on the World Trade Center on 11 September 2001 or the collapse of the Doha Round trade negotiations lead many to ask, "Is globalization over?"

Most observers, even those who are skeptical, do allow, however, that the growth of transplanetary connections has accelerated in the period following the Second World War and particularly since the late 1970s. There are varying explanations for this acceleration. At the heart of most of them is the continued dynamism of capitalism coupled with the innovations in information and communication technologies that have permitted transplanetary connections to become more "supraterritorial," to use a common term, and they are less bound by the physical locations or the nation-state boundaries within which people live. These technologies have permitted more connections to become planet wide, and the growth of these connections has meant that they intrude more into the daily lives of more persons than before (with Dirlik's caveats noted above) and that they are quickly made (Held et al. 1999). Scholte (2005, 61) refers to transworld simultaneity (they extend anywhere across the planet at the same time) and transworld instaneity (they move anywhere on the planet in no time). While accepting such a view, Habib cautions in this volume that Internet sites are still located and managed from a particular local site, which influences the perspectives and emphases of the content, even when conceived in the context of a global struggle.

These new forms of planetary connections and their consequences are only now beginning to be understood. Economists argue that they appear to make financial crises more severe and more difficult to overcome. Wars such as the US invasion of Iraq, the conflict between Israel and Hezbollah, and the civil war in Sri Lanka tend quickly to become global spectacles, leading Michael Hardt and Antonio Negri (2004) to coin the term "global civil wars." Others suggest that imaginations are expanded by these changes. Roland Robertson (1992, 8) refers to "an intensification of consciousness of the world" or increasing globality in many societies, where globality refers to the consciousness of the world as one place. Appadurai comes at the same issue differently and speaks of a changing role for the imagination. He suggests that, under present globalizing conditions, particularly the global movement of people and electronic media, imagination becomes a social practice, "a form of negotiation between sites of agency (individuals) and globally defined fields of possibility" (1996, 31). In this understanding, individuals place themselves in a world context and are more likely to imagine themselves doing new things in different ways. In this volume, Schagerl and Slemon deal most directly with particular types of a global imaginary, in ways that caution against too enthusiastic an embrace of its potential for enhancing a broadly based autonomy.

This analysis of transplanetarity and the emphasis on supraterritoriality highlight the emphasis on changes in the structures of spaces in these discussions of globalization. There is a danger in such an emphasis to overlook another key phenomenon, that of place. For our purpose of seeking an understanding of community and autonomy, the relationship between globalization and place is a crucial one. The literature has tended to equate the global with space, capital, history, and agency and the local with place, labour, and tradition (Escobar 2001a, 141). Manuel Castells' (1996) distinction between "spaces of flows" and "spaces of places" reflects this kind of

9

emphasis. This tendency is unfortunate because it privileges the powerful when it comes to agency and can lead to misunderstanding how communities are changing with globalization and what these changes might mean for their vitality and their survival.

Dirlik (2001) argues that behind this thinking is an imperfect understanding of the scalar terms "global" and "local." This binary, global-local, is seen to parallel the space-place one. The emphasis in globalization studies has been to argue that the local cannot be conceived without reference to the global. But the reverse is also true: "The global cannot exist without the local which is the location for its producers and consumers of commodities, not to speak of transnational institutions themselves" (ibid., 29). Dirlik adds that, "instead of assigning some phenomena to the realm of the global and others to the realm of the local, it may be necessary to recognize that in other than the most exceptional cases these phenomena are all both local and global, but that they are not all local and global in the same way" (ibid., 30).

This argument against asymmetry in the relations between global and local scales extends to how we then understand a second keyword, *place*. Arturo Escobar (2001a, 140) defines place as "the experience of a particular location with some measure of groundedness (however unstable), sense of boundaries (however permeable), and connection to everyday life." Groundedness refers not to an immutable fixity but to a link to topography and to socio-cultural practices. People build boundaries around this topography and these practices, albeit often permeable ones. In these respects, as Escobar notes, places are constructed whether by people's work, their narratives, or their movements (ibid., 147). What is important here is that these constructions are not solely determined by capital or global forces, although these factors will affect placebuilding through the political economy of work in particular and through changing patterns of consumption and the routines of daily life. The cultural construction of identities, subjectivities, and differences can lead to forms of agency that challenge the global, if not change it. Wendy Harcourt (2001, 301) writes, "the politics of place deliberately challenges the sense of polarity between local and global — as if the local is here and the global far away. Instead it positions the global as very closely mapped onto the local. People live with the global in their own lives and indeed shape the global at the local level." How people shape the global through community action in places is a major theme of this volume.

Part of this process includes place-based challenges to how globalization unfolds. The new information and communication technologies permit what Escobar (2001a, 144) refers to as the "concatenation" of places, networks of places tied into struggles to reshape global spaces. Harcourt (2001) emphasizes the importance of these networks of places in her analysis of women's struggles against domestic violence and poor health care. Women become "networkers" and "netweavers" in place-based politics linked in cyberspace. This "place-based politics ties localities into a global network society, redefining possibilities for women's sense of self, position in the community, and access to the public arena and decision-making venues" (ibid., 320). Escobar makes similar points in analyzing the place-based politics of indigenous peoples in South America.

The growth of transplanetary connections, some of them supraterritorial, and the changing constructions of places in response to and in the reshaping of those connections have direct relevance to community. Historically, communities formed in places that, in turn, often became defined by those communities. The experience of location, with a measure of groundedness and boundaries, helped to foster the communication and imagining needed to develop the sense of belonging that is central to community. Admittedly, the resulting isomorphism between community and place could also end up reinforcing inequalities and oppressions internal to those places, and colonization often added another layer of oppression to such dynamics. Just as globalizing processes change the politics of place making as noted above, they also challenge these isomorphisms. New means of communication, coupled with the expanded potential of the social imagination noted by Appadurai above, open alternative avenues for constructing and grounding senses of belonging. The sense of proximity, what is "nearby," changes in that it can grow out of the "networking of social relations across large tracts of time-space, causing distant events and powers to penetrate our local experience" (Tomlinson 1999, 9). In short, the opportunities for networking, netweaving, and the concatenation of places that come for some with contemporary globalization may provide a base for communicative processes shaping "new cultural codes of belonging" (Delanty 2003, 191). Accordingly, changing forms of place making lead to new politics of places, which permit the imagining and constructing of new communities or the reconstructing of old ones. They also provide new opportunities for rethinking autonomy and the relations it involves.

In asking what is at stake in understanding community in relation to globalization, we have chosen to focus on the problematic philosophical concept of *autonomy*, our third keyword. Autonomy, as the capacity for self-determination, has emerged as a particularly contentious site for understanding globalization and community in recent years. Within some contexts in a local form, it may also appear as a practical solution to the threatened disintegration of multicultural states. James Stacey Taylor concludes that "these are exciting times for both autonomy theorists and all who draw upon the concept of autonomy" (2005, 3). Many are now concluding that autonomy seems to be the value most at stake within such contentious areas as disputed political concepts of democracy, citizenship, and personhood; within disputed cultural concepts of communitarian, identity, and minority politics and associated notions of civil society and the public sphere; and within philosophical discussions ranging from moral philosophy to applied ethics. For Ranabir Samaddar, "we find in the problematic of autonomy, the congealed presence of several outstanding elements impinging on the present politics of dialogue, namely, the minority question, the issue of self-determination, globalization, and the twin strands of rights and justice" (2004, 108-9). The individual case studies that follow investigate each of these issues. Unpacking that "congealed presence" within the problematic of autonomy occupies many recent studies within a variety of fields. In locating itself within the triangulated sphere of globalization, autonomy, and community, our volume makes room to negotiate across the disciplinary divisions that tend to address these questions in isolation from one another.

Whereas globalization and community are part of an everyday vocabulary, autonomy remains a more specialized term that has not yet entered the vocabulary of keywords. Still, the concept signals major areas of concern within globalization studies. As Kwame Anthony Appiah argues, "to have autonomy, we must have acceptable choices" (2005, 30). In other words, the conditions in which a person or collectivity can exercise autonomy appear to be changing, partially as an effect of living in an interconnected world. The nature of the choices afforded by globalization is one of the main bones of contention between those satisfied with existing trajectories of globalization and those seeking alternative pathways through different processes. For many, autonomy, choice, and agency are what seem to be at stake in globalization. Many believe that, while globalization threatens community and national autonomy (usually understood in terms of self-governance and cultural distinctiveness), globalization simultaneously enables certain forms of individual autonomy. This point is probably made most clearly in the chapters by Cook and Schagerl, which address the ways in which global mobility might enhance the ability of some women to gain increased personal autonomy, either individually or as part of an imagined community. The majority of chapters in this volume explore the ways in which individual and communal autonomy may be self-reinforcing. The question posed in a recent article, "Who deserves autonomy, and whose autonomy deserves respect?" (Beauchamp 2005), reminds us, however, of the deeply evaluative nature of most uses of autonomy and their embed-dedness within hierarchical systems of power.

Since autonomy is used to describe the self-government exercised by individuals and by the groups they form, it is not always easy to determine which form of autonomy should take precedence. When the nation-state was believed to constitute the main form of group identity, individual and community autonomy could be seen as co-constitutive — that is, as shaping and complementing one another, but only by bracketing the needs of women and racialized groups within the polity. As globalizing processes have led to changes in the functions of the nation-state, other forms of collective identity (some new but many previously repressed) have emerged to claim autonomy, both within and beyond the nation-state on the international scene. Negotiating these autonomy demands places pressure on how a community constitutes itself and understands its limits. Thus, changes in how communities understand their boundaries both contribute to what we call globalization and are affected by it.

In this volume, we explore these kinds of changes by looking at the experiences of a variety of existing and mostly self-identified communities to evaluate claims about how globalization, autonomy, and community work in the world today, within the interscalar range from the local to the global or the global to the local. Using a case study approach developed from a variety of disciplinary perspectives, contributors to this volume have worked collaboratively to create a collective transdisciplinary analysis of the ways in which a variety of communities exercise, enhance, or find their autonomy limited in relation to different globalizing pressures. Our interest lies in following John Dunn's lead in considering to what extent autonomy might be used as a metric for judging social achievement under globalization (2003, 59-60). As he argues, "it remains a question of the keenest interest how far globalization has in practice enhanced the autonomy of different groups of human beings, and how far such gains in autonomy as it has delivered have been applied in practice for the advantage or disadvantage of other human beings" (ibid., 53). In seeking to answer this question, we examine the pressures that globalization may place on community autonomy and the ways in which that autonomy may be exercised to influence globalization.

Globalization may well claim to be the dominant keyword for explaining, justifying, or opposing economic and cultural change in the late twentieth century. In this context, notions of community may more often be invoked to describe ways of life once valued and now threatened by globalizing processes. Nonetheless, the rhetoric of globalization has also been skilful in reinvoking community in various, sometimes contradictory, ways, leading critics such as Iris Marion Young (1990) to question its utility for a transformative politics in contemporary conditions and Arjun Appadurai (2006a, 7) to cite Philip Gourevitch's reminder, in relation to Rwanda, that "genocide, after all, is an exercise in community-building." Whereas Williams could conclude in 1976 that "unlike all other terms of social organization (*state, nation, society*, etc.) [community] seems never to be used unfavourably, and never to be given any positive opposing or distinguishing term" (66), such is no longer the case today. Philosophers such as Jean-Luc Nancy (1991, 2000) and Giorgio Agamben (1993, 1998) argue that the histories of fascism and communism require a fundamental rethinking of the kinds of investment in community that these ideologies represented. Chapters by Schagerl and Slemon revisit Williams' claim to query his idealization of community from the perspective of postcolonial critique. We conclude that *community*, our fourth keyword, has both defenders and attackers among a variety of old antagonists, so that it cannot be seen as the property of either traditionalists or iconoclasts, of either the left or the right. Our interest in this collection, however, is less in considering community as a normative ideal and more in describing its manifestations and how it functions in relation to globalization and autonomy.

In 2004, J. Hillis Miller revisited Williams' work to conclude that "assumptions about individuality and inter-subjectivity largely determine one's ideas about community. Williams's community is only one possibility within a wide spectrum of recent concepts of community. These concepts are incompatible" (16). That sense of incompatibility among alternatives, rather than a universal consensus about value and meaning, seems to characterize our current global moment. As Perin Matteo explains, "Nancy's thought of existence makes it impossible to think about human beings in the individualistic terms of a doctrine of natural law" (2005, 335-6), a direction that challenges understandings of autonomy as "individualistic freedom" or total independence. When the autonomy of one community is achieved at the expense of another, evaluative decisions must be made on the basis of other criteria. How to legitimate these criteria remains a complex question. While Miller is correct in identifying community as a complex terrain of contemporary dispute, he evades rather than addresses the issue by shifting the grounds that determine community back onto another set of terms, individuality and intersubjectivity. These terms, however, are just as problematic and in turn may be said to rely on implied concepts of community or social justice for their own constitution. Appiah, like Miller, assumes that in the final analysis individuality trumps community. He argues that "we should defend rights by showing what they do for individuals — social individuals, to be sure, living in families and communities, usually, but still individuals" (2005, 72). But communities need not be constituted solely through the logic of individual rights thinking assumed by Appiah. Despite the confidence of such claims, common sense about individuals as the primary category and rights as the primary value is itself a historical and possibly culturally specific development. It is questioned on many fronts, including within major branches of philosophical, indigenous, feminist, literary, and postcolonial theory (Barclay 2000; Herz 2004; Matteo 2005). Certain feminist theorists are arguing for the necessity of refiguring autonomy in relational terms. Catriona Mackenzie and Natalie Stoljar (2000, 4) employ "relational autonomy" to designate "a range of related perspectives" premised on the "conviction that persons are socially embedded and that agents' identities are formed within the context of social relationships and shaped by a complex of intersecting social determinants, such as race, class, gender, and ethnicity." Their focus on the intersubjective dimensions of selfhood and identity is questioned in turn by philosophers working within deconstructive traditions.

Such contemporary philosophers have begun to theorize sociality (understood as the tendency of human beings to form social groups) beyond dependence on identity, individuality, or intersubjectivity in ways that carry major implications for how we understand autonomy and community. Giorgio Agamben (1993, 1998), Maurice Blanchot (1988), and Jean-Luc Nancy (1991, 2000, 2007) have contributed to current thinking about how alternative forms of collectivity and an alternative politics might be imagined. Best known among the attempts to work through some of the implications of their work is Hardt and Negri's influential perspective on globalization through the conceptual lens provided by their ideas of empire (2000) and multitude (2004). Many critics of Hardt and Negri concur with Gary Hall (2007, 73) when he concludes that they "are conspicuously unable to answer the question in *Empire* as to how any such synthesis between commonality and singularity can be achieved."[2] This is not necessarily a defect, however, because it involves thinking about dialectics differently and seeing that it is "the disparate, indefinite, open nature of collective struggle in Empire" that "gives politics its 'chance,' as well as 'a chance to change'" (ibid., 73). In the characteristic language of this school of thinking, "it's a process of 'synthesizing without synthesis', unification without unity, 'community without community'" (ibid.). Nonetheless, the difficulty of translating such insights into action remains. Hardt and Negri are not alone in finding themselves caught between older ways of thinking and the emergent new. What "community without community" could mean in practice is a challenge currently engaged more extensively in theory than in practice, although the unhappiness with traditional concepts of community signalled through this phrasing and the concomitant utopian investments in a "coming community" (Agamben 1993) characterize many elements within the activist community associated with the World Social Forum.

Our study puts this kind of questioning and resituating of community (most evident in chapters by Nyers and Slemon) into dialogue with theorizations of community that derive from other intellectual traditions, including those from indigenous communities. Joanne Barker's thoughtful introduction to her edited collection, *Sovereignty Matters: Locations of Contestation and Possibility in Indigenous Struggles for Self-Determination* (2005), explains the historical and contemporary logic behind the strategic deployment of discourses of sovereignty by many indigenous nations in their quest for collective self-determination. As she explains, "the *making ethnic* or *ethnicization* of indigenous peoples has been a political strategy of the nation-state to erase the sovereign from the indigenous" (16). Such an effort, by collapsing "indigenous peoples into minority groups" (17) or communities, tends to deny indigenous peoples their right to autonomy — that is, the right to speak for themselves in terms established by themselves. For such reasons, indigenous theorists remain wary of the trap of describing themselves through Western concepts while insisting on their right and their ability to adapt and redefine such terms for their own purposes. Chapters by Russell and Mulrennan elaborate these negotiations in contemporary global contexts.

As Marie Battiste points out in her introduction to her edited collection, *Reclaiming Indigenous Voice and Vision* (2000, xx), attention to indigenous knowledge enables those trained in other traditions to perceive both "the singularity of Eurocentric thought" and the dominance of its "prevailing authority." Aboriginal views of relationality, which "assert that all life is sacred and that all life forms are connected" (Henderson 2000,

259), challenge European-derived views of the autonomous and individuated self as a form of being existing in tension with community.

In basing our approach to community on a foundational respect for the autonomy of all persons and collectivities engaged in larger systems of communal interaction, we are explicitly embracing an approach quite different from that articulated by advocates of community cohesion as a new framework for approaching race, culture, and diversity (see Cantle 2005) and different as well from communitarians who see advocating community as implying a moral choice (see Etzioni 1995, 1996). As Jon Burnett (2007, 117-18) notes, the community cohesion approach often relies on simplistic premises with roots in earlier imperialist assumptions about civilizational superiority and inferiority, leading it to embrace its own "civilising mission" and to "mistakenly pit diversity against solidarity." Social cohesion theory has been used within neoliberal discourse to deny difference and thus to deny the need for or the value of renegotiating community. Our approach, on the contrary, charts a more complex route but one that holds more promise for thinking and enacting community without enforcing hierarchized forms of homogenization or invoking a specific nationalist or moral agenda. Rather than placing community in opposition to globalizing fragmentations, as these discourses tend to do, this study examines the ways in which communities renegotiate their identities and their functions within changing global circumstances, sometimes finding new ways to cooperate across differences and forging new alliances and sometimes solidifying older patterns of exclusion.

Recognizing the need to reconfigure the relation between autonomy and community in contemporary times, Benhabib (2004, 217) asks, "how can democratic voice and public autonomy be reconfigured if we dispense with the faulty ideals of a people's homogeneity and territorial autochthony?" The chapters in this volume suggest that we should not so readily assume that the notion of a people's homogeneity is necessarily linked to territorial autocthony — that is, to notions of belonging by virtue of birth or origin only. Increasingly, analysts are finding such ideals either flawed or insufficient for describing community, even indigenous community, in global times. For those of us working in settler colonies in particular, it is important to look more closely at exactly what territorial autocthony might entail. From the perspective of the world's indigenous peoples, territorial autocthony and a responsibility for and to place are not necessarily coupled with assumptions about homogeneity. They may well prove compatible with the kind of "vision of *just membership*" that Benhabib advocates (ibid., 3).

We cannot resolve these questions here. Even among ourselves, we work within scholarly traditions that frame the very terms of this discussion differently. Where we do agree is that debates around community consti- tute the moment when autonomy becomes useful for understanding how self-consciousness, self-determination, solidarity, and sociality are being reconfigured as the world globalizes.[3] In this volume, some contributors focus on the ways in which the process of community building involves the simultaneous exercise and production of autonomy, whereas others are more interested in the ways in which community autonomy may be strengthened and instrumentalized to realize common goals.

Our Structure and Its Argument

We employ the first-person plural throughout this introduction because the collaborations across disciplines in which we have been engaged for the past four years have not only encouraged us to think about commun- ities but also contributed to a growing sense that we ourselves have now formed a particular type of interdisciplinary community. The work has be- come collective, and we have been changed in the process. Several of our chapters are written in the first person, a mode that is common to some of our disciplinary practices and uncommon to others. We maintain it here because to our way of thinking it reinforces the importance of situated- ness, the place (multiply constituted by different communal involvements) out of which a perspective emerges. It is important that each contributor situate his or her work within at least two perspectives, that of his or her individual discipline and that of the interdisciplinary negotiations of the interplay of autonomy, community, and globalization that have structured our collaboration. Each contributor needs the space to nuance his or her differences in the approaches taken to these questions, thereby enrich- ing the contribution of the whole. Each chapter renegotiates the terms of encounter, resets the terms of discussion, and readjusts the lens for seeing, thereby adding to the nuances of our text when read across disciplines and a range of approaches.

The volume is divided into two complementary parts that recognize the embeddedness of different communities within larger structures and the ways in which they are both shaped by them and may play a role in influencing them. Our first section, "Global Capitalism and Community Renewal," attends to the economic dimensions of globalization as ex- perienced on the ground in a variety of localized communities. Our second section, "Building Transnational Communities," focuses on the political and cultural dimensions of globalization across a range of scales. These dimensions include global negotiations across differences of place and in response to global flows. The contributors recognize that economics and culture interact. Furthermore, the historical legacies of colonialism and communal deterritorialization emerge as unifying themes across these divisions. Each chapter approaches the problematic of globalization, autonomy, and community in a singular way that has been developed in close dialogue with the others to reveal the tensions at play within this dynamic as it is currently understood.

Opening Part 1 are three chapters examining indigenous place-based communities that are engaging globalization on terms grounded in their histories. These chapters use indigenous cases to make important points about the complexities and dynamism of communities and their interactions with larger state, policy, and corporate processes. These communities do not function as "anachronistic remnants yet to be fully engaged by globalization" (Russell, page 34, this volume), as often assumed. Instead, these communities (often perceived as only traditionally rooted) are globally linked through relations of conflict, collusion, and negotiation on a variety of scales. These chapters support Colin Scott's (2001, 4) assertion that, "as Aboriginal societies elaborate strategies for autonomous development within myriad contexts, usually against daunting odds, they are actively challenging and revising commonplace theories about the necessities inherent in mass market economies and state monopolies of power." Wendy Russell and Dick Preston look at two northern Canadian communities based on opposite sides of James Bay, the challenges they face, and how they are addressing them. Russell argues that, when place is denied its relevance under the pressure exerted by global diamond mining in the late twentieth century, there are consequences for the operations of autonomy. These consequences are still being worked out. Russell recognizes two types of community interacting in the Nishnawbe Aski region of her field research: first, communities defined as traditional constellations of residential groups based on the sharing of resources; second, communities functioning as regional artifacts of the colonial era created for control of the people. These contrasting experiences of community, which map different relations onto the land in question, are both in play as the territory is opened to capital development. At this stage, it is not clear to what extent the conditions exist for successfully achieving autonomy in conformity with indigenous notions of reciprocal community.

Preston, in contrast, focuses on a particular Cree community's reinvention of itself and the development of the notion of Cree citizenship through gestalt practices. He sees the Nemaska band story as an example of best practices that succeeded, largely because conditions enabling autonomy were present in their case at the time they made their own choice to relocate. With the resources and support to undertake a community consultation and the power to elect their own leaders, they were successful in imagining a new social scale of autonomy in concordance with their values. They were able to transform their sense of identity and cohesion through the collective performance of community that took place through their managed community consultation. What the future holds as leaders change and new challenges emerge cannot be predicted, however, as community autonomy must be continually re-enacted.

Monica Mulrennan considers the social and political dynamics involved in community-based conservation (CBC), especially as manifested through the experiences of the small island of Erub in the eastern Torres Strait. Building on the work of Russell and Preston, she argues that recognition of nested and intersecting levels and scales of community has major implications for community-based conservation. Understanding the links between resource conservation and the larger political agendas of indigenous communities can provide much-needed perspective on their roles in CBC. Like Russell and Preston, Mulrennan is concerned that the complexity of the local remains understated, with potentially negative implications for local autonomy and with reduced opportunities for scientists and policy makers to gain insights from local models. She reminds readers that indigenous communities are making substantial strides in the strategic use of globalizing discourses and networks (i.e., enhancing their autonomy). At the same time, she cautions that "community" is not a preferred category for indigenous representatives in domestic or UN settings, where "nation" is often the preferred term for achieving external recognition of group sovereignty and its associated autonomy. Our book begins with three indigenous, place-based communities and a relatively intimate scale to challenge romanticized versions of indigenous community while complicating understandings of how local rootedness, historical memory, and attachment to place may operate under a variety of global, market, and state pressures.

The following two chapters consider new communities that arose in the face of duress as a result of the stress and crisis created by an emergency in which people felt compelled to stand their ground, in part, because they had few options. As such, they fit some of Peter Baehr's criteria for a "community of fate" (2005). Baehr argues that such a community must be distinguished from Ulrick Beck's risk society. The solidarity that emerges from such a situation must be experienced "as a rupture with the recent past" and with "normal times" (Baehr 2005, 182). Such is the case for the two communities examined here. Scott Prudham examines the quest for social and environmental justice of a local BC NGO, the Youbou TimberLess Society (YTS), formed after the closure of a local mill, when ownership was transferred from one company to another and the workers were abandoned by their province and their union. Amanda White investigates the rise of a new community movement within the traditional community of Galicia, Spain, that arose in response to an oil spill off the Atlantic coast, the kind of environmental disaster that accompanies increased global trade. This community saw itself moving from "servitude to dignity." In each case, the new community that arose in response to a specific crisis of identity dissipated as the context of emergency disappeared.

Prudham's chapter shares with the opening three chapters an interest in how global capital engages resource-dependent communities and the different ways such communities try to respond. For Prudham, the importance of the YTS is the challenge it poses, through its struggle for greater local autonomy, to a global consensus that saw corporate or government responsibility to workers rendered redundant under neoliberal theory. The shifts in self-understanding of this community, as it sought to identify allies in its struggle, highlight the ways in which the search for justice eclipses narrower understandings of self-interest. They remind us of the ways in which "community turns on the ambiguous politics of social claims mobilized in opposition to market self-regulation" (page 101, this volume). This chapter reminds readers of the fragile and provisional character of many communities wrestling with the new challenges of globalization. Similarly, the sinking of the ship *Prestige* examined by White provides the opportunity for local communal autonomy to be debated. Here, a complex process of historical continuity and change shaped public reaction and activist claims within a long-standing framework of ethnic, linguistic, and geographic difference. White's chapter focuses on a historical region as a community; it documents transformations in regional identity due to events and activism related to globalization; and it analyzes the processes of reimagining regional identity within a federal state system itself embedded in the European Union (EU) federation of states. These multiple layerings link forward to later chapters that investigate transnational networks and institutions.

While the preceding chapters address community and autonomy in predominantly resource-based communities undergoing changes due to economic globalization, Peter Nyers addresses migration and the emerging movement of undocumented migrants in Canadian cities. The city has emerged as an important locus for reimagining community under conditions of globalization. Undocumented migrants put pressure on established forms of communal identity such as citizenship, challenging the boundaries drawn between alien, resident, and citizen that fracture unitary conceptions of human rights. Inspired by the International Parliament of Writers global network of autonomous "cities of refuge," Nyers extends the concept beyond its initial focus on the individual high-profile refugee. He considers the implications for community and autonomy once the "city of refuge" is opened to *masses* of people whose legal status forces them "to live on the borders of belonging." Once again an argument is made for thinking through the ethical implications of globalization in conjunction with its economic developments. This chapter forms a pivot between the locally grounded communities examined in Part 1 and transnational communities of various kinds examined in Part 2. Nyers addresses the ways in which the boundaries between the local and the transnational are blurring with the movements of people across the globe in search of refuge and work. Their quests for autonomy provoke questions about the nature and political status of the community. As Nyers notes, they carry implications for rethinking the modalities of membership that constitute a community and the potential imagining of "solidarities yet to come." Like the other chapters in this first section, Nyers considers what happens when global processes appear to move into local communities, changing their dynamics and their self-understandings. Taken as a whole, these chapters demonstrate the ways in which global movement and interaction are changing self-understandings and collective actions across both rural and urban communities in ways that challenge some conventional understandings of the urban/rural divide.

The chapters in Part 2, in contrast, focus on communities organized on broader global, national, or regional scales. This section considers a new set of issues surrounding the building of non-territorial, cross-border communities as sometimes providing new means for the exercise of autonomy. We open with Michael Webb and Patricia Young's review of some UN-supported transnational women's movements and global social policy activists, on the one hand, and some women's and policy activists working within the European Union, on the other. Their comparative review of these disparate groups helps to clarify the difference between networks and communities and stresses the importance of the process by which activists consciously attempt to build community in the face of difference through dialogue. Like Preston, they stress the importance of dialogue for generating trust and enabling consensus to emerge across differences. Certain transnational women's communities operating with UN support were able to generate such dialogue. Where opportunities for dialogue and a willingness to negotiate are absent, they conclude, networks often fail to gel into fully operative communities. Perhaps their major point is that such transnational networks do not merge into full-fledged communities automatically but often depend on external interventions and policies (e.g., by UN or EU agencies), on processes of development over time, and on the willingness and ability of participants to make a greater personal investment in the process.

Similar issues are noted in Robert O'Brien's chapter, especially in relation to specific developments within the history of the Southern Initiative on Globalization and Trade Union Rights (SIGTUR), a loosely regional labour organization that has made concerted efforts to create community across differences within its diverse membership. The identity of this nascent community entails contradictions in geography, nationality, ideology, organizational forms, producer and consumer interests, and gender so that its efforts to forge community constitute a particularly interesting study. O'Brien frames this discussion within a more generalized analysis of the relationship between globalization and labour autonomy in the post-1945 era. He asks if it is possible that new transnational identities and alliances between workers could compensate for setbacks at the national level. To answer this question, he argues that it is necessary to distinguish between workers in the North and in the South and between protected and unprotected workers. While it is possible to generalize that globalization simultaneously undermines and strengthens labour autonomy, its impact is uneven depending on other factors. In the North, worker autonomy has been undermined by globalization, while in the South some workers experience increased political autonomy but decreased market autonomy. While workers face immense difficulties in addressing globalization, transnational cooperation may help to ameliorate conditions. O'Brien's study of SIGTUR identifies three community-building strategies designed to create an instrumental community with the goal of increasing labour autonomy at the expense of capital or business autonomy. These strategies include running cultural exchanges, devising new symbols and documenting group experiences, and mounting joint campaigns. These community-building strategies help to compensate for differences within the group without necessarily succeeding in creating the kind of coherence associated with traditional place-based communities.

Jasmin Habib considers the cyberactivism of transnational activist groups in relation to organizing around the Palestinian right to return. She explores how social justice networks may find their projects intersecting with Palestinian communal efforts to remap an erased homeland through the medium of the Internet. In other words, she shows how a territorially based community, when deprived of its land, may reconstitute its identity and its struggle by establishing a global presence on the web and forming a strategic alliance with other transnational activist groups. Importantly, Habib notes the continued emplacement of such globally activist groups, making their performance of virtual community less a non-place (as is sometimes argued by globalization theorists) than the result of practices filtered through multiple webs of interpersonal relations, some of which still derive from place-based interactions. Working within constrained circumstances, the Palestinian community organized around the right to return demonstrates its ingenuity by discovering new ways to expand its autonomy but remains far from achieving the full autonomy that remains the goal of the movement.

The final cluster of three chapters revisits the question of continuities between colonialism, imperialism, and globalization as examined in our opening three chapters. Looking back to the early twentieth century, Jessica Schagerl notes how memberships in communities of the Dominion of Canada and the British Empire were seen as complementary rather than competing identities for women active in the Imperial Order Daughters of the Empire (IODE). These women showed through their activities that it was possible to stay in Canada but act in awareness of a global consciousness, even though their global consciousness and the organization it developed were in fact quite circumscribed by privileges of class, race, and religion. In examining one of the historical, gender-based communities that preceded the UN-based women's communities studied by Webb and Young, Schagerl considers the ways in which the desire for autonomy of one group of women in a male-dominated society implicitly and sometimes explicitly excluded other communities of women.

In a similar vein, Nancy Cook's chapter demonstrates the ways in which transnational development workers in northern Pakistan near the end of the twentieth century continued to subscribe to a global consciousness developed under empire, similar to that which had motivated the IODE. In each of these instances, certain Western women gained autonomy through consolidating gendered communities that were implicitly bolstered by racial and class privileges. Their communal autonomy was often implicitly, and sometimes explicitly, maintained at the expense of the autonomy of racialized others. These communities were built around gender, class, and race in ways that compensated for gendered exclusions from public space by capitalizing on racial and class privileges. As a result, the limited autonomy that they achieved seems to be compromised by their inability to imagine a more inclusive community.

In keeping with the volume's skepticism toward many of the dominant assumptions governing celebrations of community in current contexts, Cook's and Schagerl's chapters deny easy generalizations that might see women's community building as liberating for everyone or transnational communities as escaping the historical problems of place-based ones while remaining attentive to the genuine needs that community can meet. Stephen Slemon's chapter similarly balances recognition of the investments individuals make in community with a critique of its more problematic dimensions. Slemon concludes the volume by analyzing the international mountaineering community as a "brotherhood of the rope." This chapter extends Cook's and Schagerl's focus on gender-specific communities constituted through class privilege to analyze the homosociality of mountaineering, as it has developed from imperial times into the global present, including its imbrication in contemporary capitalist commodity culture. His chapter spans the twentieth century to show how a gendered mountaineering community arose in conjunction with British imperialism and has since been transformed through global capital. He asks three questions: (1) Why is it that mountaineering produces representative "heroes" who can never represent "the mountaineering community"? (2) Why does it go into panic when women, or clients, end up representing the practice? and (3) Why is it that commodity fetishism now stands in for "the mountaineering community" among consumers in the more wealthy countries? Slemon notes the ways in which a community may build itself upon structured disavowals of its material practices and contingent relations to such an extent that its capacity for autonomy in the contemporary period must be questioned. Taken as a whole, these analyses lead us to reframe the terms of debate around globalization, autonomy, and community in ways that resist setting globalization in simple opposition to either community or autonomy.

Conclusion

The chapters in this volume investigate the ways in which communities can operate productively on a variety of scales and they identify some of the obstacles preventing the exercise of communal autonomy in global times. We show how overly simplistic notions of the local and of community, including romanticized representations, may ignore or misunderstand how communities actually function and what is currently at stake regarding issues of resource use, environmental protection, or democratic practices. Our investigations challenge many of the stereotypes of particular communities that still function in contemporary writing about globalization and community. These include stereotypes of indigenous communities as timeless or trapped in the past, stereotypes of online communities as participating in a virtual reality beyond place, or stereotypes of logging communities as necessarily in conflict with environmental or indigenous groups. The reality is more complicated. We conclude that communities are always being negotiated, both internally and in relation to external forces. Local identities may be redefined, as in the evolution of a community of loggers into a timberless society (Prudham) or the transformation of a marginalized community "from servitude to dignity" (White), but such redefinitions do not necessarily result in increased communal autonomy.

Our contributors examine a range of communities, from those that seem to be integrated and deeply bonded (Russell, Preston) through communities that seem to be more broadly based yet still effective in achieving certain forms of collective agency (O'Brien, Webb and Young) to those that appear to be quite fragile (Cook, Slemon) or no longer tenable (Schagerl). These latter chapters raise the question of how deep such an association must run before it can viably be considered a community. In answering this question, some of our contributors privilege the phenomenological experience of those for whom the relations described generate a meaningful sense of belonging, while others stress the extent to which common goals may be realized through communal action. Some put less stress on the notion that a truly effective community has to be formally organized into a common unit or has to achieve collective agency as long as individuals may attain autonomy within it, while for others collective autonomy is the goal by which a successful community may be judged. We agree, however, that a community, while capable of evolving from traditional forms, remains more than a network.

A network refers to a set of nodes or sites that are in regular communication with one another for functional, strategic, economic, or political reasons. Each node has a certain independence from the other, and communication between nodes can vary from highly frequent to rare, depending on circumstances. The recent developments in information and communication technologies have made it easier for individuals, groups, and communities to form networks and to maintain them at extensive, even global, scales. Examples often cited in globalization studies include contemporary financial markets and women's activism (Sassen 2004, 2006b) and the individuals, organizations, and groups that came together to oppose the Multilateral Agreement on Investment or to support the treaty to ban landmines. After the goals of the network are accomplished, communications become more quiescent between nodes until revived for another financial transaction or political campaign. Such networks could evolve into communities if social relations become more dense, less episodic, and invested with emotive content, including a sense of responsibility and commitment to the goals of the group. In contrast to Sassen's findings, such seems to be the case within the transnational women's movements associated with the United Nations described by Webb and Young.

Our team project is based on the premise that globalization introduces complexities of such magnitude and particularity that an interdisciplinary approach is best suited to understand and address them. As a result, individual chapters engage with the debates of their own disciplines and those that emerged from collaborative work on this volume. These debates crosscut in multiple ways. Our research confirms the prevalent belief that in some ways the idea of community and the values associated with it are currently in transition. Autonomy remains a value, but the conditions in which it might be understood and exercised are changing. The desire for community may be met through a variety of social relations and collective actions. Communities are human creations, capable of renewal and adaptation, and constituted by internal diversity as well as by what lies outside communal boundaries, whether they are defined in cultural, geopolitical, or other terms. Communities are reproduced through the interplay of past, present, and imagined futures. Their renewal or creation involves a mix of cultural values, institutional structures, and communicative practices.

While the relation to place for many communities, old and new, is changing, places remain the sites for the politics of globalization and autonomy engaged in by communities. In this volume, we focus attention on the changing circumstances in which communities find themselves and the functions that they serve. We ask how communities are formed and sustained in a variety of circumstances and how they are changing in response to global developments. The dimensions of globalization that have emerged as most salient for our studies include cultural movement and belonging associated with increased intensity and extensity of connections enabled by empire or development initiatives, new technologies, institutions such as the United Nations or the European Union, or migration. The formation of transnational connections across previously defined cultural differences or between formerly isolated places based on these dimensions can also become crucial for community building. We have not exhausted the range of influences or the types of community formed through contemporary pressures, but we hope to have shown why such studies remain important for scholars today.

We began this project with an interest in the interplay between individual and collective autonomy. Looking back, we can now see that, when studying community, our focus is usually on collective autonomy: why it is necessary and what it can achieve. For us, how autonomy is negotiated is crucial. We ask: Autonomy for whom? At the expense of whom? Is autonomy negotiated in the name of reciprocity or exploitation? These questions must enter the balance in determining the nature and achievements of autonomy, what it means, and what it can signify for different collectivities. In attending to the full complexity of autonomy in its current usages, contributors to this volume hope to deepen understanding of changing notions of individual and collective agency, as exercised through evolving understandings of community and its relations to civil society, state institutions, and the public sphere. We unpack the notion of community as a monolithic construct by distinguishing among a variety of long-established and emerging forms of community. In rethinking the conventional oppositions between grounded and virtual communities, we suggest that autonomy, too, is evolving as a concept from its Greek roots. Because community as a concept operates pivotally but differentially across the humanities and social science disciplines, we hope that this book may also serve an integrating and reorienting function for the range of groups engaged with community studies, from the most theoretical to the most practical. Although each of the volume's three animating concepts (with place an important fourth component) has individually attracted considerable research attention, we believe that this is the first comparative study to systematically consider the linkages and disjunctures among globalization, autonomy, and community.

Part 1: Global Capitalism and Community Renewal

chapter 2   Globalism, Primitive
                 Accumulation, and Nishnawbe
                 Aski Territory: The Strategic
                 Denial of Place-Based
                 Community

                 Wendy Russell

GLOBALIZATION IS OFTEN IMAGINED to be happily ungrounded and
rootless, and sometimes it may be so. Popular representations of globalization depict a borderless and instantly accessible world or a world of
mingling leading toward total convergence. Whether globalization offers
global citizens a "shopping mall of cultures" or seamless, homogeneous
world unity (Trouillot 2001, 4), space (as literal and imagined distance) is
largely rendered irrelevant, in part because we can triumph over the limits
of physical distance (with technology) and in part because "we" are all in
contact. Here I argue that, in the extension of this triumph over space,
places (as specific locations) are thus also rendered irrelevant as they are
redefined relative to the imagined global whole. "Place" has a restricted
repertoire under the enthusiasms of globalism, that is, and appears only as
an imagined point of origin for ideas, bodies, "cultures" — the everything
that we imagine getting caught up in global flows (see Tsing 2005). In this
chapter, I consider the ways in which place continues to trouble any attempt
to imagine such a certain global whole by comparing and contrasting a
variety of discursive constructions of the same "place," the Nishnawbe Aski
Nation. As a territory newly opened to a flood of mineral prospecting, the
region is simultaneously being reinserted into a global whole as part of
various global discourses, specifically as a new resource frontier for capital,
as a pristine environment, and as an indigenous and colonized homeland.
At the same time, this place is also actively reimagined as a "community"
built in the mundane and material acts of immediate daily life, and it is this

31

process of community making that is most evidently muted in the broader discourses that are mapping it into the global. Drawing on interviews and participant observation, this chapter presents the argument that the assumed irrelevance of place and location is not only an illusion but also more fully a subordination of place to the global and thus a strategic denial, a denial that serves to defeat the real material autonomy afforded by localized processes of building community or of building community in place. I argue here that understanding these competing place-making projects will move analysis beyond a simple defence of place-based community as narrowly traditional or romanticizing it as "lost" to understanding. Place-based community is always unsettling, resisting, defeating, and competing with the forces of "globalization." I turn now to a brief introduction to the ways in which discourses of modernity and globalization have naturalized this strategic denial.

Modernity, Globalization, and the Problem of Place

There are both similarities and important distinctions between the rhetoric of modernity and globalization with regard to how each construes (and uses a version of) "space." Accomplishing modernity relied on identifying and championing distinction from "others" (the premodern), and in turn this logic offered the rationale for modernization — literally the appropriation of labour, land, and resources at the margins of the modern centre (Pratt 2001, 36). Like the rhetoric of modernity, the rhetoric of globalization rezones all "space" and creates new ways to imagine, give meaning to, and appropriate that space. The convenience of defining marginal premodern zones was that these zones simply became available space, open space, and space to be incorporated to the modern centre. Arif Dirlik argues that these "views of place ... that were products of modernity, that produced places as locations for parochialism and changelessness that the inhabitants of places never intended ... in the end resulted in an inexorable urge to erase places by incorporating them into the spaces of modernity" (2001, 21). Modernity, further, was defined both by capitalism (ibid., 21) and "developmentalism," or the inexorable urge to make places "developed" (Escobar 2001b, 195-6). Under modernity, capitalism, and developmentalism, places were awaiting entry into new modern orders, and place-based communities could be construed as sites for the defence of anachronistic ways of being, thinking, and acting.

Globalization's version of space differs from modernity's, however, because globalization does not require the creation of spaces containing parochial "others" but embraces that difference, though on its own homogenizing and encompassing terms ("we are all one"). Globalization's rendering of space is not quite so obviously equipped to justify projects to take over and appropriate some "backward" places in that part of space deemed peripheral and marginal. Rather, the irrelevance of space most powerfully naturalizes the idea that we simply all share one "system" or one way of interacting. "Differences" are superficial to the newly natural commonalities we all share, and those differences are neutral and readily consumable across modernity's old boundaries. Communities vested in places are reinserted into the global fold on globalization's homogenizing terms but stripped of their significance as sources of informed agency, selective engagement, and productive knowledge. History, grievance, and radical difference, which challenge easy mutual understanding, are also erased through this process. In the case I consider here, an indigenous territory, it is this radical difference (in the social relationships that constitute community and consequent human-place relationships) coupled with historical grievances against both capitalism and modernity that is most significantly effaced by the rhetoric of global unity

I say "significantly" here because of the ways in which globalization is creating new demands to reincorporate space: globalization extends modernity's project of capitalist expansion and developmentalism to its extreme in the guise of economic globalization. By rendering space irrelevant and all places simply part of the larger whole (in a manner identical to the universalism of modernization), by definition economic globalization cannot be easily identified as a "place-based project" because it is instead proposed to create commonality and mutuality. And so, even though material global flows emanate from and enrich places, this specificity is hard to identify in a world rendered one and homogeneous as it is under the false unity of globalization's rhetoric. Modernization and globalization hide the same process — the deliberate political and material work of appropriation of land, labour, and resources to enter into global flows. Where modernization's "progress" disguised this work of creating uneven flows behind the logic of "progress" (Pratt 2001, 36), globalization's rhetoric of unity helps to conceal the raw realities of new enclosures, loss of livelihood, and destruction of places. Like "progress," the naturalization of the triumphs of global commerce conceals the calculated work of primitive accumulation — the deliberate, political redefinition of lands and resources as the exclusive property of capital (Perelman 2000, 13-37). Globalization rhetoric successfully obscures this dual subordination of "place," whether its own roots in places or the notion that there is some independent integrity to life in the places it is licensed to incorporate to its own project. Denial of the relevance of place is thus currently strategic as a way to override competing claims to places.

Globalization and Place-Based Community

The ongoing process of primitive accumulation, now masked by globalist enthusiasm, renders some places apparently defensible as they are incorporated into a homogeneous globe (Dirlik 2001, 41). But at such frontiers, the expression of place is more clearly the expression and defence of community at myriad nodes in the global network of politics, capital, and space — nodes (places) sprung up from myriad particular historical interactions within, across, and among a myriad of places. The most celebrated of such expressions is that of the Zapatistas, but the same claim can be made of women assembly workers unionizing their factories: the globalized world is characterized by a multiplicity of projects that analyze and demand modification of the way in which global capitalism lands in and reforms particular "places." These projects manifest "community" as something focused and immediate: nodes. These nodes in the operation of global-scale capitalism are communities, and while each may cultivate links to transnational supporters, international organizations, and supranational institutions, as in the case I discuss below, there is some recognizable distinction between these nodes as they are lived and competed over and are productive of experience and the abstract "global" community. Place-based communities, then, are those nodes of interconnection that are productive of linkages to a variety of scales — regional, national, supranational — linkages that might just as easily be links of conflict as of collusion. These are communities "grounded" at the specific nodes they are defending, reproducing, and producing but not anachronistic remnants yet to be fully engaged by globalization.

But is this "groundedness" merely obscured by globalization rhetoric, or is it more materially defeated by the effects of globalization (especially economic globalization)? Gerard Delanty argues convincingly that modernization (and by extension globalization) uproot and atomize human interaction — community — which has led to a new longing for community but one that can be accomplished under the conditions of modernity. Those conditions produce insecurity as the state and nation are no longer available as protection or as a source of belonging — community must be created, and Delanty argues that this creation relies on the "communicative forces within modernity" (2003, 193). Delanty's "community" is "post-place" in its search for meaning and belonging, which poses a problem for both place and community in the context of modernity:

> The revival of community today is undoubtedly connected with the crisis of belonging in its relation to place. Globalized communications, cosmopolitan political projects and transnational mobilities have given new possibilities to community at precisely the same time that capitalism has undermined the traditional forms of belonging. But these new kinds of community — which in effect are reflexively organized social networks of individual members — have not been able to substitute anything for place, other than the aspiration for belonging. Whether community can establish a connection with place, or remain an imagined condition, will be an important topic for community research in the future. (Ibid., 193)

There is a certain truth to Delanty's assertion that place is already lost to community, in its consistency with globalization's demand that we privilege flows "above" encounters "on the ground." Globalization here is able to both confound and rebuild community, though place can now only be recovered from within ungrounded and subsequently rebuilt communities. This makes "sense" in globalization's terms, shored up by much thinking about deterritorialized and diasporic communities in which place functions only as an imagined origin.

Such characterizations of "community" hold in the case I examine below, though the contrary is also true. That is, in this case versions of community "above" place coexist (and I will argue) compete with place-based performances of community, opening a new frontier of potential and actual conflict. This is most clearly also a conflict generated by the real material work of economic globalization — the appropriation of land and resources — that here is the process that acts to uproot community. Contrary to Delanty, however, I argue that this is a process that does not just uproot community but also, more powerfully, strategically denies the legitimacy of a link between community and place, a denial that is aided by popular rhetoric about globalization and that normalizes primitive accumulation as a "shared" project.

35

Places and Globalization/Community at New Scales

The region under study here is the territory bounded by the jurisdiction of the Nishnawbe Aski Nation, the highest-level tribal council for the more than forty-five First Nation settlements in northern Ontario. The Nishnawbe Aski Nation is itself divided into eight smaller tribal councils, each composed of a smaller number of First Nations, which share a common language and historical ties. Each of the constituent First Nation settlements in the territory, associated with fur trade and missionary centres, has a resident population ranging from under 100 to 1,200 people. Each small settlement is also the locus of a larger territory used for harvesting, camping, recreation, and social and religious pursuits. Taken together these territories (which overlap one another in practice) make up Nishnawbe Aski Nation territory, which in turn makes up nearly two-thirds of the province of Ontario, an area roughly contiguous with the part of Ontario above the Trans-Canada Highway.

Since 1997, changes to provincial legislation regulating Crown lands in Ontario have spurred an unprecedented resource rush into all of the Crown lands in Nishnawbe Aski Nation territory: that is, into the vast majority of Nishnawbe Aski Nation territory, excepting only the tiny reserves associated with most of the Nishnawbe Aski Nation settlements. As most harvesting and other land-based activities in the region take place on Crown lands, the opening of the territory to resource developers is thus imposing a competing use of most Nishnawbe Aski Nation territory. The current rush to investigate and stake mineral claims in Nishnawbe Aski Nation territory seems to have largely emanated from De Beers Canada's 1999 announcement that it had identified a source of high-grade diamonds (the Victor site) near Attawapiskat, an Ininew[1] settlement in Mushkegowuk territory on the west coast of James Bay. In the wake of this announcement, a large amount of Nishnawbe Aski Nation territory has been studied and staked by prospectors.

The speed with which this complete redefinition of Nishnawbe Aski Nation territory has proceeded is unprecedented in the region. The sums being spent on prospecting and the anticipated costs of opening a mine in the region are staggering and provide a stark contrast to prevailing economic and social conditions in the region. Most of the Nishnawbe Aski Nation territory has no roads, many communities have no sewerage or running water, none has adequate housing available for its residents, few have easy access to all but the most rudimentary health care, and few have adequate educational facilities. The region's cash economy is built almost entirely on federal funds used to run band and community institutions, funds that are almost immediately reinvested in the national economy through the purchase of food and other supplies shipped from "the South." This degree of leakage is a symptom of the general lack of a business infrastructure within the communities represented by Nishnawbe Aski Nation. Instead, cash spent in Nishnawbe Aski Nation communities concentrates in the enterprises at the immediate southern edge of Nishnawbe Aski Nation territory that have the capacity to ship goods into the North. The region's economy, however, is not solely defined by the formal cash sector, as a large quantity of land-based resources, estimated at 25 percent in Mushkegowuk territories, contributes food, fuel, medicine, and materials for making household goods to household economies. Much of this wealth is irreplaceable, either because no imported item is of comparable quality, its replacement is too expensive, or it is socially valued for its intrinsic qualities. Each settlement also sustains its own very small but locally controlled business sector that is largely informal and provides local services.

The region is thus made up of myriad highly particular places, made specific and immediate in the practices of community building and community reproduction that make up day-to-day life in each settlement and its associated territory. While there are broad cultural and linguistic similarities throughout the region, and while English is the only common language (there are three related but mutually unintelligible languages spoken in Nishnawbe Aski Nation territory), the "region" is largely unified only on paper. However, the region's population is in various ways and at different scales being reconstituted as a "community" as the enormity of impending mining activity in the region comes to light and as new capital enters the region.

The active production of place and community has become a growth industry, and the region and its settlements are represented at various scales and by every actor currently engaged in the territory. Within this discourse, redefinitions of the region illustrate the traits of globalization, as I outlined them above, as well as Delanty's (2003) definition of community as "communication" under conditions of globalization.

In 2001 the De Beers Canada's website had a description of its Victor project that included a partial world map on which only the names Attawapiskat and Southern Africa appear. The map illustrates nothing about geography, though it does spell out the vision of a world held together and defined exclusively by the relations of industry: these two locations are tied together in the "real" world by personnel (initially most of De Beers Canada's executives are South Africans), by technology (their expertise comes from work in South African mines), and by capital (the governing board of directors is in South Africa). This is a map, in short, that shows what globalization means to industry: it is not "transnational" but "extra"-national, as if industry, investment, and profits exist outside nations themselves. This map is a record of the kind of triumph over space and boundaries that capitalists operating at a global scale both pretend to perform (see Tsing 2005) and actually perform all the time.

In the publicity and public discourse about the mine, De Beers Canada's use of a seamless globe is matched by groups complicating the progress of mining development in northern Ontario. In an April 2004 op ed piece in the national *Globe and Mail* by the Deputy Grand Chief of Nishnawbe Aski Nation (Kooses 2004), the author draws a parallel between De Beers' operations in Canada and Botswana, placing particular emphasis on the dispossession of the San and their replacement in their territory with the diamond-mining giant, a case publicized and supported by Survival International. "Are diamonds," the article asks, "the Crees' best friend?" The Cree of northern Ontario are cast in a global drama, and thus Ininew join San as citizens of the global Fourth World. Similarly, environmentalist groups (in primarily web-based campaigns) stake their claims on protecting "the environment" without reference to territorial, provincial, or often even national boundaries. In trying to complicate and modify De Beers Canada's presence in Nishnawbe Aski Nation territory, both the Nishnawbe Aski Nation and environmental protection groups operate at the same scale as De Beers Canada. Furthermore, the premises on which they base their claims (to have their interests in the region recognized) are the popular premises of globalization, unity, and mutuality.

The mobilization of these popular premises is true to Delanty's (2003) definition of community as based on communication and in this case shows how communication can help to create a community that shares imagined "stakes" in some territory. That is, environmentalists can lay claim to the inherent value of this previously "undeveloped" part of the boreal forest, valued primarily because it stands in stark contrast to other developed regions of Canada. Similarly, the Nishnawbe Aski Nation mounted a 2005 campaign to commemorate the centenary of Treaty 9 (which covers a large part of the territory) in a series of events held at the sites where various parts of the treaty were signed. Elected officers and staff of the Nishnawbe Aski Nation visited and spoke at these events, representing their position that, given existing treaties, any mining activity permitted in the region must secure the economic future of the region's First Nations. Nishnawbe Aski Nation staff designed a logo of the commemoration activities and produced and distributed high-quality booklets detailing the history of the treaty signing. Both environmentalist and rights discourses have thus created definitions of the territory that compete with those of resource developers and create "community" primarily through the work of communication.

As of January 2006, environmentalist efforts to halt and modify the mine have yielded some operational changes but have not achieved the goal of substantially delaying the development of the mine. However, bodies representing the region's First Nations economic interests have been remarkably successful and have both altered the proponent's plans and added new legitimacy to the notion of "regional community." In 2001, the Mushkegowuk region's Five Nations Energy successfully lobbied De Beers Canada to hire the newly "regionalized" electricity provider to power the mine, providing a crucial client for the regionally owned (and indebted) utility. This effort was aided by the rejection, for environmental reasons, of the proponent's plan to use diesel generators to power all of the mining operations, which would have required the importation of massive quantities of diesel fuel by tanker into James Bay and by smaller barges into the estuary at the mouth of the Attawapiskat River. In January 2006, De Beers Canada announced its contract with a new air service, Cree West, a collaboration between the regional airline Air Creebec (owned and operated by the culturally, linguistically, and historically related Cree of Eeyou Astchee of northern Quebec) and Mushkegowuk First Nations that was created specifically, in consultation with De Beers Canada, to service the mine. Both the contract with Five Nations Energy and the creation of Cree West demonstrate a newly substantive practice of "regionalism" that has been successful in cooperation with the mining proponent and in fact has significantly modified the proponent's operational plans.

True to the enthusiasms of globalization, the remapping of Nishnawbe Aski and Mushkegowuk into both a resource frontier (for transnational capital) and a regional "community" with economic interests at that frontier demonstrates the creation of new versions of community and new forms of cooperation. That this regional community now includes other Ininew separated only very recently by a provincial boundary demonstrates even the possibility of a kind of regional "expansion" for both the Ininew of Ontario and the Cree of Quebec. The pressures on the mining proponent to avoid the appearance of conflict in the territory or environmental destruction and to demonstrate a responsiveness to the economic needs of the indigenous population have come solely from communities based on communication, communities brought into collaboration most expertly by the region's First Nations representatives. These successes are also truly unique to the current global moment in that it has been the advancement of capital into this region coupled with the reduction in provincial and federal intervention into the operation of the region's First Nations — neoliberalism and devolution — that has created the context in which the regional governments and enterprises could act. Their agency in this context — their autonomy — is demonstrated especially in the directness of band and regional leaders' negotiations with De Beers Canada, almost completely unmediated by governments. In Dirlik's terms, the villages in the Nishnawbe Aski Nation and Mushkegowuk territory have been left to "fend for themselves," and this has provided new opportunities for self-determination (2001, 41).

The same devolution, however, is partial since the fundamental motor of the current resource rush into the territory, primitive accumulation, is not challenged by the successes of this new regionalism. The current resource rush is driven by the legislative transfer of resources and territory from one "community" (indigenous inhabitants of the region) to another, in this case "capital" and the alliances built around it. This "transfer" technically took place with the 1670 declaration of the Nishnawbe Aski Nation as part of the Hudson's Bay Company's (HBC) Rupert's Land and through the treaties of the early twentieth century. But this transfer has never been fully realized because most of the land remains entirely under the use of the region's indigenous peoples. One attempt to acknowledge the prior claim that this use implies (and that the current process counts as primitive accumulation) is a provincial bill (Bill 97 2004) that would award revenues from resource development in the territory to the region's First Nations. The Resource Revenue Sharing Act (if passed into law in 2008) would require the provincial government to relinquish its control over some mining royalties and would thus acknowledge the existence of tensions over the process of primitive accumulation at work in the region. In the meantime, that tension remains alive.

At the first community consultation De Beers Canada held in Fort Albany (one of the Mushkegowuk bands that will be affected by the mining operations) in 2001, the first statement from the floor dramatically disrupted the flow of the mining proponent's polished PowerPoint slide show and left the five De Beers Canada presenters scrambling as the lights in the room came up. That first statement started (in Cree) with the words "in 1492." Ninety minutes later, when it was clear that the meeting was ending without De Beers finishing its presentation, a young woman asked (in English), "Aren't you from South Africa, and wasn't South Africa racist? Why should we trust you here?" These were postmodern moments in that they foregrounded the multiple ways in which colonialism has divided and captured the world — how it configured space. Both statements, however, also identify colonialism as defining contemporary relations within Mushkegowuk: Chris Metatawabin's recollection of 1492 is an assertion about the relationships of this territory to colonial forces. Mushkego is colonized space, and De Beers Canada has entered this territory under the conditions set by colonialism. The new forms of cooperation and the successes of those "extra-place" alliances represent, at best, a partial de-colonization of the territory and the endurance of a fundamental conflict over the territory itself. Most prominently, this conflict was expressed in direct action in 2005 when the winter ice road that De Beers Canada uses to access its mine site was twice blockaded where it passes through Kashechewan territory (Fort Albany's immediate northern neighbour). Both episodes were officially attributed to the failure of De Beers to negotiate a sufficient use agreement with the Kashechewan Band and the presence of Ontario Provincial Police on the road, which signalled the return of a provincial police force into the region, effectively replacing the regional Nishnawbe Aski Police Services. Unofficially, in Fort Albany, some people attribute these blockades to an event on the newly "taken over" road: two young men from Kashechewan were stopped by the provincial police from harvesting firewood along the side of the road. In one regard, the distinction between these two explanations is minor, as both seem to be based on regional rights. Upon reflection, however, only the second version identifies the problem that primitive accumulation — the "real" loss of control of resources — poses in this territory. The latter explanation identifies the blockade as a substantial manifestation of the assertion made in Metatawabin's recollection of 1492. But the latter explanation also exposes that the new regional alliances do not address the problem of primitive accumulation. In the following section, I pursue this limitation, arguing that it resonates with globalization's strategic denial of "place" as a source of community-making projects.

Community as a Place-Based Process

In anticipation of writing this chapter for this volume, in July and August of 2005 I included the simple question, "what is community?" in a number of the interviews I was otherwise conducting in Fort Albany First Nation, one of the Nishnawbe Aski Nation settlements in Mushkegowuk territory on the west coast of James Bay. Each response intersected with the others in various ways, and the traits and qualities of "a community" that each of my interlocutors identified resonated in both broad and specific ways with the *performance* of community through the activities of daily life I previously studied in Fort Albany.[2] The interview I have selected to summarize below stands out since it was a response to this question delivered as a forty-five-minute narrative. Adam[3] proceeded to answer the question as a reflection on the barriers to the performance of community in Fort Albany today. Instead of producing the entire narrative here, I provide a conceptual summary of the defining characteristics of an ideal community, preserving the speaker's comparative method and the order of the traits as they appeared in the narrative.

Adam opened our conversation by distinguishing between two types of community. The first is the traditional constellation of residential groups spread throughout the Ininew territory at any given time, "up and down the river" that is the central feature of the landscape. This form of community was constituted through kinship, mutual knowledge, and, just as importantly, shared orientations toward one another and the land base. The contrasting form of community is an artifact of the colonial era: the settlement created first by the HBC operations in the region (immediately after Rupert's Land was established in 1670) and later (at the turn of the twentieth century) elaborated to aid the work of missionaries, the federal Department of Indian Affairs, the Royal Canadian Mounted Police, and the provincial Ministry of Natural Resources. The settlement, that is, is defined by those institutional forms that required the settlement to perform "control over the people,"[4] while the previous form of "community" Adam identified privileges human interaction. Adam's definition of the "human" community is realized in two processes, sharing (of resources, territory, and work) and what I will identify here as "mutuality," or processes of complementing, recognizing, and aiding others.

Adam identified the first quality of community as the sharing of resources (especially food), a common practice in the settlement within extended families of as many as fifteen interrelated residential households.

In the days prior to making this statement, the redistribution of wealth through extra-family sharing networks had been especially apparent as, first, a funeral feast had just passed (at which a large amount of donated purchased and wild food had been consumed) and, second, a very large amount of wild food (fish, frozen geese, and at least one frozen caribou) had been gathered for an upcoming feast for a community cultural celebration. In the narrative, Adam contrasted this practice with the pressure to accumulate resources,[5] especially cash and purchased goods, both of which were identified as colonial impositions.

Relatedly, Adam contrasted the practice of sharing territory (or acknowledging shared access to a common land base) with the provincial Ministry of Natural Resources' system of "traplines," instituted in the mid-twentieth century as a conservation measure. Traplines were identified as discrete territories assigned to individual male heads of households.[6] This remapping of the terrain implied the undoing of the collective system of resource management and allocation established within Ininew practice in the territory, and it has always been both adhered to and flouted, creating conflicts within Ininew society (among trappers) as well as signalling a fundamental conflict between the state and the Ininew. Furthermore, however, Adam argued that this atomization of the social map of the territory into discrete units, each assigned to one man, similarly atomized "work," as these men were turned into independent producers rather than considered part of a unit working together on a given territory. The reassignment of territory to individual male producers meant that their other kin (required members of the harvesting group) became subordinate members of the group. Each man's male kin (siblings and parallel cousins), wife (and her female kin), and children were shut out of his territory.[7] This process of "sharing" is also thus clearly a process of "localization," or creating thick and immediate links among humans and their territory, links that make up a place-based community.

The second process dominant in Adam's narrative, again drawn out in comparison with other institutional orders, is what I want to identify as "mutuality," that is complementing, recognizing, and aiding others. In this part of the narrative, the institutional order used for contrast is the residential school, the missionary-run and federally mandated institution that dominated the lives of Ininew in the territory for the years between 1903 and 1974. Along with the Hudson's Bay Company, the Ministry of Natural Resources, and the police, the local residential school figures prominently in all discussions of colonial influence with people in the settlement over the age of forty-five. Along with these other ordering institutions, the residential school and the mission's projects are generally identified as the institution that most forcefully remapped life for the Ininew. Specifically, the functioning of the residential school and the mission's settlement economy required the reassignment of people into roles appropriate to the mission's projects: by age (student versus adult), by place in the nuclear family (child, father, mother), by gender (men were identified as "breadwinners," and women's work was subordinate), and by economic role (men travelled alone because women were encouraged to stay in the settlement).

The residential school thus atomized Ininew society in much the same way as the remapping of the territory did, by creating individuals who were not acting in relation to one another (in a complementary fashion) but acting to fulfill the aimless order of discipline that was the dominant goal of day-to-day operations for both children and workers in the residential school. That is, Adam contrasted "knowing how to act appropriately in a community" with "knowing an individual rote performance of obedience" solely in relation to authority. Mutual recognition was largely denied in the space of the residential school as children were "strangers" because they were only made a community on the basis of the most superficial commonality, their age. Furthermore, because they were forbidden to speak to each other in their own language, it was assured that the newly interned children could only slowly come to know and be known by others in the school. However, it is mutual aid as a process that Adam identified as subverting the order of the residential school through a story about learning from three other children in the school how to stay warm by playing when they were locked outside the school for recreation in extremely cold weather. It is significant that in the narrative Adam insisted that he "followed their lesson" and thus gained the capacity to resist beseeching the supervisor to let him inside the school (i.e., to be "a victim"). If he had not been a willing learner, the other children's aid would have been wasted, while he retained his own self-determination in relation to the school. Taken together these expressions of "mutuality" identify community as built from human interactions within a frame of mutual respect and obligation (here obligations to acknowledge and aid each other), traits that in his life have always been in tension with the enforcement of order by "colonial powers."

Adam's definition of community as manifest in processes of sharing and mutuality within his context contrast with Delanty's account of community as dissipated. Instead, Adam's account represents a "traditional" form of community in Delanty's terms in that it "maintains" its ties to place and to traditional forms of belonging based on kinship, family, and class (2003, 188) and so is "still" something that may coexist with the modern but is not thoroughly modern. But this definition is troubling because there are similarities among modernity's account of these links as "premodern," a rhetoric of globalization that privileges connection and linkage "above," and a rhetoric of development that does not address the ugly effects of the operation of capital to appropriate people's resources. This is precisely the kind of community — "place-based" — that I argue is shut out of globalization, that is the "traditional" to the "modern" and the "undeveloped" subject for developmentalism and that Adam reminds us was also the "backward" subject of the civilizing mission. That is, Adam's story acknowledges that it is precisely this kind of place-based, localizing, and grounded community that is denied, denigrated, and "ignored," while the tie between place and community is not necessarily cut. Taken with the resistance to the process of primitive accumulation and what that resistance to the mining proponent's project represents, I would argue that this denial is in fact strategic, precisely because these are the communities that already define the appropriate uses of and control over territories and resources that are being taken over by capital.

Conclusion

The denial of community that colonization, missionization, modernization, and development have in common has thus opened a new frontier of conflict as primitive accumulation denies the capacity of this kind of community to tie itself to place. What is unique to the current moment in this territory is that this conflict has now been "downloaded" to the new regional forms of community that, as Delanty (2003) points out, have not "replaced" place-based community. But these new regional communities are now going to have to deal with this strategic denial.

My point in drawing out these contrasting expressions of community — one located "above" at the regional scale and one located within a kind of substantive enacting of community — is not to claim that they are irreconcilable or that one is more legitimate than the other. It is rather to keep in play the assertion that Metatawabin made about 1492: the current moment of open and flexible community building is haunted by history, by radical difference, and by the bare facts of primitive accumulation. While new forms of autonomy, new infusions of capital, and new forms of community will forge new ties to place, these continue to take place co-incident with deliberate attempts to sever other kinds of ties. The analytical challenge is to identify the ways in which the "uprooting" of community from place is naturalized and powerfully strategic and how community reasserts its ties to place in the face of its denial.

chapter 3

Twentieth-Century Transformations of Native Identity, Citizenship, Power, and Authority

Richard J. "Dick" Preston

IDENTITY TRANSFORMATION, NEW PERCEPTIONS of citizenship, and the transformation of power and authority may be studied at several levels of social scale. It is my conviction that, the smaller the scale, the more we can discover what is actually going on. This is especially true when we are trying to understand the formation of a community in the setting of a culture that is different from our own. Local community changes may be particularly revealing of global processes in action. This is true not only for us as readers but also for the people in the small communities who are newly aware of the possibilities for reimagining and re-creating their identities as community members and as citizens of their regions of Canada. I propose to focus on the emergence of local community autonomy, viewed against the background of emergent regional Native self-government (the latter as the formation of a Native state within the Canadian nation-state). This has included the development of a "nested" sense of Cree citizenship (discussed below). More specifically, this case study is a concrete example of "best practices" in the exercise of the right of self-determination, a right now being pursued by indigenous peoples globally.

In the James Bay lowlands of northern Canada, in the early decades of the twentieth century, there were vigorous colonial/modern transformations of power and authority that were disruptive of Native communities and cultures and destructive of lives, most markedly on the Ontario side of James Bay (Preston 1986, 2004). The low point was when the cumulative impact of industrial capitalism and disease resulted in the dying out of all but two Indian families of the New Post Band.

The 1970s presented an opportunity for reversal: postcolonial transformations enabled a re-creation of identity and the development of a perception of citizenship in a Cree state, which was most noticeable on the Quebec side of James Bay. Arjun Appadurai's "culturalism" — the collective imagining of social transformation — is appropriate as an explanatory framework for the cultural high point of this latter period, the remarkably successful relocation of one community. "It is the imagination, in its collective forms, that creates ideas of neighborhood and nationhood, or moral economics and unjust rule, of higher wages and foreign labor prospects. The imagination is today a staging ground for action, and not only for escape" (Appadurai 1996, 7; see also Preston 2004).

These two examples show how indigenous local dynamics have had widely varying linkages with exogenous forces of modernization, with consequences that range from the near destruction of one community to the successful creation of another.

While it is a truism that globalizing processes relating to natural resource development are damaging to indigenous peoples in most times and places, we should also recognize that, while this is chronic, it is not inevitable. Globalizing processes relating to the collective imagining of social transformation may be enabling for indigenous peoples in some times and places, even though the events are in response to very similar natural resource developments, such as hydroelectric generating stations and opening access via a railway or a highway. A close examination of the collective imagining processes and the follow-through implementation in one specific time and place provides an empirical case study of success that, with careful modification, may be used as a model by other collectivities in other times and places. It constitutes a "best practice."

At a more abstract level, the case illustrates the practical application of a globalizing theoretical process. The gestalt "school" of psychology developed by Max Wertheimer and a few colleagues in Europe in the 1930s was given practical application when Kurt Lewin developed "T-Groups," which guided the imagining processes of "individualist" American corporate executives in the 1950s into a more democratic or egalitarian collaboration in "visioning" (as we now call it). Later, and at a much more general level of application, these T-Group principles were extended to guiding the transformative imagining processes of far less competitively selected or "worldly wise" rural or remote collectivities in the 1970s, including people of radically different cultural traditions. Why Lewin's gestalt applications, which worked very well in Madison Avenue T-Groups, should also be so successful in the bush of northwestern Quebec (and small communities elsewhere in the world) is an intriguing question. It is a practical strategy for encouraging the deliberate imagining, by people in local communities in diverse places in the world, of transformations of identity, citizenship, and the proper locus of authority.

Introducing My Perspective on Community

Autonomy implies a political position. Autonomy is political because it is a relationship of both freedom and responsibility that exists between individuals, families, communities, regional governments, and nation-states. I believe that this is as true for you and me as it is for the Crees. So what is my political position? Or, put more subtly, why do I care about community? Like Cree writer Tomson Highway, I deeply believe that cultures thrive when there is a strong and coherent spiritual basis for living well with others and that only then can political and economic factors make a substantial difference in people's life chances. In 2005, when I made this comment to Nemaska chief Josie Jimiken, he remarked, "that's just common sense." I care deeply about human life chances or the potential to live "a good life." I believe that you as readers also have, each in your own way, a similar concern with human life chances (for discussion of the concept, see Ignatieff 2000). Consistent with my Quaker convictions, I choose to support those aspects of people's personal experience and life chances that contribute toward living a good life.

Why do I care about the transformations of Cree communities in particular? I care because it interests me and has done so for over forty years, and because I believe that I have learned from the experience. I do not presume that what I write will be the final word on the subject, but it will be my approximation, and it will be an informed and thoughtful opinion. We have a great many topical and community studies, from all over the globe, but we understand far too little of the actual transformations that have taken place in these communities. And how would I be able to discern them? By asking the people who have been there during those years, taking an active, often leading, part in working toward those transformations. Their words form the substance of this chapter.

I began this study in 1963 with an interest defined for me by the interests of John Blackned, my principal Cree mentor. He was born "in the

49

bush" in 1894, and "the old ways" spiritual domain was the milieu of most of his life. Contemplating this milieu and sharing his stories so that I could record them intrigued and pleased him. For reasons of birth and biography, it somewhat differently intrigued and profoundly influenced me, and our interests converged over the years of our association (Preston 1999). So I care because it matters deeply to some Crees that I have regarded as friends and because it enlightens me. I am a spiritually deeper person for having known some Crees fairly well and fairly long.

Nemaska: A Singular Success

I am focusing primarily on the formation of a new physical, social, and spiritual community and the new practices of everyday life that are entailed when a few hundred indigenous people come together for an increasingly sedentary life at a new location, with the self-conscious purpose of building their new settlement. Living in this new settlement entails "the continuous saga of growing up as a community" (George Wapachee, personal communication, 2005) — a sustained process of building new housing, transforming social relations and shared understandings, and thus reshaping everyday life. Out of this collective imagining grew new personal and political notions of autonomy, which allowed indigenous people to develop significant control of their community and to choose how they will articulate some globalizing processes.

Other relocations of this sort (e.g., Davis Inlet in Labrador, Grassy Narrows in western Ontario, New Post in eastern Ontario, or Easterville in Manitoba) have been traumatic, diminishing people's identity, power, and authority and thereby diminishing their life chances. Moved against their will to a reserve location they would not have chosen, people found their environment disrupted, their security as hunters on the land impaired, and government decisions challenging their sense of Native autonomy. But, as we shall see, Nemaska is an exception and a success story.

In all five cases named above, traditional social relations and shared understandings were similar. They concerned hunting-trapping families whose primary home locus was their ecological range, the series of places deemed desirable for the hunting of each of several species that were expected to be found at particular times and locations. This range of locations constituted their respective family hunting grounds, except for a summer gathering time near a trading post. In the bush setting, each family was a portable, personal, life cycle microcommunity (Preston 1975). What we as scholars conceptualize as autonomy was primarily to be found at the level of this small community, where each of two to perhaps thirty individuals became a self-consciously self-regulating member of a mobile family group (Preston 1980).

It will be helpful to consider the meaning of the word *primarily* in the preceding sentence. What about individual autonomy, especially in a hunting culture where so much is "left up to the individual" in instrumental, social, and spiritual actions? What kind of self-consciousness did these hunters and other members of their families have? What sense of identity as persons or as families?

I am convinced that the "traditional" or "bush-centred" Cree sense of individual identity was more "bred in the bone" than fully articulated. People were born into their family group, in their environment, with minimal "outside" influences, and from this basis people matured their sense of who they were. Identity as a self-consciously articulated claim to culture or to citizenship is more likely to arise in reaction to a significant external challenge to a people's legitimacy in their characteristic way of getting a living and relating to others — including their spiritual basis for guiding their intentions and actions.

Spirituality, as a guiding, integrating perspective for living well with others, is what I want to focus on to orient us to the Nemaska case. In the extensive discourse on globalization, most of the emphasis has been on topics relating to political economy, environmental change, and global media networks. The spiritual dimension (including religions) is at risk of being neglected. (I speak to this shortcoming also in my chapter in the volume *Indigenous Peoples and Autonomy: Insights for a Global Age* in this series; see Blaser et al., forthcoming.) In the Cree traditions of spiritual living, their mythic charter begins, felicitously, with a mythic being whose individual autonomy is so extreme that his example teaches cautionary lessons about autonomy and responsibility.

The prospect of living free of responsibilities to others, and without aid from others, would be recognized by most Crees as possible but rarely desirable. In fact, the "first-born" mythic teacher-transformer that we call Trickster lived this way in most cultures of the world most of the time (Hyde 1998). Trickster was a mythic model of a life of solitary and indomitable opportunism that we find deeply instructive (Highway 1989; Preston 1990). The Cree Trickster's experiences on the boundaries of predictable social life lead to a series of absurd, sometimes creative, and sometimes damaging consequences. The humour in the narratives is deep, at once ridiculous and profound examples of undisciplined desires and unintended consequences that we can recognize only too well. Only a mythic spirit could survive for very long in a life of this much irresponsibility, although some humans occasionally appear to try. Gradually, the Trickster-transformer Tcikabesh-wolverine becomes self-conscious but also finds the social morality of life on this paradox-ridden Earth too dispiriting and remains, in our minds, out at the edges of chaos, grinning at us, still teaching us with feats of reckless abandon, so that we will know better — know from the consequences of Trickster's actions how we should try to live well together, in our complex and contingent world. From Trickster's lessons, we draw our own measure of disciplined social responsibility and our respect for the autonomy of myriad others. The whole of Cree oral tradition documents this "fallout" from the many-faceted Trickster's transformations of the world. Without these teachings, we will wither spiritually into one or another moral dogmatism based on notions of an elegantly but distantly ordered universe or into moral apathy.

Autonomy in this tenuous and ultimately mysterious world is achieved primarily, then, at the level of the coordinated activities of a family, where each individual can contribute responsibly to sustaining the group. Together a man and a woman not only make the nurturing of children possible but also allow the hunter to focus his time, energy, and concentration on the hunt and his wife to maintain the hearth, the safety of children and the infirm, and the composure of the community. But gender roles were not rigid. A man could be a midwife; a woman could hunt to sustain her family (Preston 1982, 1986). During periods of food scarcity, their mutually complementary roles sometimes proved to be of life-and-death importance. At less dire times, it was a practical and congenial way to live well.

Cree family autonomy was gradually eroded by colonial influences, though living in the bush protected the family for most of the year. Then, after the spring breakup of the ice on the rivers that were Cree highways, the Crees gathered for a week or longer at the trading post. There the men of the families brought their furs to the trading post manager, exchanging them for supplies for the coming winter. And with their families, they enjoyed the excitement of socializing in the brief summer community of many families whom they had not seen for nearly a year, totalling as many as a few hundred people. These summering groups were called "bands" by Canadian government administrators and usually named after the location of the trading post. While this larger summer community was also recognized and named by its members, the family was still the primary locus of identity and loyalty. For the most part, fur traders and missionaries also viewed family as the locus of identity. Only government personnel thought of the band as the primary social unit until well into the twenty-first century.

But, as people stayed near the trading post community for longer periods and built houses there, a stronger sense of this larger group's identity as a "post community" home emerged. There also emerged a greater acceptance of the influences of white men in determining where they would hunt and for what, the religious values that were preached, and the medical assistance that was offered, as well as welfare credit, schooling, and other government interventions. The larger scale of group identity brought with it the incorporation of white men's authority and the consequent diminishment of Native autonomy (Morantz 2002). This coalescence and loss of autonomy was nearly universal across the Canadian North (actually the entire Circumpolar North) by the mid-twentieth century, but its "progress" toward assimilation into Canadian mainstream society was not at all inevitable, as we shall see.

With the traditional culture and environment so similar across the subarctic regions, and the external forces of colonialism and modernity so similar, why is the Nemaska Band story so different? The causes are many, but they can be listed as follows:

1 The Nemaska people made their own choice to relocate at a time when this choice was protected by law (James Bay and Northern Quebec Agreement, 1975, hereafter referred to as JBNQA).
2 They made their own choice of a congenial location that would not be flooded for hydro projects, retaining the access to their traditional bush hunting grounds — their "home" locus.
3 They made their own choice in accepting the offer of their grand council to provide a planning strategy, the "community consultation," with a support group of Cree personnel, non-Native consultants, and an explicit participatory process for developing a practical action plan.
4 They were provided with financial and material support by their grand council and by government fiscal responsibilities as specified in the JBNQA.
5 They elected and re-elected capable local leaders, and they sustained their action plan initiatives and scheduled activities over several years of establishing their new housing and buildings for social services.
6 They were successful in imagining and maturing a new social scale of autonomy, transforming the family level to include the community level.

Following a brief comparison with New Post, I will examine these reasons in some detail, ending with the situation at the time of writing (2006).

Nemaska and New Post Compared

The New Post people felt the effects of modernity a half-century before the civil rights movement, before popular sympathies for the situation of northern Native peoples and the northern environment emerged, before important legal decisions regarding Native land rights occurred, and before government policy changes were made. While the New Post hunters were on the northern frontier of Canadian expansion in the early 1900s, they were still "traditional bush hunters" in the sense described above. They continued to be able to hunt for their living, though they had to accommodate increasing numbers of strangers on the land. Few were fluent in English, and few had the technical and social skills to join the wage-earning whites at work sites or in towns. New Post people found their hunting grounds being exploited by white trappers, many of them from the gangs of labourers who worked on hydro projects — two projects in the midst of the New Post grounds had as many as one thousand men working there for several years in the 1920s and again in the 1930s (Preston and Long 1998).

No longer secure to provide for their families on their land, they lived as opportunities appeared, or as changes in the environment dictated, trying various places and activities associated with the development of railways, mining, timber cutting, and the construction of hydroelectric generating stations in the region. Mortality was extreme, with depression, disease, and accidental deaths cutting their numbers to only two surviving Indian families (Preston 2001), both of whom left their impoverished hunting grounds to live in frontier towns for several years. After decades during which the two family heads worked as wage labourers, their numbers began to recover. The two family heads also constituted the legal band administration of a chief and a councillor, who continued for many years in an essentially modernist fashion, periodically trying to pressure the federal Indian Affairs bureaucracy to take action in planning and building a new reserve community.

The original reserve location, specified at the time of the 1905 treaty, was never built on or occupied, though some timber rights were sold in the 1950s, and a hydro right-of-way was negotiated in the 1960s. Finally, in the mid-1980s, a reserve was established near a town, and housing was constructed, but even into the 1990s the residents (about fifty) shared the same family name, while the other extended family remained in a town. In 2005, both extended families finally had residences at the reserve, and a man of the second family was chief. He summarizes the New Post situation in these words:

> We went from having control over our territory to government control. Presently, we administer poverty, not wealth, our future is dictated by dollars and cents, not heart and will. We spend most time arguing and fighting over control and power, not what is best for our future generations.
>
> I have seen much change in our small community over the last few years that I have lived here. I came to think that "Would my great-great-grandfather Chief Esau Omakees ever have signed the treaty had he known that his people would practically disappear off the face of the Earth into the ever-changing world of uncertainty and unknown?" I have come to the realization that Headman Omakees would have not signed the treaty had he known what would eventually happen to his future generations and their title over the lands and waters.
>
> I look around and see that our true Ojibway tradition and language have all but disappeared on our reserve and within our family; the only thing that I have left in this world that ties me to Esau is the lands and waters which are paramount and the few pictures posted in INAC's website that I look at every once in a while on the white-man's Internet. (Chief Dwight Sutherland, open letter via e-mail, November 2004)

Tensions between the two kin group-families have continued, with initiatives taken to split the band and form a second reservation.

In the 1960s, the Nemaska people, in a more remote area, were still relatively traditional bush hunters, with little trouble from white trappers and only occasional visits by government people, whose authority was not as effective as that of the Hudson's Bay Company (HBC) post manager. But the advance notice of a hydro megaproject, declining fur sales, and the anticipated cost of renovating the company buildings at Lake Nemaska led the Hudson's Bay Company to give a year's notice of intent to close down. With the actual closure in 1969, the Nemaska people went to other summer trading post locations, but most continued wintering on their family hunting grounds. The people found that summer living for several years during the 1970s on the edge of Waskaganish or Mistassini was not a good substitute for their feeling of being at home, in Old Nemaska, and this loss of well-being was a major source of the desire to relocate. Also, some people called it "forced relocation" since Hydro-Québec subsequently did not proceed with its plan to flood Old Nemaska, and many people felt misled.

A major factor was the James Bay and Northern Quebec Agreement (1975), which provided a legal basis for the re-establishment of their community, provided this was done within a period of five years. This deadline created a reason for taking the initiative of choosing and establishing a new community site, and leaders decided that, rather than wait for the government to act on their behalf, they could and would take autonomous action, employing a multinational firm to coordinate a "community consultation" (Wapachee and Jimiken 1977). This firm had recently conducted a management consultation for the grand council staff, who found it very helpful. The globalizing process on which the rest of this chapter focuses is the consultation's collective imagining of social transformation — specifically the creation of community and its results over the following three decades.

The Nemaska consultation was initiated at the request of George Wapachee, then the Nemaska representative on the grand council, with the advice and consent of some of the hunting group headmen. They accepted the offer of their grand council to provide a support group of Cree personnel, non-Native consultants, and a clear, participatory strategy for developing an action plan. I was an invited participant. In October 1977, families came from their lands, and the staff and consultants from more distant points, and gathered at a promising location for a "New Nemaska" settlement. The sandy site on Champion Lake was suggested by George Cheezo, the family headman whose hunting lands it was on. His generosity has proven to be fortunate for the community but personally costly for him, as I will sketch later in the chapter. The place was chosen because it was well suited for a townsite, not too far from Old Nemaska and thus convenient to the traditional family hunting grounds and at a higher elevation that made it safe from future hydro flooding.

For four intense days, people focused on a process of collective imagining of their new community. The community consultation was organized by staff of a transnational corporation (Peat, Marwick, and Associates) in collaboration with some staff of the Grand Council of the Crees. The immediate result was a transformation of social consciousness. At the close of the fourth day, one hunting group headman spoke publicly (in Cree), "in the past I have always thought of my family. Now I know that I must also think of my community."

Soon after the community consultation, the consulting firm produced a detailed, well-organized compilation from statements made during the consultation — a Nemaska action plan that the people regarded as their own. George Wapachee told me that the action plan proved to be a very practical guide to construction of the new site, and the long-term result is the present Nemaska community. The specifics of the consultation strategy and the details of the action plan were outlined in my previous article (Preston 1982). In this chapter, I emphasize the aspects of the consultation that contributed most directly to transformations of Native identity, power, and authority. These transformations progressed as follows:

1 *from* a tacit sense of identity as part of their family hunting group
   to an articulated identity that combines family, community, and region.
2 *from* power in their competence to perform and nurture survival skills
   and mutual respect relations with animals and other persons in order
   to hunt and live well *to* power in their competence to perform and
   nurture skills and relations so as to balance bush, town, and world.
3 *from* authority over their own personal and family affairs *to* wider ·
   spheres of authority. This authority is "nested" (see Mulrennan, this
   volume) within successively larger scales of identity and political
   autonomy, first within Nemaska community relations, then from
   participating democratically in the Grand Council of the Crees and
   administratively in the Cree Regional Authority, and through these
   Cree entities articulating with Quebec provincial politics, Canadian
   national politics, and the United Nations. In the UN Working Group
   on Indigenous Peoples and the Permanent Forum on Indigenous
   Issues, the grand council is regarded by many as the "cutting edge" of
   indigenous representations on self-determination, a right established in
   article 1 of the Covenants on Civil and Political Rights, and Economic,
   Social, and Cultural Rights, of the UN Human Rights Committee. This
   is an example of Charles Taylor's "politics of recognition" and John
   Child's ethics of respect (see Brydon and Coleman, this volume).

The very fact that 102 Nemaska men, women, and children came to-gether as a collectivity, in a new location, and for the common purpose of trying the new idea called a community consultation was itself a step in community building. Apportioned into five distinct task groups that included staff and consultants, we assembled each morning to hear a report on the previous day's results and then some general guidelines for the new day's tasks. Then we spent the rest of the day in our groups on the next steps. Because the grand council staff had recently gone through their own consultation process, they were prepared by that experience. In particular, they were skilled in facilitating and recording but not saying anything that might intrude on the consensus-building statements of the Nemaska people. We consultants were also told clearly that we were not to take any initiatives in the discussions, and only ask questions to draw people's thoughts and feelings out into the open and to provide information if and when we were asked.

The topics were as follows: day one was to ask what people would like to see for Nemaska in ten years; day two was to discern what obstacles were likely to interfere with these goals (recognizing the obstacles became opportunities for people to agree to adapt their perceptions); day three was to innovate practical strategies for getting past the obstacles; and day four was for calculating a schedule of work that articulated all the projects and costing estimates (Preston 1982). Each person's ideas were written on tear-sheet charts and kept taped up and visible, so that we listened respectfully to every person's contribution. In my task group, on band organization and community life, I noticed that one young father with a child on his lap was writing his own notes on our contributions — a manifestation of the extent to which he estimated the words to be "owned" by the Nemaska people and of the importance he attached to keeping track of the ideas for future reference.

This brief narrative has described a process whereby the locus of autonomy increases in social scale. The locus expands, in this case, from its traditional nexus of individual and family to a newly formed community composed of many families. But of course this is typical of community formation. For example, the Davis Inlet Band was formed as a result of the success through several generations of one family in raising several adult sons who lived and hunted in the same vicinity (Preston, forthcoming). The point of interest in the study of globalizing processes is that one of these newly formed communities used deliberate, intensive, and sustained social imagining as its basis for a transformation of identity, power, and authority. Since the consultation, the Nemaska leadership, particularly through representations of George Wapachee, has taken initiatives to assert their autonomy on a number of occasions over the preferences of Quebec and federal authorities. The results have been affirmative for the Nemaska people and impressive for others. It is an instructive model of how to do community transformation successfully. There are many important supporting factors, as I have indicated, but given the right context I argue that it is a global "best practice" for the formation of community and autonomy.

The Nemaska Example of Community Development

The consultation began with a request for a near-utopian vision, unencumbered by the practical realities of which all had some sense. The query was, "What would you like to see here in ten years' time?" The purpose of this beginning was to disembed the people of this consultation from the attitudes of dependency on government direction and to move from this disembeddedness (Taylor 2004, Chapter 4) into a social imaginary that reflected the Nemaska people's unencumbered aspirations. First on the 119-item action plan wish list was a church building, to be shared by the three or four denominations active at that time.

That church was built and well used but in a few years proved too small, and it has been replaced by a much larger one, still shared by the several denominational groups, including Anglicans, Baptists, and Pentecostals. Also used for powwow sweats and healing meetings, the church continues to be important to many. I would suggest, however, that the spirit of community is a pragmatic and ideological combination that goes beyond, or perhaps even underlies, the various contemporary religious practices. The challenging phrase "spirit of community" came to me in a letter from Albert Diamond, who had been the consultation's coordinator. Although Albert is a pragmatic person and businessman, he told me that, when he had visited Nemaska in the 1980s, he was impressed not only by the progress of building the townsite but also with the spirit of community. I want to take his observation seriously and explore the concept in some detail, since I think that its basis is also the source of transformations of identity, citizenship, power, and authority.

First, I believe that the spirit of community has a labour and materials component — the process of obtaining the funding, materials, and skilled work that literally build a community. Another member of the consultation, Lawrence Jimiken, predicts that in ten years' time (by 2015), we may expect about fifty more houses and a second large sports arena. He notes that they have even built places that have no occupants, such as the new multi-purpose building for physically or socially disabled persons, plus new housing for their staff. He would like to see more emphasis on employment outside the band council and Cree Regional Authority (CRA) enterprises. At present, the only private enterprise is the small convenience store, owned and operated by a non-Native. Lawrence reflects that in all the work of building "we forgot about the people!" He says that many people here are not aware of the past, not having been a part of the planning, funding, building, renovating, and allocating. Now people can get a subsidized rental, pay for ten years, and then have ownership of the house.

Respect toward persons and respect worked into environmental management are not as strong as in the 1970s. Respect is normally learned within the family. When parents grew up in residential school settings, this respect failed to be learned, so sometimes their ability in life skills, including parenting, is defective. Lawrence observes that most young or middle-aged people are now pretty sophisticated with regard to home appliances, video, and computers. For example, when taking a youth to the bush, he found it also involved taking a generator, a TV, and video games. Finally came the lad's request to "turn off the generator and ... go down the river."

Still, if the pragmatics of building the community left the people to mature as a community with little manifest guidance other than the behaviour and attitudes of the community leaders, the experience has apparently been a series of socially and spiritually constructive examples. There is pride in having built it themselves. Issac Meskino, another of the consultation participants, says that Nemaska, unlike the other newly built Cree towns of Oujé-Bougoumou or Chisasibi, had only their regular funding, Cree Programs, and a loan from the Cree Board of Compensation. Since the Cree-Naskapi Act of 1982, they have done their own budgets, and Indian Affairs is not an authority to which they have to go. Managing with their own funding, along with building their housing on their place of choice, is part of the pragmatic basis of the spirit of community.

Nemaska as a whole community is doing very well and has even absorbed problem teens from another community, most of whom have settled down now and are raising families. George Wapachee told me in 2000 that they had achieved 105 of the 119-item action plan wish list. In 2005, as in 1977, I found the community to be a friendly place.

Beyond the pragmatic basis is a sense of unity in the community enterprise and being witness to surprisingly rapid growth in population and in housing — from 95 people living in tents in 1977 to over 600 in 2005, and from the first 5 houses completed in 1980 to over 120 houses and many major buildings in 2005. The centre of the community is the site of the architecturally impressive CRA building. It represents the successful accomplishment of another one of the consultation wish list goals, to attract one of the grand council entities to Nemaska. This would show recognition and approval of New Nemaska — a kind of regional legitimation and prestige. The CRA is the central administrative agency, and the move to Nemaska was a reason for local pride, though it was not without its challenges.

Eddie Diamond, director-general of the CRA, told me that the impact of the relocation to Nemaska was more noticeable than if it had been in a larger Cree community such as Mistassini, due to the CRA bringing in a lot of "strangers" that the Nemaska people saw walking around their community. In addition, the general level of education in Nemaska was somewhat lower than in other Cree communities, so fewer Nemaska applicants qualified for jobs with the CRA, and, to make matters worse, the CRA salary levels were quite high compared to the band office employment, especially when Indian Affairs set the salary levels before the Cree-Naskapi Act of 1982 brought autonomy to the Cree region by replacing the Indian Act. The result of these factors was an elite group of strangers, both Native and non-Native, and many of these people went out to fish, hunt, and gather berries in the immediate area. But as the community has grown, and as some Nemaska people have obtained CRA jobs, the impact has lessened.

Nemaska is a gathering place with a history, with unity in its choice, building, and use, and so it is one locus of home. But family lands also have their histories of management and harvesting, and raising families, and so they are another locus of home. Therefore, a person living, learning, and teaching for himself or herself, in the bush or in the town, where the group members are free to decide and act for themselves and without interference from the Hudson's Bay Company or the Department of Indian Affairs, has a locus of home and a basis of autonomy to adapt to and incorporate the new and to collaborate with others in these adaptations. Individual autonomy may be defined by example: Issac does not drink, and he does not keep track of the length of time since he stopped, because counting the days is showing a continuing attachment. He says that trying to find a cure in a group in the south is not much good — it is something a person has to do for himself, and the best place is the bush.

Issac observes that the old people have two homes now — New Nemaska and Old Nemaska; whereas in the 1970s they had no home, they only lived in villages of other Crees, and that was never home. The gist of Issac's statement is that the spirit of community is manifested by a feeling of being home. The locus of the spirit of community is within the individual spirit — looking within yourself for resources, fortitude, and hope — "being at home with yourself." In this case, the locus of the spirit of community is also within the family, where the family hunting grounds are home; it is also within the community group — home is the gathering place, where customary access to hunting grounds begins. The three loci are complementary.

But the benefits of all this complementarity and successful town build-ing are not an unmitigated success, and the community's management (or lack of management) of conflicts is instructive. For example, the spirit of community in a hunting ground home may be compromised by unwel-come disturbances. As I mentioned above, in 1976 George Cheezo of-fered a site on Champion Lake for the new community to be built. What looked like a friendly and generous offer has impacted George's family in unexpected ways, and as his children grew up they also grew away from his lands, leaving him alone there. George may have thought in 1976 that twenty or so traditional families would not have much impact on his own family or on his lands, because Champion Lake would just be their sum-mer gathering place and each family would then go out to winter on their own lands for hunting and trapping. Perhaps most other Nemaska adults would have thought the same thing at that time.

George probably had no idea that in 2005 there would be a year-round place of residence for over 600 people, many of them living a less traditional lifestyle and some of them not feeling much respect for his wish to use his land without interference. Probably no one thought that hydro plans would change from the flooding of Old Nemaska to a different diversion. Now hydro is impacting George's lands with two construction camps as part of the diversion project, and his son has been denied access there.

But the most disturbing consequence for his personal community is that George's children could grow up to be able to choose and to get a good living without taking part in traditional pursuits on their family lands because of the rapid way that the town of Nemaska has developed. George may feel that his way of living on the land has been rejected by his adult children. He spends his summer days on a bench by the store, near the CRA building, watching people pass by, most of them unaware that their com-munity is built on his land. Probably most of today's elders in Nemaska and in myriad other places in the world have some of these feelings of the world passing them by.

The region-wide distress about the Cree leaders' signing with the Quebec leaders to allow further hydro development was strongly expressed in Nemaska, especially by younger men. The conflict was aired publicly, then it eased, and the Paix des Braves Agreement (2002) was locally accepted, though not without resentments and political consequences. Political solidarity was shaken by the lack of consensus building prior to the agreement, but the confidence in Cree political autonomy at the personal, family, and community level was not undermined in Nemaska or in the other communities. It remained strongly family and community based, and this was affirmed when, in the 2005 elections, the people elected new leaders, giving the previous leaders "a rest." This is very similar to the response to the Cree chiefs' signing of the James Bay and Northern Quebec Agreement in 1975. Many people felt that, if those elected leaders could make such a momentous change in relations with provincial and federal governments, they might take other major initiatives that were not fully sanctioned by popular advice and consent. Best to give them a rest and let others proceed at a less radical and more widely understood pace. The defeated candidates were not dismissed from the political arena but found other, less conspicuous, leadership jobs, and some continue to this day. My point is that the way in which a community handles political conflicts is indicative of people's connectedness, with their concern for its consensual basis. The way they deal with these regional-level conflicts is very similar to the ways they handle external threats (federal or provincial authority, hydro projects, forest fires) or internal tensions (youth misdemeanours).

George Wapachee has been the most central person in building the Nemaska community. He comes from a family of devout men; his grandfather, William Wapachee, was a widely known Anglican catechist. George feels that he never left Old Nemaska because he was away in London, Ontario, working during the summer of 1969, when the Nemaska people gave up and left. He worked in Saskatoon for five years (1972-6) and shifted to the Grand Council of the Crees of Quebec in 1976 when it set up their offices in Val d'Or. While working on the Nemaska file at the grand council offices in Val d'Or, he persuaded them to let Nemaska, rather than a more sophisticated community on the James Bay coast, try out the community consultation. After helping to coordinate the consultation and reviewing the action plan, George, with a core group of four to six men, set about building the first five houses. It took them two summers, learning house carpentry as they went along. One old man was even paddling his little canoe between the access road and the community site with bags of cement on the floor. Elected chief by acclamation in 1979, George resigned from the grand council to be "on board at all times," to guide "the saga of growing up as a community." The construction proceeded, averaging five houses a year. George said that people would pitch in for a while and then back off for a while. In time, some of the core group got their own ideas, and one of them ran against George for chief and won. George later teamed up with a non-Native engineer as project manager for the construction of the CRA building.

The unexpectedly rapid growth of the population reflects recognition and approval of the community, where more than once someone who is marrying-in winds up bringing the extended family to Nemaska. George sees such rapid growth as potentially becoming an obstacle. How much success would it take to overshadow the spirit of community?

For all his pragmatic skills and years of physical work, George sees himself as primarily a teacher. He believes that he has done what he was set on this Earth to do, and he would like to continue. George has been several times elected chief and either re-elected or "booted out," but he always sustains his sense of being put here for a purpose. He has learned to accept being booted out from time to time. Once he asked his brother why it happened, and his brother told him that people "want you to take a rest." When I spoke with him during his 2005 election campaign for deputy grand chief of the Grand Council of the Crees of Quebec, he gave me one of his brochures and explained that he chose a photo that made him look like a grandfather. The choice of portraying himself as an elder is appropriate. He has been a leader and worker for twenty-five years and has been an influential teacher by letting the example of his life show his industry and morality. He is remarkable for his community-transforming ability and sense of spirituality. George suggests that Old Nemaska could be a retirement community, like Elliot Lake. The band gave him a cabin there, on the old HBC manager's site — he even has a computer there. Although he did not win the 2005 election for deputy grand chief, George does not seem likely to retire yet. The saga has not ended, for George, for Nemaska, or for the Cree region. The globalization of media has made it easy to send drafts of this chapter to George and receive his comments.

Conclusion

And here my report on the Nemaska Crees' development of identity, citizenship, power, and authority rests for now. The democratic ideals of Lewin and his gestalt strategy group of the 1950s were realized again, in the 1970s, in the Nemaska community consultation, where each individual's words were respected and contributed to a collective practical action plan and to a spirit of community. The action plan was implemented in the 1980s with the participation of many community members, and few places in the world have managed success in realizing so many of the tangible goals they have laid out for themselves. Beyond the tangible achievements, and surviving the exceptional population growth, the spirit of community is still strong thirty years later. It is shown in the people's sense of belonging, commitment, and performance. Near the main intersection there is a sign: "It's your community. You be the judge."

chapter 4
Reaffirming "Community" in
the Context of Community-
Based Conservation

Monica E. Mulrennan

THIS CHAPTER IS AIMED at an improved understanding of the social
and political dynamics involved in community-based conservation (CBC).
Building on the critiques of Preston and Russell within this volume as well
as on a wider literature, two main arguments are presented: first, that the
recognition of nested and intersecting levels and scales of "community" —
up to and including global communities of indigenous leaders announcing
the special responsibility of their constituents as environmental stewards
— has major implications for community-based conservation; second, that
understanding the links between resource conservation and the larger political agenda of indigenous communities can provide perspective on the
recent achievements of indigenous peoples and affirm the centrality of
their role in community-based conservation.

In recent decades, "community" has become widely, and for the most
part uncritically, acclaimed as the appropriate unit for the implementation of resource conservation and environmental management. Among the
factors that have contributed to this recognition has been an increasing
disillusionment with conventional centralized and hierarchical approaches
to conservation and management (Blaikie and Brookfield 1987; Redclift
1987; Wells and Brandon 1992) and a broader questioning of the authority of Western science (Wilson and Bryant 1997). Calls for a move from
conventional, top-down, specialist-driven approaches to models centred
on a greater role for non-government actors or stakeholders fell on fertile ground, as witnessed by a proliferation of approaches focused on local

grassroots involvement and participatory research as well as integrated adaptive management and holistic ecosystemic perspectives (Berkes 2003; Borrini-Feyerabend, Kothari, and Oviedo 2004; Johannes 2002; McCay and Jentoft 1996; Roe et al. 2000). A defining characteristic of these approaches and the related discourse was that they consistently privileged "community" as the appropriate scale or unit for consideration. Formerly regarded as an obstacle to resource conservation and progressive social change, "community" was propelled to centre stage as the vehicle for decentralization, local empowerment, cultural survival, and biodiversity conservation. Not only were the goals of conservation and the interests of local people no longer incompatible, but also a counterposition was established in which conservation and community development were twinned as mutually dependent projects (Brown 2002).

Not surprisingly, indigenous peoples were swept up in the wave of support and enthusiasm generated for "community." The release of the World Commission on Environment and Development's (WCED) report on sustainable development in 1987 was a defining moment in this respect. A brief, highly generalized statement on the contribution of indigenous communities to environmental protection confirmed their status among other resource-based communities while also distinguishing them by virtue of their superior knowledge and practices and longer-term connections to their traditional territories: "These *communities* are the repositories of vast accumulations of traditional knowledge and experience that link humanity with its ancient origins. Their disappearance is a loss for the larger society, which could learn a great deal from their traditional skills in sustainably managing very complex ecological systems" (WCED 1987, 115-16).

In the years that followed, the agenda of indigenous communities was taken up in a range of national and international forums dedicated to human rights and environmental interests. International conventions, such as Agenda 21, the Convention on Biological Diversity (1992), and the Draft Declaration on the Rights of Indigenous Peoples, together with a host of legal and political developments at the domestic state level, have brought about significant changes, both positive and negative, in the lives of indigenous peoples. At the same time, the experience of CBC efforts has been mixed (Kellert et al. 2000). Initially, the "feel good" neoliberal associations of CBC approaches buffered them from reproach (Shore 1993), but toward the end of the 1990s mounting evidence confirmed the failures and shortcomings of many projects (Campbell and Vainio-Mattila 2003).

In response, a series of debates in the conservation literature focused on the merits of community-based approaches and prompted a long-overdue critical analysis of the field (Agrawal and Gibson 1999; Berkes 2004; Bradshaw 2003; Brosius and Russell 2003). Much of this critique and the recommendations that emerge from it are directly relevant to the experience of indigenous peoples — in particular that the tendency to reify, homogenize, and depoliticize local communities has greatly undermined efforts to understand and support locally based conservation initiatives and associated political agendas.

Unfortunately and somewhat ironically, as the following analysis reveals, a major failing of the emerging critique of CBC approaches is that, despite calls for a more political approach to the understanding of community-based conservation, the complexity and contribution of local social and political dynamics continues to be understated. For example, few if any of the available critiques acknowledge the extent to which local and/or indigenous communities have resisted, appropriated, articulated, and/or translated the discourse of community conservation as well as other globalizing discourses to advance their political interests and the often related goals of conservation and environmental protection. Instead, a focus on the limited resources and power of communities and their dependence on external agencies has overestimated their marginality even among those researchers and advocates who support an increased role for local communities in conservation and environmental protection initiatives.

Drawing on the experience of Torres Strait Islanders in northern Australia, we discover not only that many of the ideas and agents of community-based conservation have failed to gain a foothold among Islanders, but also that they have moved opportunistically to explore the utility of other discourses, particularly those centred on small boat fisheries and indigenous sea rights, which may hold greater promise of providing them with security of tenure, economic opportunities, and the wherewithal to protect and manage their lands, seas, and resources as they see fit. The case highlights an important predicament. An overly narrow commitment by conservation scientists and policy officials to what community-based conservation is and how it can be achieved may be at odds with local political realities on the ground and in the water. The implications are threefold. First, it may yield a distorted understanding of how and to what extent CBC approaches are working. Second, in cases that depart from the conventional expectations of community-based conservation, it can deny local communities the much-needed resources and support they require from external agencies to maintain and implement local management initiatives and advance their aspirations for local autonomy. Third, it reduces opportunities for scientists and policy officials to gain insights from local models and understandings of how local ecosystems function and are best managed.

The Concept of Community

Before reviewing the concept of "community" as currently applied in the conservation and resource management literature, it is necessary to review some of the factors that contributed to the recent preoccupation with the concept (see Agrawal and Gibson 1999). There is no doubt that the failure of preceding decades of top-down conservation policies and practices provided the most powerful argument for an alternative approach focused on community (Wells and Brandon 1992). In particular, the limited capacity of the state to coerce citizens into conservation projects translated into major problems at the implementation stage (see Wilson and Bryant 1997). The spread of democratic political structures that insisted on public participation in a range of social spheres also served to enhance the political appeal of community-based approaches. The growing recognition that indigenous peoples were gaining influence through the courts and media further highlighted the centrality of community. International conventions and accords, together with the enhanced role of non-governmental organizations (NGOs) at local, national, and international levels accelerated this recognition and sharpened interest in the contributions of local and community groups.

The emergence of community-based conservation also coincided with a significant conceptual shift in ecology and applied ecology. The emergence of a radically alternative view of environment, termed the "new ecology" (Botkin 1990; Scoones 1999) and focused on the non-linearity, self-organization, and uncertainty of complex systems, raised questions about the relevance of a deterministic science that seeks not only to predict but also to control and manage outcomes. This new understanding of nature and appreciation of its profound spatial and temporal variability also found resonance in many "traditional" understandings of nature. The latter, while acknowledging an underlying cyclic pattern to events, also commonly recognize the continuous intervention of unpredictable forces (Barsh 1999) that can be mediated and manipulated through social relationships that extend to all living and non-living things (Langdon 2002). Interest in indigenous worldviews and associated knowledge and management systems — both in their own right and for their potential relevance to the revision of conventional perspectives and approaches — strengthened support for the establishment and/or maintenance of community-based resource management regimes.

Having enjoyed more than a decade of uncritical acclaim, the role of community in conservation has recently become the subject of intense debate. At one extreme, a group of conservation biologists claim that community-based conservation initiatives are either inherently contrary to the goals of biodiversity conservation or are at best an unacceptable compromise that in the long run is doomed to fail (Terborgh 1999). Others, while acknowledging poor conservation outcomes, suggest that the problem is less fundamental, stemming from weaknesses in the application of the concept of community as well as failures at the implementation stage (Brosius, Tsing, and Zerner 1998). The former include the use of generalized representations of "community" centred on overly simplistic notions of community: community as "small spatial unit," community as "homogeneous social entity," and community as "shared norms and common interests" (Agrawal and Gibson 1999, 633). These representations are said to "ignore the critical interests and processes within communities, and between communities and other social actors" (ibid.), and thus shed little light on matters of resource use and environmental protection.

The association of community with "small size and territorial affiliation" (Agrawal and Gibson 1999, 633) has resulted in a widespread and naive application of the concept to all or any nucleated populations centred on basic service infrastructure. The complexity of interpersonal relationships and political processes at work in the negotiation of these spatially constrained and often vigorously defended and controlled shared spaces is all too often ignored, making it impossible to appreciate the link between such communities and successful resource management. A further problem that arises from the latter is the conflation and confusion of community as "social organization" with community as "village/settlement." Because of the limited attention given to internal interests and processes, much of the literature seems to operate on the flawed assumption that the loosely defined or undefined concept of "community" is a single unified local scale level at which management authority currently prevails or should prevail. Little account has been taken of the nested levels of institutional structures and authority operating within and between local and regional political arrangements or how they articulate with resource management regimes or with processes and agencies beyond.

Another problem with much of the conservation literature has been the tendency to romanticize indigenous peoples specifically and "traditional" communities generally (Wilshusen et al. 2003). Advocates of marginal peoples have frequently represented local communities as derivatives of three key determinants — scale, place, and identity — and used these shared qualities of "community" as a packaging device to connect marginalized groups from disparate parts of the world. Notwithstanding the negative impacts of the "invention of community" (Brosius, Tsing, and Zerner 1998), the representation and promotion of indigenous and traditional peoples as idealized, homogeneous entities has served a twofold purpose: fostering valuable transnational alliances and networks among indigenous peoples and promoting the rights and interests of indigenous and traditional communities at the international level (Nacher and Hickey 2002). The following statement speaks to the political power of the latter, uncritical premises notwithstanding:

> The community is important because it is typically seen as a locus of knowledge; a site of regulation and management; a source of identity and a repository of "tradition"; the embodiment of representation, power, authority, governance, and accountability; an object of state control; and a theater of resistance and struggle (of social movement, and potentially of alternate visions of development). It is, then, an extraordinarily dense social object and yet one that is rarely subject to critical scrutiny (not least by those, such as the post-structuralist critics, who sing its praises). It is often invoked as a unity, as an undifferentiated thing with intrinsic powers, that speaks with a single voice to the state, to transnational NGOs, or to the World Court. Communities are of course nothing of the sort. (Watts 2000, 36-7)

Agrawal and Gibson (1999, 640) similarly note "a widespread preoccupation with what might be called 'the mythic community' ... [that] fails to attend to differences within communities." Efforts to counter this trend generally fall short of the mark. For example, Redford, Brandon, and Sanderson (1998, 458) assert that "it is clearly not that communities are 'bad' but rather that they must not be stereotyped. Some will actively work to conserve some components of biodiversity; others will not, and have not." Unfortunately, such concessions provide a poor basis for moving forward. Redford and Sanderson's (2000, 1364) hope of establishing an alliance with forest peoples premised on recognition and acknowledgment of their dichotomous perspectives rings empty. They refuse to accept that forest peoples speak for the forest but offer a compromise position: "They may speak for their version of the forest, but they do not speak for the forest we want to conserve." Others, such as Oates, take the argument to its limits with no place for qualifications; he does not believe "that the park or reserve concept should be rejected because of the possible difficulties such a protected area may cause for a few people" (1999, 239).

Beyond problems with the concept of community, the effective implementation of community-based approaches has been found to be "extraordinarily complex and difficult" (Kellert et al. 2000, 713). According to Chapin, while conservation agencies were quick to jump on the bandwagon of community-based conservation, on the ground these initiatives "were generally paternalistic, lacking in expertise, and one-sided — driven largely by the agendas of the conservationists, with little indigenous input" (2004, 20). A lack of social science training, combined with little previous experience working with local communities and the dismissal of issues linked to the defence and strengthening of indigenous resource and property rights as "too political," is said to have undermined the relevance and legitimacy of many externally driven conservation initiatives at the local level. The fallacy of this depoliticization is underscored by Zerner:

All nature conservation and environmental management efforts are inevitably projects in politics. To ask questions about justice and environment in the late twentieth century means a vigorous engagement with politics, governance, and power. Certain species, landscapes, and environmental outcomes are privileged, while others are peripheralized or disenfranchi[s]ed. Each park, reserve, and protected area is a project in governance; in drawing boundaries — conceptual, topographic and normative; in implicating a regime of rules regulating permissive human conduct; in elaborating an institutional structure vested with power to enforce rules; and in articulating a project mission rendering the management regime reasonable, even natural. (2000, 16-17)

Notions of community, nature, and environmental conservation are inextricably tied to relations of power and agency, local and beyond, that must be addressed in the implementation of community-based management regimes. Efforts to reassert the validity and promise of community-based conservation approaches must acknowledge and embrace the political complexities and socio-economic realities of communities if they are to have any relevance and achieve results.

Toward a Revised Concept of Community

A common theme that emerges from the current critique is the primacy afforded to the role of institutions and institutional linkages at a variety of scales. Agrawal and Gibson (1999) suggest that the focus of community-based conservation should be on (1) the multiple interests and agents within the so-called community, (2) local politics and collective decision making and their links to external actors, and (3) institutions that impact decision-making processes. Kellert et al. (2000) also call for greater attention to institution building, organizational reform, and public education. Berkes (2004) emphasizes a cross-scale approach to conservation, governance, and community that would involve bottom-up planning but include horizontal and vertical linkages across various levels of organization. Similarly, for Hulme and Murphree (1999), the achievement of conservation goals is a matter not of identifying the right actor but of establishing institutional linkages and governance processes that allow the state, community, and market to function in the related fields of conservation and development.

The current wave of enthusiasm for the shift from a focus on community to the role of institutions ironically echoes the recognition given by the WCED to the importance of institutions almost two decades ago: "The recognition of traditional rights must go hand in hand with measures to protect the local institutions that enforce responsibility in resource use. And this recognition must also give local communities a decisive voice in decisions about resource use in their area" (WCED 1987, 115-16). A move toward a more political approach focused on "institutions" rather than "community" (Agrawal and Gibson 1999) may offer greater scope as a framework. Less burdened by the baggage and blind spots associated with the concept of community, this revised approach has the potential to contribute a more textured understanding of cross-scale interactions at different organizational levels (Berkes et al. 2005; Ostrom 1998). Community, as the foregoing discussion suggests, has been too blunt an instrument even at the local level to take account of the multiplicity of scales and dynamics at play, let alone linkages beyond the local. However, while an examination of the roles played and the tasks performed by various institutions has the potential to facilitate some unpacking of "community," the risk remains that the dynamics of social organization underpinning local institutions will remain invisible unless the role of political agency through institutional fields is understood. What counts as an "institution" also depends on a sharpness of ethnographic definition not to be taken for granted. A local institution such as kinship may be low in the relevance estimates of conservation and development planners but prove to be decisive in ordering the social field in which resource management "regimes" come to bear. It may define lines of cohesion and cleavage within and beyond local residential communities. So too with the social identities that inhere in extended family and clan, both differentiating and interconnecting identities based on community of origin. In short, the ethnographic terrain of institutional orders, and the manner in which local actors negotiate it, are as crucial to a non-reified institutional focus as to a non-essentialized perspective on community.

Community and Institutional Realities on Erub, Torres Strait

The small island of Erub in the eastern Torres Strait illustrates the weakness of notions of community that hinge merely on small size, co-residence, and assumed shared norms. Whatever degree of harmony may have existed in the past when Islanders lived in several small villages adjacent to beaches around the island, new challenges accompanied the move in the late 1800s, at the behest of the London Missionary Society, to a single settlement centred on the church and other infrastructure. While one might hypothesize that the move facilitated greater interaction and a stronger "sense of community" among Islanders, in reality relocating people to lands, beaches, and adjacent reefs to which many had no customary entitlement created significant tensions and conflicts that continue to be felt today. At the same time, relocation distanced many from garden plots and fish traps to which their identities and livelihoods were tied and undermined their ability to regulate and control access to those resources.

Ownership of and custodial responsibility for Erubam land and sea are tied to group identities at several institutional levels. Households inherit rights to certain garden lands, fish traps, and in some cases reef areas beyond the home island. They do so through membership in patronymic lineage segments, in turn nested within broader lineages, each descended from an apical ancestor, *lu giz* in Meriam or *Hed rut Blo pamle* in *ailan tok* (Torres Strait "broken" or creole). Lineages in turn identify with one of four major clan groupings: Seisarem and Peidu are associated with northwesterly winds, or *koki,* on the more fertile monsoon-facing side of the island and enjoy reputations as excellent gardeners, while Samsep and Meuram, associated with the trade wind on the southeast side of the island, are linked to land less suitable for gardening that adjoins an extensive home reef. They are considered the better fishermen. *Ged* (home place/territory) provides an important spatial marker of clan identity and territorial ownership. The institution of totems *(lubabat)*, and there are many for each clan, reinforces social and spiritual connections to components of terrestrial and marine environments. Totemic affiliations underline duties of care and cooperation between humans and the natural world and feature prominently in human social and symbolic exchange. Knowledge of place, networks of named places, and the charter myths of clans, island communities, and inter-island alliance groups are integral to the ordering of tenure and resource management (Scott and Mulrennan 1999).

In modern times, beginning with the colonial administration of Queensland, officially endorsed forms of local government authority were bestowed on island councils. In recent decades, external funding and resources of growing importance to local economies have been channelled by Queensland State and Australian Commonwealth administrations through these councils (Mulrennan and Scott 2005). A parallel local institution — the Erubam Le Traditional Land and Sea Owners Corporation — was established under Australia's Native Title legislation in 2001. Although starved of resources and external funding, as the official authority for Native title issues this body can wield considerable clout on sensitive issues of land and sea title that at times involve open and direct conflict with the island council as well as various families and factions within and beyond the community.

Thus, at the local level, community operates as nested and intersecting levels and networks of difference and alliance. Intra-island strife is often focused on land disputes between families that involve complex negotiation of customary rules, revealing contested interpretations of the strength and extent of ownership and access claims. Such disputes are played out in various forms, including religious affiliations, choice of marriage partners, adoption practices, and bylaws. A long and once violent history of contact with, and incorporation of, outsiders has made this a community both deeply committed to defending home territory and receptive to outsiders and outside ideas. Incentives of external funding and the achievement of political status in local and regional politics by individuals who successfully work "the system" have produced constant innovation and hybridization at the interface of indigenous and imported practices.

Beyond the level of the island community, at least two other additional levels operate: subregional island groups (Erub belongs to the eastern island Maiem or Meriam group) and a Torres Strait Islander region-wide identity.

In the past, elaborate networks of trade, marriage, and alliance dictated political associations. Some of them were quite stable, underwritten for eastern Islanders, for instance, by mythical journeys of the god Bomai and his son (or nephew) Malo from mainland New Guinea or present-day Irian Jaya through the western and central islands to Erub and Mer in the eastern Torres Strait (Scott 2004). This and related mythology has been brought into play in contemporary politics of identity and cultural renewal. Eastern Islanders point to shared language, culture, and mythology in speaking for the reef and sea spaces of eastern Torres Strait as distinctive from those of central and western Islanders. At the same time, mythical journeys criss-cross the Torres Strait region from west to east, and from south to north, providing ample grist for the mill of solidarity building, even as ambitions and jealousies anchored at subregional and local levels continually test and challenge that solidarity. In relation to local environments, "community" extends to other living things and places through the institution of totems, connections to named places as lineage and clan prerogatives, and rituals of respect and reciprocity maintained by hunters and fishers. Hence, Torres Strait Islanders articulate identities and cooperation in or as "community" in different contexts and at different scales,[1] the dynamics of which become apparent to outsiders only through detailed ethnographic analysis.

While region-wide connections, alliances, and animosities predate the colonial period, the idea of a regional Islander identity (which subsumes significant linguistic and cultural differences at the subregional level) is a function of shared experiences of colonialism and of resistance to the colonial enterprise (Beckett 1987). Islanders engaged in tactics of labour organizing as early as the 1930s, participated in the anti-racist activism of the 1960s, and assumed a strong voice in the Australian indigenous rights movement from the 1970s onward. In each context, Islanders have been "managed" as a distinctive administrative category by the state and in some ways treated differently from Aborigines of the Australian mainland. Their sense of themselves as a regionally distinctive political community, then, has emerged through a dialectical process of state imposition and grassroots resistance. At the same time, their treatment in Australian law and policy strongly parallels that of mainland Aborigines, who are the large major-ity of Australia's indigenous people. For certain purposes, then, the phrase "Aboriginal and Torres Strait Islander" evokes a further nested identity as the community of indigenous peoples of Australia.

Most recently, nested layers of community have reached outward to embrace the transnational through the development of a network of communication and alliance with other indigenous communities.[2] Islander leaders have attended international gatherings, including UN meetings in Geneva and NewYork, to speak to and meet with representatives of indigenous peoples from many corners of the world. In the words of Getano Lui Jr., former chair of the Torres Strait Regional Authority, "Torres Strait Islanders have turned to global environmental and sustainable development currents, and to spreading 'first world' standards accommodating indigenous autonomy and self-government, in order to bring some fresh air to discussions about their future" (1995). Discussions with other sea-faring groups facing similar challenges in relation to recognition of traditional sea territories and fisheries development issues have influenced Islander political strategies (see the chapter by Scott and Mulrennan in Blaser et al., forthcoming). At the same time, Islanders have used the international stage to highlight some of the adverse environmental impacts of globalization. In an address by George Mye, former ATSIC (Aboriginal and Torres Strait Islander Commission) commissioner for Torres Strait, to the UN Working Group on Indigenous Populations, the new realities and risks that globalization brings and the limited extent to which Islanders might resist or reverse them are deliberately underscored:

In a world where the global priorities are changing and humble custodians like ourselves are being called upon to advise on ecologically sound options necessary for the preservation and sensible management of our environment, let me just say that it is ironic that the age of industrialization has finally caught up with my people in the Torres Strait, and we are now beginning to experience the threat of pollution from mining wastes ... We stand a high risk of inheriting massive pollution — principally from the Ok Tedi Mine in the Western District of Papua New Guinea — despite countless appeals made to the authorities in Australia and Papua New Guinea. Additional risks of pollution are now being experienced with the opening of the Kutubu Oil Mining operation in the Papuan Gulf, which will open other shipping routes and increase heavy shipping traffic in amongst the narrow and shallow channels of the Torres Strait. (1992, para. 14)

The political dynamics that operate within and between nested layers of autonomies are central to how Islanders articulate their rights to resources. Strategic choices are involved — sometimes embracing Western models and adopting transnational discourses, at other times insisting on difference and distinctiveness. The local imagination on Erub is shaped, in part, as the cultural memory of journeys of cultural heroes and historical figures, embodied in terrestrial, marine, and celestial features, shaping human social identities at various levels and authorizing local institutions of land and sea tenure. Practical knowledge remains strongly indigenous in character — the vast majority of the hundreds of named marine creatures, for example, and cycles of tide, wind, moon, and season, are known by their Meriam names, even for Islanders for whom ailan tok creole has become the primary everyday language. Models of ecological relationship are finely tuned to the specific resources and by islander fishers and divers, and are geared both to subsistence activities and to over nearly a century and a half of involvement in commercial marine industries. At the same time, contemporary Islander discourses are also heavily influenced by conversations with scientists, particularly fisheries biologists, government officials, and such media sources as the Discovery Channel, so Islanders have learned to relate such concepts as sustainable yields, biological diversity, and fisheries stock assessment to their own context. These interactions are often seamlessly integrated into local discourses, where they are found in dialogue with both mythical and local practical knowledge-based discourses. Through metaphors and model building, links to the Old World are confirmed, and the relevance of new ideas is explored.

The discourse of sustainable fisheries development has been embraced with zeal by Islanders in the promotion of their small-boat fishery. While the Torres Strait Treaty provides for exclusive Islander fisheries, and Islander aspirations for Native title to the sea may result in more exclusive fisheries based on inheritance from indigenous ancestors, Islanders have found utility in exploring other rationales to support their cause (Mulrennan and Scott 2000). In particular, Islander leaders operating at national and international levels call upon various sources of authoritative discourse, including the WCED (1987), the Convention on Biological Diversity, and Agenda 21, and introduce them into ways of talking about and defending their rights to livelihood, territory, and autonomy. In declaring Exclusive Economic Zones of ten or twenty miles in radius around their home islands, the Meriam of eastern Torres Strait model themselves after the somewhat arbitrary and bureaucratized conventions of UNCLOS (United Nations Convention on the Law of the Sea) rather than Islander tradition, another strategic appropriation of globalizing discourses by Islanders. Leaders at the same time are actively forging metaphors to make the sea and their indigenous relationship to it more comprehensible to the rest of us: the "sea as our garden" rather than a vast emptiness. Their use of the courts, the Australian legal system, direct action on the seas against commercial operations seen as unsustainable, and media tactics invoke a heady mix of the customary and traditional, with rhetoric of human rights and environmental responsibilities that amount to a positioning within not just a wider Australia but also a transnational community of concerned global citizens.

Relational Autonomy in Torres Strait

Concepts of community-based conservation and resource management, externally derived, generally encompass only the levels or scales of "community" tending toward the local end of the spectrum and even then with limited appreciation of the institutional and political complexities. In so doing, they fail to take account of what Scott (2005) has termed the "relational autonomies" involved. This may be acceptable for certain narrow purposes, but it fails to recognize the multiple levels and modalities in which "community" functions. Isolating or privileging one level or modality over another reveals a distorted and incomplete assessment of Islander politics and establishes an unstable base for the establishment of partnerships linked to community-based conservation. The success or failure of any externally introduced initiative depends ultimately on successful negotiation and engagement of the nested layers through which relational autonomies are realized. For example, it would be folly to deal only with local island councils, or island-level fishermen's associations, while ignoring the Torres Strait Regional Authority; conversely, it cannot be assumed that consultation with, or approval by, regional-level Islander leaders is capable of effecting predictable outcomes at the local island level.

Accommodating and navigating these multiple levels of Islander autonomy poses a major challenge for any external agency with interests in Torres Strait while also going to the core of concerns about legitimate Torres Strait Islander representation within their own governance structure. A legacy of Australian Commonwealth and Queensland State policies in relation to Torres Strait, combined with contemporary funding formulas and procedures, is perceived at more local levels to compromise the autonomy of the Torres Strait Regional Authority and its legitimacy as the regional Islander government. The enormous difficulties involved in accommodating variable and sometimes disparate interests at intra-island and inter-island levels also hamper efforts by the regional leadership to move forward on a united front. The opportunity to amplify these sources of dissonance is not lost on state-level governments. A recent strategy by the State of Queensland for resolving Native title to islands in Torres Strait applied an inconsistent prescription that not only served to dilute the content of Native title but also exacerbated tensions among Islanders at a variety of levels.

To their credit, Islanders have learned from these experiences and understand well the synergistic value of enhanced horizontal and vertical linkages involving all levels. The emergence of a grassroots fisheries task force in the eastern strait in the late 1990s and the support it generated across the region underscored the importance of inter-island (horizontal) solidarity. At the same time, the success of these efforts, involving protest and controversial direct action, depended on the diplomacy and legitimacy of the Torres Strait Regional Authority to mediate and consolidate political gains. The subsequent restructuring of fisheries management within the strait was in many respects an attempt to replicate and promote this power dynamic. The endorsement of inter-island regional groups within this structure is aimed at bridging the distance between individual families and clans on isolated islands and a regional government based on Thursday Island. These groups enjoy considerable legitimacy through the membership of active fishermen, while a Torres Strait Regional Authority commitment to fund and support their participation provides continuity and stability — as well as the prospect of regionally efficient administrative measures over which Islanders are institutionally equipped to exert some control. While this revised management structure has been greeted with enthusiasm by Islanders, the Torres Strait Islanders' prospects for achieving increased autonomy over their lives and resources depend as much on their ability to mobilize political support from the nested levels of "community" active within Torres Strait as on negotiating the terms of such an arrangement with Canberra and Brisbane.

Community-based conservation programs — whether driven by external or internal agents — face similar challenges and depend on mobilization of similarly complex bases of institutional support. The success of these initiatives will depend in large measure on the extent to which the conservation agendas that inform them tie into the political agendas and processes of Torres Strait Islanders at all scales. While this engagement of local support may necessitate some compromise of conservation priorities in the short term, the convergence of Islander aspirations for economic and political autonomy with the long-term health and sustainability of the Torres Strait environment presents abundant opportunities for enhanced resource and environmental protection. The establishment of protected areas represents

one such opportunity, with the potential to fulfill the twin goals of reinforcing customary marine tenure while also enhancing sanctuary for species
during critical life cycle stages. Other approaches, such as the current initiative by CRC Reef and James Cook University to instigate species-specific
community-based management plans in the region, tend to offer less scope
for at least two reasons: first, they may fail to connect with a fundamental
element of Islander harvesting strategies (the importance of multiple species harvesting, the rhythms of which are attuned to seasonal fluctuations
in the availability and condition of the resource); second, they do not fit
themselves to the broader socio-economic and political context of resource
harvesting and management in the region. Thus, despite their designation
as community-based programs, in reality these are programs developed by
outsiders to advance an agenda designed "to assist Indigenous fishers to
develop an understanding of the scientific principles, techniques, and underlying reasons for collection and analysis of fisheries data and how the resulting data influences subsequent fisheries management decisions." Rather
than mapping onto local agendas and attempting to engage Islanders in
a productive and meaningful dialogue, non-Islanders sometimes condemn
Islanders for their limited participation in and support of these programs,
which in turn, from the outsider's perspective, "defeat the purpose of developing and initiating community-based management" (CRC Torres Strait).

Conclusion

Approaches to community-based conservation, if they are to fulfill their
potential, require a fundamental reassessment. As a first step, unpacking the
nested and intersecting levels and scales of "community" is needed, followed by recognition of the social and political dynamics operating within
each level and between levels. That they are not capable of orchestration
from outside must also be realized, which explains why, in situations where
outside advocates of community-based conservation impose their own
agenda, they so frequently fail to touch ground with local institutional
dynamics. Effective community-based management is not about educating
locals in the ways of Western scientific research or appointing community representatives to management boards. Creating the conditions under
which indigenous knowledge and local management authority prevail
requires enabling local institutions to function on their own terms —
buffered from state interference, while drawing autonomously on useful
information resources that the latter may be able to offer.

If even the most enlightened government interventions from the centre can erode the very thing they are trying to protect just by being there, then more productive alternatives must be explored. The challenge before us is to identify the circumstances under which local institutions are afforded the authority and autonomy to do what they do well. Greater attention to discourses of sustainable resource use, environmental protection, and indigenous rights may help, if these discourses can ground themselves in local realities. A better appreciation of the ways in which indigenous peoples articulate and translate local relationships to nature and territorial rights in the context of these discourses — and under conditions of formidable political, economic, and cultural pressures — should reduce skepticism about the "reality" of communities. Notwithstanding the naive representation of communities as homogeneous and depoliticized entities, indigenous peoples are not sitting idly by as passive recipients but are making substantial strides in the strategic utilization of globalizing discourses and networks. The processes involved in translating and adapting these discourses into vehicles to advance local agendas are acts of collective resistance — often subtly and strategically conducted — and of reconstruction, often toward goals not so much at odds with the central goals of many conservationists.

Globalization has afforded indigenous peoples the opportunity to extend their nesting of community transnationally; indeed, indigenous peoples have enjoyed what Minde, Nilsen, and Jentoft refer to as a "fruitful international mobilization" (2003, 307) at this level. A key aspect of their success has been their ability to forge communities of interest with other indigenous people while making linkages to "larger worlds of power, discourse and institutional allies" (Zerner 1999, 5). In the act of "translating" (ibid.) transnational discourses, not just in linguistic form and appearance but also in substance (in making the meanings and intentions of these discourses their own, transforming and refracting them into local political and cultural contexts), indigenous communities have understood that they must relate to external legal and political interests and institutions. What emerges is new but familiar enough both to find its place in the "mainstream" and to be meaningful within particular cultural and political contexts. The multiplicity of strategy, deployed through the horizontal and vertical linkages of indigenous politics, generates what are sometimes too hastily dismissed as inconsistencies or paradoxes of indigenous culture. Ironically, the orchestration of this very heterogeneity, and the navigation of these paradoxes, are the conditions of effective political "community."

chapter 5

The Moral Economy of Global Forestry in Rural British Columbia

Scott Prudham

> This argument [about the double movement] can be taken
> further not only by noting the different economic and political
> programmes and ethico-political visions into which economic
> liberalism is articulated but also by considering the range of
> counter-hegemonic projects that can be developed to resist the
> onward march of liberalism. *For if society's fightback is to move*
> *beyond dispersed, disorganized and mutually contradictory struggles,*
> *attention must be paid to the ways in which "society" acquires a relative*
> *unity and cohesion* in resisting capital's unhampered logic.
> — Bob Jessop, "Regulationist and Autopoieticist
> Reflections" (emphasis added)

ON 26 JANUARY 2001, the Cowichan sawmill in Youbou, British Columbia, closed. More than two hundred people were put out of work in a community and a region where few comparable employment opportunities existed. The owner, a prominent forest multinational, had decided the mill was redundant and no longer profitable. Paralleling as it did many similar mill closures in the province during recent years, the Cowichan mill would have been easy to write off as one more casualty of a fickle, increasingly footloose industry tied more closely to global markets and centres of capital than to places like Youbou.

But the employees of the mill were unwilling to accept this script. Instead, they formed a non-governmental organization (NGO) called the

Youbou TimberLess Society (YTS) and began to lobby for social and environmental justice. At first, they focused on evidence of corporate and bureaucratic wrongdoing. They argued that the company had an obligation to the workers and to the local community, a responsibility prescribed in the lease governing the company's exclusive, private access to state forest lands in the area. Facing little chance that the company would change its mind, and largely abandoned by the state, the group nevertheless persisted and broadened its vision. The YTS increasingly challenged the industrial model of forestry that had sustained the mill, embracing community-controlled forest tenure, stronger protections for jobs, high value-added production, and forest practices emphasizing ecological sustainability. At the same time, the group's political affinities, affiliations, and subjectivities changed. The group increasingly networked outside trade unions, forging ties with environmental and First Nations groups and with broad coalitions advocating for enhanced local autonomy via greater control over forest management and harvesting rights. In so doing, the YTS emerged as one of the more compelling voices for changing forms of forest control and governance in British Columbia.

This chapter is not about a social movement that won; the YTS has yet to win much of anything tangible. But it is about a group that challenges the very idea of a globalization consensus, and at the same time it explores the dynamics of an evolving, self-organizing social collectivity struggling for greater autonomy in the context of contemporary globalization. The chapter draws on an ongoing collaborative research relationship with the YTS and on documents pertaining to its campaign as well as from ongoing discussions with other contributors to this volume. The main goal of the chapter is to explore the challenges of defining and redefining claims for community-based "autonomy" as a form of counter-globalization, particularly as these claims invoke moral economies of work and nature.

To develop these ideas, I draw on the work of Karl Polanyi (1944) and his analysis of the politics of the nineteenth-century laissez-faire international order (a precursor to contemporary globalization), with emphasis on his idea of the "double movement." I argue that the theory of the double movement remains salient for numerous reasons, not least because it renders globalization in political terms as a struggle between contending autonomies, one seeking to enhance the freedom and flexibility of capital and market processes (pursuing what Polanyi terms the "self-regulating market"), the other seeking to protect and enhance the autonomy of a somewhat loosely specified self-organizing society. While Polanyi's formulation usefully illuminates the "problem" of globalization in political terms in ways that I argue remain highly salient, at the same time it leaves unresolved what a successful counter-hegemonic vision might look like. As the YTS struggle demonstrates, this is a question of moral economies: namely, what rights and obligations (whose autonomies?) govern economic activities and relationships? But it is also one of political subjectivities involving the definition and redefinition of "community" in political terms. Ernesto Laclau (2005) has usefully discussed this as the problem of "populism," which is none other than to define a counter-hegemonic political community. However, I argue that this problem is both enabled and constrained by territorially based notions of community, familiar in the taken-for-granted sense of the word *community* but now also enjoying a renaissance thanks to widespread enthusiasm for community natural resource management, including community forestry in British Columbia. If such programs afford opportunities for reinvigorated, territorially based communities organized around a new politics of place, they equally challenge the potential formation of progressive, less territorially based communities necessary for the kind of populism Laclau has in mind. In this sense, the political problem of counter-globalization has interconnected geographical and moral dimensions.

The Cowichan Sawmill, BC Forest Policy, and the YTS

Youbou's Cowichan sawmill was owned and operated by TimberWest Forest Limited, a company headquartered in Vancouver. The mill was supplied with logs primarily from provincial Tree Farm Licence (TFL) 46, a swath of state forest land covering over 99,000 hectares of the midsection of Vancouver Island, near Cowichan Lake. Although leased on an exclusive basis for twenty-five years, the TFL remained nominally state-owned land, governed by an Annual Allowable Cut (AAC) limit and by provincial regulations on forest practices. The Cowichan mill relied on TFL 46 for 75 to 80 percent of its total log supply,[1] producing finished lumber intended primarily for export to Japan.[2]

At its peak, the Cowichan mill employed in excess of seven hundred people. However, successive rounds of restructuring and technological changes reduced the workforce to under 250 by the late 1990s. Former employees maintain that the mill remained profitable up to the time of its closure. Yet it is clear that TimberWest had little long-term interest in its operation, having tried several times to sell the mill prior to its closure.

Former employees also report that the company had ceased to process top-quality logs at the mill and that investments in equipment replacement and renewal had ceased to keep up with minimal requirements. Moreover, an inquiry into the mill closure after the fact revealed that TimberWest had in years prior discreetly investigated how the mill might be closed given provincial restrictions requiring that it be operated as a condition of retaining the rights to TFL 46.

In fact, these restrictions were a crucial link between the Cowichan sawmill at Youbou and TFL 46, tying the fortunes of the broader Cowichan Lake region to TimberWest and its global connections. The mill and the TFL were two places where a distinct set of political ecological relations between land, labour, and capital became territorialized, reflecting and reinforcing what can be understood as a particular spatial fix for forest-based capital accumulation in British Columbia. Two key institutional facets of this fix are of particular note. In the case of the workforce, the Cowichan mill was represented by the Industrial Wood and Allied Workers (IWA) Local 1-80 under the terms of a pattern agreement between the IWA and Forest Industrial Relations Limited (representing forest products companies) that covered the coast region of the province.[3] In the case of the TFL, the terms of the lease specified cutting amounts and practices but also, as noted, tied harvest from the TFL to the Cowichan mill via an appurtenance clause. This clause, known simply as "Clause 7," stipulated that the leaseholder "will not cause its timber processing facility at Youbou to reduce production or to close for a sustained period of time, unless, and to the extent that the Minister, or his designate, exempts the licensee from the requirements of this paragraph" (cited in Gelb 2001, 2). The clause, in place until 1997, further required the company to manufacture roughly 330,000 cubic metres of logs from TFL 46 at the Cowichan mill every year.[4] Failure to comply would open the company up to the potential loss of access rights. Indeed, the company's own legal counsel had warned management that the clause would not allow the mill to close or reduce production: "If such reduction or closure is anticipated, it would be prudent to obtain the Minister's exemption from the requirements of Clause 7. Failure to do so might subject TimberWest to a host of remedies, not the least significant of which might be a suspension and, possibly, cancellation of the license."[5]

This raises the question of how this clause was removed from the lease in 1997, allowing the company greater flexibility and autonomy in its allocation of the harvested wood volume, a central question motivating the initial formation of the YTS. The Ministry of Forests has since maintained that it was an administrative error involving replacement of specific language in Clause 7 with more generic conditions that did not name particular facilities or harvest volumes. YTS members and local residents affected by the mill closure have been skeptical that a simple administrative error can explain what happened. The coincidence in timing indeed seems suspicious given evidence that the company was actively seeking a way to sell or close the mill and had been advised to seek relief from the clause by striking a deal with the IWA in order to present a proposal endorsed by the union to the government.[6] The IWA, in collaboration with the YTS, filed suit over the mill closure and the removal of Clause 7, naming both the government and TimberWest. Although the IWA has now dropped the suit, it is still pending, and being pursued exclusively by the YTS.

"Globalist" Political Economy in BC Forestry

The exceptional circumstances surrounding closure of the Cowichan sawmill unquestionably helped to fuel outrage among the mill's workforce and in the wider communities of the Lake Cowichan region. But it is critical to highlight the connections between this isolated mill closure and systemic features of a distinctly globalist system of forest products production and regulation. Many facets of the Youbou story, including the social and institutional relations tying together capital, the local state, and rural economies in a project of forest appropriation and transformation, are reflected in the Cowichan mill case. These features point to a long-standing "structured coherence" of political economic and ecological relationships that have provided a particular kind of socio-spatial fix for forest-based capital accumulation in the province. And it is just as much these wider systemic features that YTS organizing has come to highlight and target.

By invoking David Harvey's (1985) twin notions of a structured coherence and a socio-spatial fix, I refer to the specific political economy and geography of both capital accumulation and capitalist regulation (social and environmental) that prevailed for much of the period subsequent to the Second World War and that in British Columbia underpinned a spatially extensive and environmentally intensive model of commodity production as well as a particular geography of social life.[7] The "spatial fix" is Harvey's phrase for the particularly geographical or territorialized ways in which the inherent crisis tendencies of capital accumulation may be offset or resolved (if only temporarily) by particular socio-spatial relations, only to become obstacles in subsequent rounds of restructuring, when capital seeks autonomy from these very spatial configurations. Harvey's notion draws on regulation theory, but also spatializes it, and includes all manner of institutional, regulatory, and technological dimensions of "the partial, temporary spatial fixes of accumulation as capital seeks to resolve crises through geographical expansion and uneven geographical development" (Jessop 2004, 481). Most of the inspiration for Harvey's thinking along these lines has been in relation to cities and the particular ways in which the spatial organization of urban landscapes is made and remade under capitalism. Rounds of urban restructuring are driven by the changing imperatives of fixity and mobility, as fixed spatial configurations are first created to enable and regularize capital accumulation but then become subsequent obstacles to the flexibility and mobility (i.e., autonomy) of capital required to facilitate subsequent rounds of typically accelerated accumulation (Harvey 1982, 1985). Although Harvey does not say much about ecological transformations as facets of socio-spatial fixes, the centrality of forest-based capital accumulation and the dramatic remaking of the BC forested landscape over the past century by industrial forestry demand that material ecological conditions be considered constitutive elements of, and not merely incidental to, the spatial fix of British Columbia's globalist forestry model.

The political and institutional relations sustaining this spatial fix comprise a structured coherence (also Harvey's phrase) that has lasted more or less intact since the end of the Second World War. This model featured access rights to public forests granted to increasingly large-scale and globally integrated private capital mass-producing relatively generic commodities mainly for export markets. It also featured state-centred, top-down, and expert-dominated bureaucratic administration of science-based forest regulation, guided by maximum sustained yield forestry. And it featured a form of institutionalized paternalism toward forest-dependent rural economies and communities, with the state making conditions such as local wood processing a quid pro quo for capital's access to provincial forest lands. From a political standpoint, the structured coherence of this model was sustained by what has been called British Columbia's exploitation axis (Burda and Gale 1998; Burda, Gale, and M'Gonigle 1998; Salazar and Alper 1996) — political ties binding organized labour, capital, and the state together in the project of liquefying British Columbia's green gold (i.e., its old-growth forests).[8]

All of the features of this model are evident in the case of the Cowichan mill. For instance, the mill's orientation toward international and specifically Japanese markets is consistent with the provincial forest industry's emphasis on exporting most of its output to the United States, Europe, and Japan in the form of largely generic, mass-produced commodities (Burda and Gale 1998).[9] This reliance on international markets was in fact critical as an outlet for the industry's dramatic expansion during the middle of the twentieth century (Hayter 2000; Marchak 1983; Marchak, Aycock, and Herbert 1999).[10] Yet globalism in BC forestry is also apparent in the dominant role of multinational capital. While public land accounts for about 95 percent of forest land in British Columbia, most of it is leased to large, international corporations, as in the case of TFL 46. Never a "natural" phenomenon, this has been by design in the province's model of globalist forestry. Specifically, large-scale capital has been consistently courted, based on the now questionable faith that larger companies would prove more stable and thus a better bet for the economic future of British Columbia's hinterland (Bengston 1994; Tollefson 1998).

In return for retaining access rights, companies were obliged by their unionized employees to provide relatively high wages and benefits and by the provincial government to maintain processing facilities in often remote forest-dependent areas. The latter commitment frequently came in the form of explicit appurtenance clauses inserted in forest leases naming specific mills in particular locations, an example of which was Clause 7 in the lease governing TFL 46. This territorialized capital in a particular way even as it reflects and reinforces in turn a particularly territorialized conception of "community" tied to interwoven and proximate spaces of work and home and embedded within the state.

Yet, if the Cowichan mill and TFL 46 reflect and reinforce the political ecological relations of the socio-spatial fix in British Columbia's forest sector, so too does the sudden closure of the mill reinforce a long-standing sense that this fix is unravelling. The BC forest industry has been wracked by fluctuating levels of performance and profitability since the 1970s (Hayter 2000, 2003; Hayter and Barnes 1997; Marchak 1983). Many areas of the province like the Cowichan Lake region have experienced the pain of layoffs and mill closures (Barnes and Hayter 1992; Barnes, Hayter, and Hay 2001; Halseth 1999a, 1999b; Hayter 1997, 2003; Ostry 1999; Reed 1999). This turmoil is related in part to the ecological exhaustion of conventional, industrial, sustained yield forestry as valuable and voluminous old-growth timber stands have become increasingly scarce in British Columbia (Dellert 1998; Demeritt 2001; Green 2000; Marchak, Aycock, and Herbert 1999). Not coincidentally, active political opposition to conventional industrial forestry in British Columbia has grown. Highly publicized campaigns seeking to preserve remaining old growth in places like Clayoquot Sound (located on the island, not far from Lake Cowichan) have been complemented by a resurgent First Nations nationalism seeking a stronger voice in forest management (Braun 2002; Hayter 2000, 2003; Magnusson and Shaw 2003; McManus 2002; Rayner 1996; Rayner et al. 2001; Satterfield 2002; Wilson 1998). And it is in this context, building first on the immediate and seemingly exceptional circumstances of the Cowichan mill closure, then increasingly drawing on and contributing to a wider political community dedicated to forestry reform, that the YTS has emerged to become one of the more compelling voices advocating a different kind of forestry in British Columbia.

The Youbou TimberLess Society

The Youbou TimberLess Society was actually formed in December 2000 in advance of the mill shutdown, after TimberWest announced the mill would be closed. Reflecting the immediacy of the threat, the group focused first on publicizing and impeding the company's plans. In the initial aftermath of the mill closure, the YTS attempted to block the mill's disassembly in the hope that TimberWest could be forced to reverse its decision, sell the now-closed mill and the TFL, or (as a somewhat unlikely third option) have the IWA own and operate the mill directly. Hope was first placed on provincial enforcement of Clause 7 based on the erroneous belief that the clause was still in place as well as on IWA efforts to buy the operations. But the local state proved unwilling to act, not least because (as soon became apparent) the clause was no longer in place. And talk of the IWA buying the mill evaporated quickly, in part because TimberWest imposed an extremely tight timeline for the development of any union proposal.[11]

While early efforts failed to stop either the mill closure or the April 2001 decommissioning of the Youbou site, they did contribute to organizing and building solidarity among the displaced workers, helping to establish the YTS as an independent NGO. On 11 January 2001, the IWA and the YTS staged a rally outside the provincial legislature in Victoria, successfully drawing attention to the impending mill closure. The YTS also conducted and publicized a log truck count in the first days after the mill closed, documenting the continued flow of unprocessed logs from TimberWest lands via the company's log export docks in nearby Crofton.

This count helped lead to the first policy issue highlighted by YTS organizing, specifically raw or unprocessed log exports. The theme proved to be critical and successful in gaining political resonance because of the broad, clear appeal of opposition to unprocessed log exports and because it helped the YTS to bridge a long-standing chasm between labour politics and environmental politics. While the IWA has traditionally resisted open opposition to log exports because of the influence of its logging division, other unions and groups concerned with local economic development have opposed the apparent export of jobs attendant with the international sale of unprocessed logs. At the same time, environmental groups have opposed raw log exports based on the perceived link between low value-added production and ecologically destructive high harvest volumes. Pushing this issue, the YTS helped to organize a highly successful protest against raw log exports in front of the provincial legislature on 24 February 2001, which was featured in a widely circulated film entitled *Exporting BC's Future* (Williams 2001) produced by the Western Canada Wilderness Committee (WCWC).

The log export rally and theme allowed the YTS to shift and broaden both its mission and its organizing strategy as well as to build bridges to diverse organizations seeking forest policy reform in British Columbia. By the time I first met members of the YTS on 23 July 2002, this transformation was well under way. On a hot, dry Wednesday evening, I attended a general meeting of the Youbou TimberLess Society in the IWA Local 1-80 Hall, just east of the downtown business district in Duncan. As was explained to me that night and the next morning by members of the YTS executive, the group's membership had by this time grown to more than two hundred, with half the membership composed of people who had never actually worked at the mill. Most, but by no means all, of the members I met were men, and most, but again by no means all, were of apparent Anglo-European descent. At the meeting, most of the talk concerned the YTS's entry of a float in the Duncan Summer Festival parade on Sunday, 14 July, which had won first prize. The theme was a tree seedling giveaway, and the YTS had distributed 1,300 seedlings to people at the parade. An effective organizing and outreach activity, the seedling giveaway also signified the group's broadening vision and its growing engagement with what was termed "community"-oriented and more "sustainable" forestry.

The raw log theme, prominent a year earlier, had helped to precipitate these changes by bringing the YTS into contact with a prominent environmental group and by highlighting a tension in the group's initially conservative, reactive position on what needed to be done. Opposition to raw log exports became an entry point for dialogue linking higher value-added production with more selective, less damaging forest practices and lower-volume harvests. YTS collaboration with the WCWC on the film highlighted these connections, as did a warming relationship with the BC Sierra Club.

The connections with environmental groups in turn helped to bring the YTS into contact with ideas about social and environmental alternatives to the kind of globalist forestry dominant in British Columbia through-out the postwar era. Among these alternatives is the idea of "community forestry." In recent years, a widespread international consensus has formed in activist and policy circles advocating "local," "community" control as an alternative to corporate and state-centred natural resource appropria-tion and regulation.[12] While the province has formally granted a limited number of such tenures since the late 1990s, there is broad support in the NGO community for expanding this program. And despite entrenched, open hostility to the idea by the IWA, the YTS has increasingly gravitated toward community forestry, seeing itself as a potential owner of, or partner in, a community forest tenure. Reflecting enthusiasm for this idea, mem-bers of the YTS attended the BC Community Forestry Forum, held at the University of Victoria, 14-16 March 2002, featuring activists, academics, and policy analysts from around the world with an interest in community-based forestry.

Favourable disposition toward community forestry also helped to pro-vide a bridge to First Nations groups seeking their own form of enhanced local, community autonomy in forest tenures and management. The YTS began to actively network with First Nations, crossing another typically frosty divide between BC First Nations and the trade union movement, particularly the IWA. Signifying this rapprochement, dancers from the nearby Cowichan First Nation performed on the YTS float in the Duncan Summer Festival parade of 2001. And YTS members have cited coopera-tion with both the Cowichan (Cow ut zun) and the Ditidaht Nations on issues surrounding community forest tenures and greater local autonomy in forest ownership and governance.

Throughout, a key piece of YTS strategy keeping the group linked with its origins has been the aforementioned lawsuit pertaining to the mill closure. Backed by the YTS and former members of the Cowichan sawmill, IWA Local 1-80 initially launched the suit in May 2001, naming the provincial government and seeking damages for allowing Clause 7 to be removed. However, the union's lawyers, in a letter of 25 April 2003, ex-plained that all evidence gathered to that point indicated that the minister of forests must have known that Clause 7 was being removed. That is, and ironically contrary to ministry staff claims that the clause had been erroneously replaced by a more generic processing clause, the union's legal team concluded that then-minister Zirnhelt had endorsed the move.[13] Acting on its lawyer's advice, in June 2003 the IWA dropped the suit. The YTS, however, refused to accept this decision, further alienating the YTS from the union, and in July 2003 relaunched the suit filed by YTS member Ken James. On 6 May 2004, BC Supreme Court Justice Dean Wilson certified the case as a class action suit, and it is still in progress as of this writing.

The twists and turns in the tale of the lawsuit are further evidence of YTS persistence, resourcefulness, and resilience, but they also point to genuine obstacles and setbacks the group has faced. None of these seems more puzzling and unfortunate than the divergence of the YTS from the IWA and the deterioration of relations between the two. While the IWA initially supported the YTS in tangible ways, friction has been evident from the outset. To a large degree, this is a function of the YTS's broadening network of relations with groups dedicated to forest policy reform, some of which have been and remain critics of the IWA. Union leadership has been openly critical of the YTS for this reason. In 2002, the IWA local withdrew access to the union hall for YTS meetings, ostensibly because the former mill workers were no longer union members but also, as numerous people indicated, because the union's leadership was angry over YTS collaboration with groups such as the WCWC and the Sierra Club.

The significance of this split is not merely to be judged in terms of the changing networks of relationships in political organizing but rather points to the changing individual and collective subjectivities of YTS members constituted by a struggle that increasingly targets the structured coherence of globalist forestry in which these individuals were, until the mill closed, embedded. Changing conceptions of what forestry is and should be for YTS members go hand in hand with changing conceptions of themselves but also, significantly for this volume, reflect changing ideas of community. Specifically, the evident meaning of "community" reflected by the YTS has changed or become more polyvalent. While the word, as this volume attests, is problematic and slippery, it always refers to associations of some sort. For YTS members, one might conceptualize the changing connotations of community as having moved away from the more territorialized connotation of interwoven associations among workplace, home, and place (literally the geographical agglomerations where mill workers lived). It has shifted toward a connotation less strictly territorialized or place bound and more overtly constituted in political terms by geographically disparate actors seeking reform. In this sense, mobilizing against one facet of actually existing globalization (globalist forestry in British Columbia) has precipitated a profound change in the character and composition of the "communities" of which the YTS and its members are a part. In the remaining portion of this chapter, I explore the significance of this shifting notion of community as it pertains to the YTS and consider it in relation to questions about globalization, autonomy, and the politics of alternatives.

The YTS, Community Autonomy, and Counter-Globalizations

In some ways, there is not much to get excited about when it comes to the YTS. It is not my intention to romanticize or gloss over important problems and obstacles facing this group. By strictly material standards of success, the YTS has accomplished little. The workers did not get their jobs back. The YTS does not own a mill, nor does it have direct access to fibre. And the YTS remains a relatively small, obscure, locally based organization, bounded in important respects by workplace and territorially based notions of community. Most of the members are from the Lake Cowichan region, and the group's profile remains highest there. Although the YTS has opened the door to new organizational chapters in other locations, it does not yet feature any. The YTS can claim little by way of effecting significant policy change, despite successful campaigning in the most recent provincial election.[14] And the former mill workers, members of the YTS and otherwise, continue to suffer adverse effects from the mill closure (as of this writing) more than six years after the fact. (For more details on lasting effects of the mill closure, see Prudham and Penfold 2005.)

But measuring success in strictly material terms cannot capture, much less explain, the formation of political discourses and subjectivities that themselves will underpin any eventual material gains. Such measures cannot capture or do justice to the persistence of the group, which in and of itself is a form of success. And perhaps most importantly, it is arguable that there is as much to learn from so-called failures as there is from successes. Put differently, exclusive emphasis on material gains will not offer insights into how and why groups such as the YTS constitute themselves as political communities engaged in the search for alternatives to actually existing globalization. It is these processes that are central to the lived experience of globalization and to the questions of social and environmental justice invoked by an examination of globalization as contending autonomies. In this way, globalization as outcome and as consensus carries less salience than as struggle(s) over whose autonomy is enhanced, whose is compromised, and whose capacity to act and transform human and non-human geographies is reinforced or reduced.

In these respects, I am struck by the ways in which working with the YTS has reinforced a sense that *this is globalization*. Seemingly endless rounds of defining globalization as something ostensibly unique and different about the contemporary period must be complemented by a close examination of the ways in which particular places and spaces become the crucibles for the same kinds of debates and definitions. That is, globalization must be seen as emergent from the innumerable dialectically connected political moments that produce and construct meaning around increasingly distantiated political, economic, and cultural relationships stretched by globe-spanning processes. As Gillian Hart argues, this is not just about our conceptions of globalization but also about our conceptions of the *spatiality* of globalization. Localities (often described as "communities" in a strictly place-bound, territorial sense of the term) such as Lake Cowichan, Duncan, and Youbou are not merely the concrete places and spaces where abstract globalization occurs; rather, they are "constituted in relation to one another through power-laden practices in the multiple, inter-connected arenas of everyday life" (Hart 2004, 22). And in this they are constitutive of globalization and our understandings of globalization (see also Burawoy 2000; Hart 2002).

This is not to deny, however, marked differences in the institutional, material, and discursive "resources" that can be brought to bear in shaping globalizing outcomes, perceptions, and representations that enhance or reinforce one form of autonomy or another. Given, for instance, the pronounced differences between the YTS and TimberWest in their respective capacities to act in ways that transform places, both human and non-human, it is tempting indeed to think in terms of "nautonomy," David Held's (1995, 170-1) term for the "asymmetrical production and distribution of life chances which limit and erode the possibilities of political action." However, I would not advocate the adoption of this term if it in any way overlooks groups such as the YTS for precisely the ways that they *do* act politically.

Here I find it useful to draw on the insights of Polanyi to reflect on and interpret aspects of the YTS campaign and its relevance in relation to the politics of globalist forestry and community autonomy in British Columbia. In his best-known work *The Great Transformation,* Polanyi (1944) argued that the advance and retreat of economic liberalism, spanning from the middle of the nineteenth century through the two world wars of the twentieth, could be conceptualized in terms of two contending political movements for and against laissez-faire capitalism or what he called the "self-regulating market." According to Polanyi, contradictions in this project of market self-regulation reside in the "fictitious" commodification of money, land, and labour. Focusing on his argument about land and labour, his logic is deceptively simple: if a commodity is that which is produced exclusively for sale (as Polanyi specifies), then land and labour cannot be commodities because they can never meet this condition. Rather, their production is inherently "embedded" in a wider political ecology.

The relevance of *The Great Transformation* as a key text for scholars of globalization has been revisited by others (see, e.g., Block 2003; Burawoy 2003; Jessop 2001; O'Riain and Block 2003), and I will not dwell on it here. However, one of Polanyi's central arguments I wish to consider is how the fictitious character of land and labour as commodities gives rise to political conflict between market and non-market claims to each. Polanyi called this the "double movement" for and against market self-regulation. In his words, the double movement

> can be personified as the action of two organizing principles in society, each of them setting itself specific institutional aims, having the support of definite social forces and using its own distinctive methods. The one was the principle of economic liberalism, aiming at the establishment of a self-regulating market, relying on the support of the trading classes, and using largely laissez-faire and free trade as its methods; the other was the principle of social protection aiming at the conservation of man and nature as well as productive organization, relying on the varying support of the market — primarily but not exclusively, the working and landed classes — and using protective legislation, restrictive associations, and other instruments of intervention as its methods. (Cited in Jessop 2001, 221)

A key insight here is Polanyi's emphasis on the development of a more market-governed society as something that must be *made* to happen. Transcending widely held and still prevalent dichotomies between politics and economics, Polanyi's thesis has a "levelling" effect. It defines politics not as that which is opposed to the "normal" or the "system" but as a contest between contending moments. It renders "the economy" not as something given but as something made. For example, in his discussion of the Poor Law reforms of 1834, which eliminated relief and forced workers into either factories or workhouses, Polanyi emphasizes how decisive state action was needed to remove social welfare provisions, "freeing up" labour to market coordination (with devastating effects) and giving the lie to any notion of the natural, apolitical unfolding of a purely economic logic.

Polanyi's emphasis on the political remains an important counter to the tendency to see globalization as something that "happens" to local places and that comes to be resisted. It also avoids what Jessop identifies as the frequent diminution of the political in political economy, a tendency that elides what he calls the "inescapable political dimension" of state action and the struggles of various social movements in constituting the economic (2004, 492). The relevance of this view in relation to the YTS and globalist forestry is evident. It is very easy to see groups such as the YTS in political terms. It is less easy, particularly in public discourse, to render the "structured coherence" of globalist forestry in such terms. Yet this "system" is the culmination of numerous, key, contingent, and intentional choices, including, for example, the initial establishment of the modern forest tenure system and the privileging of large firms in granting leases.[15] More recently, it includes the myriad ways in which the BC state has attempted to respond to persistent political economic and ecological crisis and stagnation in the province's forest sector, alternating between what has been called a "neo-pluralist" reformism of the 1990s (McManus 2002) and a distinctly more neoliberal flavour in recent years. This combination has led to the establishment of community forest tenures, for example, and has produced some significant reforms in forest practices (McManus 2002; Rayner et al. 2001; Wilson 1998). But it has also largely entrenched business-as-usual globalist forestry, not least by enhancing capital's autonomy via the outright elimination of all appurtenance clauses tying commodity production to particular places. As the authors who write under the persona of J.K Gibson-Graham argue in their work on the politics of global capitalism (1996), to avoid seeing groups such as the YTS as strictly particular, territorially bounded resistance movements facing immutable globalizing processes, we need to see these globalizing processes as themselves contingent, dialectically related to (and produced by) "the local" (Rankin 2003).

Seen from this vantage point, and again drawing on Polanyi, groups such as the YTS become constitutive of the formation of a politics that opposes self-regulation, a politics that draws on social and moral (see below) imperatives other than market worship to embed economic processes. And in this sense, as Michael Burawoy has forcefully argued, Polanyi's *The Great Transformation* (and his subsequent work) make a central contribution to the development of a viable notion of society, one occupying "a specific institutional space within capitalism between economy and the state, but where 'civil society' spills into the state, 'active society' interpenetrates the market" (2003, 197). While it is not always clear exactly what political and institutional form this society will take (see below), what is clear is that Polanyi believed that the politics of land and labour, under the dual movement, would be constitutive of both the specific trajectory of capitalism and its wider social context and the relation between the two. It is intriguing in this sense to consider the ways in which the YTS has moved from being a largely labour-based organization resisting the unregulated commodification of labour to one that offers a highly compelling vision of different use values governing the transformation of provincial forests for human ends — that is, one seeking stronger social controls over the allocation of land and labour. Moreover, if Polanyi's emphasis was squarely on the disjuncture between the economic and the social under liberalism, groups such as the YTS, through their organizing, highlight the ongoing salience of neoliberal economic doctrine. In this sense, the YTS offers a caution to those (e.g., Scholte 2003) who would emphasize the differences between contemporary globalization and nineteenth-century liberalism; these differences can be overstated if they overlook important continuities with the past (Weaver 2003).

Yet, if the YTS invokes the politics of Polanyi's double movement, this invocation reflects and reinforces important ambiguities in his thesis and in his idea of the social. It is here where the profoundly ambiguous and politically elusive notion of "community" comes to the fore, explicitly in the group's embrace of community forestry and otherwise in the logic of YTS political organizing. If globalization and counter-globalization may be conceptualized as a series of modern-day double movements, Polanyi offers little insight into the specific politics of moves to protect society from the ravages of commodifying land and labour. One can imagine, for instance, that such movements could (and do) run from radical to reactionary. Similarly, whether these countermovements specifically organize against market self-regulation and commodification (i.e., whether they become explicitly anti-capitalist movements) as opposed to reform movements that work within and through capitalist states is an open question.

And if Polanyi offers little guidance on the substantive content of moves to protect society from market self-regulation, he also does not offer much concerning how it is that disparate groups might become joined into broadly based counter-hegemonic coalitions. The latter is a political problem that, as Laclau (2005) has argued, goes to the heart of the notion of populism, invoked explicitly or otherwise in various discussions about the politics of counter-globalizations. The question, in Laclau's terms, is whether and how such groups can contribute to a "chain of equivalences" necessary to unite disparate, fragmented social demands into a counter-hegemonic populist force. Here the formation and reformation of collective subjectivities are dialectically related to the articulation of moral economic claims that not only counter the logic of self-regulation but also stand a chance of presenting viable alternatives.

There are two key aspects of this politics that I wish to highlight here, one pertaining to the geographical logic of linking disparate, local, territorially bounded particularities, the other pertaining to the moral content of economic embeddedness. Each of these aspects invokes the "problem" or ambivalence of enhanced community autonomy in relation to actually existing globalization. The geographical problem pertains to the spatial scale and logic of political action and social regulation (Brenner 1999; Peck 2002; Swyngedouw 1997; Swyngedouw and Heynen 2003). Jessop, in his comments quoted at the outset of this chapter pertaining to Polanyi's double movement, clearly recognizes both facets in his reference toward "dispersed, disorganized and mutually contradictory struggles." Although not fully specified in such terms, the adjective *dispersed* reflects Jessop's insight into the problem of political geography, one that pivots on whether "communities" as collective political subjectivities are strictly territorialized and place bound or whether they are able to transcend this place-bounded character to become linked in a "chain of equivalences" across space. If localized moves to enhance social autonomy (however specified) are to transcend their particularities, there remain profound challenges to the "scale jumping" (Smith 1992) required to mobilize a truly counter-hegemonic globalization.

The second problem is that of the moral content of alternatives. Returning to Laclau, his argument is that populism per se has been misunderstood because it cannot be evaluated as a politics that is necessarily about anything in particular (i.e., in terms of its substantive logic). Populism is neither inherently progressive nor reactionary. Instead, as noted above, populism is a contingent political *logic* involving the coalescence of discrete, particularistic "social demands" that, despite being different, become linked by a "chain of equivalences" into a politically unified movement.

Yet, if there is an implicit geographical problem to be worked out here, there is also a moral or normative one. As Laclau (2005, 12) goes on to ask, "to what extent does the logic of equivalence dominate [the movement's] discourse?"

At stake here is the idea of moral economies: that is, the moral content of "embeddedness," the now ubiquitous (Polanyian) term to reflect the politically and socially constituted character of the economic. The notion of a moral economy has a complex lineage but can be traced to E.P. Thompson's (1968, 1975) work on how popular movements have resisted perceived violations of traditional rights of access to land and resources, typically related to enclosures of various kinds. One of the key insights of this notion is that the "economic" is frequently if not always underpinned by moral imperatives that guide behaviour (Booth 1994). Related to the Polanyian notion of embeddedness, the moral economy idea has been used to explain why typically marginalized individuals and groups act in certain ways in response to transgressions of what are perceived as their rights. It provides a rationale for approaching knowledge and truth claims or worldviews as situated, and it encourages careful empirical, ethnographic, and historically situated approaches to political conflicts (McCarthy 2002; Scott 1976).

Some critics have argued that Polanyi made the "mistake" of treating economic liberalism as an exception to this rule rather than dissecting the moral codes underpinning liberalism. This, the argument goes, constructs moral economies as unique to marginalized, traditional, non-Western, and non-liberal settings or (in Polanyi's case) to the social claims opposed to market self-regulation. Ascribing moral economies only to the politics of resistance or to the non-liberal "other" would contradict Polanyi's own insistence on a thoroughly political double movement. But more importantly, it would overlook the norms, rights, and obligations that underpin economic (and other forms of) liberalism that have become so taken-for-granted and naturalized that they are often overlooked (until resistance to their sometimes violent imposition serves to remind). Whether this is a fair or accurate reading of Polanyi is not the point (see Block 2003; Block and Somers 1984; Booth 1994). Rather, what is important is to consider the broader question about the overarching normative imperatives that determine what kinds of behaviours are right and wrong, and, perhaps most radically in the context of a capitalist globalization addicted to and dependent on growth, to what end(s) the "economic" is to be directed.

The question of "community" then becomes critical not only as an issue of political geography but also of prevailing moral codes. What is the political and geographical basis of a community, and how does the community constitute itself in relation to norms, beliefs, and ideas about a social order in relation to those of prevailing, actually existing globalization? The ambiguous but also ambivalent character of community in my view resides in large part on the basis of these two problems: namely, how do disparate, particular, and largely territorialized communities constitute themselves into more spatially extensive communities, and from what set of moral imperatives do they draw? There is reason to be both hopeful and apprehensive, which in my view is why the very word *community* seems to elicit such mixed reactions among left-critical observers (see Watts 2004), every bit as much as does invoking the word *morality*. Community, in these respects, turns on the ambiguous politics of social claims mobilized in opposition to market self-regulation, critically, as Polanyi argues, vis-à-vis land and labour.

Consider the YTS in these respects. One of the most striking things about the YTS is the way in which the group (and individual members) have undertaken broad, open-ended, and reflexive processes of constructing and reconstituting political subjectivities. This is not to say that YTS members are saints or that they have wholly overcome their historically and geographically constituted subject positions. The group remains overwhelmingly though not exclusively male and has in my experience never explicitly dealt with issues of gender. The group is about as diverse as the population of the region overall (roughly 15 percent immigrant, largely white Anglo-European, with significant and growing Indo-Canadian populations). But the executive committee of the YTS, where most of its activism comes from, is all white and all male. In addition, class politics and tensions continue to manifest themselves in the YTS, primarily in the composition of the executive. Of the four men who have taken the most prominent leadership roles, only one held a shop floor or production line job at the mill; the others all had "white collar" or professional positions, for example as engineers or accountants. Latent class tensions around these divisions of labour are evident in comments made by members of the group about one another. These politics arguably inform the group's orientation toward "big picture" reforms as opposed to more localized strategies aimed at securing employment (permanent or otherwise) and relief for former members. And if a broader agenda of reform draws the group toward less strictly territorialized strategies for community autonomy, it also potentially compromises the longer-term chances of the YTS "winning" something tangible in the Cowichan Lake area.

But all of this reflects and reinforces that these are complex people involved in complex negotiations over how they define their political subjectivities and how they constitute themselves in relation to the wider world, even as they seek to change that world. In this sense, it is difficult not to be struck by the ways in which the YTS quite profoundly challenges the now stale dichotomy between "old" (i.e., labour-based) social movements and "new" ones. The YTS has moved from being a labour-based and territorially bound organization embedded within a trade union to being one still motivated by social justice questions in relation to work but now cast in broader political and geographical terms. These terms now include engagement with access to and control over forests (means of production?), commodity production, a wider politics of social justice (including race), as well as a willingness to challenge business-as-usual forestry in the name of environmental sustainability. This willingness has made environmental and First Nations groups closer political allies to the YTS than the IWA, and this is very difficult to understand in terms of a strictly materialist, interest-based politics. In fact, the YTS has adopted positions on forest policy reform that could well undermine its chances of securing access to forest tenure by antagonizing both the Ministry of Forests and the IWA, two pillars of the exploitation axis in British Columbia (and the YTS can hardly expect favours from the third). Indeed, according to the group's main spokesperson, YTS organizing has compromised his prospects for future work in the area since he has been branded a "troublemaker" by potential employers. At the same time, the group's widening political networking and changing collective subjectivity have, somewhat paradoxically, led it to embrace the now ubiquitous but also politically ambiguous call for "community" control over natural resources, in this case forests. This is both a tactical manoeuvre (seeking to capitalize on existing institutions and political momentum) and a genuinely hopeful invocation of community natural resource management as an alternative to business-as-usual forestry. If this is not everything I (we?) could hope for, it is at the same time about as hopeful as anything else I have seen.

chapter 6   **From Servitude to Dignity?**
A Community in Transition

Amanda White

ON 19 NOVEMBER 2002, the *Prestige,* a Bahamian oil tanker, sank some
seventy-five kilometres off the Galician coast in the Atlantic Ocean with
approximately 70,000 tons of fuel oil in its tanks.[1] Over 1,000 kilometres of
the 1,121-kilometre Galician coastline, parts of the Spanish Cantabrica, and
coastlines in France and Portugal were eventually contaminated. Similar
to case studies presented in this volume (see chapters by Prudham and
Preston), this event sparked intense public debate about belonging and social justice. In this chapter, I consider how the ecological disaster, a product
of economic globalizing processes, incited new modes of collective action
and redefined analytically rich concepts such as community and autonomy.
I show that this "critical event" (Das 1995) helped to open a public space in
Galicia for claims to a shared community identity and the opportunity for
communal autonomy to be debated. Specifically, I examine the dominant
discourse of activists in Nunca Máis (Never Again), the social movement
that emerged in Galicia following the ecological catastrophe that foretold
a cultural shift in the identity of the regional community from "servitude
to dignity."

Setting the Scene

The Spanish state is characterized as "federal-regional" (Prieto de Pedro
1998, 68). Geographic regions are the central focus of pluralism. Since the
end of the Franco regime, Spain's democratic model has been organized

Amanda White

around territorial levels: the state, the autonomous communities, the provinces, and the municipalities. The Spanish Constitution of 1978 allowed for the establishment of autonomous communities. The Constitution recognizes them as decentralized territorial political units. These units "act out the self-government of the different 'nationalities' and 'regions' of Spain" (Prieto de Pedro 1998, 69). There are now seventeen such communities in the Spanish state. Autonomy is regionalized within Spain's state structure (Greenhouse and Greenhouse 1998, 7). Prior to the commencement of the Civil War in 1936, Galicia was granted the status of a non-state nation during the second republic (Roseman 1995, 4). As a "historical nationality," Galicia, like the Basque region and Catalonia, gained the status of "historical autonomous community" following the death of Francisco Franco in 1975. According to Galician anthropologist José Antonio Fernández de Rota Monter, as a nationality the autonomous community "takes on the main task of defending the identity of Galicia and its interests and promoting solidarity amongst the Galician people" (1998, 130).

Since 1981, Galicia has had a regional government known as the Xunta. Galicia is also officially bilingual, using both Galego, the Galician language, and Castilian Spanish. The Xunta has control over areas of government administration such as health care and education and the construction, tourism, agriculture, and fishing industries, among others. Manuel Fraga, a former minister under the Franco regime and the founder of the political party Alianza Popular (later known as Partido Popular), has been president of the Xunta, governing with an absolute majority, since his initial inauguration in 1990.[2] At the time of the sinking of the *Prestige* in November 2002, the right-wing Partido Popular held power in Spain's National Assembly and in the regional Galician parliament. As I document below, for many activists in Nunca Máis, the perplexing situation of semi-integration in this model of the "federal-regional state" limits the ability to act in an autonomous manner. Significantly, the majority of Galicians harmoniously combine a sense of collective Galician identity with self-definition of the Spanish state.

Legacies from the Galician Political Economy

Galicia has long identified itself as an ethnically distinct, rural, and peasant region, economically marginal in the Spanish state and in more recent times within the integrated markets of the European Union (Bauer 1987, 1992; Beiras 1997; Gulevich 1995; Roseman 1993, 2003, 2004; Villares

1998). Since the end of the twentieth century, however, there have been significant changes in Galician socio-economic and political conditions as a result of the shifting interface between regions, nation-states, and the EU. At the beginning of the 1970s, for example, approximately 53 percent of Galicians were engaged in agriculture and fishing, whereas about 26 percent were employed in the service sector (Villares 1980, 275). By the last decade of the twentieth century, the service sector surpassed the primary sector as the number one employer of Galicians (Gulevich 1995, 68). Spain, however, has one of the highest unemployment rates in the European Union. It is estimated that by 2010, with continuing urbanization occurring in Spain and in Galicia, 66 percent of Galicians will reside in semi-urban and urban areas (see the Instituto Galego de Estatística website). Since Spain's entry into the European Economic Community, later the EU, in 1986, the "financial incentives to become involved in large-scale capitalized agriculture were replaced with price subsidies and inducements to encourage small-holding agriculturalists to abandon farming altogether and even commit to taking their land out of production as the newly expanded European bloc confronted the problem of 'overproduction'" (Roseman 2004, 16).

Despite these recent changes in the political economy of Galicia, political activist and academic Xosé Manuel Beiras argues in the most recent edition of his book *O atraso económico da Galiza* (Galicia's Delayed Economy) that "Galicia's economic backwardness [continues to be] a fact, like [Galicia's] exploitation" (1997, 11, 14-15). As I show in the following sections, similar to Beiras, Nunca Máis activists problematized the legacies of the Galician political economy in their representations of the Galician regional community and in their debates about regional autonomy.

The "Critical Event"

The *Prestige* oscillated in the open ocean for seven days before sinking. That monumental week sparked the beginning of media frenzy, political declarations and negations, and public discussions about government officials' decision-making practices and the rights of citizens to partake in this process. Journalists from the region, from Spain, and from other European countries made their descent into what would become popularly known as Galicia's "ground zero," those areas most affected by the ensuing oil slicks. Reporters meticulously recorded events surrounding the Spanish government's decision to deny the tanker port entry in one of Galicia's harbours, a denial that quickly became the target of open criticism levied against Spanish government authorities. This situation was made worse when the vice-president of Spain, Galician-born Mariano Rajoy from the right-wing governing party Partido Popular, told his fellow Galicians in a live television broadcast not to worry, that the amount of fuel oil seeping into the ocean was negligible: "The coast would suffer as a worst case scenario only trickles of fuel oil [*hilillos*]," he said in earnest (16 November 2002).[3] More than 50 percent of the Galician population live along the coast. Approximately 12 percent of Galician employment relies directly on the fishing industry, which is just over 10 percent of the Galician gross national product (GNP). For these Galicians, it was clear from the beginning that the economic consequences would be deeply palpable despite Rajoy's hopeful evaluation.

In sharp contrast to the Partido Popular's downplaying of the potential impact of the oil slick, already by 16 November villagers along a coastal area in northern Galicia known as the Costa da Morte in the Galician language or "Death Coast" in English awoke to the horrors of raining fuel oil, which blew in from the ocean, covering the coastline and their streets, businesses, and homes. In the context of the government's tactic to minimize the situation, journalists who inundated coastal Galicia to follow the development of the story were themselves unprepared and "stupefied by the great impact of the oil slick" (Catalán Deus 2003, 89). In the words of one Spanish journalist, even before the sinking of the vessel "people were drenched in *chapapote* [colloquial for fuel oil]. A dense layer of it covered cliffs and rocks" (Catalán Deus 2003, 99). In media portrayals of the eventful sinking, statements made by Spanish and Galician authorities from the Partido Popular on the disaster were set against the actual experience of villagers and juxtaposed alongside sensationalist images of birds, marine life, rocks, homes, and people shrouded in fuel oil. These counterpositions helped to solidify an emerging gap between two distinct realities, one where political representatives forwarded the view of *hilillos* and the other depicting ordinary citizens' experiences of the successive waves of ravaging oil slicks. Although there were competing readings of the disaster, a dominant interpretation emerged: the sinking of the tanker was *not* an accident. It could have been avoided, it was argued, with the execution of safety measures and with the adoption of an alternative decision that would have allowed the tanker to dock at a Galician port in order to transfer the remaining fuel oil on board to another vessel's tanks. In short, government representatives from the Partido Popular were largely blamed for the extent of the ecological depravation even though the EU was also involved.

The *Prestige* itself reflects economic globalization through the presence on the seas of increasingly large ships carrying huge amounts of petroleum usually to distant markets. The EU is involved in these transactions in two ways. First, the United Kingdom has become a major producer of petroleum through its offshore resources. Norway, an adjunct state to the EU through the European Free Trade Area, is also in this position. Second, the EU countries are increasingly dependent on petroleum resources to fuel their economies. The tanker was registered in the Bahamas, which is not a major producer but a country of convenience for a world shipping industry seeking to maximize profits and remove itself from nation-state scrutiny and regulation. In essence, a registration in the Bahamas or Liberia "erases" nation-state identity from the ship and signifies its global identity. This registration also signifies the global character of shipping in general and oil transport in particular. Hence, oil slicks like the ones that occurred in 2002 become much more likely as economic globalization intensifies.[4] The public blame of the Partido Popular should come as no surprise, however, since there was an ever-widening discrepancy between what officials from this political party said and what Galicians experienced. This gap coalesced into growing civic frustration, and unrest formalized itself into a Galician-based social movement, Nunca Máis.

Nunca Máis: A "New" Social Movement

What began as a small gathering of concerned Galician artists, intellectuals, regional politicians from the left-wing Galician nationalist party (the Galician Nationalist Bloc), and the Galician Confederation of Unions only three days after the sinking of the *Prestige* would eventually grow into a monumental social movement never before seen in the Galician context.[5] Within a month of the first meeting, the social movement formalized, adopting the name La plataforma cidadá Nunca Máis (Never Again, the movement of citizens). In a statement on the group's website, the reason for creating the social movement is made clear: "It was the ocean, our life was under threat, and we saw the ocean abused and without defence [*Era o mar, a nosa vida, o ameazado e víamolo maltratado e indefenso*]." The group wanted to bring together "citizens' responses to their government's treatment [of the sinking of the *Prestige*], which culminated in the ecological disaster." In the words of Maria, a university professor in her late thirties at the University of Santiago with almost two decades of experience in Galician-based social movements, Nunca Máis is "a movement of the citizens ... It serves citizens independently of any organization. It represents you" (interview, 4 June 2003).

More than five thousand pages in one of Galicia's regional newspapers, *La voz de Galicia* (13 November 2003, 26), were dedicated to the sinking of the *Prestige* over the course of a year. Throughout the year, other sectors of society focused on the event and the societal response that was Nunca Máis. Indeed, from November 2002 to November 2003, the sinking of the *Prestige* and the theme of Nunca Máis overshadowed most organized events and rituals in the Galician context (e.g., soccer and basketball matches, work strikes, parades, other protests organized against the state in response to the government's support of the US-led war in Iraq). Galicians and other Spaniards openly talked about their governments' management of the disaster and their response to the oil slick on radio and television programs.

Nunca Máis was depicted as distinctively different from other movements because, as one activist said, "all kinds of people," including Galicians who normally do not participate in protest, came together under the unifying banner of Nunca Máis to challenge the regional and Spanish governments' treatment of the sinking of the *Prestige* and to demand the resignation of politicians deemed responsible for the extent of the ecological disaster. Experienced activists interpreted this level of commitment as being unusual in the Galician context. Nor was the movement localized or specific to those Galicians directly affected by the oil slick. In the words of Maria, Nunca Máis "unified all of Galicia [*unío todo Galicia*]." For another Galician academic, "the waves of solidarity put an end to the sentiment of living in a geographic corner far from everyone and forsaken by those who administer" (Arias Veira 2003, 21).

Thus, the movement brought "together fishermen's organizations, environmental, student and other like-minded groups" (Aguilar Fernández and Ballesteros Peña 2004, 33). Although I describe the struggle between activists in Nunca Máis and the regional and national branches of the Partido Popular, these opponents do not, in the words of Jane Schneider and Peter Schneider, "face off on opposite sides of a battlefield as identifiable armies" (2003, 4). Rather, like the anti-mafia struggle that they examine in the Sicilian context, this struggle in Galicia is "embodied in the divergent attitudes and practices of people who occupy the same social spaces" (ibid.). Even though activists whom I interviewed were against the Partido Popular, it cannot be assumed that all activists opposed this political party.

Initially, the goal of Nunca Máis activists was to coordinate an organized effort to raise awareness about the *Prestige* disaster and to offer a civic space for frustrated and disgruntled Galicians who were morally outraged with the Partido Popular regional and national governments' response to the catastrophe. Activists who were already opposed to the Partido Popular government hoped that the oil spillage would translate into an opportunity to modify the political situation in Galicia by non-electoral means (Aguilar Fernández and Ballesteros Peña 2004, 44). In the words of Susana Aguilar Fernández and Ana Ballesteros Peña, "the *Prestige* was initially perceived as a window of opportunity in order to introduce changes into a static regional political scenario" (ibid.). Indeed, recall that at the time of the disaster the Partido Popular had been governing in Galicia for twenty-three years with Manuel Fraga as the regional president during the last fifteen years. "His leadership," as Aguilar Fernández and Ballesteros Peña state, was never "questioned either by his party or by the Galician electorate" (ibid., 37). Despite the fact that the opposition parties failed to oust the Partido Popular in the first elections following the disaster (the municipal-level elections in May 2003), activists' ongoing consciousness-raising activities fostered debate about the status of the region as one of Spain's autonomous communities.

Nunca Máis Debates Communal Autonomy

Nunca Máis activists described the relationship between Galicia and "the state" as deeply problematic owing to the region's chronic dependency on institutional economic aid. According to Ricardo Beiras, professor of environmental studies at the University of Vigo in the Galician province of Pontevedra, the "democratic and autonomous institutions of Galicia" did not play a role in the management of the crisis, and he analyzes this inactivity as symptomatic of the region's continuing dependency on the Spanish state (2003, 22). For activists in Nunca Máis, the sinking of the *Prestige* brought to light the still relevant question of what kind of autonomy is available in regions such as Galicia. Moreover, statements made by Partido Popular representatives such as the minister of agriculture, who angrily declared that "those [Nunca Máis] signs don't put food on your table, we do," perpetuated the image of an omnipotent, paternalistic, and arrogant state (Beiras 2003, 25). Activists blamed the state for abandoning Galicia in the crisis, thus implicitly indicating that they desired the presence of the Spanish state. However, they envisioned a state presence removed from the entangling system of political cronyism and patronage that was interpreted as further entrenching the imbalance of power between Galicia and the Spanish state and between the political class and civil society. Activists in Nunca Máis addressed the lingering question about the region's autonomy by encouraging public debate and non-contentious actions against the Partido Popular government. In this way, "for the first time," according to another activist, "Galicians showed dignity, becoming the dignity of the *pobo*" (interview, 28 May 2003).

The Galician economic and political conditions were also scrutinized and viewed as severely limiting the region's ability to act autonomously. The view of Galicia as transforming from the Land of Servitude to the Land of Dignity emerged in relation to these constraints. The sinking of the *Prestige* marked a symbolic "disruption" in the way that Galicians narrated the relationship between the region and the Spanish state (from Roseman 1999). Although activists framed their struggle in the context of the Spanish state, it seemed to me that to write about "the state" was out of step with the growing bodies of literature on the importance of neoliberal transnational corporations and other actors such as refugees, immigrants, and global justice activists whose daily crossings of state boundaries challenge territorial sovereignty. Despite Galician friends' attempts to help me establish connections with activists from transnational organizations such as Greenpeace that had a presence in Galicia during the oil slick, I was repeatedly reminded of the salience of the state in the Galician context. Nunca Máis activists, for example, openly criticized Greenpeace for focusing on the environmental consequences of the oil slick without consideration of the particular historical and institutional conditions of the Galician region that are perceived as legitimizing environmental disasters.

Despite forecasts of a withering state, since the Second World War the number of "states has more than quadrupled" (Aretxaga 2003, 394). As Begoña Aretxaga attests, "the desire for statehood continues to be intense in many parts of the world" (ibid.). "Globalization," she asserts, "is not only compatible with statehood; it has actually fueled the desire for it" (ibid., 395). In addition to Nunca Máis activists' regard for the state as the guarantor of rights, debates on the status of the region were framed in the context of the state. Thus, far from having little relevance, for activists in Nunca Máis the state is perceived as structuring belonging in the "new" Europe. Nunca Máis brought together citizens' moral outrage and articulated this widespread sentiment in the form of organized debate on the status of the region as one of Spain's autonomous communities. It is also true, as previous anthropological research in Galicia attests, that public debate about the status of the region is not new or confined to this environmental disaster (e.g., R. Bauer 1992; Gulevich 1995; Kelley 1994). Significantly, with the sinking of the *Prestige,* culturally relevant fears and hopes about a transformation in the Galician political community were fastened to a particular view of the state.

The Cultural Shift: From Servitude to Dignity

I examine activists' rendition of a cultural transformation from servitude to dignity in light of what the Schneiders (2003) analyze in the Sicilian context as "reversible destiny." They develop this concept in their study of the anti-mafia movement in Sicily. In their description of the interconnected histories of this movement and the mafia since the Second World War, they trace Sicilian activists' efforts to reverse what seemed to be inevitable: a "mafia-infused Sicilian 'destiny'" (ibid., 290). In their investigation of the anti-mafia movement's challenges to the mafia culture problem, they argue that "assigning a centuries-long pedigree to purportedly Sicilian attributes of character is a way to essentialize without appearing to" (ibid., 112). Similarly, the story that I document here of a cultural transformation in the identification of the Galician region from servitude to dignity is framed by essentialist assumptions about the Galician culture, character, and value system.[6] Like the movement that the Schneiders describe, the dominant storyline that transpired in Nunca Máis evoked a shift from one discursive location to another, challenging "the idea of culture as constant" (ibid.). At the same time, however, the discourse from servitude to dignity is structured by notions of a "Galician culture." Categories such as "Galicia," "Galicians," and "Galician culture" are, in the words of anthropologist Yael Navaro-Yashin, "far from being natural or straightforward concepts" (2002, 11). Indeed, they are the "products of historical agency and contingency" (ibid.). Activists' descriptions of a cultural transformation in the identity of the Galician region attribute a reversal of essentialist categories, from the "old" Galician conservatism to the "new" progressivism, from political passivity to political activity, from silence to vocality, and from servitude to dignity. This binary logic is not new, as anthropological research in Galicia attests. It is a logic that is typically associated with either rural or urban Galicia (e.g., Gulevich 1995; Kelley 1994; Roseman and Kelley 1999).

Galicia as the "Land of Servitude"

There is a well-known saying in Galicia. To paraphrase one of the region's most beloved and controversial figures, Alfonso Daniel Rodríguez Castelao, "Galicians don't protest, they emigrate." Castelao, who participated in the agrarian movement in Galicia and in the Galician regionalist movement in the early part of the twentieth century, and who later wrote in earnest in exile about his *terra* (land), would certainly not have recognized the changes afoot nearly a century later. Contemporary Galicians could hardly believe the change in collective action themselves.

Narratives of a shift in Galician character soon began to circulate in headlines in regional newspapers, in everyday conversation, and in formalized public debate. In conversations and activities organized under Nunca Máis, Galician participants depicted themselves and fellow Galicians as emerging from silence and invisibility toward vocality and visibility, as shedding off the chains of servitude and stepping onto the fresh ground of dignity. So central is this narrative of silence and emergence from servitude that it was common to read posters in street protests and other organized activities such as "O silencio é peor que o chapapote" (Silence is worse than fuel oil) (for a visual example, see *Nunca Máis: Xornal da plataforma cidadá,* a journal published by the movement, May 2003, 2). In his article "Prometeo encadeado" (Chained Promise), Galician writer Suso de Toro describes this transformation in community. The first community is depicted as sad, without hope, desolate, and entrapped in chains from the past, and the latter is portrayed as jumping free from bondage and optimistic in its future (2002, 87-92). In a later reflection on the significance of Galicians' support of Nunca Máis, he wrote in the inaugural issue (February 2003) of *Nunca Máis: Xornal da plataforma cidadá Nunca Máis,* "they [the government] thought we were a defeated and servile *país.*" Later that month, in a passionate plea to the more than 300,000 protesters who stood in the Plaza del Sol in Spain's capital shouting in unison "Nunca Máis! Nunca Máis!" Manuel Rivas, another Galician writer, declared in Castilian Spanish through loudspeakers from a stage that had been erected for this protest in Madrid, "the government has to assume once and for all that Galicia has awakened; that we don't believe in fairytales told to put us to sleep; that Galicia does not have a price. They have to understand that we are not a *país* of servants" (excerpt from Nunca Máis manifesto in Paz and Vázquez Carpentier 2003, 52-3). The spokespeople for the movement were not alone, however, in their characterization of Galicia as a place having previously been subservient to established authority. For another Galician commentator on the sinking of the *Prestige,* Galicians as a people (*pobo*) have rebelled against stereotypes that characterize them as submissive. "The society organized itself, rejecting resignation and silence, protesting against the deficient handling of the crisis" (Beiras 2003, 15). For others, such as Maria, the university professor whom I introduced above, Galicians are "more than submissive. We are servile. But our movement shows another kind of Galicia" (interview, 23 May 2003).

This other kind of Galician community was the topic of a public forum one evening in early March 2003. Four speakers, three male presenters from Galician nationalist political associations and one male Galician journalist from *La voz de Galicia,* debated the evolving Galician political context since the sinking of the *Prestige.* The speakers characterized Galicia before the sinking as *"calada e pasivo"* (quiet and passive). The image of male fishermen drenched in fuel oil with their handmade tools was offered as representative of Galicia's "new and surprising" change toward *"unha Galiza viva"* (a live Galicia), a self-reliant Galicia. The speakers surmised that since the oil slick Galicians no longer believed in what their governments told them with "a blind faith" (*unha creencia cega*), instead rising up, taking to the streets, and expressing their discontent (public forum, 6 March 2003). As I show in the following section, two areas in coastal Galicia were made symbolic of the *pasivo* and *viva* or "old" and "new" communities, a symbolism that emerged within a few months of the disaster.

Card-Playing Villagers: Faces of "Old" Galicia

Around a dozen volunteers, including myself, from the city of Lugo made our way to a beach one early morning in April 2003 in the province of A Coruña to collect fuel oil. Before slipping into our white synthetic uniforms, rubber boots, and protective face masks, we stopped at a local café to have one last cup of coffee. The small café in the local village was crammed, and the air was sticky, hot, and thick with smoke from cigarettes. Two Galician women in their early thirties and I sipped our coffee near an open window that overlooked the beach. Glancing over at the tables, I noticed that several groups of people were playing card games. Since we were at this café on Saturday, I thought the scene typical, especially since one of my roommates had told me stories about playing card games every weekend in his natal village. One of the women standing beside me, however, talked critically about the activity, portraying villagers along this coast, the Costa da Morte, as being grateful for the oil slick. "As a result of the oil slick," she argued, "they could sit around all day, collecting government subsidies, playing cards, and watching volunteers working on their beaches." For my Galician friend, the image of villagers playing cards provided proof of the well-worn circulating stereotype that depicts Galicians as "passive and quiet," "thinking only of themselves," and "content with handouts."[7] In contrast to the derogatory terms used by Nunca Máis activists to talk about villagers along the economically depressed Costa da Morte, the fishermen from the lucrative fishing areas in the *rías baixas,* an area in the southern Galician province of Pontevedra, were deemed the heroes of 13/N (13 November, the day when part of the single hull ruptured on the *Prestige*). Images of their scarred and blackened faces drenched in fuel oil, their arms swinging handmade tools in the ocean in desperate attempts to collect the toxic substance before it could reach the shorelines, circulated around the world. For activists in the social movement, these fishermen became representative of the emerging, self-reliant Galician community.

Galicia as the "Land of Dignity"

In some of my interviews and conversations with Nunca Máis activists, I attempted to break through assumptions about Galician character, pushing my interlocutors toward elaboration beyond the stereotypes. Ana, a member of a feminist group, was very active in Nunca Máis. In one of my interviews with her, she mentioned her surprise about the Galician support for the movement. "We have the reputation of being submissive (*sumisa*), you know?" she said. "No, I don't," I replied. "Perhaps you could say more about that?" "*Bueno.* It's a well-known fact [*echo*] that we are conservative and accept what is. Any history book draws your attention to this" was her explanation. Nonetheless, I pressed her for more elaboration about this taken-for-granted *echo,* apparently so obvious that further clarification was not required. Ana briefly but patiently chronicled how Galicians typically emigrate during hardship as opposed to remaining in Galicia and challenging governments to improve employment options. "Galicians choose," she said, "to remain silent [*callada*]" and hand over decisions that impact Galician livelihoods to government representatives in Madrid. Ana explained that, with the sinking of the *Prestige,* a radical change in the Galician mode of action had transpired, making Nunca Máis "historical" (*un echo histórico*) (interview, 8 May 2003). In a separate interview, another self-identified feminist elaborated on Ana's characterization of Galicians as "submissive." Patricia, who was born and raised in Catalonia, had been living in the city of Lugo for nearly twenty years at the time of our interview. She narrated Galicians as being "very conformist. They are hard-working people, but *aj* they are preoccupied with their own things. They don't think beyond that [*en el más allá*]. They are servile with [those in] power [*servil con el poder*]. But with Nunca Máis," she concluded, "this changed" (interview, 7 April 2003). Like de Toro and Rivas (see above), these women drew a connection between a change in Galician character from accepting "what is" to an active stance. Like their Galician counterparts active in Nunca Máis, Ana and Patricia were hopeful that this change in character and action signalled a transformation in the Galician community. The collective past was narrated as being marked by silence. This past was also characterized by Galician subservience to established authority and a location geographically and symbolically "far from everyone." In the words of Catuxa, a stay-at-home mother of two young sons and an active participant in the social movement, "we were a people who kept quiet, and now I see Galicia as shedding off its sadness, blooming in the process [*florecemento*]" (personal communication, 7 May 2003). By the end of June 2003, a book featuring photographs of the oil slick entitled *No país do Nunca Máis* (In the Land of Never Again) captured the discursive move in representations of Galician character, sense of community, and place (Lobato 2003). Nunca Máis was interpreted as bridging the dichotomy between people and government, mediating a shift in Galician character from subservience to self-determination. The social movement became symbolic of Galician dignity, "the people's dignity (*o dignidade do pobo*)," in the words of another seasoned activist. In addition to the discursive representations of the old Galician location as "far from everyone" and the old Galician character as "servile and quiet," activists in the social movement contrasted the powerful images of card-playing villagers with those of self-reliant fishermen. This difference in the perception of villagers' behaviour in the Costa da Morte and in the *rías baixas* was symbolic of the old and new Galician communities. Catuxa vocalized this shift as Galicia's shedding of sadness toward the *florecemento* of dignity.

In another article, de Toro explained that "for Galicians [the ecological catastrophe] has become a collective existential crisis" (2002, 90). This crisis expressed itself in the form of popular debate about the identity and autonomy of the regional community. The debate was structured as a shift in collective identity from servitude to dignity. Indeed, for another commentator on the disaster, this "collective existential crisis" was characterized by the emergence of popular heroism in the face of institutional desertion and despite stereotypes of Galician political passivity (Beiras 2003, 21). Servitude was portrayed as being rooted in the feudal history of the Galician countryside and associated with the practice of emigration and complacency to the state. Dignity, on the other hand, was described as emerging in the actions of activists who gathered under the banner of Nunca Máis and especially in the conduct of the fishermen in the *rías baixas* who collected fuel oil with their handmade tools without the assistance of state actors.

The new Galician community would emigrate not out of need but out of desire. In much the same way they argued for the right to information during the *Prestige* crisis (see above), activists contended that Galicians had the right to work at home as opposed to emigrating. Shouting across a crowd of activists and spectators, one of the Nunca Máis spokespersons declared, "here is dignity, here is a consciousness liberated, here is a live people [*pobo*], here is Galicia's honour" (Manifesto, 1 December 2002, in Paz and Vázquez Carpentier 2003, 50). Certainly the notion of dignity expressed in the social movement differs from the kind that Castelao conceptualized and developed in his political essays in the early part of the twentieth century ([1944] 1977). Castelao and his contemporaries mainly linked the concept of dignity to the question of Galician sovereignty. Since that time, however, universal rights discourses and norms have far exceeded the geopolitical territory of the sovereign state. As political scientist Georg Sørensen argues, "human rights have expanded beyond a conventional list of civil rights to include such social and economic rights as employment, education, health care, nourishment, and housing" (2004, 87). Significantly, this expansion of human rights discourse is apparent in the Galician case through the contemporary experiences of Galicians seeking employment in the region. Indeed, the notion of dignity cannot be separated from the Galician experience of migration and unemployment. Moreover, the concept of dignity was used by Nunca Máis activists within the context of a view of excess state corruption and institutional desertion. Nunca Máis chose as its slogan to commemorate the one-year anniversary of the sinking of the *Prestige* "365 Days of Dignity and Incompetence," capturing this tension between Galician self-reliance and abandonment and corruption by government institutions. In his speech on this anniversary, Rivas "referred to the waves of dignity, memory, truth, solidarity, freedom and hope, amongst others, and brought the event to a climax with a toast 'to the sea and to dignity'" (Aguilar Fernández and Ballesteros Peña 2004, 51).

From Servitude to Dignity?

De Toro and other Galician commentators on the *Prestige* disaster reflected on the strategy of activists in Nunca Máis to openly and directly protest against government representatives. "Was another kind of Galician community emerging?" they asked. Activists interpreted their own actions and especially those of the fishermen in the *rías baixas* as opening a public space in which to build civil society, weaving a tapestry of dignity, and in this way exercising autonomy in the context of the Spanish state. A woman who participated in my research explained the importance of getting, in her words, "the job thing sorted out. When you're working and you can have your dignity, then you can take that dignity and convert it into a space of action. Then you can work on opening up political and social spaces" (interview, 26 November 2003). Another activist shared a similar view: "We're creating openings, *huecos,* and that's a good contribution *y ala*" (an expression that conveys a sense of satisfaction) (conversation, 22 July 2003). Not only was Nunca Máis articulating a vision of transformation in Galician political culture by openly debating the kind of autonomy in the region and problematizing complacency and political corruption, but more importantly Nunca Máis activists were building civil society (Schneider and Schneider 2003, 3). In the words of Ana, "NM helped to raise the capacity of citizens to self-organize [*auto-organizacion*]" (conversation, 16 July 2003).

In their analysis of the Sicilian mafia, Jane Schneider and Peter Schneider argued that, because the mafia was perceived as being "rooted in the [Sicilian] regional society and intertwined with national as well as regional and local politics," it was considered Sicily's "destiny" (2003, 3). In their examination of the history of the mafia and the anti-mafia social movement in Sicily since the Second World War, they focused on how the social movement consolidated its efforts to "reverse what seemed inevitable" (ibid.). Likewise, Nunca Máis activists challenged the view of political corruption as an inevitable part of the Galician political culture. The language of this new struggle against the Partido Popular, from servitude to dignity, perpetuated old social divisions mediated through the conceptual spatial map of the Spanish state and its autonomous communities. Even though the discourse of the struggle suggests a complete transition from a beginning point, servitude, to an ending point, dignity, the process is never complete.

Social Movements, Community, and Global Restructuring

Without getting into too much detail about the scholarly debates regarding new social movements, Nunca Máis can be analyzed as belonging to this type (see, e.g., Edelman 2001). In the post-Cold War era, social movements such as Nunca Máis have largely "parted ways with the politics of class struggle" (Schneider and Schneider 2003, 161). In light of the unfulfilled promises of parliamentary democracy and global capitalism to usher in more economic development, more equality, and less injustice, sociologists Boaventura de Sousa Santos and Joao Arriscado Nunes argue that it should hardly come as a surprise that, "as different forms of resistance and opposition to the dynamics of neoliberalism emerged, the debates on the theory and practice of democracy and on its links to social, environmental, cognitive and cultural justice gained in visibility and intensity" (2004, 1). As suggested in the growing literature that analyzes protest and collective action in Europe, Nunca Máis activists mobilized resources made available to them by European integration (e.g., directives on the environment and human rights; see, e.g., Imig and Tarrow 2001). Importantly, however, and despite the challenges of neoliberalism, Nunca Máis is not an entirely new phenomenon. "Political baggage," to use the Schneiders' terminology, and memories of the past along with traditions of local struggle and popular action shaped Nunca Máis and governmental responses to it (2003, 162).

Similar to other post-Cold War movements, Nunca Máis activists expressed moral outrage in the context of the environmental disaster using the language of human rights, specifically Galicians' right to information, their right to participate in decisions that directly affect the economy of the region, and their right to work in the region as opposed to emigrating. However, initially I was stupefied by the discrepancy between my view of Nunca Máis and the interpretations of Galicians. I wrote in my field journal on 24 February 2003 that, "from the disaster, something truly wonderful has happened. And the people that I've met because of this disaster are so dedicated, leading the way forward, taking control of a situation that politicians say is not theirs to take into their own hands. Their progressive and defiant actions against their government [are] inspiring. I know I'm getting carried away but I am hopeful like [Galician activists], that this movement will translate [into a change in government] in the coming elections." My buoyant optimism was rooted in a somewhat romantic concept of participatory democracy shaped by my reading of evocative compilations on the power of grassroots movements to destabilize the market as the arbiter of decisions. This optimism was not based on examples of particular, historically contingent, and place-based interpretations of redress. I eventually recognized, however, that the frame of reference structuring my feelings of hope was not the same as the one shared by my Galician counterparts. The more I involved myself in Nunca Máis, the more aware I became of the fundamental differences in our analyses of the "critical event." Galician activists talked about shedding the chains of servitude and emerging as a free and dignified community without abuses of state power in the form of political cronyism and patronage. Although expressing its agenda in the new language of human rights, Nunca Máis was simultaneously invoking older, essentialized social divisions between, for example, the Galician region and the Spanish state. To understand more fully this interplay between newer and older forms of arguing for redress in the language of rights in the context of the state and in relation to the question of regional autonomy, it is necessary to turn to a discussion of European political and economic restructuring.

A wealth of literature now exists on the transformations of culture and community in the "new" Europe (e.g., Anderson, O'Dowd, and Wilson 2003; Berdahl 1999). "In Europe," the editors of a recent volume on European borderlands argue, "there has been a growing interest in how border regions and border peoples have developed their own reasons for redefining their relationships to their metropolitan centres within their own states" (Anderson, O'Dowd, and Wilson 2003, 15). As a historically marginal area within the Spanish state, Galicia is one such border place. Importantly, national boundaries and national identifications are not "necessarily imposed from the political centers of power but may arise on the peripheries locally and according to local needs" (Fernandez 1997, 726). For James Fernandez, this popular cosmology works against the idea of a Europe without frontiers.[8] However, I argue that recognizing the impact of place-based historical contingencies for community and identity-making practices does not foreclose the possibility of solidarity within and beyond the local milieu. The magnitude and visibility of the ecological disaster, a collectively shared agenda, and a common grievance against the Partido Popular at the regional and national levels ensured the success of a popularly supported social movement that crosscut geographical and conceptual divides. The tension between place-based and global action remains, but it is less an anomaly than a product of the current moment, a moment that historian Arif Dirlik (2003) has analyzed as the condition of "global modernity." This condition is qualified by two seemingly contradictory developments — "economic and political globalization that is taken generally to point to unprecedented global integration, and the resurgence of religions or, more broadly, traditionalisms, that create new political and cultural fractures, or reopen old ones" (ibid., 147). This reopening occurs in part at least in the case of Europe because of territorial restructuring. As political scientist Thomas Christiansen argues, "political groups have changed their course of action, their demands and their discourse, but such developments would not be significant without a change also in the underlying matrix [the EU, member states, and regions], and the structural framework for territorial politics in the mid-1990s is very different from the situation, say, only 10 years ago" (1996, 15).

In other words, the novel political arrangements that have resulted in the weakening of borders in the EU have also helped to create a space in which minorities can contemplate their rights and possible futures that involve securing more collective autonomy. Behind the possibility of change from servitude to dignity is the "synergy between local citizens' activism and the opening provided by the shift in the national and international context" (Schneider and Schneider 2003, 4).

Fundamental to the reorganization of territoriality in the EU is the ceding of sovereignty by member states. Indeed, not only did the media, the long-festering discontent toward the Partido Popular, and the environmental and economic impacts of the spillage play important roles in the emergence of Nunca Máis, but also Spain's membership in the EU is a contextual condition that helps to explain the timing of the movement's appearance. With the turn toward democracy in the late 1970s and Spain's subsequent inclusion in the EU in 1986, the Spanish state moved away from its strongly centralized stance that existed under Franco to one where considerable regional autonomy is exercised in its seventeen autonomous communities. Galician activists in Nunca Máis were to some extent able to take advantage of the availability of the political spaces opened up by the EU to build community in ways that departed significantly from the anomie and dependence characteristic of their past.[9]

Anthropologists have noted that, as a result of historical economic difficulties in Galicia, Galicians talked about the region and themselves in disparaging terms (e.g., R. Bauer 1992; Gulevich 1995; Kelley 1994). Since the end of the twentieth century, a revival of customs considered typical, the love of tradition (Fernández de Rota Monter 1998, 124), and the new prestige of the Galician language (Núñez 2002, 232) indicate a shift away from this derogatory attitude. Indeed, José Antonio Fernández de Rota

Monter suggests that "the argument that the Galician people should be treated with more respect and dignity has also met with approval" (1998, 124). The metaphor of a cultural transformation from servitude to dignity is therefore reflective of this larger change in the political economy and in the self-perception of Galicianism. This shift in attitude is also attributed to Galician regional institutions' increasing interest in reclaiming the Galician language, the memory of migration, Galician cuisine, and what is vaguely defined as "Galician traditions" such as music, festivals, and folklore.[10]

Conclusion

As a "critical event," the sinking of the *Prestige* opened a public space in Galicia for claims to a shared community identity and debate about communal autonomy. Global political restructuring and economic changes and activism rooted in specific local historical, cultural, and economic contexts shaped perceptions of regional Galician autonomy and the popular interpretation of a cultural transformation from servitude to dignity. With the sinking of the *Prestige,* culturally significant fears and hopes about the idea and practice of group autonomy projected themselves onto the environment. The reinvigorated debate about the question of status as an autonomous community acted as a guiding principle toward dignity, a communal destiny.

The culturally salient explanation of a change in Galician regional community is dominated by dichotomies: rural versus urban, political passivity versus political action, and servitude versus dignity. These dichotomies are mapped onto the particular view of the Spanish state as both righteous and corrupt. In their interpretation of a shift from servitude to dignity, Nunca Máis activists resorted to the long-standing framework of ethnic, linguistic, and geographic differences that are always heavily charged with histories of vulnerabilities and asymmetrical power relationships. Indeed, a complex process of historical continuity and change shaped the activists' framework of interpretation and qualified their actions.

In many ways, Nunca Máis belongs to a genre of social activism that emerged worldwide in the 1980s and 1990s, exposing political cronyism and corruption, all the while promoting an informed, what can loosely be termed, "civil society" (also see Schneider and Schneider 2003, 300-3). However complex the question of belonging to the Galician community is, it is clear that the concept of belonging has become salient in the context of the European Union and its controversial processes of integration and expansion. For activists in Nunca Máis, the Galician community is distinct from other regions in the Spanish state. The sense of belonging to a collective community is in dialectical relation to the idea of a strong, centralizing state. That the Spanish state as a political community continues to structure belonging may at first appear as an anomaly in the context of Europeanization. However, the process of "re-organisation of territoriality and peoplehood" fuels the desire for "the state" (Borneman and Fowler 1997, 487). The narration of a shift from servitude to dignity is framed by historical contingencies and the newer circulating rights-based ideologies and actions.

Presented in the language of recognition of and reparation for previous grievances and injustices, the narrative from servitude to dignity suggests an ongoing metamorphosis in Galician collective subjectivity and in representations of the Galician homeland more generally. The story of Galician servitude and Galician dignity emerges in the context of the long-enduring stereotype of Galician political passivity and is influenced by the expansion of human rights discourse.

The employment of the concept of dignity in Nunca Máis in connection to political dissent is not new. Galician intellectuals toward the end of the nineteenth century had already wrestled with this concept in their exercise of political self-determination (see Castelao [1944] 1977). I therefore analyzed the narration of a cultural transformation from "servitude to dignity" as an enduring struggle cast in the new language of rights.

chapter 7

Community without Status: Non-Status Migrants and Cities of Refuge

Peter Nyers

Immigrants, today's proletarians.
— Étienne Balibar, *We, the People of Europe?*

IN HIS CELEBRATED ESSAY "On Cosmopolitanism," Jacques Derrida challenges us to rethink the terms and conditions of hospitality and community in relation to the global movement of people. The essay is based on the keynote address he made in 1996 to the International Parliament of Writers (IPW). In considering the current possibilities for a hospitable cosmopolitics, Derrida finds inspiration in the theorizations and practices of the IPW and in particular their global network of "cities of refuge." Established in 1993 with Salman Rushdie as its first president, the IPW has been successful in establishing a network of autonomous cities of refuge for dissident writers and intellectuals who have been forced into exile. The participating cities are extremely diverse and include historical sites of sanctuary (Strasburg), "global cities" (Berlin, Paris), major metropolises (Mexico City), and even kitschy tourist towns (Las Vegas). Cities of refuge provide a candidate nominated by the IPW refuge, protection, and a stipend to live on for one year. In solidarity, Derrida (2001, 4) calls the theory and practice of cities of refuge "audacious," both to imply a certain insolence to established authority and a daring to go beyond the acceptable bounds of normality. The insolence of the IPW's audacity resides in the fact that cities of refuge take on practices that are fundamental to the sovereign state. These practices include making decisions about asylum and the control of movement more generally. Locating these practices at the level of the city, and not the state, is no small move since the sovereign state has historically claimed a monopoly over what counts as political space, identity, and practice. Thus, Derrida also calls the members of the IPW "audacious" also because of their courage, their sense of daring, in that their acts imply that a new politics can be constructed, one that does not rely on the sharp distinctions between insider and outsider that come with the practices of sovereignty. Cities of refuge, Derrida hopes, will "re-orient the politics of the state," "transform and reform the modalities of membership," and participate in the construction of "solidarities yet to be invented" (ibid., 4). Derrida speculates that it is in the space of the city that we can find new hospitalities, new solidarities, and new communities that do not impose divisive qualifications such as nationality, formal citizenship, or proper documentation.

There is much to admire and learn from the way Derrida situates his cosmopolitanism within the work of the IPW. Cities of refuge provoke a number of critical political questions. What is the fundamental category of our politics: city or state, polis or cosmopolis? Is it possible for political subjectivity to emerge outside the codes and practices of state sovereignty? Who is the object of hospitality, and who is the subject? To the extent that cities of refuge might open up possibilities for community, hospitality, and political practice that challenge or evade the powers of inclusion/exclusion of the state, we can see in them the possibility for an emerging politics. At the same time, however, there are significant limitations to the city of refuge model. While I feel a great deal of solidarity with the efforts of the IPW, its model is nonetheless a highly individualistic form of hospitality since cities of refuge sponsor only one exile per year. More to the point, however, this individual is typically someone who fits with the classical figure of the refugee: the outspoken critic who speaks truth to power and suffers persecution because of his or her words. As Derrida says, the principal beneficiaries of cities of refuge are "intellectuals, scholars, journalists, and writers — men and women capable of speaking out ... in a public domain that the new powers of telecommunication render increasingly formidable" (2001, 6). While certainly deserving of hospitality and protection, the recipients of refuge retain a close conceptual — and deeply political — relationship to our received understandings of citizenship. Citizenship here is not only the marker of belonging but also signifies who can develop a political subjectivity, display agency, and evoke a *presence* in the public realm. The refugee, from this perspective, is someone who, because of his or her excess of citizenship practices, has lost citizenship. The loss of citizenship, ironically, leads to the end of agency and the beginning of victimage. Refugee and citizen, therefore, appear as a binary couplet — they are twins — and each term relies on the other as its condition of possibility. The agency of the citizen is mirrored by the victimage of the refugee; the citizen's secure place within the polity is mirrored by the insecure displacement suffered by the refugee (Nyers 2006). What is admirable about cities of refuge, however, is the way they provide refugees with a space to assert their voices as political subjects. That this space is conceived of as the city, and not the state, represents an important departure from and challenge to state-centric conceptions of citizenship and political subjectivity.

Nonetheless, the success of the IPW is due in part to the fact that states seem to be quite capable of tolerating individual transgressions of their prerogative over matters of immigration and asylum. The questions that animate this chapter, by contrast, are concerned with the implications for community, autonomy, hospitality, and other key political concepts once cities of refuge are opened up to *masses* of people whose legal status has forced them to live on the borders of belonging. This is a politics based not on the individual but on the mass of undocumented people living without full legal status. This shift from individual to mass raises a number of problems for political community as well as for who can count as a political subject. Should citizenship and non-citizenship be seen as variations in *legal* status, or are they forms of *practice* that are up for the taking (Honig 2001; Nyers 2003; Rancière 1999)? Is it possible to have a political community *without* status?

This chapter engages with these questions by focusing on the political practices of various "non-status immigrant" communities in Canada. The major demand that underscores every campaign undertaken by non-status immigrants and their allies is for a program that would allow all non-status immigrants to "regularize" their status in Canada. What is notable about these campaigns is that they are being directed at both the state and the city levels of governance. These are two sites in which claims and counterclaims about community, belonging, and citizenship are being made by, for, and against non-status immigrants. In each case, migrant political agency is asserted in places meant to deny, limit, or repress it. The significance of these sites, I argue in this chapter, is that they allow migrants themselves to act as *mediators* — translators — between established and emerging forms of political community.

Non-Status Lives

Many words are used to describe people without full legal immigration status. Some are legalistic ("aliens"), others are pejorative ("illegals"); some are descriptive ("undocumented"), others are analytical ("irregular migrant"). All of these terms are political, and they need to be examined critically and deployed cautiously. In a way that is perhaps revealing of my own politics, I use the phrase "non-status immigrant" because it is the term used by the self-organized political action committees of non-status immigrants in Canada (e.g., Action Committee of Non-Status Algerians). Put simply, non-status immigrants are people who do not possess the legal status that would allow them to live permanently in Canada. It is uncommon for a person to become non-status by entering the country in a clandestine manner. More often people have travelled to and reside in Canada quite legally until their legal status expires. For example, their refugee claim could have been rejected, they may not have access to official identity documents, or they may have remained in the country after the expiration of their student visa, visitor visa, or work permit. The government does not collect official statistics on people living without status, so it is difficult to say how many non-status immigrants live in Canada. However, recent estimates suggest that there are up to 400,000 people in Canada with less than full legal status, with the majority living in the cities of Toronto, Montreal, and Vancouver.

The binaries of status/non-status and citizen/non-citizen imply that there are two fixed identities at stake. This is misleading. These sharp distinctions suggest that "status" and "non-status" are two separate ontological conditions or states of being. However, being non-status is not so much a given condition or state of being as a product, the result of state practices of inclusion and exclusion. Non-status is not a fixed identity but the experience of moving across a border. Souyma Boussouf, a member of the Action Committee of Non-Status Algerians, remarks on her experience of living without status: "When it happens to you, even then it takes a lot of time to realize what it really means in your everyday life" (quoted in Lowry and Nyers 2003, 67). Note her choice of words: *when it happens to you*. Like an accident, becoming non-status is something that happens; it appears as the unexpected result of some act; it imposes real and, to the person affected, arbitrary limitations on personal autonomy and self-determination.

As a practice, the designation "non-status" works to negate individual autonomy and efface personhood. For example, non-status immigrants are often defined as being invisible, marginalized, and superfluous to the nation-state. They have been described as the "excluded among the excluded" (Balibar 2000, 43). They are said to occupy a "space of nonexistence" (Coutin 2000, 177) and a "space of forced invisibility, exclusion, subjugation, and repression" (De Genova 2002, 427). To be sure, people without official legal status suffer from having severely limited access to the range of rights and entitlements of citizenship. T.H. Marshall's (1950) classic account of social citizenship speaks very little to the realities faced by growing numbers of non-status immigrants. The rights of social citizenship outlined by Marshall — including political rights (e.g., the right to vote, to be present in the public sphere), workers' rights (e.g., the right to join a union, to earn the minimum wage, to be treated fairly by the boss), and social rights (e.g., public education, health care, emergency services) — are largely denied to people without full legal status. Non-status immigrants have restricted access to legal support, public education, social housing, health care, social services, and even public recreation and sports facilities. While most non-status immigrants work, they are not protected against unfair and dangerous working conditions and are not eligible for workers' compensation if they are injured on the job. As one non-status person said, "a lot of employers are delighted to hear that you have no papers, because they can overwork you and exploit you."[1] People living in Canada without legal status are vulnerable to abuse by employers and landlords and exploitation by immigrant consultants and lawyers. Exiled from both the space and the subjectivity of citizenship, they lack what Arendt (1968, 295) called "the right to have rights."

Non-status immigrants live in constant fear of detention, deportation, and surveillance by the authorities. An activist in the Toronto Philippine community is depressingly honest about what advocacy work amounts to: "We're getting our people ready for deportation." A non-status person describes the state of the Latin American non-status community in Toronto: "There are many people who live like ghosts." A pervasive fear overcodes non-status life, making it difficult for non-status people to go out in public, let alone emerge as dynamic political agents or even participate in a "focus group" meeting. A participant at a focus group meeting held in a non-status community in Toronto gave her opinion on why certain people from her community were absent: "I asked a person to come to this meeting, and this person said to me, 'you go, and if you get anything let me know.' What do you call that? Laziness." Another participant in the focus group responded, "no, that is called security."

Despite all the major impositions it causes in daily life, the matter of status is nonetheless experienced as a rather abstract, arbitrary, and at times ambiguous moment. One non-status woman from Toronto's Caribbean community speaks to this point: "When you come to Canada, you're not focused on getting status. You want to get a job, send money home, and shop in the mall. *[laughter]* Only later do you realize that status and papers are important." An active member of the Action Committee of Non-Status Algerians in Montreal makes a similar point: "I think it is important to note that most of us didn't know what 'non-status' meant before we came here to Canada. I personally didn't know what it was. I had never heard of it before ... Even though you are a non-status person, you do not even realize it. You are working; you have friends; you go out; you try to have a life despite all the barriers, despite everything — which is just normal, just human. You are not going to stop living your life" (Lowry and Nyers 2003, 67). Status is not something that overcodes identity but a power relationship that is revealed whenever a border is crossed. These borders, moreover, are not just international lines that separate one state from another. As we shall see below, they are also internal bordering practices that are suffused throughout the social order.

The Ubiquitous Border

Where does Canadian border policy occur? This is a difficult question because the location of the borderline itself is a complicated matter. Borders increasingly involve temporal barriers as much as spatial ones. They work to limit and constrain life and autonomy. Rob Walker (2004, 249) makes the point that sovereign power increasingly has "more to do with life, with being in time, than it does with the freezing of human life in territorial space." The action committees of non-status communities often make this point. They use the language of "self-determination" to describe their struggle and to bring attention to the borders that they constantly run up against. The border is less of a "line" across a specific piece of territory than a complex network that is projected both far beyond and well within the territorial space of the state. Borders no longer simply signal the external limits of states. They are complex practices that cut deep into the heart of contemporary polities in order to produce difference, create unequal hierarchies, and force entire communities to live permanently "at the border," neither inside nor outside the state (Balibar 2004).

Borders are both visible and invisible. Some are only perceptible to non-status people themselves. In this way, borders are "polysemic" (Balibar 2002, 82) because they are experienced in vastly different ways depending on one's legal status, country of origin, race, ethnicity, gender, age, and so on. For example, one community worker whose agency serves non-status people spoke about the problems that come when even a limited amount of their funding comes from the Canadian state:

> I work at an agency where there is a very large Citizenship and Immigration Canada billboard right beside the main reception area. I find that sign to be one of the biggest barriers to providing services for non-status people. For people just walking in, *even if they know that we offer services to non-status people,* they see that billboard from Citizenship and Immigration Canada and just walk away. They re-member the billboard as the same one they saw at the passport office and the Immigration Review Board: the places where they were rejected in the first place! This is a huge barrier to people thinking that they would be safe and treated any different from the institu-tions that had previously rejected them, making them non-status.

The implication of this statement is that borders can be drawn irrespective of any intention. In the province of Ontario, for example, well-intentioned social workers who intervene to protect a child from an abusive family situation will call the Children's Aid Society. But this agency is mandated to inform the police when any abuse is occurring. If the family, or even just the parents, are without legal status, then the police will, in turn, call the Canadian Border Services Agency and inform it of the family's lack of status. What began as an effort to protect the child ends up as a deportation of the entire family.

For non-status immigrants, the borderline is not just at physical entry points at ports, airports, and land crossings. Rather, the border exists wher-ever and whenever they try to claim the rights of social citizenship. The border is therefore widespread and ever-present, emerging in such places as health centres, social housing cooperatives, schools, food banks, welfare offices, police stations, and other sites where social services are provided to community members. For obvious reasons, non-status people often lack basic identity documents, such as a driver's licence. This can create enormous barriers to accessing basic services. For example, food banks in Toronto are mandated to serve particular communities and so make it a practice to ask for ID to ensure that they are serving members of their catchment area. City-run shelters require identification, and there are shelters that have called immigration authorities on people without status. One client support worker at a multicultural health care centre that services non-status people stated that "my referrals are embarrassing. I refer people to more barriers. They report back to me consistently, 'I went to that agency you referred me to, and the minute they asked me for my documents I just walked out the door.'"

For non-status immigrants, simple, everyday activities — working, driving, and going to school — are at risk of being transformed into criminal and illicit acts with dire consequences (De Genova 2002, 427). Minor transgressions such as jaywalking across a city street can be magnified out of proportion and land the non-status immigrant in immigration detention. Activists who volunteer within Toronto's Heritage Inn immigration detention centre report that many women are incarcerated there as a result of trying to access social services (Padgham 2005). There are many documented cases in Toronto of non-status women who end up in detention (often with their children) after they telephoned 911 and asked for emergency services. For example, women making a legitimate demand for police protection from domestic violence and abusive partners have been placed in detention and eventually deported once their lack of formal status is discovered (Keung 2004). Here we can see the highly discretionary — as opposed to law-based — aspect of immigration law (Pratt 2005, 53-72), as city police make it a practice (although they are not directed to do so) to pass on details about immigration status to the deportation arm of the Canadian state, the Canadian Border Services Agency. What begins as a legitimate demand for protection ends up as a cruel form of discrimination and exclusion from the community. Similar complaints have been made against various school boards, social housing buildings, and health clinics. By trying to access basic social services, these failed refugee claimants end up triggering a deportation apparatus that implicates individuals and agencies well beyond those who directly work for Immigration Canada, the Canadian Security Intelligence Service, or the Canada Border Services Agency. One of the effects is that it is increasingly unclear who is actually a deportation officer: border security officers, immigration officials, local police, campus security, housing workers — or all of the above?

Migrant Autonomy and Agency

Understanding the ways in which refugees, migrants, and non-status immigrants are being stigmatized, securitized, and marginalized is of obvious importance. Social justice perspectives take care to outline all the various ways that statist forces are rendering these populations abject and insecure. This is a crucial and important task. It is not, however, the only task. In the effort to catalogue all the calamities of non-status lives, what risks being displaced are the various ways in which these communities are politicizing themselves — becoming political subjects — on their own terms. The autonomy of non-status immigrants is a topic that Sandro Mezzadra has discussed extensively. Migration, he argues, is not simply an inevitable *response* to "objective" structural forces such as war, persecution, environmental catastrophes, and disparities in the global economy. Instead, migration involves "an autonomous space of subjective action that can force significant institutional transformations" (Mezzadra and Neilson 2003, 22). By insisting on the freedom of movement, what Mezzadra (2004) calls the "right to escape," migrants pose significant challenges to our received notions of political community (state) and identity (citizenship). The main target of displacement is the one not from territorial space but from the subjectivities that allow people to assert themselves as human beings — political beings — with all the rights and dignity that such assertion implies. By taking the subjective aspect of migration seriously, we can be better attuned to how migrants are active agents in the process of their own political subjectification.

In Canada, diverse communities of non-status immigrants are actively reframing the terms of their political relationship with the state and the city. As one activist with the Toronto group No One Is Illegal explains, "one of the interesting trends is that so many different community groups are coming together to support themselves and each other. Like the Philippines, the Bangladeshis, the Iranians, the Palestinians, the Algerians ... We're really seeing a new trend of self-organized committees coming out of different communities. People in these communities are trying to figure out strategies for lobbying, mobilization, and public actions. This is something unique, and we are seeing more and more of it." The number of these self-organized and autonomous "action committees" of non-status immigrants has indeed grown dramatically in Canada, especially since the aftermath of the 9/11 attacks. A partial list of the action committees includes the Solidarity without Borders coalition (Montreal), the Coalition

Against the Deportation of Palestinian Refugees (Montreal, Toronto), the Action Committee of Pakistani Refugees (Montreal), the Action Committee of Non-Status Algerians (Montreal), the Human Rights Action Committee (Montreal, Brampton, Surrey), Refugees Against Racial Profiling (Vancouver), and many others. Mohamed Cherfi, a leading activist with Montreal's Action Committee of Non-Status Algerians, sums up the attitude of this movement: "People who are directly affected need to be the ones fighting and creating this movement with allies. We need to be radical. That is the best way we are going to grow and be effective" (Lowry and Nyers 2003, 71).

Political acts can be described as practices that work to expose the arbitrary foundations of superiority, hierarchy, and inequality (Isin 2002, 276). Consequently, when non-status people come together as a group to expose the arbitrary constraints on their autonomy and capacity for individual self-determination, they also constitute themselves as political subjects. The action committees that non-status people have organized in major Canadian cities are highly revealing in terms of how notions of community and citizenship are being renegotiated and reframed by non-citizens.

Regularization Campaigns and the Problem of Exclusion

If non-status immigrants are to be understood as emerging political subjects, what is their politics? What are their central demands? Due to cross-national networking, the non-status action committees in Montreal, Toronto, Vancouver, and other Canadian cities have developed a series of key demands. They include an end to deportation, an end to the detention of migrants, immigrants, and refugees, and the abolition of "security certificates" (a measure in Canadian immigration law that allows non-citizens deemed to be a threat to "national security" to be held in detention indefinitely, without charge, and under secret evidence). However, the demand that tops the list of most of the non-status action committees and their allied groups is for the Canadian government to implement a program to "regularize" the status of non-status immigrants (Wright 2003).[2]

A regularization program allows non-status immigrants to apply for official legal status so that they can permanently reside in Canada.[3] Although often called "amnesties," both governments and activists have notably avoided using the word, the former because they do not want to give the impression that every non-status immigrant will benefit from such a program, the latter because the word implies a wrongdoing on behalf of non-status immigrants and sets up the state as a patriarchal figure that has a monopoly on forgiveness. As a result, the preferred lexicon includes words that are non-committal ("review"), imply a process of selection and normalization ("regularization"), or suggest a one-time exception to the norm ("special procedures"). The most popular term — *regularization* — has the unmistakable connotation of implying that a process of normalization is occurring. For everyone who is "regularized" and can make a claim to normality there is also someone whose application is rejected because he or she is deemed to be undesirable for inclusion in the body politic. To be sure, the Canadian state has always employed restrictive criteria in its regularization programs. These criteria — such as criminality, medical inadmissibility, economic wealth, length of residency, level of "integration," family connections, and country of origin — work to produce the figure of the "good" and "desirable" immigrant who may, one day, become a full member of the political community as a citizen (see Honig 2001).

The demand for regularization is always politically tricky as the Canadian state has historically proven to be quite adept at excluding large numbers of non-status immigrants in its past regularization programs. To be sure, while regularization programs are usually pitched as a humanitarian act of a compassionate government, the political reality is much more complex. Governments, for example, often introduce regularization programs when they are planning major changes to Canadian immigration law. Regularization programs allow for people who were still in the old system to be dealt with before new — and usually more restrictive and exclusionary — immigration procedures are introduced. In this way, regularization programs can go hand in hand with the imposition of tighter border regimes, more restrictive immigration controls, and harsher punishments on non-status immigrants.

Every regularization program introduced in Canada has included a long list of eligibility requirements. These criteria — such as length of residency, criminality, medical admissibility, and the level of one's "integration" into Canadian society — pose serious barriers and end up excluding many people from getting full legal status. Even the massive Adjustment of Status Program (1973) was no general amnesty; it assessed applications on a case-by-case basis and judged them according to certain criteria, including family relationships, length of residency, and financial stability. By imposing restrictive criteria, regularization programs can actually *increase* the number of non-status immigrants in detention and under deportation orders. Regularization programs always budget for significant increases in resources for monitoring, apprehending, and deporting failed applicants. As well, more restrictive criteria force people who think they will not be accepted to avoid the risk of making an application — thus remaining "underground" and perpetuating the whole problem of social exclusion faced by non-status immigrants.

The criteria used in regularization programs are part of the complex set of practices that work to produce and stabilize notions of citizenship and belonging. As a method of categorization, these criteria separate those worthy of legal status, permanent residency, and eventual formal citizenship from those deemed undesirable, unworthy of status, and potentially dangerous to the national body politic. The action committees of non-status immigrants are savvy about this aspect of their demand for regularization. As a result, they have developed campaigns that target some of the most problematic criteria, such as criminal inadmissibility. Criminality is part of an exclusionary discourse that casts the non-status immigrant as a threat, a source of fear, and a danger that must be "screened" and "contained" to prevent the "contamination" of the political community (Pratt 2005, 139-84). For example, many non-status immigrants who participated in this study pointed out that exclusion on the basis of criminality does not address the systemic racism, classism, and sexism within the policing and criminal justice systems in Canada. As one woman said, "you shouldn't be punished again after you've served your time. Plus, not everybody really commits a crime. There's a big problem with false imprisonment and unfair judges. And today is a very stressful world we live in; people make mistakes." Another person expanded on the problematic practice of deporting non-status immigrants because of criminal activity: "For example, a child comes to Canada when they're two years old; they grow up in Canada. If he 'turns bad' here, he should stay here, not be sent back to his country of birth. Who are you sending him to? How will he survive?"

As these comments attest, non-status immigrants who are criminally charged often face a "double punishment": they are punished once according to the Criminal Code and again by way of deportation. Citizens, in contrast, are punished only once. It is not surprising to find that most non-status immigrants consider criminal inadmissibility unfair and arbitrary. As a non-status activist from Montreal pointed out, "We are humans; we are individuals. And if an individual did some kind of gesture that is criminal, then they can be punished through the justice system. Why specifically target a whole set of human beings based on these criteria, for who they are?"

The history of regularization programs in Canada shows that people with serious medical conditions will likely be excluded. Like criminality, this criterion is implicated in a nationalist production of fear and reinforces the racist discourse that constructs the immigrant as dangerous and diseased — to be screened, tested, monitored, and contained. Again, the non-status immigrants who participated in this study typically described exclusion on medical grounds, like criminality, as extremely problematic, discriminatory, and inhumane. As one non-status immigrant said, "people who are ill should be treated equally with others." Another person pointed out, "sometimes you get the disease here, and they want to send you back to your country. That's not right." People with physical disabilities, or who have chronic illnesses such as kidney disease, HIV/AIDS, leukemia, or tuberculosis, are often found "medically inadmissible" for landed status, despite the reality that non-status immigrants often get sick as a result of the unsafe and dangerous work conditions they are forced to accept. As one non-status immigrant explained, "the job that you get as a non-status immigrant is a job that is going to get you sick."

As a way of regulating belonging and restricting inclusion within the national community, it is important to recognize that the various criteria utilized in regularization programs work together. Consider, for example, the criteria of "integration." Many, if not most, of the non-status immigrants who participated in this study thought, at least initially, that this could be a fair condition. At the same time, they pointed out that it could be difficult to get involved in activities that are generally associated with integration, such as learning English or French, going to church, and volunteering with community organizations. One participant summarized this difficulty by saying that, after working many hours of overtime and looking after the family, "there is very little time left for integrating." Another non-status participant said, "if other people don't participate in things it's because they work — not because they don't want to, but it's because they work. And working is also a way to be incorporated into society. Because they don't only work with people from inside their communities — no, they work with different communities." In a way that echoes Mezzadra's comments about migrant autonomy, one non-status participant rejected the criterion of integration altogether: "Who cares how well you get along! People are people." Members of non-status action committees similarly viewed the criterion of integration with suspicion, considering it to be a largely discretionary and arbitrary category, with its meaning often determined on a case-by-case basis by the immigration officer in charge.

Revisiting Cities of Refuge

A regularization program is obviously of critical importance to the directly affected people living without status in Canada. At the same time, however, the systematic exclusions that have historically been enabled by such programs are cause for real concern. Asked what kind of regularization program she would like to see, one non-status person replied, simply, "I would like something that liberates you." Consequently, the idea of regularization is not something to be abandoned, but it occupies such a difficult political terrain that both caution and some daring are necessary. Because regularization programs bolster the state's power to authorize and enable distinctions between "desirable" and "undesirable" immigrants, any regularization program that employs selective criteria is inevitably going to create more (not less) people without full immigration status. Well aware of the exclusionary character of regularization programs, campaigns by non-status immigrants and their allies are beginning to direct their advocacy at levels of governance where the state's power to exclude can be avoided or minimized.

One can see this kind of political activity within refugee and migrant rights movements, especially in their efforts to implement innovative public policy at the municipal level of governance. City-based policy initiatives are of interest to social movement campaigns demanding a national regularization program for non-status immigrants. The difficulty with state-based initiatives lies in the fact that, as described above, all previous regularization programs in Canada have employed restrictive criteria (e.g., medical admissibility, economic wealth, integration) that end up excluding large numbers from qualifying. While the power to grant "status" is the prerogative of the federal government, municipal authorities can side-step this issue by providing services on the basis of *residency,* not legal status. To be sure, many cities have learned through experience that failing to provide services to *all* residents, regardless of their legal status, can lead to unhealthy and unsafe communities. When non-status immigrants are afraid to present themselves for medical treatment, send their children to school, or complain about unsafe working or living conditions, local authorities begin to have legitimate concerns about the overall public health and welfare of the city.

In response to such concerns, refugee and migrant rights groups across North America are active in creating "sanctuary cities." One dimension of this movement's politics is to lobby municipalities so that they adopt some version of a "don't ask, don't tell" (DADT) policy with regard to immigration status. These policies prohibit municipal employees from asking about an individual's immigration status ("don't ask") and stop them from sharing this information with immigration or other government authorities ("don't tell"). A DADT municipal policy would therefore ensure that city services are available to all city residents on the basis of need and without discrimination on the basis of immigration status. It would also ensure that municipal funds, resources, and workers would not be used to enforce federal or provincial immigration laws.

In the United States, over fifty municipalities have adopted some kind of DADT policy. In Canada, a DADT campaign was launched in Toronto in March 2004, with over forty community organizations as active participants. Groups in Vancouver and Montreal are considering similar campaigns. In a short period of time, the Toronto DADT campaign has built momentum and has received serious attention from the media, city councillors, and the community at large. A DADT campaign advocates for city services to be given on the basis of residency, not immigration status. If successful, it will effectively constitute a de facto regularization program. This is a savvy recognition of the exclusions that are always built into state-level regularization programs. Those who were excluded from such a program would continue to be able to fully access health, education, police, and other city services without the fear of having their lack of status exposed and reported to immigration officials and border police. As well, to the extent that the city becomes a site of immigration policy making — a prerogative reserved for the state — this may be a form of "municipal foreign policy" (Hobbs 1994) that poses a serious challenge to the state as the site for a transformative politics. Is there the possibility that, like Derrida (2001, 4) hoped, DADT cities will "reorient the politics of the state," "transform and reform the modalities of membership," and participate in the construction of "solidarities yet to be invented"?

Conclusion

It is now common for social justice activists to argue that "another world is possible." But the substantive content of this new world is often left vague and undefined. Meanwhile, refugee and migrant activists and their allies are busy trying to build *communities without status* where *no one is illegal*. What kind of politics would allow such a community? What kind of citizenship regimes would allow no one to be illegal? The history of regularization in

Canada shows that these programs are at once a moment of inclusion (for those whose applications were successful) and exclusion (for those whose weren't). In response, the city has emerged as a site where a community without status can be constructed and is meaningful to the majority of non-status immigrants. The political campaigns and social movements by and in support of non-status immigrants provoke serious challenges to our received notions of political community (state) and individual autonomy (citizenship). The chants of this movement — "no borders, no nations, no deportations" and "neither here nor elsewhere" — are indicative of a radical critique of the categories and practices of the modern state. What turns the four words *no one is illegal* into such a radical proclamation is that statist political communities *require* that some human beings be illegal. To say that no human is illegal is to radically call into question the principles and practices of state sovereignty — *as well as the sovereign political subjects (citizens) that state sovereignty makes possible.*

Balibar introduced the expression "citizenship without community" as a way to evade the conventions, routines, and unhelpful dichotomies offered in the debates about nationalism and cosmopolitanism, communitarianism and libertarianism, state and international civil society, et cetera. Citizenship without community enables a radical deconstruction of the notion of "commonness" implied by community and insists that "all the admitted representations of a common — historical and, even more so, natural — identity must be put into question" (2004, 76). Citizenship without community describes a form of citizenship that recognizes its constitutive relationship with an outside. Citizenship is constituted from without, and those without status constitute citizenship. The significance of the political activism of non-status immigrants and their struggles for regularization is, therefore, not limited to a discourse about the expansion or widening of the space of citizenship. Rather, there is a transformative effect, with a recasting of the terms of belonging that is based more on residence, not nationality, freedom of movement, not sedentary territorialism. As Balibar (2002, 4) puts it, "to be a citizen, it is sufficient simply to be a human *being, ohne Eigenschaften* [without qualities]." This philosophy of citizenship and community is echoed in the words of one non-status woman: "I think that nobody should be prevented to go somewhere, because the world is for everybody."

Part 2: Building Transnational Communities

chapter 8

Transnational Women's Groups and Social Policy Activists around the UN and the EU

Michael Webb and Patricia T. Young

COMMUNITY HAS TRADITIONALLY BEEN defined primarily in territorial terms, with the pre-eminent community being the nation linked to a defined and bounded territory. Following the territorial logic, autonomy has previously been considered a quality of territorial communities such as the national state, and many commentators believe that economic and cultural globalization erodes senses of national community and undermines the autonomy of national states. However, if we think of globalization in terms of the deterritorialization of social relations, then some of the same phenomena that challenge the autonomy of territorially defined communities also open up new possibilities for individuals and communities to work with others who share their values, identities, and interests across national borders. Emerging transnational communities do not replace traditional national-territorial communities but instead provide another possible level of community attachment. Individuals can feel a sense of belonging to multiple overlapping communities, including so-called virtual communities based on shared beliefs and values rather than on geographic proximity, with each community contributing something to the multiple dimensions of that individual's identity.

The term *community* is generally applied to people who share a sense of belonging to the group (Delanty 2003). By analyzing transnational non-governmental organizations (TNGOS) as communities, we suggest that the interaction among these groups may involve elements of belonging and shared identity that provide a stronger, more constant basis for action than the shared material interests and issue-specific values implied in terms such as "activist networks" and "coalitions." A network is simply the existence of institutionalized links among distinct groups, while coalitions are "collaborative, means-oriented arrangements that permit distinct organizational entities to pool resources in order to effect change" (cited in Tarrow 2005, 163-4). In contrast, belonging to a community involves a sense of obligation to other community members that goes beyond the instrumental calculations that underlie networks and coalitions. Key indicators of this sense of obligation in activist communities include openness to dialogue among diverse actors and to consideration and accommodation of the values and interests of relatively marginalized groups within the community. Openness and dialogue are an essential first step in building shared identities. We see recognition of difference rather than its suppression as an essential element of transnational community building, even though traditional communities often were associated with the suppression of difference (as noted in the introduction to this volume). The recognition of differences of race, class, and national context among others is, however, compatible with joint political action and an element of common community identity if norms of inclusivity guide the interaction between different groups within the community (Weldon 2006).[1] The boundaries of community can be defined in either a negative fashion (i.e., what the community is not) or in a positive fashion (i.e., positive values and goals shared by members of the community); the former corresponds to what feminist theorists call reactive autonomy, while the latter corresponds to relational autonomy (Code 2000; Sylvester 1992).

Following David Held (1995), we understand autonomy as requiring both self-awareness and a capacity to act by the autonomous person or community. These two dimensions of autonomy correspond to a basic distinction found in the social movement literature — between interest-based explanations such as resource mobilization theory and identity-based approaches such as new social movement theory, which focuses on struggles over symbolic resources and rights to difference (Edelman 2001). Self-awareness links to identity, while capacity to act relates to the resource or interest dimension. Autonomous action therefore cannot be understood without considering both kinds of factors, and we will investigate the connections between interests and identity as the basis for transnational activist communities.

Among factors that affect the degree of autonomy experienced by various groups and impediments to their autonomy, we examine both the internal politics of potential transnational communities and the external environments — especially globalizing pressures and the influence of intergovernmental organizations (IGOs) such as the European Union (EU) and the United Nations (UN). Not surprisingly, common concerns generated by globalizing pressures have been crucial to the development of transnational activist communities, but our case studies also show — consistent with Sydney Tarrow's argument (2005) — that the growth of IGOs and international meetings provides a critical element of the political opportunity structure in which transnational activist communities have developed.

We analyze the building of transnational activist communities in four cases: the global women's movement, global social policy activists, relations between women's groups based in Western and Eastern Europe, and relations between social policy activists in Western and Eastern Europe. These cases allow us to examine transnational cooperation across potentially sharp divisions of interest and identity. We recognize, like the authors of other chapters in this volume (Cook, Prudham, Schagerl), that the autonomies of differently located groups are sometimes in opposition, and we reflect on how participation in transnational activist communities can enhance or impede the autonomy of constituent groups.

Women's movements are a particularly interesting case for studying the relationship between shared identities or shared interests and the development of autonomous communities because they have confronted identity issues in a particularly self-reflective fashion. Social policy groups provide a good point of comparison with women's movements because they are newer actors in the transnational arena,[2] and thus have had less time to develop a sense of community, and because their identity as a community has a stronger reactive element. In turn, the choice of the European setting for our empirical research allows the comparison between a global and a regional setting, helping us to better understand the role of IGOs, and the significance of the extent of value differences present in each potential community of NGOs. Some of the implications at the EU level are specific to this regional setting, depending on the institutional shape and powers of the EU versus the UN and on the longer history of interaction among NGOs centred on the UN. We believe, however, that the processes of community formation of EU-centred NGOs are similar enough to those of the global-level groups that the study of NGO interaction at this level provides valuable insights into transnational activism in general.

On the basis of these case studies, we argue that globalization can encourage the development of new forms of non-territorial community accompanied by feelings of belonging and obligation but that this is far from an automatic or spontaneous process. Political institutions and processes determine whether and how transnational activist communities emerge. A particularly important external influence is the role played by intergovernmental organizations such as the UN and EU, both of which have encouraged the development of transnational activist communities that have some autonomy from national governments and societies. Internal processes of identity development and capacity building reveal that shared interests alone do not generate community; rather, agents must consciously seek to build community based on shared interests and values while remaining sensitive to differences. Finally, we find that the development of autonomous transnational activist communities has mixed implications for the autonomy of their constituent units (which often are territorial). Transnational connections can enhance the autonomy of those units in relation to national governments and societies, but those units may sacrifice some autonomy in relation to other elements of the transnational activist community.

The Global Women's Movement

Transnational connections among women's groups have a long history and have been intensively studied. Our purpose here is to examine how shared and divergent interests and identities have shaped the movement and to assess the degree to which it can be understood as an autonomous transnational community.

At first glance, transnational action by women's groups might appear to rest on shared interests arising out of the structure of patriarchy and from the gendered character of economic globalization, which implies a reprivatization and intensification of the burden of social reproduction (Marchand and Runyan 2000). Despite these shared interests, efforts to organize women at the global level have revealed a number of overlapping differences of identity and interest — differences that must be negotiated if the global movement is to develop the characteristics of an autonomous community. Three key dimensions of difference have been widely discussed in the literature: North versus South, identity as "feminist," and grassroots versus internationally organized groups.

Perhaps the central dimension of difference is that between groups from wealthy Northern countries and those from Southern developing countries, reflecting contrasts of both interest and identity. Because of their relatively privileged position in the global capitalist system, women's groups from the North tend to identify gender as the key structural problem, whereas women in the South often focus more attention on class and racial divides seen to underlie the marginalized positions of women and men alike in southern countries. North-South differences in the status of women in society generated different approaches to mobilizing against patriarchy. In the South, women usually organize locally along the lines of traditional gender roles and often around the concept of motherhood (Ray and Korteweg 1999, 48, 51). Mobilization around traditional identities can allow women's groups to develop the capacity to act that they need in order to extend their demands to broader issues of power (Lind 2000; Peterson and Runyan 1993; for examples, see Linkogle 2001; Ray and Korteweg 1999; Tamale 2001).

Nevertheless, there is a tendency among some Northern groups to interpret Third World women's mobilization as representing a lower level in the hierarchical structure of consciousness (Rowbotham and Lingkogle 2001), based on a distinction between practical and strategic gender interests.[3] Practical gender interests are those that address immediate needs without challenging underlying gender dichotomies, while strategic gender interests directly seek remedy for the wrongs of patriarchy. Northern middle-class women's groups tend to focus on "strategic" interests, and they were often perceived to be critical of Southern groups' focus on "practical" interests.

A second source of difference was grounded primarily in identity. Many women in developing and post-communist countries do not identify with Western feminism, which they perceive to be different from their local struggles (Basu 1995; Beck 2000; Karam 2000; Schirmer 1989). Third World women were particularly skeptical of the dominant Western approach to women's movements in the 1980s, which assumed that women experience common conditions of oppression worldwide (Basu 1995).

The third source of difference, which often largely coincides with the South-North difference, is between grassroots organizations and internationally active organizations (Geske and Bourque 2001; Lind 2000). Both are non-governmental; however, while the former generally deal with issues that directly affect their members, the latter focus on shaping broader patterns of governance and often claim to speak on behalf of broader constituencies. Furthermore, internationally active NGOs often disburse funds (frequently on behalf of Northern governments and aid agencies), while grassroots organizations in the South are mainly recipients of funding. While some women's groups in Southern countries have developed strong institutional links with internationally active TNGOs (Geske and Bourque 2001), Southern grassroots movements are largely left out of the internationalization of Third World feminism.

The difficulties associated with building a common approach in a varied feminist landscape can be seen in the history of the women in development (WID) approach, which was most influential internationally in the 1970s and 1980s. It aimed to involve women more fully in conventional (i.e., liberal, market-oriented) economic development by removing barriers to women's participation in the formal economy and access to education. WID developed largely as an initiative of UN agencies in response to pressures from Western feminists, even though it was intended to address problems in Southern countries. The UN also played a key role in stimulating the growth of women's NGOs in the South (Snyder 1995, 110) and in creating a sense of international community by opening up a space for discussion at a series of global conferences on women, human rights, and social development beginning in the 1970s. UN support of a role for civil society in global deliberations was one of the main factors facilitating the transnational exchange of ideas among women's groups (Stienstra 2000).

However, many elements of the transnational women's movement that developed in response to UN encouragement opposed important elements of WID, meaning that WID could not provide a normative basis for a transnational activist community. Some Southern NGOs (and many Southern governments) insisted that the unstable nature of the global economy and the effects of apartheid, racism, and colonialism had to be addressed, as these factors imposed "double burdens" of exploitation on women (Snyder 1995, 100). These criticisms, combined with poor results from WID programs, led to a widespread recognition that economic discrimination cannot be rectified simply through market-based economic means (Keck and Sikkink 1998; Kerr 2002).

The exchange of ideas among elements of the movement was not equal — Northern groups had more access to the women's caucuses of official UN conferences because of better financial opportunities and access to technology (Stienstra 2000) — reflecting global structural inequalities, but the debate did encourage an openness to dialogue and to consideration and accommodation of the concerns of relatively marginalized groups within the community. For example, the Association of Women in Development organized forums on themes such as "A North-South Dialogue" to overcome perceived North-South divisions, expanded its membership and activities in developing countries, and brought southern and Eastern

European representatives onto its board of directors (Kerr 2002). This example reflects the specific efforts within the global women's movement to identify and overcome obstacles to global collaboration. .

While the WID approach had emerged largely from IGOs in the UN system, the next focus of NGO action — women's rights as human rights . — was to a larger extent initiated within a global civil society strengthened by earlier UN efforts. Problems with the WID approach had encouraged a shift in focus to women's rights, and this shift helped to build links between women's groups and vibrant transnational activism on human rights issues. Within the women's rights approach, the issue of violence against women has had the greatest impact, both as a catalyst for building a shared identity among diverse groups and in terms of enhancing the autonomy of the women's movement in the global political environment.

As a unifying normative framework, the focus on violence had the advantage of being practical; specific abuses could be identified and specific actions taken to remedy them. Moreover, gendered violence was a personal and evocative issue for women from different backgrounds who believed that they shared a common interest in combatting violence in all of the different forms it took in different parts of the world (Keck and Sikkink 1998). Nevertheless, the violence against women approach did not emerge as a spontaneous consensus; rather, it evolved from broad women's rights concerns through assiduous work under the leadership of a small group of activists led by Charlotte Bunch and the Rutgers Center for Women's Global Leadership.[4] Activists emphasized the interconnections among different forms of violence and recognized that the "violence against women" agenda was an opportunity to cross the divide between Northern and Southern women's issues (ibid., 175-80).

However, the depth of the shared identity around violence against women should not be overstated. An important element of the consensus is the strategic joining of forces between Northern and Southern groups. The influence of the women's rights framework outside the Northern core is supported by financial and organizing aid to those women's organizations that are sympathetic to this framework. Some groups may declare their interest in the issue only to receive much-needed funding (Keck and Sikkink 1998, 182-3). Thus, the convergence around violence against women demonstrates that a capacity to act can be built around foci of agreement, without an all-encompassing common consciousness. The experience of working together to achieve shared interests can then give impetus to the development of a shared sense of identity.

Such a strong focus of agreement allowed the global women's community to exercise autonomy in global politics by putting pressure on the UN to recognize violence against women as a global concern. The UN played an important role in lending legitimacy to this consensus by adopting in 1999 the Optional Protocol to the 1979 Convention on the Elimination of All Forms of Discrimination against Women (CEDAW). CEDAW allows NGOs to report violations of the agreement directly to UN committees set up to periodically review governments' implementation progress. The recognition by the UN that gender violence is a global problem means that women's NGOs can now pressure states to be accountable for their actions, which enhances the autonomy of these groups relative to national states.

Another way in which the autonomy of civil society groups has increased is the acceptance by other actors (mostly the UN) of their knowledge claims. The role of testimony in bringing prominence to the issue of violence against women has to be emphasized here (Keck and Sikkink 1998, 183, 187). The increased acceptability of testimony as a form of knowledge has significantly improved the prospects for global civil society to create shared understandings and influence governments, because civil society groups have better direct access to this embodied form of knowledge. A vital weapon for women's groups in influencing governments is the Internet. States can be shamed into improving their record on issues such as violence against women when the UN's opinion on their progress on the implementation of UN conventions such as CEDAW is publicized against their will.

The overall effect of global mobilizing has been to enhance the autonomy of women's groups in relation to national governments, but this effect should also not be exaggerated. Southern women's movements have varying degrees of independence from corresponding national states, as is the case for Northern women's movements. In some Latin American countries, the feminist movement has been in part incorporated within state structures (Geske and Bourque 2001; Icken Safa 1995), while in Islamic countries much of women's organizing conceives of gender issues only within the confines of state religion (Karam 2000; Ray and Korteweg 1999). Some commentators argue that women's groups are autonomous agents only if they exist outside state institutions,[5] but when it comes to the implementation of international accords state cooperation is vital. This is an irony of autonomy: for women's groups to be autonomous, they need the cooperation of the actor whose autonomy they are undermining in the process. If and when states are more concerned with their image in the international community than with resisting NGO attempts to encroach upon their autonomy, the mechanism of reporting violations to international conventions will enhance the autonomy of women's groups.

This autonomy should be understood not only in relation to national states but also in relation to other women's groups. In this respect, in spite of the important reporting role for local organizations, TNGOs dominated by Northern and elite Southern groups have gained the most autonomy by taking advantage of the opportunities created by globalization. Their focus on violence against women not only managed to attract the attention of the UN but also enabled these groups to influence the priorities of local organizations. The ability of TNGOs to channel funding to smaller organizations can be fairly persuasive in putting violence against women on the agendas of the latter. For instance, UNIFEM (United Nations Development Fund for Women) and IWRAW (International Women's Rights Action Watch) are organizing global to local training sessions to help local NGOs become familiar with CEDAW and capable of reporting on their governments' violations of the convention (Geske and Bourque 2001, 251, 253). Despite these efforts to involve grassroots organizations, some see a discrepancy between the political, cultural, and financial capital of women's organizations that operate in the global community of international governmental meetings and those that operate at the local level (Alvarez 2000). Indeed, to the extent that locally oriented groups have gained autonomy in relation to local governments by virtue of these groups' involvement in the global women's movement, they have correspondingly lost some autonomy in relation to a global civil society overwhelmingly shaped by groups and ideas from the North.

This review of the development of the global women's movement suggests that it represents an important element of transnational community that is deeper than a simple interest-based network or coalition. Activists at the transnational level do appear to share a sense of identity as women in a world characterized by common elements of patriarchy, though differences of material circumstance and belief mean that this sense of identity as women coexists with regional and national senses of identity that are sometimes in opposition. The shared sense of identity also includes a commitment to respect for difference, a commitment that emerged in response to instances of difference experienced in the process of building the movement. The sense of community builds on some shared interests emerging out of those elements of patriarchy that are common to many regions of the world (e.g., violence against women), but it did not emerge spontaneously; activists guided by norms of inclusivity were crucial in figuring out how to frame issues in a way that made a shared sense of identity possible.

Global Social Policy Activists

The 1990s witnessed an explosion of transnational activism around the issues of global poverty, inequality, and social dislocation. To study the phenomenon in a manageable fashion, we focused on activism surrounding the World Summit on Social Development (WSSD), one of a number of major world conferences organized by the United Nations in the mid-1990s. Several thousand representatives from hundreds of NGOS participated in the conference and the parallel NGO forum. We are particularly interested in seeing whether transnational social policy activists constitute a community that can act with collective autonomy, rather than simply a coalition or network, and in identifying the bases (in interests or identities or both) for the elements of community that do exist.

Global social policy activists do have a distinct set of shared values that collectively unite them and set them apart from states (Northern and Southern) and the international financial institutions (IFIs). Most NGOS at the WSSD approached questions of global social policy from a social democratic perspective, in contrast to the liberal perspective favoured by most states and the IFIs. This was most apparent in joint position papers such as "The Quality Benchmark for the Social Summit" signed by a large number of NGOS involved in the preparatory meetings (van Reisen 2001, 37) and the "Copenhagen Alternative Declaration" adopted at the parallel NGO forum (NGO Forum 1995). Their readiness to criticize dominant institutions demonstrates that NGOS have substantial autonomy from the forces behind market-oriented globalization, even though many rely on states and IGOS for some of their funding. These reformist views are shared by a large number of NGOS based in the South as well as the North, challenging the notion (see, e.g., Pasha and Blaney 1998) that NGOS are simply another mechanism of Northern hegemony. Some of the strongest and most consistent NGO positions were their critiques of free markets and institutions such as the World Bank and the International Monetary Fund (IMF), which is consistent with the suggestion that "opposition to neoliberal globalization [may be] an emerging master frame" among transnational activists (Della Porta and Tarrow 2005, 11). Thus, the boundary between community members and non-members (e.g., the small number of liberal groups that also participated in the WSSD) was defined primarily by *values* rather than by territory or other traditional bases of community. More traditional is the fact that this element of shared identity reflected a *reaction against* an other presumed to have different values, suggesting also that the idea of reactive autonomy is helpful for understanding this transnational activist community.

At the same time, there was a shared consensus around positive proposals for measures needed to achieve shared NGO values, and this consensus emerged through a deliberative process. The specific concerns of each group gained coherence and strength through their association with related proposals and with the joint adoption of a human rights framing of problems of poverty and social development, not unlike the issue of violence against women for the global women's movement. In particular, framing macroeconomic issues such as structural adjustment as violations of universal social and economic rights enabled Northern human rights groups to join with others (including Southern grassroots groups) motivated more by macroeconomic issues (van Reisen 2001, 25).

The consideration shown for diversity and difference took a strong form in this case. Groups from different economic backgrounds agreed on the need for global social policy to reflect the views of those most affected, particularly marginalized poor people. NGOs from the North and South were very critical of the tendency they saw at the WSSD (and in the IFIs) to portray people living in poverty as victims in need of external intervention rather than as active agents who could meaningfully contribute to poverty eradication (*Earth Negotiations Bulletin* 10, no. 22, 1995). To promote the latter, NGOs agreed strongly on the need to empower local communities in relation to the IFIs (and transnational corporations) and to give grassroots social movements and citizens' organizations a stronger role (NGO Forum 1995). Local community empowerment is a key value for transnational activists on a wide range of issues (Friedman, Hochstetler, and Clark 2005, 54-6).

In contrast to their strong normative consensus, however, NGOs did have some difficulty developing institutional mechanisms to help them pursue their shared goals. Most contentious were issues of leadership and who would speak on behalf of the large number of NGOs that shared the values just described. There was tension between groups such as the International Council on Social Welfare (ICSW), which had a long history of involvement with the UN and formal consultative status with ECOSOC (Economic and Social Council) (groups such as this are sometimes labelled "CONGOS" because they participate in the Conference of NGOs in Consultative Relations with the United Nations), and nationally based grassroots groups active on social policy issues and between groups from the North and groups from the South. The UN was making greater efforts to expand involvement of non-traditional NGOs in its work (especially NGOs from the South), and it granted conference accreditation to all NGOs that participated in the first preparatory meetings, regardless of whether they met the stricter ECOSOC criteria (Disney 2000; van Reisen 2001, 33-4). UN openness efforts challenged the special status of the CONGOS as points of entry for civil society into UN processes, as did the improved access to information about UN meetings provided by the Internet (van Reisen 2001, 16-17, 22-3, 29-33). For their part, the CONGOS feared that many of the newer groups did not understand how the UN worked, were not prepared to contribute in the necessary spirit of compromise, and made "extravagant claims of representativity" (Disney 2000, 17 [quotation], 13, 18-20). The CONGOS attempted to create an International Facilitating Committee under their leadership, but it was not acceptable to the other groups (Disney 2000, 10; van Reisen 2001, 31-3). Collective disarray at the first meeting of the WSSD preparatory committee (*Earth Negotiations Bulletin* 10, no. 11, 1995) highlighted the need for more effective coordinating mechanisms, and NGOs subsequently grouped themselves into a number of caucuses, among which the most prominent were the ICSW, the Development Caucus, and the Women's Caucus (Disney 2000, 10, 12-13; *Earth Negotiations Bulletin* 10, no. 22, 1995; van Reisen 2001, 29, 34-5). This was possible only because some particularly well-resourced and experienced Northern NGOs such as Novib (Nederlandse Organisatie voor Internationale Bijstand) (in relation to the Development Caucus) and WEDO (Women's Environment and Development Organization) (in relation to the Women's Caucus) felt a sense of obligation to reach out to other groups and share leadership with grassroots Southern groups wary of being pushed aside (this is discussed in greater detail in the chapter "Transnational Actors and Global Social Welfare Policy: The Limits of Private Institutions in Global Governance" in Pauly and Coleman 2008). The willingness to compromise within the activist community reflected both the shared values described earlier and the shared interest in increasing NGOs' collective influence vis-à-vis powerful actors pursuing more liberal approaches to social policy.

The activist community that emerged around the WSSD persisted beyond the immediate campaign. NGOs have taken full advantage of the opportunities the Internet provides to build international networks among people who share similar values but not territorial contiguity. A particularly important NGO initiative was the establishment of Internet-based Social Watch (www.socialwatch.org). It provides annual reports on government progress (or its absence) toward meeting the Copenhagen commitments based on reports prepared by national groups of NGOs, and it produces its own analyses of country policies, social conditions, and global trends. Social Watch can best be understood as an *international* network that strengthens *national* groups in the pursuit of *transnationally* shared values, and it is a prime example of how the building of transnational communities can help NGOs to gain autonomy vis-à-vis national states.

Our study of NGOs involved in global social policy shows they do have collective normative autonomy, though their policy impact is more limited. As in the case of violence against women, there is a shared sense of community based on shared values, including, importantly, a commitment to inclusiveness, particularly for groups marginalized in conventional political and economic processes. These values have been developed and refined through deliberative processes and are expressed by NGOs from the South as well as the North. The study also shows that the development of a sense of community among transnational social policy activists has depended heavily on support from the UN, again mirroring the evolution of global women's groups.

Women's Groups and Social Policy Activists in Western and Eastern Europe

Our review of the transnational women's movement and global social policy activists shows that two crucial factors in the development of transnational activist communities are the actions of intergovernmental organizations such as the UN and the process by which activists consciously attempt to build community in the face of difference through dialogue. We can gain further insight into the dynamics of transnational community building by taking a closer look at these points in a more restricted regional setting, one in which cultural and value differences are not as marked as at the global level. To do so, we conducted interviews with representatives of women's groups and social policy activists (including trade unions)[6] in Western and Eastern Europe.[7] Our intention is to understand activists' experiences in relation to questions about the development of autonomous communities at the transnational level, in this case the level of "Europe."

Economic globalization and regional integration present women's groups and social policy activists in Western and Eastern Europe with some common challenges, though in other respects their circumstances differ greatly. The common challenge is to defend and develop progressive social and gender policies in the face of economic and ideological pressures to limit social welfare programs in the name of enhancing international economic competitiveness. Generally speaking, groups in Western Europe are attempting to protect past achievements at the national and EU levels from retrenchment, while in Eastern Europe the challenge is to develop progressive social and gender policies appropriate for a market-oriented economic system after the collapse of communism. Western Europe has a much longer tradition of vibrant civil society, including a large and highly organized NGO sector represented by EU-level lobbying organizations. These EU-level organizations are characterized by shared values and trust in the ability to resolve conflicts that might arise democratically and have an institutionalized place in the EU policy-making process. It therefore makes sense to consider these groups as constituting a transnational activist community. In the case of social policy activists and union confederations, agreement centres on strong support for the European social model, with its emphasis on inclusiveness and social cohesion. In contrast, the development of civil society in Eastern Europe is a phenomenon largely of the post-communist era (the dissident movements of the 1970s and 1980s notwithstanding), and the nascent NGO sector is relatively divided and weakly developed. Paralleling the North-South divide discussed earlier, groups in Western Europe are far wealthier than those in Eastern Europe, in part because the former can draw on extensive financial support from national governments and the EU. These differences suggest that the development of autonomous transnational activist communities spanning Eastern and Western Europe is not a straightforward process.

TNGOs and the EU

Attempts to develop transnational activist communities at a pan-European level have been heavily influenced by the policies of the EU, just as the development of global-level communities of women's and social policy activists was heavily influenced by the UN. The EU supports the development of pan-EU NGO networks by providing financial assistance and opportunities for networks to consult with the commission. EU support encouraged the development of highly institutionalized NGO networks in Western Europe before the EU's recent eastward expansion.

The eastward enlargement of the European Union is an important reason why Western European networks want to include members from Eastern Europe. The impending opening of Western European labour markets to workers from Eastern Europe means that groups from both regions face pressure to find ways to collaborate. Western groups such as the European Trade Unions Confederation (ETUC) hope to avoid a race to the bottom in labour and social policy, while Eastern European NGOs and trade unions want to gain access to EU policy making that will affect their countries. These concerns have indeed led to a wave of cooperation among groups on the two sides of Europe. For instance, the Social Platform, a network of thirty-nine European NGOs, federations, and networks, has an enlargement taskforce and used the occasion of EU enlargement in 2004 to issue a declaration in support of civil society organizations in Eastern Europe. Thus, the coming together of NGOs from different locations is due partly to changes in the international institutional environment, not just to processes internal to NGO communities themselves. Increased East-West collaboration reflects the shared interests of these groups (rather than a shared identity) in gaining influence at a level of governance that is becoming more important.

European NGO networks depend on financial support from the European Commission (EC) for their enlargement, and this support provides more evidence that international organizations are critical to the ability of differently located NGOs to establish strong, lasting connections. When it is available, EU funding can promote east-west NGO cooperation. For example, the EU sponsored a training and information conference for Hungarian social policy NGOs organized by the European Anti-Poverty Network (EAPN), and this conference generated close connections between the EAPN and some Hungarian social policy NGOs. But in our interviews, representatives of EU networks pointed to the absence of funding for partnerships with organizations from Eastern Europe as the reason why collaboration is often limited to sporadic, project-based contacts, while Eastern European NGOs lamented the fact that Western European networks only collaborate on projects for which EU funding is available.

Relatively secure EU funding allows Western European lobbies to concentrate on policy work, and this work contributes to their ability to engage in self-reflection and develop an element of common identity based on shared values. In contrast, Eastern European organizations have to apply for project-based funding to a variety of donor agencies, and this requirement contributes to their tendency to focus more on service provision than on policy work. The different funding-related orientation of Eastern and Western European NGOs — service provision versus policy lobbying — can make it difficult for groups to relate to each other's concerns and impedes the development of a shared identity at the pan-European level.

External funding for civil society development has been instrumental in the growth of Eastern European NGOs since the collapse of communism. However, the external impetus behind the formation of such NGOs means that many struggle to define their own identities outside donors' needs.[8] In our interviews, some women's organizations in both Hungary and Romania noted that the level of external interest and funding had subsided since the early 1990s and that external funders increasingly insisted that the eastern organizations focus on service provision to become financially sustainable. However, this view was not universally shared. The head of a women's NGO in Romania explained that her group had learned to frame the projects it wished to pursue using whatever keywords were attractive to donors, though rapid change in these keywords (e.g., from violence against women to ethnic minority rights) could impede continuity in their efforts to successfully address social problems.

Finally, we should note that the EU is not the only IGO shaping the development of European activist communities; the World Bank also supports the development of civil society in Eastern Europe. One Eastern European social policy activist we interviewed claimed that it was easier to obtain funding from the World Bank for the projects considered most urgent by activists and that World Bank funding came with fewer conditions. The EU was also criticized for not understanding the importance of community activism and the building of social capital. This example shows that the orientations of IGOs influence the kinds of activism possible in local communities. It also shows that EU-espoused norms do not have a monopoly on NGO identities in Eastern Europe, though they do provide a framework that helps to define the terms of discussion and, implicitly, the borders of NGO communities. IGOs are thus, even in this regional environment, pivotal to the ability of NGOs to form communities.

Negotiating Differences of Identity and Interest

EU-funded project-specific cooperation between groups from the two parts of Europe has been going on for some time now. In this section, we discuss how this interest-based cooperation shapes the possibilities for building shared identities and a sense of community among activists in Eastern and

Western Europe. We argue that cooperation has so far not been extensive enough, and in some cases not open enough, to forge shared identities. Some encouraging signs in this direction do exist, however, which leads us to cautiously optimistic conclusions about the possibilities for creating autonomous communities at this level.

Apart from the funding issues discussed above, obstacles to interest-based cooperation include the hierarchical structure of EU-level networks. They take the form of networks of national umbrella organizations, each comprised of numerous NGOs, and they can only accept national networks as members. But national networks have been slow to develop in Eastern Europe. The formation of national networks of women's groups has been slowed by the conflict between "new" and "old" women's organizations. Old women's groups are the successors of Communist Party women's organizations; they run women's clubs and claim to have large memberships. New NGOs formed after the fall of communism often define their identity more closely in line with their transnational counterparts in Western Europe and accuse the old organizations of failing to promote women's rights and of attempting to suppress dissenting views. This conflict shows that national NGO communities are no more "natural" than their transnational counterparts.[9] National social policy activist networks have also been slow to form, perhaps because this type of activism is very new in Eastern Europe, though extensive contacts with European-level networks (as in Hungary) can hasten their formation.

Concrete conflicts of interest also limit the development of what might appear to be natural communities, as in the case of ETUC and Eastern European trade union confederations. While ETUC provides information and advice to Eastern European counterparts on a variety of topics, Eastern European union representatives whom we interviewed did not feel their links with ETUC were close.[10] Key to this weakness is the issue of labour mobility across EU borders, which leads Western European labour organizations to fear wage competition and the erosion of higher Western European social standards. In contrast, Eastern European trade unions favour labour mobility and flexible regulations to ensure their members have access to Western European labour markets. This difference in views is so sharp that the topic usually is avoided in discussions among trade unions; ETUC prefers instead to foster unity by defining the main adversaries as multinational corporations. However, avoiding the issue rather than addressing it (however difficult that may be) limits the potential for developing shared identities and building a sense of community.

Identity differences between women's NGOs from Eastern and Western Europe are not as marked as those of Northern and Southern groups at the UN. The founding principles of most new women's NGOs in Eastern Europe were much influenced by the "women's rights as human rights" framework. Laura Grunberg (2000, 318) noted that, at the time of her writing, the concept of women's rights had not been fully internalized by Romanian women's NGOs because the discourse of rights was not yet meaningful in a country still marked by a collectivist culture. However, at the time of our interviews for this study, representatives of women's NGOs whom we interviewed did not criticize the human rights framing of their work despite some resentment about the need to use specific keywords to attract external funding (e.g., Roma minority rights, trafficking of women). Acceptance of the human rights discourse by eastern European NGOs suggests that this framework has now been internalized into the identities of these groups.

Moreover, some identity differences that we would expect to thwart efforts at transnational community formation do not appear to be very salient. One is the issue of feminism. Organizations in both locations are generally reluctant to define themselves as feminist due to the suspicion the term provokes in many circles. In spite of their more service-oriented nature, women's NGOs in Eastern Europe see their job in much the same terms as do Western European groups. Training on gender-related issues for various professional groups, hotlines for battered women, lobbies for changes to the legal system, and campaigns to change public attitudes toward women's rights are activities that bridge practical and strategic gender interests in ways that are relevant to Western and Eastern European women's groups. NGO identities seem to be closer for women's groups than for social policy groups. For the latter, while there is a fair amount of agreement on desirable long-term objectives, Eastern European groups regard the social issues they address as transition specific, and they appear not to share their Western European counterparts' goal of extending the European social model eastward; this is not a declared aim for Eastern European social NGOs.

In spite of this uneven picture of the extent of shared identities among Eastern and Western European NGOs (greatest for women's groups, less for social policy groups, and least for trade unions), there are signs that east-west interaction contains an element of openness to dialogue that prefigures a sense of mutual obligation specific to communities. Especially important here is the willingness on all sides to engage in dialogue and learn from their counterparts, which was revealed in our interviews. Women's groups in Eastern Europe mentioned trust issues in their early interactions with Western European groups, arising from the apparent belief among Western European NGOs that women in Eastern Europe were victims of communism in need of foreign intervention. This view triggered defensive attitudes from women in the east. However, the NGO representatives whom we interviewed agreed that such inequalities have faded in importance, because the growing self-confidence and expertise of women in the east has gained them Western European respect and because Eastern European groups have chosen to cooperate only with organizations that treat them as genuine partners rather than as subordinates.

Even in the case of trade unions, while funding inequalities persist, Eastern European unions believe that communication with their Western European counterparts is now on a more equal footing and that the initial tendency of Western European groups to look down on Eastern European groups is diminishing as the latter gain strength and experience in their own countries. The Interregional Trade Union Councils set up for the EU frontier regions are another example of an attempt by a Western European-based organization (ETUC) to deal with differences through dialogue. The work of these councils is said to represent "a laboratory for the practical implementation of a genuinely European trade union policy in the social and economic field, and ... a significant contribution to European trade union identity" (ETUC 2003, 32). These councils suggest openness by ETUC towards negotiating differences (though perhaps falling short of full engagement with the issue of labour mobility) and a keen interest in building a joint European identity.

Emerging transnational activist communities are also strengthened by growing personal networks that connect activists from Eastern Europe with their counterparts in other regions. Once someone is on a distribution list and has made personal contacts with other activists, she gets invited repeatedly to international conferences, where she often sees familiar faces, all of which helps to create a sense of belonging to the community. The opportunity to meet face to face with other group members has been identified by some social movement theorists as a key reason for the greater strength and coherence of national as opposed to transnational NGOs (Tarrow 1998). However, funding constraints mean that many Eastern European activists miss out on these networking opportunities, just as grassroots activists in developing countries have limited opportunities to network with their Northern counterparts in the global women's and social policy movements.

In conclusion, there is a mixed picture of the prospects for community building on the basis of interest-based cooperation between Eastern and Western European NGOs. Inequalities between the differently located groups still exist, but there are signs that they are not insurmountable. Limited interest-based cooperation still constitutes the bulk of the interaction between these NGOs, but the opening of dialogue is a good sign for the prospects of these groups to form stronger communities.

The Autonomy of Emerging Pan-European Activist Communities

In this section, we consider the impact that the growing transnational connections just described have on the capacity of different groups to act with autonomy in relation to other political institutions and actors, particularly national governments and the EU. The activist networks that developed in the EU before its recent eastward expansion have considerable autonomy because of their strong domestic NGO foundations, shared values and senses of identity, and institutionalized roles in the EU. Their autonomy is manifested in their significant independent influence on the European Commission. For example, policy proposals from European NGO networks became part of the Lisbon Agenda, a ten-year EU program of social and economic commitments devised in 2000, and, as one of our interviewees noted, the EC now funds these NGOs to work specifically on proposals that the NGOs themselves helped to design. Their ability to participate in the definition of dominant European social policy and gender values enhances these NGOs' autonomy relative to other actors attempting to influence EU norms, including individual governments or business representatives. Expanding membership to include groups from Eastern Europe will help the European networks to maintain their roles in the enlarged EU.

However, having influence with the EC does not necessarily translate into a greater capacity for direct action. EU-level women's and social policy NGOs suffer from having an overly specialized relationship with the commission. The relationship with the Directorate General (DG) for Employment and Social Affairs is very good for all EU-level NGOs interviewed, but these NGOs have little contact or influence in more powerful parts of the commission, such as DG Competition, which limits the overall influence of NGO networks on EU policies. The Western European networks also have a low capacity for mobilization because their relationship with member organizations is highly institutionalized and leaves little room for the more spontaneous enthusiasm that characterizes many Eastern European NGOs.

Even ETUC, whose involvement in policy consultation is one of the pillars of the EU system of social partnership, has a limited capacity to act beyond its role in policy consultation because its connection with workers and trade union members is not particularly strong (ETUC 2003).

Eastern European groups are interested in cooperating with Western European networks in part because they hope to use their influence with EU institutions to gain leverage over their own governments. The autonomy relative to the state thus potentially afforded to these NGOs is analogous to the situation of the global women's community, where Southern NGOs can gain leverage on their own governments by allying themselves with Northern groups around the UN. The closer a country is to EU membership, the more its NGOs benefit from an EU-dictated stable, institutionalized relationship with their state. In Hungary, for instance, consultative mechanisms shaped according to the EU model (e.g., a Social Policy Council) enhance the autonomy of NGOs relative to their government by providing an opening into the national policy-making process and access to a more stable source of funding. In Romania, in contrast, NGOs complained about the lack of an institutionalized relationship with the state, reflecting the less advanced stage of this country's relationship with the EU at the time the interviews were conducted.

So far, however, Eastern European NGOs (in particular social policy NGOs) have not made full use of the EU's policy leverage on their governments. The groups are engaged primarily in providing services rather than policy lobbying. Similarly, Eastern European trade unions' capacity to act as social policy actors is mostly an unfulfilled potential, in spite of institutionalized relationships with states, because of the weakness of the union movement in most countries (on union problems, see CNSRL Fratia 2004).

These configurations of autonomy for women's and social policy groups regionally show some similarities and some differences to those at the global level. In terms of the autonomy of northern/western groups relative to their southern/eastern counterparts, the European case study does not present the same degree of contending autonomy between the two types of groups as was apparent in the global cases. Unlike Northern women's and social policy NGOs, European networks already had a more established policy position within the EU when they started collaborating with Eastern European groups. Such collaboration was thus not as necessary for enhancing the western networks' autonomy relative to the EU or to their national governments. In terms of the potential autonomy of

Eastern European groups relative to their national governments, however, the similarities with the Southern women's groups are evident.

Conclusion

Our examination of the global women's movement, global social policy activists, and European NGO networks shows that globalization can encourage the development of new forms of deterritorialized community but that such effects are not automatic or spontaneous. The developments discussed in this chapter rely on globalizing pressures and phenomena such as advances in communication technologies and the rise of international governance. All the case studies point to the crucial roles that intergovernmental organizations play in shaping the conditions of possibility for transnational activist communities. Of course, IGOs and their conferences provide focal points for transnational organizing, but the UN and the EU also play much more active roles — encouraging the development of TNGOs in developing countries and Eastern Europe, providing funding, and legitimizing TNGO concerns. The role of IGOs has some important implications for TNGO autonomy. For example, IGO efforts could channel TNGOs into a dominant framework, or dependence on funding from IGOs could lead TNGOs to alter their positions to avoid alienating benefactors. Other political circumstances, such as the enlargement of the EU, also create important opportunities for community formation among NGOs.

We can also think of the influence of globalization as enhancing the ability of NGOs to reach broader consensus by building more reflective worldviews. Such worldviews are built during the process of negotiation of difference. Efforts to mobilize around sweeping claims to common identity had limited success (sisterhood is global, WID), compelling NGO leaders to define issues so as to appeal to groups with different experiences and to avoid disputed terms (e.g., "feminism" in the case of European NGOs). It is not clear to what extent these reflective views are fully internalized or are simply adopted to create strategic alliances. This problem is particularly acute for groups from the South and East, whose funding often depends on the adoption of these new keywords.

The TNGO coalitions examined in this chapter do not constitute closely knit communities. Territorially derived political and economic differences continue, at least in terms of access to funding but also often in terms of the issues of concern. But elements of inequality are common in most communities. What matters for the making or breaking of community is just how divisive these inequalities are and whether a sense of belonging exists despite inequalities. On the one hand, inequalities could be expected to be quite divisive due to the absence of many other bases for community (e.g., language and history in national communities). On the other hand, activist communities have strong incentives to overcome divisive inequalities to gain the capacity to act and to take advantage of the opportunities for joint political action offered by international organizations. But the perception and pursuit of common interests does not emerge spontaneously; groups must work consciously to identify points in common and resolve or avoid points of difference. There has indeed been much progress in facing differences in some movements, such as the global women's movement, though other areas of activism have been slower to take on the negotiation of difference (e.g., the European trade unions). Groups and movements that can develop respect for diversity and difference within can find that to be a source of strength (Gill 2000; Klein 2001), in contrast to traditional theories that have tended to see internal diversity as undermining collective strength (Tarrow 2005, 176-7).

Strategic considerations have been important in encouraging Northern and western groups to increase their openness to dialogue with groups from developing countries and Eastern Europe, but the effect of such dialogue is often to force the rethinking of bases for identity, making these communities stronger in the process. Thus, strategic attempts to increase capacity to act are associated with strengthening the elements of joint identity. Negotiation to build commonality of interests and identity is an indispensable part of creating autonomous communities.

Finally, we should note that the development of autonomous transnational activist communities has mixed implications for the autonomy of their constituent units, which often are territorially based. Transnational activist communities can enhance the autonomy of member groups in relation to national governments and to other social and political forces, but at the same time those member groups may lose some autonomy in relation to the transnational community. These opportunities and pitfalls of engagement in transnational communities, the subtle back-and-forth negotiations involved, and the open-ended nature of the outcomes demonstrate that the development of transnational communities is just as much a political process as are relations among states.

chapter 9

Labour, Globalization, and the Attempt to Build Transnational Community

Robert O'Brien

THE INTENSIFICATION OF GLOBALIZATION in the last quarter of the twentieth century has opened the issue of shifting group and individual identities and their relationships to changing forms of community and autonomy. This chapter presents a case study of an attempted community transformation in the global labour movement. The goal is to shed light on how the concepts and practices of identity, community, agency, and autonomy can intersect in an increasingly globalized environment.

As outlined in the introduction to this volume, and in a number of its chapters, the form and nature of community in a global era can vary substantially. Some communities may be deterritorialized, such as the climbing communities in Slemon's chapter. They may exist only in the imaginations of individuals or in literary form. Some communities may be seeking to reterritorialize their existence, as is illustrated in Habib's discussion of the Palestinian right of return movement. Some of the communities are of inheritance, such as the indigenous communities discussed by Preston and Mulrennan. Other communities are more accidental, such as the Western women development workers described in Cook's chapter. Communities may sit on a continuum between affective groups of people and instrumental networks.

These varieties of experience resist generalization, except perhaps to say that there are multiple patterns of community transformation. This chapter highlights a case where particular agents are attempting to build new transnational communities in an instrumental fashion for the purpose of mobilizing forces in pursuit of a political objective — increased labour autonomy. In this case, community is viewed as a prerequisite for sustained contentious interaction designed to secure labour autonomy. The boundaries of the community-in-waiting are porous and shifting, but it is clear that particular groups are excluded from membership (capital, state-controlled and Northern-based labour groups). Perhaps more so than in other cases in this volume, the practice of autonomy is viewed as a zero sum game. Labour autonomy can only be secured at the expense of capital or business autonomy.

The chapter is divided into two major parts. The first part provides an overview of labour, globalization, and autonomy. It argues that the process of globalization has had a multi-faceted effect on workers' autonomy and sense of community, depending on the type and location of labour being conducted. Globalization simultaneously undermines and strengthens labour autonomy. As well, it breaks existing patterns of local community and provides opportunities for the creation of new forms of transnational community. Although the overall balance leans to the negative side, it is not yet fixed and remains the object of considerable conflict. It is this negative relationship that provides the incentive for creating new forms of community.

The second part of the chapter presents the case study of the Southern Initiative on Globalization and Trade Union Rights (SIGTUR). After introducing SIGTUR, I examine its self-defined identity to highlight the many tensions in transnational identity formation. This examination is followed by sections that examine SIGTUR's efforts at community and autonomy building. SIGTUR's example provides both evidence of transnational community building and caution about the difficulties involved in such a task. The conclusion presents the arguement that the issue of labour's autonomy in the globalization process is still very much subject to political struggle and that transnational labour community is one consequence of, and response to, that struggle.

Labour Autonomy on a Global Scale

There are several reasons why an examination of the relationship between globalization, labour autonomy, and community are warranted. First, from the perspective of globalization studies, the impact of globalization on labour is highly contested. Many labour organizations condemn globalization in its present form and lay many sins at its door. Simultaneously, others argue that globalization is lifting millions of workers out of poverty and offers the best hope for human betterment. Second, from the perspective of labour, a central issue in the globalization debate is whether its ability to act, or autonomy, is being impaired under globalization. The perceived impact of globalization on labour autonomy has significance for labour's attitudes toward the state, the economy, and global governance. Third, from the perspective of those interested in shifting forms of community, labour offers a significant case study. Labour organizations were among the first modern internationalists, yet most recent academic study of transnationalism has neglected labour organizations. Given the centrality of capitalism and economic factors to globalization, the transformation of labour communities has significant implications for the notion of community in a global era.

Key Terms

Before launching into my argument, it is necessary to clarify key terms used in this chapter because concepts such as "globalization" and "autonomy" are used in many different ways. Following Scholte (2000), the word *globalization* refers to a process of relative deterritorialization or supraterritoriality. The uneven compression of time and space on a transworld basis creates new forms of social relations. It also creates new forms of authority beyond the state such as international organizations or market actors.

Labour experiences globalization in particular ways. In general, the rise of transnational corporations, global financial markets, and instantaneous communication technologies has increased the competitive pressures on most workers. Simultaneously, workers tend to be hobbled by cultural and linguistic barriers that some elites are able to surmount in their globe-spanning interactions.

The concept and practice of *autonomy* range from a simple formulation as the ability to make informed choices about what should be done and how to do it to the more advanced notion of "critical autonomy," which involves the ability to agree to or change the rules that govern a culture or political economy (Doyal and Gough 1991, 53, 67). This chapter pays attention both to the ability of groups to act as agents (minimal autonomy) and to their ability to negotiate and shape the environment in which they live through political participation.

The concept of *community* refers to collections of people who self-identify as a group with common interests or experiences. A community takes both an organizational and an intersubjective form. Communities create organizations or institutions to facilitate their operation. One can think of civic associations, states, and international organizations as evidence of particular communities. Communities are also composed of groups of people who think or feel that they have a common link. This intersubjective notion of community is much more fluid than the organizational manifestation. The intellectual community is constantly changing as individuals or groups redefine themselves as being part of this or that community or drop out of other communities. Given the macro focus of this chapter, it is not possible to investigate the intersubjective nuances of various workers' communities because that would take an immense volume of research. As an alternative, communities will be inferred from organizational structures with the caveat that more fluid communities surround the institutions.

It is useful to differentiate between types of workers to distinguish varying patterns. Although there are several typologies one could use, I employ a rather general distinction between protected and unprotected workers. The term *unprotected workers* refers to non-established workers or producers lacking power in the world labour force (Harrod 1987, 38-9). This is in contrast to *protected workers* who have been able to develop some personal or social power to defend their interests. Protected workers usually have an organization such as a trade union, political party, or state to assist them. Protection is not an either/or category but a question of degree. Workers lie on a continuum between very protected and very vulnerable. While the distinction blurs close to the centre, it is clear at the extremes. For example, one can contrast a unionized worker in an advanced industrialized state with a street vendor in a developing country. However, the distinction is not confined to different countries. One can also contrast the same auto worker with migrant labour in her own country or the street vendor with a high-tech worker in his own country.

Because labour and workers' organizations and situations vary so greatly across the globe, it is difficult to make a blanket generalization about the relationship between globalization and workers' autonomy. However, it is possible to discern some broad trends when labour is disaggregated according to geographical location and degree of protection. The greater we disaggregate, the more precision we will have, but the more difficult it is to make generalizations. Thus, this section identifies four broad, overlapping categories of labour: Northern, Southern, protected, and unprotected. Exceptions to trends in these four categories will be addressed where they are judged to be significant.

Protected Workers in the North: Autonomy Undermined

Intensification of globalization since the early 1970s has coincided with, and contributed to, the almost universal undermining of protected workers' autonomy in advanced industrialized countries. Workers have lost ground both in the political arena and in the industrial relations field. Politically, trade unions have seen their influence decrease as former left and social democratic parties have moved to the right and loosened ties with their labour constituencies. In the United States, this was most vividly illustrated during the debate over the North American Free Trade Agreement (NAFTA). NAFTA was supported by the Democratic Party establishment despite the opposition of its labour constituency. During the crucial NAFTA vote in Congress, Democratic president Bill Clinton urged members of his party to join Republicans in passing the agreement. NAFTA was approved, and organized labour was left reconsidering its traditional support for US foreign economic policy. Some interpreted this split as signifying a potential radical turning point in US labour's relationship with the state (Rupert 1995).

Organizationally, autonomy has been reduced by an attack on trade union rights and a steadily declining union density in many states. The attack has been most severe in the Anglo-American states, with union density dramatically declining (Fairbrother and Yates 2002). For example, the percentage of workers belonging to unions in the United States has declined from 35 percent in 1954 to 20 percent in 1983 to only 13.5 percent in 2001. The figure for private (excluding public sector) non-agricultural industry is less than 10 percent (Graham 2003). Despite an upsurge in resources dedicated to organizing workers (Bronfenbrenner et al. 1998), there is no sign yet of recovery.

Although protected workers in the North have seen their autonomy undermined by globalization, they remain relatively more autonomous than unprotected Northern workers or protected and unprotected workers in the South. They still have access to state, union, and political party protection to assert their autonomy, even if these institutions are significantly weaker or are less sympathetic than they were thirty years ago.

Unprotected Workers in the North: One Step Back

While most workers in advanced industrialized economies enjoy some type of state protection in the form of minimum employment rights and social services, significant numbers of workers have seen their autonomy undermined by the growth of precarious employment. Increasingly, the norm of full-time employment with benefits and some degree of protection has been challenged by a temporary employment relationship characterized by casualization and insecurity (Vosko 2000). For example, in the United States in 2004, there were as many workers engaged in temporary contract work as there were members of unions (Witte 2004).

The striking element about unprotected work in advanced industrialized states is the degree to which the rest of the economy relies on this form of labour. Reliable statistics are difficult to marshal, but the extent and significance of unprotected work rises to the surface in a number of ways. One high-profile example occurred in 1993 when President Clinton attempted to appoint a woman to the post of attorney general. His first two candidates were forced to withdraw because they both had used "illegal" workers for child care. The eventual post holder was a childless woman. This incident demonstrated the degree to which professional women with children in the United States rely on unprotected, often migrant, women to perform household labour. Another example emerged in 2003 when it was revealed that an element of the retailer Wal-Mart's famous competitive advantage rested on its employment of undocumented workers to clean its stores (Saunders 2003).

The growth of precarious work conditions has combined with a transformation of the state to reduce the autonomy of many workers. This transformation has variously been interpreted as the demise of the welfare state (Mishra 1999), growth of the workfare state (Jessop 1993), or rise of the competition state (Cerny 2000). However it is conceptualized, the central element is the withdrawal of universal social services and the increased targeting and conditionality of social benefits. These changes have the effect of reducing the choices available to large sections of the paid and unpaid workforce.

Protected Workers in the South: Two Steps Forward, One Step Back

Protected workers in the South have had a variety of experiences. One pattern has been increased political autonomy and decreased market autonomy. Another pattern has been stagnant political autonomy and marginally increased economic autonomy.

Organized labour has been involved in dramatic democratization struggles around the world (Adler and Webster 1995; Bielasiak and Hicks 1990;

Eder 1997). In numerous non-Western states, labour movements have played a key role in changing the political systems of their countries and opening up new regions to the full forces of globalization. One significant example is Poland, where the solidarity labour movement challenged the power of the communist state. Its success in representing independent workers opened the first cracks in the Soviet regimes and eventually led to the elimination of communist states in Eastern Europe and the Soviet Union. These areas were then quickly incorporated into the global economy and information society. In South Africa, labour movements played a central role in ousting the apartheid regime. The newly democratic South Africa quickly rebuilt links with the international community and other parts of the world. It has moved to integrate itself into the global economy at breakneck speed. A similar experience can be seen in Brazil, where workers led the charge against authoritarian governments and were later rewarded with neoliberal economic programs.

In these states, workers both enjoyed the benefits and suffered the shortcomings of low-intensity democracy (Gills, Rocamora, and Wilson 1993). The democratization of political institutions was accompanied by a move to neoliberal economic relations. This dual transformation offered workers new civil and political rights in liberal democratic states, but they also found their political influence and power in industrial relations undermined by the newly adopted liberal economic policies. Formal democratic institutions were created, but the ability of workers to achieve their goals was undercut — a low-intensity democracy. For example, the newly democratic government of South Korea was forced into IMF structural adjustment programs following the 1997 East Asian financial crisis. These policies ended employment security and prompted widespread labour unrest. The jailing of union leaders continued after regime change to a more liberal democratic form of state. Post-apartheid South Africa rapidly liberalized its trade and investment regimes as it enshrined legal protection for its unions. The result has been increased union participation in tripartite bodies as its membership is eroded by unemployment.

A different trend has been the continued authoritarian suppression of labour autonomy combined with some improvement in labour's ability to engage in a restricted set of economic relations. Indeed, labour suppression was at the heart of the East Asian economic "miracle" from the 1960s until the mid-1990s (Deyo 1989). The most prominent and significant case in the early twenty-first century is China. China's liberalization and integration into the global economy through trade and foreign direct investment have had immense implications for Chinese and non-Chinese workers alike. Foreign direct investment in China's special economic zones has created impressive economic growth and export-oriented development. Millions have fled the poverty of the rural economy and flocked to the cities in search of employment. However, Chinese workers lack autonomous organizations to represent their interests. They are represented by the All China Federation of Trade Unions, which is controlled by the Chinese state. Attempts by workers to create autonomous organizations have been met by fierce state repression. While parts of the economy boom, many Chinese workers have few chances to advance their interests (Chan 2001).

Unprotected Workers in the South: Two Steps Back

Southern unprotected workers have been seriously disadvantaged by the globalization process since the 1970s. Two key developments are structural adjustment programs (SAPs) and the liberalization of agriculture.

For many workers in the developing world, economic SAPs are the face of globalization. Following the debt crisis of 1982, many developing countries restructured their economies to follow a more liberal, export-oriented model. This model reflected the tenets of the "Washington Consensus," which stressed balanced budgets, reductions in state subsidies, privatization, and trade and financial liberalization. Both the International Monetary Fund (IMF) and the World Bank made financial assistance in times of economic crisis or for development conditional on national acceptance of these principles. The attempt to manage the debt crisis through structural adjustment resulted in a lost decade of economic development in the 1980s followed by increasing inequality in the 1990s in many developing countries. Writing for one of the international trade union bodies, Harrod (1992, 74-9) points out that SAPs attack living standards by liberalizing labour markets, increasing unemployment, reducing state social security, and freezing/restraining/rolling back wages. These "reforms" have resulted in growing inequality and a deterioration of labour market conditions in many developing countries (Vreeland 2001).

While many sectors of society suffer through these adjustments, the burden falls most heavily on those already engaged in unprotected work and those newly thrust into it. In particular, there is considerable evidence that the highest price is paid by women. As governments implement SAPs, women are often forced to pay the price by taking up tasks performed by the state or giving up their existing sources of income (Chang 2000,

124-9). When food subsidies are cut, women often cut back on their own nutrition in order to feed their children. As health and education are cut back, women often take on the additional burden of nursing family members, or girls are kept at home to help in domestic tasks rather than being sent to school. In desperation, some women export their labour in the health care and service industries.

A second area of concern is the liberalization of agriculture. As countries attempt to find their niches in the global economy, they are increasingly faced with the "agrarian question" that was prominent in Europe in the nineteenth century (McMichael 1997). The agrarian question concerns the transformation of subsistence agriculture into commercially based agriculture and the large-scale social and political adjustments required to manage the population transfer into new forms of economic activity and new spaces of living. This is a particularly important issue for countries with large rural populations, such as China, Mexico, and India. Indeed, the situation in China is severe; it is estimated that there are approximately 150 million rural dwellers who have migrated to Chinese cities in search of employment (Yardley 2004).

In terms of global regulation, the agricultural regime exacerbates these problems. Many developing states have reduced protection for their agricultural sectors and allowed markets to be penetrated by imports. Yet developing countries have been unable to secure free access to the markets of developed states. This inability has challenged the viability of subsistence agriculture and led to social upheaval in many countries where the agricultural sector is the dominant source of employment and livelihood.

Putting together the globalization and labour autonomy balance sheet, one sees that in a few areas some labour groups have made some progress, but the general trend has been negative. Some groups have increased their autonomy as the spread of liberal political arrangements has undermined previous authoritarian states. Others have been able to increase their economic options as they are swept up in the wave of the global economy. However, other workers have had their autonomy reduced as competition increases and as the tasks of daily life become harder. The goal of critical autonomy — being able to influence the environment through negotiation and political participation — has suffered numerous setbacks as labour organizations are marginalized in political structures and discourses.

Transnational Openings

While the globalization of capital, trade, and production has increased competition between workers and generally undermined their autonomy, the information technology revolution and the reduction in transportation costs have increased the possibility of transnational contact and cooperation. Contrary to Castells' (1997, 354) pessimistic evaluation of labour solidarity in the age of network society, labour groups are forging new transnational communities. The neoliberal aspect of globalization undermines labour autonomy, but the communications revolution creates transnational openings for increased cooperation.

For unionized workers, the international organizations that represent them have undergone transformation, and new entities have emerged. At the international level, the division between union confederations produced by the split between communist and non-communist unions during the Cold War abated in the early 1990s. Thus, the communist World Federation of Trade Unions now exists only in name, while the International Confederation of Free Trade Unions (ICFTU) has gradually absorbed affiliates from around the world to become the dominant international trade union organization. In November 2006 the creation of the International Trade Union Confederation (ITUC) saw the ICFTU absorb its one remaining challenger, the Catholic-based World Confederation of Labour.

Not only has the ICFTU (now the ITUC) taken a more prominent position, its nature has also changed in response to sustained challenges from within its membership and from outside it (O'Brien 2002). New activist affiliates from the South (Korea, South Africa, and Brazil) have pushed for a more development-oriented agenda. Women unionists have advanced gender issues, and the global social justice movement challenges the ICFTU to be more engaged with radical causes. While the ICFTU is still subject to withering criticism of its conservatism (Greenfield 1998), recent changes suggest it has broadened its understanding of community to include women and people in developing countries.

Unprotected workers face more obstacles than their protected counterparts, but they are still generating transnational communities and responses. For example, small farmers and peasants from many parts of the world have coalesced around the group Via Campesina. It describes itself as "an international movement which coordinates peasant organizations of small and middle-scale producers, agricultural workers, rural women, and indigenous communities from Asia, Africa, America, and Europe" (see www.viacampesina.org). It advances farmers' autonomy by advocating for landless populations and small farmers while resisting the spread of free trade agreements, genetically modified organisms, and national and transnational agribusiness. Via Campesina has been active in the World Social Forums and in engaging institutions such as the World Trade Organization, the World Bank, the Food and Agriculture Organization, and regional integration projects. The goal is to create space in the global political economy for small-scale farmers to pursue their livelihoods.

In many developing countries, the vast majority of the population works as unprotected workers in the informal sector. Transnational cooperation between such groups is very difficult since they often lack the resources to form local or national institutions. However, there are instances of informal sector workers whose organizations become stable enough that they can develop an international presence and serve as an example to workers in other countries. One of the most prominent is the Self-Employed Women's Association (SEWA) in India (see www.sewa.org). In addition to affiliating with the established trade union international ICFTU, SEWA is building its own international networks. For example, in 2003 it hosted an international conference on organizing in the informal economy that drew participants from forty-seven organizations in twenty-three countries.

One significant way that unprotected workers have been making transnational contacts and advances has been with the cooperation of consumer groups. The movement for ethical trade links consumers in advanced industrialized countries with workers and farmers in developing countries. In its broadest sense, ethical trade encompasses two elements (Blowfield 1999). The first element is a concern with how companies make their products. This concern involves pressuring companies to ensure that the production process respects key human rights and environmental standards. Examples include companies that adopt codes of conduct guaranteeing respect for workers' rights or banning child labour. The second element is the fair trade movement that seeks to increase the financial return to poor producers as a method of improving sustainable development. Major fair trade initiatives have taken place in products such as coffee and chocolate. Both of these initiatives are designed to give workers in developing countries more autonomy in their working lives by supporting human rights or transferring wealth. The ethical trade movement requires the formation of new transnational communities joining Southern producers with Northern consumers.

One of the responses to the changing opportunities for labour auton-omy has been an attempt to build transnational labour communities. These communities are assembled to act as platforms for political action designed to bolster labour autonomy. The following section examines one of these attempts: SIGTUR.

SIGTUR as a Transnational Community

SIGTUR is a trade union network whose goal is to increase trade union rights in the face of neoliberal globalization. As a prerequisite to action, it tries to foster new forms of transnational identity and community. These new identities can then provide the launching pad for direct action against states and corporations to secure increased worker autonomy.

Advocates claim that SIGTUR represents a new form of trade union activism that is campaign oriented, networked rather than hierarchical, and open to social movement alliances (Lambert and Webster 2003). Its ori-gins lie in bilateral relations between trade unions in Western Australia and South Africa. Trade unionists from these two countries formed the core of a workshop in Perth, Australia, in May 1991. The workshop brought together activists from the Philippines, Malaysia, Sri Lanka, Pakistan, Indonesia, and Papua New Guinea. These groups were then joined by rep-resentatives from India, Thailand, Vietnam, and Korea in the launching of the Indian Ocean Trade Union Initiative in Perth in November 1992. In March 1999, the regional coordinators of the network agreed to change its name and identity away from the Indian Ocean to the Southern Initiative on Globalization and Trade Union Rights.

At SIGTUR's core is a group of trade unions from several states with a history of activist and independent trade unions. The key members come from confederations and individual trade unions from Australia (e.g., Western Australian Trades and Labour Council, and maritime, teacher, and construction unions), South Africa (COSATU — Congress of South African Trade Unions), India (Centre of Indian Trade Unions and All India Trade Union Congress), South Korea (Korean Confederation of Trade Unions), and the Philippines (Kilusang Mayo Uno/May First Movement). The Brazilian confederation, the Unified Trade Union Federation of Brazil, has attended several SIGTUR meetings but remains at a distance.

Around this core of established left unions, network members include labour activists from unions that are less established. Biannual meetings also attract labour-friendly NGOs, activists, and labour-oriented academics. For example, Indonesian labour activists such as Dita Sari participated because of the lack of independent unions at the time. Relatively small Sri Lankan unions organizing workers in free trade zones and on plantations are active participants. As SIGTUR moves its biannual conference between countries, numerous national unions and NGOs are also brought into the process.

The SIGTUR Identity

The identities of SIGTUR members are constantly being adjusted and resist easy description. The group self-identifies as "a campaign orientated network of democratic unions in the south," but this description falls down on closer examination (SIGTUR 2001). SIGTUR can best be described as a network of leftist trade unions outside North America and Europe. There are a number of identity tensions at the heart of the SIGTUR enterprise. They include geographical, national, ideological, organizational (trade unions versus NGOs), producer versus consumer, and gender tensions. The organizations and individuals involved constantly negotiate and modify these identity conflicts.

Geographical conceptions of SIGTUR are problematic. Although it is called the Southern Initiative on Globalization and Trade Union Rights, the adjective *Southern* is ambiguous. A strict geographical interpretation of the South does not apply because of the role that the Koreans play in the organization. Geographically, they are from a northern hemisphere country. A political economic view of the South as an arena inhabited by developing countries does not capture the network because the Australians play a central organizing role. Although members may talk about the global South, it is not clear why Australia is a member of the global South while a country such as Canada is not. SIGTUR's coordinator has suggested that South denotes "a political experience of exploitation and marginalization that arose out of a particular position of subordination in the new global economy" (Lambert and Webster 2001, 345). While such a description fits many of the members, it does not capture Australia's experience.

The group also confronts a tension between national and international identities. One of the key fault lines is between those countries colonized by Western powers and those that experienced a different history. Thus, countries colonized by the United States (the Philippines), Britain (India, South Africa), or Japan (Korea) tend to have a more explicitly anti-imperialist stance than those countries that are the beneficiaries of the colonizing process (Australia). In the case of SIGTUR, these different historical experiences can pit Australians against other members because of different historical sensibilities. An example of this occurred at the congress in Seoul in 2001. Many SIGTUR members interpreted the US-led invasion of Afghanistan through the prism of a history of US imperialism and wanted to condemn the action through anti-imperialist rhetoric. This posed a large problem for the Australian delegation, which was more likely to be sympathetic to the view that military action in Afghanistan was a legitimate response to the attacks on New York and Washington on 9/11.

Ideologically, participants are on the left of the labour movement. However, they vary in their precise political orientations. The Indian unions are very close to home-grown communist parties. The South African unions have strong links with the South African Communist Party and the African National Congress. The Koreans have links with a newly created Labour Party, while the Australians have affiliations with a national labour party that is closer to being centrist than leftist. United in their opposition to corporate power and neoliberalism, the delegates do not share a common alternative utopia.

SIGTUR also contains a tension between organizing forms. It is a trade union organization but has reached out to labour NGOs in those countries where trade unions are either weak or not independent of the state. In the case of Indonesian membership, early contacts were with labour-related NGOs. Hong Kong NGOs have attended to discuss labour rights issues in China, although this discussion caused some controversy among Indian delegates. The Indian trade union delegates felt that NGOs should not speak on behalf of Chinese workers. SIGTUR has not escaped the tension between trade unions and NGOs that characterizes the broader social justice movement.

Although SIGTUR members advocate the rights of workers/producer interests, there is relatively little consideration given to their members' own role as consumers. Because the battle for labour rights is so overwhelming and pressing, little discussion has taken place on the issue of how workers' consumption patterns might impact working conditions. To date, there has been little discussion on alternative consumption mechanisms such as ethical consumption or purchasing. This omission is most evident at occasional SIGTUR events, which include time for shopping excursions. These excursions only benefit members who have enough money to spend, while others are left wondering what is taking place. The excursions are focused on securing bargains, which is surely some of the same behaviour that provides incentives to corporations to suppress trade union rights. Corporations can supply these bargains by reducing labour costs through the suppression of trade union rights.

The network also experiences some tensions over gender roles and identity. While rhetorically committed to gender equality, some delegations have lacked female representatives. At other times, some male delegates have engaged in inappropriate behaviour toward female delegates from other countries. These are not all faults of the membership. Rather, these observations indicate that the organization faces many of the same hurdles as other international and transnational bodies that attempt to reconcile relations between groups of different economic status and ethnic, national, and gender background.

Community-Building Initiatives

SIGTUR attempts to build community among its members through three main mechanisms. The first is cultural interchange. The second is rhetorical assertion of common interest. The third is common political action against identified targets. This third element is also part of the attempt to build space for labour autonomy and will be dealt with in the next section.

Cultural interchange is a large part of the SIGTUR community-building process, and it takes place on a number of levels. SIGTUR has attempted to adopt symbols and language that strike a common chord among its members. For example, the word *Southern* is used to differentiate members from "Northern" (US and European) entities. SIGTUR designed an emblem that portrays several workers whose appearance indicates that they are from a mix of ethnic backgrounds. The emblem appears on a red background that resonates with many members who are affiliated with communist parties or movements.

In the 2001 Korean meeting, participants jointly painted a large banner that symbolized the network. It featured workers of different ethnic and national backgrounds moving forward under a common flag. The innovative aspect of the banner was that it was composed of separate panels given to member organizations for safe keeping and reassembly at the next meeting. Unfortunately, the reassembly did not take place. Presumably, the pieces of the banner are still with various member groups.

Song and dance play an important role in bridging cultural differences. Meetings usually have a cultural evening where people from each country sing national songs. Host delegations usually also bring in worker musicians to put on performances of national culture for the assembled delegates.

In addition to gaining an appreciation of each other's struggles through national culture, delegates also share some common culture. For example, songs such as "Solidarity Forever" and "Internationale" are known by many delegates in English or in their own native languages.

In some cases, cultural expressions can serve to mediate conflict. For example, during the Korean congress, an animated debate evolved into a shouting match and general chaos that required a suspension of proceedings. While various delegates were engaged in discussion and debate, South African delegates brought people together by singing songs of struggle, which everyone could identify with and appreciate.

Despite these efforts, cultural barriers inhibit community building. One issue is the different cultures of union organizing and expression that can create misunderstanding between delegates. For example, Australian delegates tend to express diverse views from their unions and participate in conversations in a relatively undisciplined manner. South Africans tend to have a very strategic and coordinated approach to intervening in discussions with people and positions identified in advance. The Indian union delegations tend to give more opportunity to the most senior delegates to speak. Delegates are not always sensitive to these differences and can interpret different styles of participating in debates and discussions as being offensive or insensitive. For example, Indians may view repeated Australian interventions as disrespectful, while Australian delegates may be tired by long interventions of senior Indian delegates. The interesting thing is that these cultural misunderstandings are repeated from one congress to another without sufficient briefing and education of delegates. People who attend several meetings may be sensitized to the issues, but newcomers are not.

Autonomy-Building Initiatives

The issues of organizational structure and identity formation comprise a prelude to SIGTUR's main task, to increase worker autonomy. To this end, SIGTUR has taken on a number of campaigning issues. Key issues have been campaigns against corporations and efforts to influence state labour legislation and anti-privatization campaigns.

One example is SIGTUR members that joined the global campaign against mining giant Rio Tinto. It is one of the world's largest mining companies and has come under substantial criticism for its labour and environmental practices. The campaign has primarily been led by the industry-based global union federation, the International Federation of

Chemical, Energy, Mine, and General Workers' Unions (ICEM). SIGTUR members have assisted this campaign by organizing demonstrations and letter writing in their own countries. They help to broaden the scope of the campaign by highlighting the issue even in countries where Rio Tinto has little or no presence.

Another example has been a campaign to free imprisoned Korean labour leaders such as Dan Byung-Ho. This campaign combined standard letter writing with attempts to use unconventional tactics. One such tactic was to try to influence Korean political leaders who were Catholic by organizing interventions from Catholic leaders in other countries, such as the Philippines.

One of the significant elements of SIGTUR's activities is that, at times, it reverses the flow of solidarity efforts. Traditionally, trade union solidarity was seen as something that Northern unions did for Southern workers. A number of events in SIGTUR have featured Southern workers protesting labour standards in an advanced industrialized country — Australia. This was the case at SIGTUR's origins when South African unionists travelled to Perth to condemn changes in Western Australian labour practices, and it occurred again in 2005 when SIGTUR delegates protested outside the Australian embassy in Bangkok.

A crucial question for groups such as SIGTUR is their effectiveness. How deep does the sense of community run? Is it deep enough to trigger mass mobilizations or actions? Will it motivate members to make sacrifices on others' behalf? The extent of SIGTUR's community is difficult to gauge. Delegates who participate in SIGTUR conferences return home and report back to their respective unions. Reporting back to members allows for the distribution of messages and events to a broader union audience or union-friendly publications such as the online editions of the Liquor, Hospitality, and Miscellaneous Union in Australia, COSATU's website, or *Ganashakti,* the online edition newspaper of the Communist Party of India (Marxist). SIGTUR can point to solidarity events, but it is much more difficult to find mass mobilizations or identify policy successes.

Conclusion

Delanty (2003, 195) argues that global forms of communication have facilitated the emergence of new networked communities of individuals but that these communities are unable to resist the forces of globalization or to substitute for place-based groups. In the context of this chapter, the question is, will the new labour communities emerging in response to globalization be strong enough to mobilize political forces needed to defend worker autonomy?

This chapter has highlighted a case study of one of these transnational projects, SIGTUR, a hybrid entity sitting between the traditional interstate trade unions bodies (e.g., ICFTU) and horizontal labour activist networks. In response to reduced national labour autonomy, several prominent trade unions from "Southern" countries have been trying to build transnational labour identities that would support political action. While the community that SIGTUR is trying to form builds upon a shared history of class exploitation, it encounters numerous difficulties in nurturing transnational identities. In SIGTUR's case, the outcome is not yet clear. It is struggling to deepen and extend its activities. Members have been able to identify elements of common identity and begin some common action. Yet these attempts are fragile and may be eclipsed by other events or organizations.

The possibility of transnational labour communities compensating for the erosion of national or local labour communities has sparked vigorous debate within labour movements and between students of the movement. While most observers and activists agree that labour groups need to exert influence domestically and transnationally, there is disagreement over the relative emphasis of time, energy, and resources on these two fronts. Some, such as Sam Gindin (2004), the former research director of the Canadian Auto Workers, argue that labour groups must concentrate on domestic affairs and the attempt to influence national institutions. Effective internationalism will only spring from strong domestic players. Others, such as SIGTUR's coordinator Rob Lambert (Lambert and Webster 2003), see transnational activity as being central to increasing labour's domestic power. Transnational work can be used to bolster faltering national and local movements. There is certainly no consensus in the labour community about the most effective combination for transnational and national/local communities.

The creation and activity of new transnational communities are subject to ongoing political struggle. As this chapter outlines, the position of labour communities remains precarious worldwide. Yet one can also see evidence of labour communities rebuilding and making progress. The hesitant steps to reregulate labour relations and temper capitalist exploitation through labour clauses in trade agreements, corporate codes of conduct, global framework agreements, ethical trade initiatives, debt relief, anti-privatization struggles, and anti-slavery campaigns suggest that the global contest is just being joined. It is premature to come to judgments about whether labour groups can recover and expand their autonomy under existing global conditions. What can be said, however, is that globalization is shaping, and being shaped by, new forms of local and transnational labour community.

chapter 10

**Transnational Transformation:
Cyberactivism and the
Palestinian Right of Return**

Jasmin Habib

> *The stability of geography and the continuity of land — these have
> completely disappeared from my life and the life of all Palestinians. If
> we are not stopped at borders, or herded into new camps, or denied entry
> and residence, or barred from travel from one place to another, more of
> our land is taken, our lives are interfered with arbitrarily, our voices are
> prevented from reaching each other, our identity is confined to frightened
> little islands in an inhospitable environment of superior military force
> sanitized by the clinical jargon of pure administration. Thus Palestinian
> life is scattered, discontinuous, marked by the artificial and imposed
> arrangements of interrupted or confined space, by the dislocations and
> unsynchronized rhythms of disturbed time.*
> — Edward Said, *After the Last Sky: Palestinian Lives*

> *We are all Palestinian*
> — Bumper sticker, Washington, DC[1]

THIS CHAPTER ADDRESSES SOME of the novel ways in which members of the Palestinian community have engaged and reclaimed history,
employing the Internet to assert an autonomy denied the "stability of geography and the continuity of land," as mourned by Said in the epigraph
above. While oral histories of Palestine have become much more prevalent
and their place in the historiography of Palestine is invaluable (see, e.g.,
Lynd, Bahour, and Lynd 1994; Nazzal 1978; Sayigh 1979; Slyomovics 1998;

Swedenburg 1995), the focus of this chapter is on Palestinian-centred activism that has emerged through the globalizing technologies of the Internet. Neither entirely celebratory of community nor cynical about its contemporary ability to exercise autonomy, the chapter presents arguments for appreciating how Palestinian transnational advocacy groups (or what I call TAGS) have used cyberactivism to enter history in ways that are populist as well as political, symbolic as well as strategic, interactive as well as fixed, though not entirely or necessarily dialogical. My purpose is to argue that TAGS reinforce existing feelings of community in a Palestinian diaspora that is dispersed geographically. They give the community a means of expressing hope and of developing ways to continue living together as a community. They also take advantage of the capabilities of information and communication technologies to organize place-based politics and activism. This place-based politics is increasingly coordinated throughout the diaspora, a possibility that also tends to reinforce community. Doing things together while living in different places becomes a community building activity, similar to Escobar's "cacatenation" of places (2001a), as described in the introduction to this volume. TAGS reterritorialize a national community, strengthening dense social relationships across dispersed spaces by reclaiming history.

In his essay "Globalization as the End and the Beginning of History: The Contradictory Implications of a New Paradigm," historian Arif Dirlik reflects on Fredric Jameson's (1994) seemingly dystopic representations in *Postmodernism: Or, The Cultural Logic of Late Capitalism:* "Jameson here is clearly describing a novel predicament for EuroAmericans, especially EuroAmerican elites, who have lost control of historical narratives, and of the guarantees they provided for present and future direction. The dilemma he poses is a very real one; it faces all the descendants of nineteenth century World Fair organizers and Museum-makers who now face the prospects of returning to the savages the skeletal remnants that were supposed to preserve savagery in historical memory, but now face the very same savages as political and legal equals" (2000, 42). In response to Jameson's (1994, 57) concern that "the more people we recognize, even within the mind, the more peculiarly precarious becomes the status of our own hitherto unique and 'incomparable' consciousness or 'self,'" Dirlik replies with words that are clearly meant to be read with respect and care: "What [Jameson] does not recognize, remarkably in a scholar of his prescience and political concerns, is that this has been the condition for a majority of the world's peoples, especially those peoples who had earlier been left out of history, who now have re-entered history to disturb the First World elites' complacency about self and history" (2000, 42-3). While this chapter does not even begin to take up some of the methodological or theoretical questions posed by Dirlik, his reply to Jameson forms the starting point of this chapter.

My focus is on a number of transnational Palestinian-centred cyber-activist sites, including alternative media sites, that were designed in the mid- to late 1990s and early 2000s to generate discussions of the Palestinian narrative in the public sphere: Al-Awda, The Coalition for the Right to Return; Palestine Remembered; Electronic Intifada; and Zochrot.[2] The chapter begins with a brief overview of the right of return discourse followed by a synopsis of some of the relevant TAG sites and their links. In the final section, I discuss the methodological and theoretical concerns that are addressed by my findings and conclude with reflections on the role of utopian narratives in asserting autonomy and building communally based anti-colonial struggles and global justice movements. I conclude that participation within such TAGs, based in a single justice-seeking community, may lead to a greater appreciation of the autonomy of idealized global community formations.

What Is the Right of Return?

Numerous publications have appeared on the Palestinian right of return or right to return, but I will not explore the range of their proposals or their implications for peace (Friedman 2003; Khalidi 1998; Rempel 1999, 2000; Sabel 2003; Said 2003; Tamari 1999; Wakim 2001; Zureik 1994). My broader interest is locating what emerged as an important locus of activist concern by and for diasporic Palestinians and that now appears to have become part of the narrative of global social justice. I believe that some of this may be explained by the moment — that is, the rise of the global justice movements and their relationship to the anti-war movement — and the method — cyberactivism — that saw a long-silenced community give voice to their opposition and resistance in the emerging cacophony.

As many scholars have observed, the right of return is embodied as a right in a number of international legal regimes, including the Universal Declaration of Human Rights and the International Covenant on Civil and Political Rights (see Akram 2001; Fischbach 2002; Khalidi 1992; Rempel 1999; Zureik 1994), though advocacy for the Palestinian right of return focuses on UN Resolution 194 (III): "The refugees wishing to return to their homes and live at peace with their neighbours should be permitted to do so at the earliest practical date and ... compensation should be paid for the property of those choosing not to return and for loss or damage to property which, under principles of international law or in equity, should be made good by governments or authorities responsible" (GA Res. 194. UN GAOR. 3rd Sess., UN Doc. A/810 [1948] 24). Soon after signing the Declaration of Principles (also known as the Oslo Peace Accords) in 1993 between Israel and the Palestine Authority (PA), it became evident that Palestinians were deeply divided over the content and the implementation of what was commonly referred to as "the Accords" or simply "Oslo." While some believed that the Accords were an important step toward a just and comprehensive peace, others argued that it would simply perpetuate Israeli domination (see, especially, Aly et al. 1996; Hanieh 2001; Said 1994). According to the website of the UN Refugee Works Agency (UNRWA), set up to support Palestinian refugees in the early 1950s, as of 31 March 2006 there were 4,375,050 registered refugees, of whom 1,306,191 live in fifty-nine official camps. The Palestinian Refugee Research Net (PRRN) website estimated the total number of Palestinian refugees as 8,265,000 in 2005.

By limiting the peace proposal to a partial withdrawal of Israeli troops from parts of the militarily occupied territories of the West Bank and Gaza Strip, the main concern for many Palestinians living in the refugee camps that dot the region as well as those living in a worldwide diaspora was that the Accords had set aside the right of return. As Palestinian historian Rashid Khalidi explains,

> only by understanding the centrality of the catastrophe of politicide and [territorial] expulsion that befell the Palestinian people — *al nakba* in Arabic — is it possible to understand the Palestinians' sense of the right of return. For in an abstract sense, if this expulsion were an injustice to the Palestinian people in national as well as in humanitarian terms, and marked the beginning of a period of disasters for them, then it follows that as far as the Palestinians are concerned, the wrong done to them can only be righted, and the disasters ended, through a return to the homeland ... Rejection of the right of return is seen as a denial of the Palestinians' peoplehood and rootedness in their homeland, and thus of the injustice they have suffered. (1992, 30-1)

Although several of the Accords' pledges were implemented, including the withdrawal of the Israeli military from some of the high-population areas in the West Bank and Gaza Strip, many more were broken and or lapsed, and the Oslo era would finally come to an end with the collapse of the US-sponsored talks at Camp David in 2000. Palestinian journalist Akram Hanieh reported on the Camp David summit's discussions as follows: "The greatest failure of the summit was in the refugee committee ... Refusing to take moral or legal responsibility for what happened, the Israelis were willing only to express sorrow over what befell the Palestinians as a result of the Arab-Israeli War of 1948. And because any discussion of the right of return was taboo for Israel — in their eyes tantamount to declaring a war of destruction on the Israeli state — there could be no talk about a timetable for the implementation of return" (2001, 82). This report is consistent with other reports as well as with the Israeli position (Sabel 2003). The subsequent political fallout included the al-Aqsa Intifada or "uprising" and, by 2006, the rise of Hamas as a political alternative to Fateh in the Territories. This also coincided with the decline of the "land for peace" coalitions and the rise of a "security first" unilateralism in Israel.

At first, it was difficult for most Palestinians to grasp or even to believe that, by agreeing to the Oslo Peace Accords, their negotiators set aside such an important issue for discussions in the longer term (see Said 1993). A critical response to the Palestine "imagined" by the Accords (Anderson 1983) saw a range of Palestinian-centred TAGs gaining support and prominence since 1993. Careful examinations of the discourses of identity informing Palestinian practices have shed some light on this phenomenon (see, e.g., Artz 1996; Friedman 2003; Khalidi 1998; Rempel 1999; Said 1996; Said 2003; Tamari 1999; Wakim 2001; Zureik 1994), but there is little analysis of the shifts in TAGs working on behalf of and with Palestinians in this regard. Such organizations offer an interesting milieu to explore the emergence of daily practices of struggle that are central to individual, collective, and activist identity formation and transformation as organizations respond to contingent social and political events.

Moreover, in research conducted between 2000 and 2002 with Palestinians living in North America, I ascertained a widespread belief among many respondents that Israel-Palestine policies are made in the centres of power — the United States and the United Kingdom in the main, with the middle powers of Canada and the European Union as secondary — not regionally or locally. Thus, it is crucial to understand the role that TAGs play for diaspora communities, because TAGs enable and sustain cultural ties, produce and circulate knowledge of homeland events and crises, and, in some cases, negotiate the concerns of the diaspora to homeland political players. In what ways are Palestinian identities and imagined geographies (Gregory 1995; Said 1986) re/constituted through TAGs? In what ways do TAGs act as channels of connection between exiled and diaspora Palestinian communities and the wider global public? Can TAGs provide spaces for the exercise of communal autonomy or compensate for the loss of sustained face-to-face contact within a homeland by building community through dispersed local interactions and global exchange in cyberspace?

TAGs and the Palestinian Right of Return

In March 2000, I received an invitation to the first Trans-Arab Research Institute (TARI) conference to be held on 8 April 2000 in Boston. Although I was unable to attend, I kept the conference schedule since it was the first time I had seen reference to a right of return conference theme in the diaspora. Associated as it was with some well-known academics, including Edward Said, Noam Chomsky, Ilan Pappé, Atif Kubursi, journalists Robert Fisk, Ali Abunimah, and Lamis Adoni, the BADIL Resource Center for Palestinian Residency and Refugee Rights in Bethlehem, Palestine, and lawyers Wadie Said and Susan Akram, the conference proved to be the meeting ground for what would soon become the Al-Awda Coalition for the Right of Return.[3] Many of these names and organizations would soon be familiar to those accessing Palestinian cyberactivist TAGs. Below are brief overviews of some of the sites that I visited and that led me through the world of Palestinian-based TAGs.

At the Al-Awda (US) site, which appears to be the home base for the North American coalitions that extend from New York to San Diego and Toronto, the demographic of this TAG is identified as "the US public and International community" whose goals include "extend[ing] and coordinat[ing] educational efforts and initiatives for Palestinian rights beyond their defined geographic locations, thereby leveraging the power of networking while linking together and empowering dispersed activities." The Al-Awda (UK) site lists among its activities "lobbying for adequate financial support from Britain and the EU"; "campaigning for the indictment of war criminals, including Sharon, who have committed crimes against the Palestinian people; monitoring British media coverage of Palestinian affairs for bias and inaccuracy; organizing educational and informative talks and workshops in schools and universities; [and] organizing pickets and other protest activities." In general, the websites appear to be aimed at a non-academic, activist public interested in learning about Palestine, and they are often framed by a left-revolutionary discourse. That these sites and their users are linked to other global justice concerns was most evident by the calendar of events, posted on each site and in each locale. In the summer of 2006, the Al-Awda (Toronto) site listed stories on boycott and sanction campaigns against Israel as well as the diary of a Palestinian refugee affected by Israel's deadly violence in the south of Lebanon. Readers were implored: "Please Don't Forget What's Going on in Gaza." Another audience seems to be activists involved in allied social justice issues. For example, the Toronto site's calendar lists a range of activities, including a series of information sessions and updates on the conflict over Six Nations land claims near Caledonia, Ontario; the Homes Not Bombs campaign against biological weapons development in Canada; the Coalition of Concerned Taxi Drivers music show; the demonstration against the legalization of deportation to torture; and the commemoration of the Warsaw ghetto uprising. Between events such as a "vigil to honour the children of the hundreds of missing or murdered aboriginal women in Canada" and support for imprisoned Mapuche leaders in Chile the website lists the catastrophe demonstration: Yom Al-Nakba.

Comparatively, the US sites seem to be very concerned to respond to what is perceived as the US media's pro-Israeli standpoint. Media spokespersons and media workshops are listed. Only the New York calendar of events is as active as the Toronto site. Both sites link activist groups to one another, but the New York site tends to promote more media-related sessions.

At the time of the Oslo Peace Accords and as the peace process continued to unravel, Electronic Intifada (EI) was founded. Intended as a site for journalists and editors, activists, students of the media, and researchers looking for reference material, this is an "independent publication committed to comprehensive public education on the question of Palestine, the Israeli-Palestinian conflict, and the economic, political, legal, and human dimensions of Israel's [decades-long] occupation of Palestinian territories." Those who founded and manage EI have emerged from within the global justice arena. EI is described as a "project" whose "team" and co-founders — Ali Abunimah, Arjan El Fassed, Laurie King, and Nigel Parry — are all social justice activists and skilled journalists.

A few of EI's milestones include launching Live from Palestine, a "project featuring continually updated ... accounts from local residents detailing life under a punishing curfew and military invasion," which coincided with the March-April 2002 Israeli military offensive Defensive Shield, "the biggest ... operation in the West Bank since 1967." EI claims more than 600,000 "hits" to the site in the first month of Israel's attacks.

In May 2002, the site was credited by *Newsweek* for "making the pro-Palestinian cause more prominent with the media in recent years," while later that year the *Jerusalem Post* lauded EI as "very professional, user-friendly and well written ... the Palestinian CNN." In March 2004, Salon.com "singled out EI as an exceptional example of a successful site" for how it "tries to represent ... an electronic uprising, carrying the Palestinian struggle for a nation — nonviolently, through information, education and communication — to Palestinians beyond the West Bank and Gaza, helping to keep a unified Palestinian community that extends from Europe, to America, to the Middle East" (Christopher Farah, as cited on the EI website).

From March 2003, EI op-eds and analyses were dominated by the death of Rachel Corrie, an International Solidarity Movement activist. Corrie, a US citizen who had been working with Palestinians to prevent home demolitions in Gaza, was bulldozed to death in what Israeli officials claimed was an accident. She became a cause célèbre, particularly in the United States, where her parents released her e-mail letters reflecting on her experiences in Gaza. *My Name Is Rachel Corrie,* a theatrical review written by her parents, debuted in London, England, in October 2005.

In August 2004, EI began to cover the politics of the route and construction of Israel's separation fence or "Apartheid Wall." By July 2005, EI had been sent a leaked copy of the International Criminal Court of Justice's ruling against the wall's legality, making it the first media outlet to post the court's decision.

Like Al-Awda, EI has an extensive list of external links categorized as "Activist and Solidarity Groups"; "Divestment and Boycott"; "Human Rights Organizations"; "Humanitarian Agencies"; "Israel's Apartheid Wall"; "Palestinian Authority"; "Refugee Organizations," including Al-Awda chapters and other right of return groups; "Weapons and Arms Trade"; and EI's sister sites, "Electronic Iraq" and "Electronic Lebanon," the latter launched in response to the Israeli-Lebanon war in 2006.

Through the hyperlinks provided by the Al-Awda Coalitions and Electronic Intifada pages, I came upon Palestine Remembered, a site founded in 1999 "to create an easy medium where refugees can communicate, organize, and share their experiences amongst themselves." Palestinians are encouraged to attach their stories, memories, pictures, movies, and music files and to join discussions at the message board or use the directory listing services for refugees. In 2006, the site was a source of information about the displacement and dispossession of Palestinians from several villages and cities that had been "ethnically cleansed, looted, and destroyed by the Israeli army." While detailed accounts and photographs of some locales were more comprehensive than others, its purpose and ambition — "to preserve the memories and experiences of Palestinian people around the world" and to "amplify their voice in cyberspace" — place this site, in Web parlance, permanently "under construction."

In 2003, the al Nakba Oral History Project website was launched to provide information about the importance of oral history and how to collect it. Palestine Remembered gives Palestinians a way to reclaim their history as well as to counter the more common Zionist narrative of their dispossession. Doing so addresses another of the Palestine Remembered's goals: "To increase refugees' awareness of their rights to return to their homes, farms, and businesses."

At a time when many in the global justice community have been accused of anti-Semitism, it is also important to point to the following proclamation found in the PalestineRemembered.com mission statement: "We at Palestine Remembered do not judge all Israelis or Jewish people by the actions of the Zionist movement and its leaders. We understand that many Israelis and Jews around the world support the Palestinian struggle for justice and are willing to do their part in bringing an end to the wrongs of the past." That some Palestinian TAGs would be hyperlinked to Israeli organizations — human rights organizations such as B'tselem, Physicians for Human Rights-Israel — would come as no surprise to those engaged in Israel-Palestine activism. However, I was interested to find the link to Zochrot on many of the Palestinian right of return TAGs. Zochrot ("remembering" in Hebrew), an Israeli group organized "to commemorate, witness, acknowledge, and repair," focuses its attention on educating the Israeli public and the international community on al-Nakba. Available in Arabic, English, and Hebrew, Zochrot describes how "the Nakba is ... also an integral part of the history of the Jews ... It is a history that has been silenced and almost completely erased from the physical landscape of the country. Zochrot supports the right of return of the Palestinian refugees." To this end, Zochrot reimagines the Israeli landscape by "touring and posting signs at destroyed villages" and "hosting encounters between uprooted Palestinians and Jews residing on their lands."

After several court appearances, in May 2006 Zochrot won the right and received official authorization to post signs in Canada Park designating the villages of Imwas and Yaly on which remains the park was built. Zochrot reports that, "on May 15, 2004, the 56th anniversary of the Nakba, Zochrot held the first ever March of Return in the city of Tel Aviv," commemorating "six Palestinian villages [that] existed in what is now Tel Aviv: Jamasin, Summeil, Abu Kabir, Sheikh Muwanis, Jrish, and Salameh."

Cyberactivism as Palestinian Transnationalism

> *The most challenging political problems of our time ... arise primarily*
> *from a need to reimagine what we mean by politics.*
> — R.B.J. Walker, Canadian political theorist,
> "Both Globalization and Sovereignty"

For the past decade or so, scholars have tried to understand the role of the Internet as a means of communication in the movements for global social justice, particularly its emphasis on networking across borders and the development of alternative sources of global information and identity (Cammaerts and Van Audenhove 2005). In his critique of the use of the term "global civil society" — which he argues presupposes a global state — to describe the space of social movement activism, Thomas Olesen proposes that scholars instead "speak of a plurality of transnational publics rather than the singularity of a global civil society ... By doing this, we discover two things: first, transnational publics ... imply a transformation of space, a new way of combining the local, the national and the transnational; second, transnational publics are mediated and communicative, but ... also very much rooted in real people and places and in face-to-face interactions" (2005, 420).

What makes cyberactivist TAGS unique is their ability to form coalitions and to coordinate with other transnational and national advocacy groups and organizations. Donatella Della Porta and Lorenzo Mosca have noted how these technologies "create connections between isolated, ... unlinked networks, favouring collective action toward a common goal" (2005, 179-80), while Victor Roudometof argues that "the transnational experience should be conceived as involving several layers ranging from the construction of transnational social spaces to the formation of transnational communities" (2005, 113; see also Langman 2005). Saskia Sassen writes that "the possibility of global imaginaries has enabled even those who are geographically immobile to become part of global politics" (2004,

649). An examination of any TAG reveals its locale — as well as its transnationalism. Having explored a range of Palestinian-centred TAGS, I would argue that they are poised somewhere between transnational NGOs and the Internet-based communities that Langman describes as "large numbers of interconnected, progressive mobilizing structures, flowing across extremely complex networks of communications" (2005, 60).

While some scholars have been interested in understanding the Internet's role in assimilating immigrant communities (Staeheli et al. 2002, 990-1), and perhaps owing to the fact that Palestine disappeared from the world's maps in 1948, Palestinians always and already have to negotiate their place in the world, I have been interested to learn how cyberspaces are used by Palestinian TAGS as creative, performative sites of identity and history, mobilized to strengthen community and imagine possibility. Nonetheless, it is important to note that at least one study analyzing Arab American websites and activists that explore "citizenship, identity and transnational migration" concluded that, "by transforming the way that 'mainstream' America thinks about Arab causes and the Arab world, Arab immigrants will gain acceptance and full social and political membership in American society" (Nagel and Staeheli 2004, 16). It is clear, though, that integration/assimilation is not the only or even the primary goal of Palestinian-centred TAGS, committed as they are to designing and developing websites to do more than simply provide information or correct the misperception of certain audiences or alerting them to alternatives: Palestinian TAGS are politicizing the Web, politicizing their audiences. Integration/assimilation seems not to be the primary goal of these sites.[4]

The Al-Awda coalitions, Electronic Intifada, Palestine Remembered, and Zochrot have all contributed to remapping Palestine — towns, villages, and cities — enabling the production and representation of virtual histories, archived photos, and maps. Such remapping of place and reclaiming of history become potent exercises in asserting community autonomy. Palestine Remembered is especially interesting in this regard because it is entirely open and interactive. Any Palestinian may upload her story, the tragedy of her family's displacement, and the site(s) of the displacement into the virtual world, making real what has remained largely invisible on the global map.

Theorizing Cyberactivism

Writing against what they characterize as Slavoj Žižek's "tendentially conservative" politics, Andrew Robinson and Simon Tormey argue that "transformative politics should be theorized ... as a process of transformation, an a-linear, rhizomatic, multiform plurality of resistances, initiatives and, indeed, acts which are sometimes spectacular and carnivalesque, sometimes prefigurative, sometimes subterranean, sometimes rooted in institutional change and reform and, under certain circumstances, directly transformative" (2005, 104-5). This observation moves us away from political sociological treatments of TAGS, shifting the analysis from effect and resource mobilization toward process and praxis. This is the realm of autonomy, where communal identity is renegotiated. Robinson and Tormey observe that "it is important that radicals invoke 'utopias.' Through enacting utopia, we have the ability to bring the 'no-where' into the 'now-here'" (ibid., 105). While the Palestinian struggle for the right of return plays itself out against a Zionist backdrop that continues to deny that excursion, TAGS suggest that another world is emerging despite the political regimes that are in place to silence its inheritors. Zochrot and Palestine Remembered are two key sites for observing these creative productions, through which people within historically opposed communities reimagine their boundaries in the name of global justice.

In "Complexity and Social Movement(s): Process and Emergence in Planetary Action Systems," Graeme Chesters and Ian Welsh argue against the "rational choice theories and political exchange models" and propose instead a "neo-materialist/complexity reading" to understand the "alter-globalization movement" as "an expression of social and global complexity" (2005, 187). In this way, moments of physical interaction — such as protests — are "understood to be dynamically interconnected" with cyberactivist practices and mediations. "The 'object' of analysis becomes ... overlapping networks, and the processes of interaction and exchange between global locales, the relationship between the virtual and the real, and the interaction between new social actors and familiar forces of antagonism." What is most interesting about Chesters and Welsh's analysis is their appreciation of the degree to which cyberactivist modes are sites of engagement "shaping ... projects at local and global level[s]" and fostering "strategic and tactical reflection" (ibid., 193).

It is true that Al-Awda, the Electronic Intifada, Palestine Remembered, and Zochrot provide an architectonics of transformation and exchange:

responding to political concerns in the traditional sense — by disseminating information — while also re/constructing and re/inventing a discourse of justice (Pishchikova 2006). Palestinian-centred TAGS campaigning for the right of return have been clearly influenced by, as well as influencing, the global justice movements and their capacity to educate, coordinate, and organize for change. Chesters and Welsh observe that TAGS' practices and exchanges "produce a *community* with a commitment to a cultural politics (the opposite of political culture)" (2005, 202). This is "a politics inscribed in the slogan 'unity in diversity' and manifest in the seemingly paradoxical attempt to valorize both counter-hegemony and a proliferation of minoritarian interest, hybridized identities and new forms of subjectivity" (ibid., 203). In this way, the Palestinian-centred TAGS can express two contradictory impulses: to engage the post-national order to reterritorialize a national community. That is, coalitions such as Al-Awda can act out and organize on the principles and promises of non-state and deterritorialized (i.e., cyberspace) politics while also co-creating and advocating for a Palestinian nation-state-territory.

The examples I cite also suggest that a benefit of cyberactivism is timeliness, with instantaneous information from a variety of perspectives and a variety of official and unofficial sources (Brainard and Brinkerhoff 2004, S45). EI and Al-Awda sites were particularly useful in this regard. Both TAG sites also provide evidence of what Lori Brainard and Jennifer Brinkerhoff, writing on what they call the grassroots online sector, describe as the "organizational richness" of an activist sector replicated online (S46; see also Kavanagh et al. 2005). As Peter Ester and Henk Vinken have noted,

> the more important questions about the Internet are not about what it can do for real life or about how real life can best be mimicked with it, but about what it is as a constitutive force for the identity of people who engage in it, for the way people will experience the world and for the cultural forms that will arise from this ... For virtual identities to exist at all, there is one requirement: interaction ... It is the idea of a forever-unfinished personal identity, of real people who can be nodes in an unlimited circuit and who can freely experiment with their identity in contact with an infinite network of others (2003, 670).

Although I am less interested in considerations of "personal identity," any hyperlinked excursion through the Palestinian TAG sites reveals this observation to be largely true. People shape their individual identities through the communal narratives of displacement and dispossession, past and present; community politics emerge in the individual acts of posting events, remapping the places that have disappeared, and reacting, in large and small demonstrations, to the actions of states and the military. Through such interactions, a form of community autonomy emerges.

While noting that cyberactivism may mean fewer face-to-face meetings, Della Porta and Mosca acknowledge that cyberactivists have been able to organize and stage massive transnational demonstrations (2005, 167), suggesting that not only are they well organized but also that participants realize the importance of face-to-face (and "in-your-face") contact, though not necessarily for organizational purposes (Olesen 2005). With the anti-war demonstrations in February 2002, the World Social Forum meetings, and the 12 August 2006 worldwide demonstrations against Israel's bombing of civilian areas in Lebanon as recent examples, the use of these technologies to organize community-based action has not diminished.

In "Democratic Media Activism through the Lens of Social Movement Theory," William K. Carroll and Robert A. Hackett make the important distinction "between democratization through the media (the use of media, whether by governments or civil society actors, to promote democratic goals and processes elsewhere in society), and democratization of the media themselves" (2006, 84). While all of the TAG sites claim to be engaged in educating the general public as well as the media, only Electronic Intifada is part of the media. These alter-media or indie-media sources may lead some to bypass dominant media sources altogether. As Carroll and Hackett note, "certain kinds of media activism do focus upon issues of content, but ... a good deal of media activism presents not just a 'symbolic challenge' to elites but a challenge to the system of symbolic production — a critique of the political economy of mass communication and an effort to build democratic alternatives" (ibid., 99). In this way, Zochrot's database and Palestine Remembered provide the news for which some are searching. These alternative sources of information, like the mapping and rehistoricizing processes described earlier, provide necessary structural support and a sense of solidarity for the exercise of communal autonomy.

TAGs and Theories of Globalization

Many critics confront in globalization the signs of an unacceptable social order. I would like to suggest that TAGs seek to "occupy," for lack of a better word, global space; they seek to increase, expand, explore, and extend it. These are activists who invoke the global as a sign of the unlivability of the current order, choosing to incorporate it into their arguments, using it as their starting point for formulating new practices of intervention and new social practices and relations. They work as if they are inside the "machine," the system, while simultaneously recognizing their "outsider" status (as non-state, non-elite actors). In their practices, they project their perceptions of global justice and citizenship. It is a space that has been opened by and for them.

My focus on the more radical orientations of Palestinian activism and the right of return in particular is only partially informed by a concern with TAGs and the global context. I am also very interested in and engaged by the politics of diaspora and refugee communities and the symbols that stand for themselves (Wagner 1986). I have argued that Palestinian-centred TAGs successfully articulate and mediate between those in power and more general audiences, between the centre (the West) and the periphery (Palestine, immigrant community, refugee camp), between antagonistic and supportive groups, and between ideal and pragmatic political practices. As such, TAGs can be better understood as conduits and sets of practices than as sources of influence. Differing in both the scope and the intent of most social movement theorists and analysts, and following Chesters and Welsh's (2005) framing, I argue that the connection between TAGs, NGOs, and the "public" is not simply linear but also circular and systemic.

I do not suggest, however, that Palestinian-centred TAGs are somehow unmoored from a wider public culture of which other human rights and transnational social movement organizations (e.g., Human Rights Watch, Amnesty International, PEN) are a part and that do have power and influence. Measuring the degree to which governments respond to or shift their policy discourses as a result of cyberactivism by TAGs prevents a full appreciation of the channels of communication and mediation between different structures, organizations, and communities. This type of analysis fails to consider TAGs as communicative spaces for the imaginative re/construction of what may be more diffuse but equally important: collective identities, solidarities, non-territorially based relations.

Conclusion

My study of how the cyberactivist work of TAGs has simultaneously enabled the strengthening of Palestinian communal autonomy and of global networks seeking social justice on a broader scale leads me to agree with anthropologist William Mazzarella's critique of *Empire* (Hardt and Negri 2000). Mazzarella writes that,

> instead of taking mediation as the object of critical analysis, [Hardt and Negri] compound the problem by demonizing it as the death-dealing, freeze-frame technology of those whose global sway depends on "fixing" the dynamic, productive, and im-mediate (their word is "immanent") energies of the "multitude." By romanticizing the emergent and the im-mediate, this neo-vitalist position tends too briskly to dismiss given social formations as always already foreclosed. This is clearly an impossible point of departure for an ethnographer because the critical value of fieldwork depends on an understanding of social process as an *ongoing mediation* of the virtual and the actual, of potentiality and determination. (2004, 348, emphasis added)

To analyze and explore the give and take generated in these moments of dialogical practices through Palestinian TAGs in cyberspace reveals how cyberactivists negotiate between the "imagined community" (Anderson 1983) of Palestine and its representations by influential media sources; between the self-representations on the Internet and face-to-face contact at meetings with other activists, students, scholars, policy makers, journalists, and researchers; between the latest posting and the next protest. To simply "situate" (Haraway 1988) the TAGs as an online community would unmoor them from their own beginnings as well as deny the material consequences of their activists' goals.[5]

Palestinian TAG activities exemplify the complex geography that Palestinian political spaces cross. This geography spans two locales — the places of origin and the destination (Gilroy 1993). The linkages are also multiple, entailing connections with localities as well as states, intersecting with international human rights regimes that shape the rights and political processes that immigrant-citizens and refugees can expect to encounter. The connections are also multivalent, varying across familial, social, political, and economic realms of life.

The sense one gets from these websites is that they provide information (see also Staeheli et al. 2002). The kind of information they provide is comparable only to the extent that Palestine and the crises experienced by Palestinians are imagined along similar lines. Beyond that, however, there are differences that, I would argue, are particular to the locale of the activism. This activist emplacement was surprising to me in part because I had accepted the notion that a virtual community is not emplaced, that it is a non-place. It means that TAGs' identities and practices are filtered through multiple communities, multiple webs of interpersonal relations, and multiple identities that make up the global public realm. Throughout the 1990s, global justice movements principally called attention to the role of corporate globalization and economic injustice around the globe. Many of the same organizations were able to mobilize after the 9/11 attacks, drawing attention to the grievances of the Muslim and Arab world, and bringing some focus to the Israel-Palestine conflict. Moreover, peace activists networking along the same Web "routes" could now mobilize against the war in Iraq (Della Porta and Mosca 2005, 170)[6] and make the connections — some long-standing — with Palestinian rights organizations.

At the macrolevel, Palestinian TAGs are concerned not only with the diffusion of information to the public but also with the dramatization of the public sphere and the creation of a common cultural framework for building common identities and solidarity. These practices are elaborated through compelling narratives of communal identity and history, providing the cultural grounds for the social imaginary, an alternative global society, and the moments for understanding and engaging the public narratives of global justice. Palestinian TAGs present narrations of tragedy and loss while also offering the prospect of creating an alternative Israel/Palestine.

Palestinian TAG practices have strong affinities to some of the most significant departures from the dominant paradigm of civil society theory, suggesting a multiplicity of public spheres, communities, and associations nested within one another and within their national realm. Within these debates has been a divergence from understanding civil society as an institutional or informational space of subjects passively receiving information to become a more powerful "voting bloc"[7] to understanding TAGs as participants constructing real and ideal global communities. This emphasis on culture and agency does not imply an absence of structures and limits. It assumes that there is a history that serves to limit the interpretive frames through which audiences as actors can interpret such narratives. Palestinian TAG narratives present alternative histories and representations of the Israel-Palestine conflict, with every expectation that those who enter their spaces will always and already have been exposed to the dominant pro-Israel narrative. Yet the Internet provides them with a space for presenting and negotiating their own autonomous views.

In the literature on globalization, one finds identification with post-nationalist subjectivities — refugees, diasporas, migrants, exiles — all subjectivities of mobility, although of course most are the real subjects of borders reinforced and redefined. My work with Palestinian TAGs suggests that, despite sympathies for post-nationalism (many propose that Israel/Palestine be transformed from an ethno-territorial state to one that represents all of its citizens, without special consideration for ethnic/religious identity), these theories do little to ameliorate the conditions of those whose lives are incapacitated by the excesses of nationalized and rationalized violence. Seen in this light, Palestinian TAGs may be expressing two contradictory impulses: to fully engage the "post-nationalist order" of cyberactivism to reterritorialize a national community.

The quotations that mark the beginning of this chapter are entry points — our voices are prevented from reaching each other — and a point of critique. Internet technologies have allowed Palestinians and other activists to reach out to one another as well as to communicate with others to learn our stories. Stories passed on through the generations are now available to anyone interested in learning about Palestine and the catastrophe that has befallen Palestinians. Jon Anderson (1997), in his conclusion to a study on Arab cybernauts' use of the Internet in the diaspora, writes that "what they are creating is less a 'techno-space' of wandering signifiers ... This is not just a conversational world ... but a world where 'voice' — literally — is found and made into social action, where talk is organized social pose beyond mere discourse about poses ... not limited to assertions of identity in a literally trans-national 'space.'" The space is being created not so much 'virtually,' in techno-parlance, but 'actually' in what Anderson called 'imagined community' ... The action is at once negative, in denying sanctioning authorities, and positive, in asserting alternative legitimacies of a subtle ... sort." In the same way, Palestinian-centred TAG sites provide a way into resistance politics, global and local. Like the children's game of tag, they pass along narratives of memory, history, identity, and resistance so that, once you've been hyperlinked, "you're it." In thus narrating a national community and welcoming a global audience to share in Palestinians' pain and struggles, these sites perform a type of community that seeks to move beyond exclusions toward larger visions of reciprocity.

chapter 11

The Tensions of Global Imperial Community: Canada's Imperial Order Daughters of the Empire (IODE)

Jessica Schagerl

THIS CHAPTER TAKES AS its central focus Canada's Imperial Order Daughters of the Empire, a female imperialist group formed in Montreal in 1900 and still operative today. I speculate that the IODE, when considered at the moment of its formation, can serve as a site for exploring the ways in which one locally based transnational community was developed out of a contradictory imperial moment in Canada's history: its participation in the South African war (1899-1902). Founded as the Federation of the Daughters of the British Empire and the Children of the Empire (Junior Branch), its headquarters quickly shifted to Toronto, and its name changed to the Imperial Order Daughters of the Empire. The IODE has most often been understood by feminist imperial historians as a "sister" organization to the (better-studied and therefore more known) Victoria League in England. By shifting the discussion of the IODE toward global imperial community, I stress the historical links between imperialism and the contemporary global moment. Nineteenth-century empires, with the British in the lead, accelerated the processes of globalization by fashioning transworld economic, political, cultural, and geographical relationships. In the process, the prevalence of a shared global outlook became more common among individuals, communities, and nationalities. Those closest to the metropole in these empires took particular pride in their apparent global strength. The first generation of the sororal network of the IODE shared such a global consciousness and used it to build a sense of community, which had global pretensions of its own. The bonds of this community were possibly all the stronger for being limited by race, religion, and class privileges, elements of community that initiate some questioning of Raymond Williams' belief that "community is rarely used unfavourably" (1976, 66). From a postcolonial perspective today, the implied assumptions legitimating such bonding of community are no longer seen as self-evident. This awareness of the term's assumptions leads some to argue "against community" (Joseph 2002). While these critiques are clearly justified, my interest here lies in understanding what this community did for its members, how it functioned within the contexts of its times, and what its history might mean for understanding globalization, autonomy, and community today.

What interests me about the community of the IODE in relation to globalization and autonomy is what Miranda Joseph terms the "conservative, disciplining and exclusionary effectivity of the invocation of community." She employs community to "refer to social practices that presume or attempt to enact and produce identity, union, communion, and purity" (2002, xviii-xix). The homogenizing of other communities in order to make their own communal claims is one of the less pleasant aspects of IODE transnational community building. This aspect of their community identity lends itself to an analysis of how a privileged women's community may produce itself in the name of promoting imperial, racial, and gender structures. The feminine imperialist community of the IODE fostered a limited amount of individual autonomy for some Canadian women, especially through the local and regional projects undertaken by the Order. Communal autonomies, however, especially at the national and imperial levels, remained gendered. Autonomies available to groups of women, even if privileged, were more restricted than those available to men. Accordingly, it is worthwhile to re-examine the optimism that attends transnationalism as a potentially emancipatory project for women at the turn of the previous century — for instance, in international congresses for women's labour and suffrage rights. Revisiting the history of the IODE may also help contemporary scholars begin to understand the uneven global histories of liberal feminism.

I do not wish to rest with an interpretation of this community as merely an example of the homogeneous ethnic construction of "Britishness," binding women from colonies together as actors in imperialist projects (see Colley 2003; Pickles 2002; Wilton 2000). To do so would be to overlook other central questions. What does it mean that the IODE and others like it defined themselves through a model of community founded on sororal intimacy (as "sisters" and "daughters" of the empire)? How, and why, did the articulation of a community "across the seas and hemispheres" coincide with expressed anxieties about the role of women at the time? How was the community produced and maintained and to what ends? What can we say about the production of a social order often premised on a racial hierarchy that, it was repeatedly argued, could only be mitigated by white imperial feminist patriotism? What sorts of possibilities exist for understanding the personal and collective investment in the idea of an imperial community? While I do not propose to answer all these questions, I am interested in the curious gender gap that exists in the rhetoric of globalization's histories. Where were women in these histories? For those who made imperial patriotic service a priority and those for whom public service was important, the IODE could offer women a supportive community. It also afforded them access to the public sphere in limited ways, thereby breaking the bonds of domesticity felt by middle- and upper-class Victorian women. Moreover, the community provides a way to unpack how a form of collective imagining of the national community (contrary to Anderson 1991) depends on women imagining themselves as not fully autonomous daughters, wives, and mothers.

The Global Imperial Community of the IODE

A month before the morning meeting on 13 February 1900 in which Mrs. Clark Murray (Margaret Polson Murray) is said to have first introduced the idea of a "Federation of the Daughters of the British Empire," she wrote a reflective solicitation for members to the English-language press in Montreal. Under the title "A League of 'Daughters of the Empire,'" she called for expressions of sympathy and support, noting that "every true Canadian heart must be proudly touched at the wave of enthusiastic patriotism which is passing over the Dominion during the present war in South Africa." "Will you allow me to suggest," she wrote,

> that the women of Canada have an opportunity which should eagerly be seized to place themselves in the front rank of colonial patriotism? Why not arise as the Daughters of the Empire — the women if not the soldiers of the Queen — and invite their sisters in Australia and New Zealand to join in a prompt and rousing expression of themselves? A federation of this sort, especially if made on a permanent basis, would in itself be useful as creating an organized

means of action should a united action of colonial women be at any time necessary. At the present moment it would be of tenfold value. It would cheer the entire Imperial army to know that British women across the seas and hemispheres were fighting with them. It would startle European nations, who sneer that we are only after gold and diamonds. And, with all modesty, it might bring a gladdening throb of joy to the heart of our August Queen in her declining years.[1]

At first glance, Murray's call for a federation of imperial women seems merely to be part of the rich, and still understudied, texture of gender-inflected language of imperial feminism and colonial nationalism that was so prevalent in early twentieth-century Canada. Increasingly, however, more nuanced feminist work has emerged. Studies of empire, including British imperial history, have turned to more "politicized" understandings of empire's "ideologies, workings and effects" as a result of encounters with postcolonial studies and other cross-disciplinary work, including globalization studies (Colley 2003, 133). This work demands that researchers pay attention to women's lives, experiences, and identities as shaped by global processes such as imperialism. Perhaps not surprisingly, when the IODE has been studied, it is usually placed as a contributor "in the making of an Anglo-Canadian identity in the image of Britain" (Pickles 2002, 1). It is seen as a group that promoted "the participation and visibility of British women in Canadian society and politics" (Wilton 2000, 150). Recent scholarship about female imperialist organizations starts from the premise that women were just as involved as men in expressions of imperial patriotism, involvement manifested in voluntary organizations (Bush 2000). The term "organization" emphasizes the historical links between the IODE and other social reform movements, such as the National Council of Women (with which it shared numerous members and officers), the YMCA, local nursing and community groups, and Women's Institutes. I prefer to speak of a "global imperial community" — in contrast to "organizations" — to designate their identity. This notion places a greater emphasis on what allowed these organizations composed of "pro-British Anglo-Celtic Canadians" (Pickles 2000, 81) to form in the first instance: the transnational migration of settlers to Canada and other parts of the Empire as part of Britain's imperial project, the glorification of this project, and their desire to feel part of this larger whole.

In her rationale for founding the order, Murray mobilizes a powerful sense of identity and community under the terms of a white women's voluntary association that seems to signify something dynamic and fluid, moving across national boundaries and serving as a means of collective identification. Striking in its passionate and emotional intensity, as well as its rhetorical flourish, her call invokes the social order and stability that Murray sees as stemming from imperialist projects. The IODE was to be a racial federation guided by women, united in the idea that the white citizens of empire formed a natural unity. They believed that a federation of women "across the seas and hemispheres" was a biological reality that could be supplemented by an environmentally determinist discourse holding that the northern climate would promote healthy racial characteristics. The overt racism of this discourse suggests a general overall affinity between the globalizing imperialism in the early twentieth century and those understandings of globalization today that emphasize its links with racism, oppression, genocide, and economic exploitation. Even if, as Susie O'Brien and Imre Szeman note, "globalization cannot be reduced to simply the extension and intensification of early imperialisms" (2001, 610), those structures of domination have continued to reproduce themselves in many cultural, political, and economic facets of contemporary globalization.

At least until the First World War, many Anglo-Canadians considered the British Empire their "imagined community," placing the Empire ahead of the nation.[2] Having a notion of community not based on the nation-state matters for my analysis. Although the British Empire figured as part of the social imagination of many Canadians, the promotion of imperial sentiment that echoed the racial and religious ideals of the Empire required deliberate and sustained effort. The creation of a gendered and racialized "we" that would support often militarized imperial aims was by no means automatic. After Benedict Anderson, it is by now almost a cliché to suggest that, as Gerard Delanty puts it, "the power of community consists in the emergence of definitions, principles and cognitive models for imagining the world" (2003, 156-7; see Anderson 1991, 6). Promoters of imperialism knew that the idea(l) of imperial community had to be actively and dynamically conceived, however, and promoted wherever and whenever possible. This promotion could take place just as easily through the public performance of political speeches and personal reflections as it could through British-influenced class and gender politics.

The earliest pamphlet of the IODE details that reactions in England after unforeseen losses in the South African war were the impetus for Murray's proposal to federate as a specifically sororal group. In this account, responding to the *"atmosphere of unity"* was "contagious":

On Mrs. Murray's leaving London, she brought that burning desire across the ocean, fresh from the smoke of battle ... She thought it an opportunity when something might be done in the eyes of the European powers to silence the malignity of their hatred and envy, something in addition to the wonderful, spontaneous, magical response to the call for more men, — magnificent and soul thrilling as that has been all over the Empire, — and that something seemed to come demanded from the women — the women of the Queen, — that portion of Her Majesty's subjects in every corner of the globe whose patriotism finds expression in humble deeds, in patient endurance, in unrepining grief, in cheerful hope.[3]

Telegrams to the mayors of the provincial capitals, asking for them to call on the women of their cities to form regional chapters, were the first step in Murray's attempt to have a pan-imperial movement uniting women from "across the seas and hemispheres." In recalling the historical circumstances of the South African war, Murray develops a founding narrative for the community tied to an invocation of specific political interest. She situates a collective effort as being part of an imperial community in the act of performing the call to "federate." By 1901, when the IODE was beginning to organize itself nationally and internationally, the opening preamble of the order's *Constitution and Statutes of the Imperial Order of the Daughters of the Empire and the Children of the Empire (Junior Branch)* further suggests the transnational scope of the community: "For the purposes of planting and administering the Order in the several Kingdoms, Dominions, Commonwealths, Provinces and States of the Empire, 'The National Chapter of Canada' shall be vested with all the powers of the Imperial Chapter, until said Chapter is formed in accordance with this Constitution ... It shall be the duty of said National Chapter to organize the Order throughout the world as speedily as possible on the lines herein indicated."[4] The desire for overseas affiliation should come as little surprise since "the interconnectedness of home-building and Empire-building was to become one of the most powerful themes of Edwardian female imperialism" (Bush 2000, 68). While members of the IODE, including Murray, sought to extend the reach of the order to England, "the possibility of expansion outside of Canada ... [often] met with cold defensive opposition" (Pickles 2002, 18). Such was a global imperial consciousness.

Murray's comments are a self-conscious effort at transnational community building. Murray sought to link a group of women across disparate parts of the world in common aims and similar backgrounds, with potentially transformative goals. From the outset, the IODE defined itself with the motto "One Flag, One Throne, One Empire," linking gender, class, and belief in imperial sentiment in what Catherine Hall calls "the fantasy of ethnological unity" (2000, 2). It provided what Melissa Steyn calls "the credibility that comes with being perceived as 'of the same kind' by the international community" (2005, 128). In claiming a shared community identity, Murray's passage also points to how gender can be closely allied to both race and class privileges. Ostensibly, as the *Constitution and Statutes* reveals, membership in the IODE was accorded to "all women and children in the British Empire or Foreign Lands who hold true allegiance to the British Crown" (section 1) who have been proposed by a member (section 7), elected by a chapter (section 5), affirmed loyalty to the reigning British monarch (section 8), and paid relevant fees (sections 6, 9).

It is worth briefly noting that, somewhat like the gendered mountaineering communities discussed by Slemon in this volume, the global imperial community of the IODE comes about in discursive contradiction: the rhetoric of inclusivity gives way to a more circumscribed set of criteria designed to ensure that members of the community shared like values, identities, and interests.

One can begin to see the contours of this global imperial community: the role of invitation and decorum, proper norms of femininity and hierarchy, as well as an unspoken yet explicit emphasis on class and whiteness, appropriately understood in this context as the social positionality, economic, and political advantages stemming from European colonial expansion. Notions of belonging and connections to other members of the community were based as much on the assumption of culturally and racially homogeneous communities and on the construction and maintenance of exclusions as on common aims and desires. In emphasizing ties of belonging and identity as a central part of what will become the Imperial Order Daughters of the Empire, Murray underscores that the construction of this community is premised first on received ideas about "Britishness" and second on imperial ties that provide the conditions necessary for (some) women's collective participation in national as well as imperial life. The aims of the order were shortened or elaborated as necessary. For instance, writing to a colonial administrator in Ceylon, the national secretary in 1904 noted that "the chief aim of this Order is to promote a bond of union amongst the women and children of the Empire, to encourage the study of the history of the Empire, and to stimulate the spirit of patriotism amongst the youth in the schools in all parts of the Empire."[5] That the IODE can be read as part of "a narrative of hegemonic colonial identity" (Pickles 2000, 84) seems to be self-evident. Nonetheless, the privileges of white women's imperial identity were contingent on the performance of particular aspects of (gendered and racialized) transnational community.

One of these particular aspects of gendered and racialized transnational community was the IODE's privileging of emotional attachments as a feature of sororal community. In its earliest years, the IODE claimed access to broader global imperial community through ethnic and racial affiliation that often took the form of female friendship promoted "across the seas and hemispheres" through letters and other written correspondence. These human expressions of affiliation and obligation differentiate the IODE as a community. I read these letters as an invitation to think about Brydon and Coleman's suggestion in this volume that the emotional life of a community is an important area for exploration. A concern of members with securing affiliation overseas marks the IODE as part of a global imperial community. Accordingly, cross-cultural exchanges are particularly interesting for the ways in which members of a community defined their common belonging, employing class, gender, and racial distinctions to demarcate membership and its limits. Indeed, with its invocation of gender and empire, the IODE offers a particularly productive site to reflect on points of comparison in charting both transnational or, perhaps more accurately, "trans-imperial" (Lester 2002, 30) interactions and communal discourses. Here issues of affiliation and communicative exchange figure prominently in helping to consolidate this group as a community based on sororal intimacy. My rationale for this claim is a series of letters that passed between members of the order and like-minded women across the Empire, including several letters to the wives of high-ranking colonial administrators. These kinds of emotional attachments reinforced members' feelings of belonging to transnational as well as national communities.

On 10 March 1902, for instance, from aboard the hospital ship *Orcana*, en route to Durban in the Southern African colonies, Florence Cameron wrote to the national secretary of the IODE in Toronto:

> My dear Mrs. Land:
> Before leaving Halifax I was delighted to receive a Daughters of the Empire badge: and hoped to leave there able to acknowledge it

on my first voyage. Owing to sea sickness, I have been forced to defer telling you how much pleasure it gives me to receive this insignia of the Order, together with the good wishes which accompany it. I shall hope to meet at some future time, members of the Order at home, as well as abroad and till then beg to remain yours.[6]

Whether Cameron met any other members of the order at home or abroad is a matter of conjecture. But her correspondence, like that of many of the women involved in various patriotic associations designed to unify the Empire, reveals global processes of cross-cultural exchange. These processes include the ways in which members of a community define their common belonging through differentiated class, gender, and racial relations. Letters of introduction, likewise, served as the appropriate means of expressing the cultured imperial femininity fostered by the IODE and other members of the larger global imperial community. On 5 February 1905, Mrs. Stowton, the secretary of the Victoria League in Tasmania, wrote to introduce "Miss Fawns, Hon. Sec of the Launceston branch of the VL [Victoria League, the foremost female imperialist group in England] and her sister Mrs. Kermode, Vice-President of the VL, who are visiting Canada on their way to London."[7] A subsequent letter dated 21 March 1905, directed to Mrs. Nordheimer, president of the National Chapter in Toronto, written by Muriel Talbot, the energetic secretary of the Victoria League in England, reintroduces "Miss Fawns, who is acting as Secretary to the Victoria League in Launceston, Tasmania, and who is very much interested in our work."[8]

For the women of the National Chapter in Toronto — the order's pre-eminent chapter — a range of pressures and opportunities as a result of globalizing processes is crystallized in the letters written by and to members of the order. The IODE's attempts to form chapters and to connect with other colonies and dominions were pervasive. They extended from the Atlantic world (Canada, England, the South African colonies, Bermuda) to the Indian subcontinent and to the Australasian colonies and dominions. As Eliza Riedi notes, the "web of imperial women's networks criss-crossed the Edwardian empire, and despite the tensions inherent in 'imperial sisterhood,' survived in attenuated form through two world wars and the transition from empire to commonwealth" (2005, 1316).

By early January 1902, the headquarters and leadership of the IODE had fully shifted away from Montreal and Margaret Polson Murray. Members of the National Chapter in Toronto began to mount campaigns to secure influential women in positions of leadership for the eventual development of international chapters. On 12 January 1902, Mrs. Land, then the secretary of the National Chapter, wrote to Her Excellency, the Countess of Hopetoun, in Australia, wife of the governor general, suggesting that a member of the order be dispatched to Australia "to organize chapters in the different states." When this organizing activity was accomplished, she hoped that the countess "would consent to become Hon. President in the Commonwealth."[9] Recognizing, perhaps, that it might be presumptuous for dominion women to make such a proposal, Land ended her letter by stressing that "although Canadian in its origin this order is Imperial in its scope and Imperial in its administration being built upon the representative basis ... of cooperation."[10] In May 1903, letters were still being exchanged with the secretary of the wife of the governor of New South Wales, asking for expressions of "active interest" and continuing to advance the idea that "Canada is merely taking the initiative prior to more complete organization."[11] In 1902, a Provincial Chapter of the IODE was formed in Nassau, Bahamas, by a group of women with strong enough ties to Canada that several of them planned to leave "for Toronto ... for a long stay there."[12] This correspondence of members of the order shows how contact through letters records the tensions between national, imperial, and global identities. These letters, which I read as "communicative links as established by networks of actors" (Delanty 2003, 165-6), help to produce transnational networks and sometimes even communal identities.

The IODE's rhetoric of an imperial sororal sisterhood, where "the women of the British Empire" would be brought "into real and living touch with one another,"[13] expressed a desire for community beyond the privacy of the home as well as beyond the borders of the nation. The global social imaginary invoked by the earliest members of the IODE did not rely on a notion that national borders would dissolve. In fact, the women of the IODE were vocal nation builders, believing that it was possible, and indeed desirable, to transcend the nation in order to achieve a multi-layered belonging in the global imperial world. What the example of the IODE suggests, particularly through Murray's call and the letters that helped to bond the women of the order, are the corresponding investments in whiteness and imperialism that structure a particular form of global imaginary. Not able to achieve political agency through nation, or only able to achieve it within circumscribed parameters, some of the women involved in the IODE sought to forge new avenues of agency through imperial networks.

At a very real and visceral level, some women were given the option of getting out of the house.

The parallel with the female development workers studied by Cook in her chapter in this volume is striking. Globalizing processes created opportunities for certain individual, privileged women who were part of the imperial community. How and why it is that this particular community, which seemingly offered the scope for limited autonomy for some Anglo-Saxon women, paradoxically ended up obscuring options for political choice at the level of national/collective autonomy is the focus of my next section. What is important for the argument of this chapter is that aspects of autonomy could be privileged in one context or marginalized in another and, in both cases, impacted by gender, class, and national affiliation. Furthermore, I argue that the rhetoric of the global imperial daughter suggests tensions in how individual and communal behaviour and policies are negotiated.

Of Daughters and the Disciplining Function of Global Imperial Community

Murray's active imagining of a collectivity and the grounds on which it could be developed both nationally and internationally can point to a reading of the formation of the IODE as part of the plural nature of communities in late nineteenth-century and early twentieth-century Canada. These communities were concerned with maintaining ties to Britain and developing a set of closely related, densely integrated regulatory apparatuses (see Henderson 2003). The limited autonomy afforded to the women that made up the IODE in its first generation operated within the confines of maternal feminism, which placed white women as mothers, wives, daughters (also as educators, nurses, housekeepers). Through these roles, women became formative to national and imperial projects. Prevalent as a discourse by which women could exercise autonomy and claim citizenship (without having the franchise), maternal nationalism upheld women's traditional roles as mother and wife and constructed women's citizenship on the basis of involvement in social reform, especially (though not exclusively) through a rhetoric of protection for girls so that they could grow up to "reproduce the race." As empire and nation builders, many upper- and middle-class women and organizations such as the IODE involved themselves in benevolent reform movements designed to provide help and support to "fallen" women, families in need, and children suffering in poverty.

Understanding autonomy as the capacity of individuals to shape the conditions under which they live (Held 1995), we can see that the IODE often attempted to create the conditions for the articulation of both collective autonomy (for the order) and personal autonomy (for its membership) and the women and girls they supported.

Perhaps the best example of the limited opportunities for autonomy is the work undertaken by the IODE to honour soldiers killed in the Southern African colonies. In choosing to direct the emotional and physical energy of the community toward the raising of funds for adequate memorialization of the war dead, the IODE held true to the original impetus for the community's formation and its own expressed aims. The aims of the order, around which the community could be said to be constellated, included the stimulation of "patriotism which binds the women and children of the Empire" (aim one) and the promotion of imperial history (aim four). Other practical aims included the provision of "an efficient organization by which prompt and unified action may be taken by the women and children of the Empire when such action may be desired" (aim three). This activity included the care of "widows, orphans and dependents of British soldiers or sailors and Heroes during war, in time of peace, or under sickness, accident or reverses of fortune."[14]

The IODE had both a national and a transnational focus in its work on the Southern African graves. Nationally, the IODE took the initiative to contact the families of soldiers killed during the war, offering support and condolence. This strategic initiative followed sanctioned forms of maternal involvement in the life of a nation. The emotional reactions to the letters written to the families of the soldiers suggest that the IODE treated the emotional and sororal as a matter of citizenship and collective autonomy. In three letters directed to the National Chapter, all written coincidentally on 16 April 1902, a parent of a soldier killed in combat expressly thanked the community for its interest in the particulars of the death of his or her son. Each letter begins with an expression of heartache — how "death has made a vacancy in our home which can never be filled" — before the inevitable request for further information about the whereabouts of the body and how the death transpired.[15] Appreciation for obligations in society was applauded by others, one father going so far as to write, "I cannot help feeling that when ladies like yourself and those whose names appear on your letter head withdraw from the claims of home and society, so as to give relief to the feelings of sorrowing ones in reference to the resting place of cruel war's victims, then I feel that all heroes are not of any means of the sterner sex."[16] The convergence of the discourses of responsibility and civic-mindedness, which I see as highlighting the emotional thrust of this sororal community, signals the possibility of gendered citizenship. It also suggests the designation of proper spaces for women to engage in the life of a nation. In other words, forms of autonomy are gendered.

Transnationally, the IODE tried to be involved in raising funds for the Canadian South Africa Memorial Association as well as the Guild of Loyal Women of South Africa Graves Committee. Both organizations were working in concert with the British War Office and groups in the Southern African colonies to identify grave sites and mount memorials. The community was also stimulated by other political institutions of the time, such as the office of the governor general. Importantly, however, for the expression of autonomy for this community, the structure of these political institutions did not encourage the extension or continuation of IODE involvement beyond the initial raising of funds. On several occasions, the IODE was, in effect, sanctioned by governmental and non-governmental organizations that claimed greater involvement in the cause. Lady Minto, wife of the governor general, went so far as to request that groups in the Southern African colonies be informed that "the Canadian South Africa Memorial Association" — and not the IODE — "is working with the full approval of the Canadian Government, the Canadian Military Authorities and is in no way connected with any other organization of a similar nature."[17] The example of the IODE's sustained work with the graves in Southern Africa shows how even limited autonomy could have dramatic effects with unintended consequences for the community's interest. As the opportunities increased for national and regional involvement, the opportunities for realizing collective autonomy (e.g., in the realm of being the chief organizers of a trans-imperial network) dissipated. The IODE was sanctioned by more powerful imperial communities in Canada and Britain, such as the Victoria League or more centrally the War Office, and forced into a secondary role designed to mimic the nation's semi-autonomous status in the Empire. The constitution and consolidation of the IODE, as evidenced by the controversies surrounding the Southern African graves, throw into sharp relief what Cynthia Enloe calls the "family dynamics shaping citizen participation" (2004, 194). While on one level it would seem to afford a limited measure of personal autonomy, the naturalization of the "daughter" role signalled continuing limits on women's political autonomy.

Conclusion

Conceiving the IODE as a "global imperial community" more adequately explains the lived political and social realities of early twentieth-century Canada. It emphasizes the importance of a gendered communal relation for participants embedded in Canadian performances of racialized empire. Globalizing processes, including imperial war, enabled these women to express new forms of community tied not only to place and space but also to their racialized identity as white Anglo-Saxon women of empire. Accordingly, scholars need to understand the complex nature of these relations in order to understand the continuing power of community in the social imaginary of the IODE. While this reframing introduces another set of limitations, what I focus on here is how the specific gendered and racialized construction of this particular imperial community can complicate easy understandings and valuing of communities as transnational.

The desire to maintain imperial connections coincides with what practitioners of transnational women's history have increasingly recognized as white Anglo-Saxon women's complex, complicit (and occasionally resistant) involvement in imperial struggles over race and gender at the time. In asking about the roots of the sometimes comfortable ideology linking women's involvement in the global sphere, however, I want to nuance claims of historical geopolitics by introducing notions of autonomy tied to responsibility (as suggested by Martha Albertson Fineman 2004). Versions of feminized patriotism assume a gendered, secondary status linked to global hierarchies of power chiefly negotiated by men. Revisiting the IODE's employment of imperial rhetoric leads to a consideration of the discursive structures of contemporary claims to global sisterhood. There are similarities both in the ambitions and in some of the limitations deriving from circumscribed forms of privilege. An important consequence of understanding transnational non-governmental organizations in a historical frame, as both Cook and I suggest in this volume, is that they can be seen to fit into patterns of stratification and unequal relations within a global system. There are differentials of power and privilege: some nations, some communities, some individuals have what labour studies colleagues call (with tongue in cheek) "bargaining power."

"Community" then as now could help to secure identity and locate one's place in the world. For some members of the IODE, a sense of community was important to counter the isolating effects of women's limited involvement in the public sphere. I prefer to think of the IODE in the context of a tension-filled global imperial community, which allows for a longer historical view of the entrenched and taken-for-granted privileges that accrue to masculinity and whiteness in Canada. More interestingly, it points to how these privileges have been transformed into the ideals by which the nation defines itself. Canada's current image of itself as a just international power broker — polite, peacekeeping architect (though not follower) of the plan to devote 0.7 percent of the GNP to foreign aid — relies on a dehistoricized global imaginary that Canada invents for itself. Slotting the IODE into this imaginary, without problematizing the idea of a global imperial community (as I hope I do here) would only serve to further this deracialized understanding.

chapter 12   Development Workers,
                    Transcultural Interactions, and
                    Imperial Relations in Northern
                    Pakistan

Nancy Cook

In *Globalization and Culture* (1999), John Tomlinson argues that global-izing phenomena are essentially complex and multi-dimensional, posing complicated challenges and opportunities for nations, economies, cultures, and daily lives around the world. Communities, too, seem to be braving the eddy of globalization. But what, precisely, is the current relationship between globalization and community? My contribution to this volume is motivated by a desire to interrogate some of the global processes that produce community inequality and sustain colonial-era power relations in our postcolonial world and to provoke new understandings and alternative behaviour patterns that are more equitable and just. To achieve those ends, I provide a case study of how the global movement of a community of people, enabled by international development as a cultural institution of globalization, variously affects the (re)configuration of identity, power rela-tions, and community autonomy in a local transcultural setting.

I focus here on the lives of a transnational community of Western women development workers living in Gilgit, northern Pakistan, to de-lineate several contradictory facets of the dialectical relationship between cultural globalization and community autonomy. In this way, I share several conceptual overlaps with fellow contributors. First, with Schagerl, Slemon, and Webb and Young, I am interested in the gendered and racialized char-acter of globalization. Second, I join Mulrennan and Habib in their focus on a nested community, in my case a transnational Western community that is lived locally in Pakistan. And third, this nestedness indicates a larger point made by Russell and O'Brien: that under globalization, community practice and identity are no longer necessarily rooted in place.

Drawing on ethnographic research inspired by a concern to think through my own complicity in these processes as a Western tourist and researcher in Pakistan, I concentrate on how women development workers in Gilgit inadvertently exercise globally circulating and self-privileging Orientalist discourses of gender and race (Said 1978; Spivak 1985) in the terrain of development, as well as purposely make use of the travel and work opportunities that accompany this form of globalization (Bernal, Bissell, and Cortes 1999; Dallmayr 1994; Sutcliffe 1999), to construct fulfilling identities and gain work experiences that will also serve them well at home. My research participants, therefore, work through global institutions (in this case Aga Khan Foundation development organizations) and the transnational flows of people, ideas, values, identities, and expertise they enable to achieve their aims and interests. They also use their mobility to enhance their autonomy, finding greater personal authority, self-esteem, and self-determination in the process.

This approach to self-determined living is achieved by the women studied here in large part by employing the discourse (Foucault 1977, 1978, 1980) of autonomy, a set of ideas and practices mobilized to constitute individuals, as well as their community, as independent, authoritative, and agential. The particular (and partial) interpretation I offer here outlines how the discourse of autonomy organizes these development workers' thoughts and actions in Gilgit. For instance, as I interpret their interview comments and everyday practices, the discourse of autonomy motivates their global travel agendas, development work, philanthropic practices, and constructions of Self, as well as their representations of Muslim Gilgiti women. In all of these ways, if to different extents, these Western women exercise the discourse of autonomy, in articulation with Orientalist constructions of race and gender, to constitute their own identities as free, independent, and authoritative individuals who can influence their own way of life, both abroad and at home. But while these locally situated processes usually enhance the individual and community autonomy of these development workers at global and local scales, they also reverberate negatively at both of those scales, compromising the discursive autonomy of Gilgiti women who, through this set of knowledges and practices, are unwittingly appropriated and codified as Othered inferiors. Consequently, my chapter clarifies the ways in which globalization (which enables the autonomy of some at the expense of others) is simultaneously detrimental (to some) and enabling (for others). Like other authors in this volume, I develop the concept of contending autonomies to show how, as one community enhances its autonomy in a local setting by seizing opportunities presented by globalization, pressures are simultaneously placed on the autonomy of a collocated community. And these constraints, in turn, reconstitute processes of globalization as imperial power relations. These themes of contemporary globalization as the legacy of empire, as gendered and racialized violence, and as the disguised appropriation of Others' identity to create personal and community autonomy are key features of the current articulation of globalization, autonomy, and community.

To demonstrate empirically the ambivalence of globality as it is lived locally in this instance, I examine the complex intersection of development and autonomy in the lives of these Western women primarily by exploring the relationship between their understandings of themselves and local Muslim women as *particular types of subjects* in this transcultural setting. I argue that representations of Self and Other are informed by these women's global travel experiences, international development philosophies, and the politics of philanthropy, all of which partially recuperate colonial-era discourses of gender and race. In this way, the community of Western women I studied in Gilgit is inculcated in a process of discursive colonization (Mohanty 1984) that is enabled by globalization to realize autonomy. For example, development workers' constructions of themselves as liberated, benevolent, and globally authoritative subjects are largely forged in opposition to their imperial representations of an undifferentiated, faceless mass of oppressed, needy Muslim women who are absent objects, muted figures, foreclosed subjects with no independent condition of existence (Spivak 1985, 1988). In Gayatri Spivak's (1988, 283) words, "the ontology of the Western subject necessitates and creates the Other: the silent subaltern." As a signature of Western power, these representations colonize the material heterogeneity of Gilgit women's lives in this globalized setting so that their voices are rendered inaudible, their material realities are overlooked, and their cultural productions are disregarded. Their subsequent lack of subjecthood on the global stage robs them of political agency. Consequently, many Western women in contemporary Gilgit, like their Raj-era predecessors, generally endeavour to "enlighten" and act for local women through development initiatives that impose Western standards of hygiene, nutrition, work, love, and domestic life. Transcultural community relations in Gilgit, then, sometimes seem to be a discursive violence that Westerners do to Others because they are situated within a colonial legacy of power relations that strengthen Western women's self-images, subjecthood, and social efficacy at the expense of local women's autonomy, understood as their capacity to achieve an independent subjectivity in transcultural interactions, as opposed to the object status that has been already constituted for them through imperial discourses. If we grant that these are unintended consequences of my research participants' desires to help coupled with their quest for autonomy, then globalization (as seen through the lens of contemporary development practice in this instance) is risky business.

My argument in the remainder of the chapter unfolds in four main sections. In the first section, I introduce my research setting, larger ethnographic project, and research participants. In the second section, I trace the intersecting politics of philanthropy and self-determination that intertwine in these women's stories of departure, global travel, and work abroad. The third section outlines their constructions of the Muslim women whom they have come to help as well as of themselves, showing how Self and Other are, for the most part, constituted oppositionally. And in the fourth section, I describe how these representations infuse my research participants' understandings of their development work and what cultural power implications that activity has for the autonomy of both communities of women in Gilgit.

Transnationals Abroad

Gilgit is the largest town and development headquarters in the Northern Areas, a frontier region of South Asia that was once part of the British Raj but is now a federally administered province of Pakistan located seven hundred kilometres north of Islamabad, near the Chinese border. It lies in a steep valley at 1,400 metres at the confluence of the Hindu Kush, Karakoram, and Himalaya mountain ranges and the Hunza and Gilgit rivers.

When the Karakoram Highway (KKH) opened in 1978, the Northern Areas were connected to southern Pakistan and Xinjiang province in China via a paved road that traces one of the ancient silk routes of central Asia. Gilgit was almost immediately affected by the increased, if intermittent, economic trade and human mobility that the KKH allows. The city became the administrative, military, and economic centre of the Northern Areas, attracting international traders, tourists, village migrants, and various international development organizations. As a result, the population of Gilgit has grown dramatically and in 2002 was approximated at sixty thousand.

The Aga Khan Rural Support Program (AKRSP) consolidated and intensified development activity in the villages of Gilgit District beginning in December 1982. Next to the army and the civil administration, AKRSP is the largest employer in the region, and its Northern Areas head office is in Gilgit. Along with numerous other development projects, many of which are also funded by the Aga Khan Foundation, it employs many local people and down-country Pakistanis as well as Western volunteers on development work terms and foreign consultants and general managers. This wide-ranging development activity explains why there are approximately seventy-five Westerners living in and around Gilgit.

During the summers of 1999 and 2000, I conducted nine months of ethnographic research with Western women living in Gilgit. My purpose was twofold. First, I wanted to understand how they negotiated identity reconfigurations in the transcultural setting of Gilgit through particular discourses and social practices. Second, I was interested in how Western women, including me, perpetuate, legitimate, resist, and transform relations of domination as they imagine themselves in relation to the people among whom they live, construct communities and homes, and build careers and relationships in Gilgit. The resulting study (Cook, forthcoming) examines these aspects of the lives of thirty British, Canadian, Dutch, American, and Australian volunteers working for international development agencies, many on two-year contracts negotiated through the British agency Volunteer Services Overseas (VSO). They are health workers, teachers, librarians, English-language coaches, and teacher trainers who instruct local educators on new methods of teaching the curriculum in English.

Western women in Gilgit do not form a homogeneous community with common interests. Different groups of women, with various friendships and enmities toward each other, coexist uneasily as closeted missionaries, socio-cultural reformers, housewives, friends, housemates, and co-workers. There are significant internal tensions within this community and thus diversity and conflict among Western women. Nor is this a permanent settlement. Rather, it is a temporary group of Western women, haphazardly thrown together by the accidental and limited circumstances of development job placement, what Melissa Williams calls a "community of fate" (see her chapter in Bernstein and Coleman, forthcoming). This community is easily dismantled, fragile, and contingent. Consequently, my use of the term "community" invokes neither Ferdinand Tönnies' (1957) normative ideal designating how social relations ought to be organized nor a metaphysical logic of identity that conceptualizes community as a unified whole (Young 1990). Rather, I use "community" — as do many authors in this volume — to denote a shifting, fractured, and fragile small group that is generated as members negotiate global opportunities and is employed to achieve particular autonomy interests.

Social characteristics of research participants	
Age	• Participants were between the ages of twenty-three and fifty-nine. Five were in their twenties, but most were between thirty-seven and their early fifties. They usually identified as one of two "life" groups: young (unmarried, no children, desirable) and seasoned (married or once married, with children, past desirability, and often, in their words, "grand-motherish").
Nationality	• Four Canadians, two Americans, one German, four Australians, one Dane, two Dutch, British remainder. • All claimed Anglo-Saxon heritage, except for Germanic and Nordic backgrounds.
Formal schooling	• All but two participants were university educated. • Many had advanced degrees, teaching certificates, and English as a Second Language training.
Vocation before going to Gilgit	• One freelance photojournalist, one postal carrier, one businesswoman, one retired civil servant, two nurses, three housewives (two of whom were also part-time teachers), one doctor, one feminist lawyer. • The rest were educators (teachers, teacher trainers, or education consultants).
Religion	• For eight women, Christianity was a fundamental component of their lives. (Five of them were "closet" missionaries.) • The rest claimed to be non-practising or to have no religious affiliation.
Station	• All self-identified as middle class.
Partnership	• Three were lesbians (two of whom were partners); four were in long-term relationships with men but not married; eight were single; nine were married; five had once been married.
Progeny	• Fourteen participants had children, but only five had children with them in Gilgit.

This community is constituted based on some common social characteristics — such as being women, foreigners, and development workers — in addition to being constructed in relation to a shared territorial location. Although Western women in Gilgit speak the same language, are well educated and engaged in the same kind of work, enjoy similar food, drink, music, and travel experiences, and crave cultural belonging in an unfamiliar environment, being thrown together haphazardly through their development work means that they often have little else in common: they have not read the same books, their sexuality and spiritual beliefs differ, they range widely in age, they are not all parents, and they espouse various and competing philosophies of life (see box on previous page). While some community members would likely not choose to develop relationships with others in the West, carefully cultivated associations and similarities among these women in Gilgit not only create familiar and sustaining human contact but also aid in constructing community autonomy. The liberated/oppressed binary they exercise in their representations of themselves and Gilgiti women leads most Western women to overlook characteristics, events, and situations they have in common with local women as well as the differences among themselves, creating two ostensibly internally coherent communities that are radically different and hierarchically arranged. This "us" versus "them" community dichotomy nurtures Western women's sense of autonomy, but it also sustains colonial-era power relations in our contemporary world, inculcating members from both communities in the historical continuity of imperialism that is facilitated through development processes.

Over the course of my fieldwork, I conducted thirty-seven multiple unstructured interviews, nine months of participant observation, and several group interviews. Because my empirical concerns in this chapter revolve around collective constructions of "liberated Self" and "oppressed Other" and the subsequent effects these representations have on community autonomy, I rely primarily on my interview data in this analysis.

The Politics of Philanthropy and Self-Determination

Western women development workers in Gilgit were usually offended to be called "tourists" or "travellers," whom they understand to be temporary visitors searching for instant doses of self-gratification that exploit local culture. In contrast to these categories of foreigners, my research participants argue that they are in Gilgit not simply to holiday but also to help, to labour as development workers for a Western-funded NGO with the goal of improving local living conditions. This politics of philanthropy is an important factor that "pulled" them to travel abroad, the "official" reason most of my research participants gave for why they took development placements in Gilgit. Most women told me they felt lucky to have had a good education, comparatively satisfying and well-paid work, and materially abundant lives in the West. They want to share that *kismat* with less fortunate people by putting their expertise to work in a developing country. Joan (pseudonyms chosen by individual research participants are used thoughout the chapter), who is fifty years old and representative of the group, thinks "there were lots of reasons why I got to the point of deciding to come. My life has been rich, so I've always had it in my mind that I would like to come and work in a poor developing country at some point in my career, to help."

This philanthropic pull factor — for privileged Western women to provide for the needy through development work — sits uneasily with a general uninterest in the everyday lives of local Muslim women, much as it did in the colonial era (Burton 1990; Melman 1992; Ramusack 1990; Ware 1992). Abbie, a middle-aged American health worker, is "amazed that I can even live here, because it just doesn't interest me hardly at all. I really like [the men I work with] ... And I've liked a lot of the expatriate people. But I don't feel any draw to the [local] women. I don't want to go and visit my neighbours ... I feel like I have to have my life separate." For many of my research participants, Muslim women constitute "the needy" as opposed to poor, yet interesting, people with compelling lives. They often serve as foils against which foreign women imagine themselves as self-sacrificing benefactors.

As Joan suggests above, Western women usually have multiple reasons for travelling to Gilgit. Altruism is often mixed with "selfishness," which makes Evelyn, a forty-three-year-old Canadian teaching consultant, "realize that nobody has 100 percent pure motives ... I'm at the point where I can't define who's here because they really want to help people, or, as in my case, part of the reason for me taking the job was that I needed the *money* ... I want to do good work, but I can only take that so far." "Push" factors, such as a lack of employment opportunities in Canada, thus constitute another context of global travel for Western women development workers, one that can be embarrassing to acknowledge. For example, when I asked Susan why she decided to do development work after just getting her feet wet in a teaching career, she said, "It sounds a bit *crass*. I wanted to do something, I wanted to feel worthwhile ... If I'm honest, I'd say the main reason I'm here is for selfish reasons. The job opportunity is *great*. We get a lot of professional freedom here, which you don't get in Britain." Dolly, a fifty-five-year-old former school principal in Britain, also "needed to do something that's *worthwhile*. That sounds really *pious*, doesn't it ... That's for me, never mind anyone that's on the receiving end. That's trying to be honest about it. It actually fulfills something in me. I only feel half a person if that's not happening."

Although "push" and "pull" factors intermingle in every woman's life, my research participants tended to stress what pushed them to development work in Gilgit. Some women were unable to find well-paid jobs at home. In Evelyn's words, they came "chasing money." But this job offered Evelyn more than an income: "I'm a bigger fish in this small pond than I was at home. I found that my career there was nose-diving ... Discretionary money and consultancies were drying up. It was impossible [to find that work] anymore. So *here* I revived my career." Other women were fleeing an empty nest. Troubling family relations, including divorces, elderly parent nursing responsibilities, and bereavements compelled several others to leave home.

Becoming more self-reliant and assured fulfills one of my participants' common "emancipation aspirations," mentioned in most of their departure stories. These aspirations, which they attempt to fulfill through global travel and development work, include an urge to escape dull lives, a quest for self-reliance and self-determination, and a desire to prove themselves strong, independent, and liberated. Janet concludes that her experiences in Gilgit have improved her preparedness for old age: "If I've had an experience of having just *physically* survived here, it brings me into a slightly more confident old age in Britain ... I had hoped that as an outcome that I would be a *stronger* and less *fearful* old lady, going into old age knowing that you can cope with things and not be fearful." Gaining confidence through her work abroad has helped Dolly to escape an increasingly dull life at home: "I don't think I can settle back in the UK. It's just not enough ... I think I need the variety ... I don't know what's missing there. I've outgrown those experiences ... I wouldn't be satisfied to go back to that. But I'd quite like to go and see what's around a few more corners, now that I've got more experience of travelling and more confidence about travelling with VSO." Rosemary's desire for a life change pushed her into travel. She thinks that "probably I was looking for a total change. My kids are grown and independent, and I'd had enough of my job ... It was quite the life in Canada, and I didn't need to be there anymore. So I was very open for something different, and this place is affordable on what I've got." Travelling abroad to do development work seems not to be solely an altruistic venture for Western women in Gilgit but also, as it was in the colonial era, a means for metropolitan women dissatisfied with their lives to constitute themselves as full, independent, and authoritative individuals and thus achieve some sense of autonomy (George 1994; Ghose 1998; Kaplan 1997; Knapman 1986; Sharpe 1993; Ware 1992).

James Buzard (1993) argues that the function of travel for Europeans in the colonial era was to realize a fuller sense of Self. Janet Wolff (1993) supports my conclusion that this is still the case, especially for women who historically have had a marginal relationship to travel. The requirements of femininity involve sticking close to home, thus making travel a masculine activity. By choosing to leave home, Western women in Gilgit disrupt discourses of femininity related to travel and thereby enhance their self-definition as independent individuals. Their individualistic strategies of escape through travel enact a discourse of autonomy by initiating a form of gender power for women: entering a global world enables them to transgress gender norms at home, to shape a self-confident, somewhat elitist feminine identity, and to gain some sense of control over their lives. The feelings of independence and confidence Western women achieve from travelling help them to realize other, more autonomous, selves.

Liberated Self/Oppressed Other

When a crowing rooster interrupted our interview, Amanda shouted, "I want to kill that rooster! Every morning he wakes me up at six ... He struts around the garden, he's the boss, and all the girl hens follow behind him. Yeah, it's like the [local] women here [laughs]." By naturalizing Gilgiti women as a group of subjected followers, Amanda perpetuates two interrelated discourses of Orientalism (Said 1978) that objectify and homogenize Muslim women as an oppressed mass. She also implies that it is only Muslim women who follow. According to the Orientalist beliefs prevalent among most of my research participants, local Muslim women are radically different from Western women. "Liberated" Westerners usually contrast themselves favourably with "oppressed" Muslims. This liberated/oppressed dichotomy extends to related oppositions: progressive/traditional, uncovered/veiled, free to travel and work/confined by purdah and the veil, independent/dependent, active/passive, unique/undifferentiated.

Without prompting, almost all of my research participants painted fairly uniform portraits of Gilgiti women in our interviews based on assumed knowledge of local women's everyday lives. As Amanda, a thirty-seven-year-old Dutch teacher, proceeded to discuss her maidservants' various health-related ailments, she launched into a more extended description of local women's putatively onerous lives: "Here the women are always suffering. They give too many children birth. And they let men handle them like weak people. That's their lot. They can't be seen or heard. That's a big problem here for me, the plight of Pakistani women." Local women's apparent lack of agency to fight their "lot" is almost as bluntly represented by twenty-six-year-old Andy, who was "brought up in the UK to know that I did have a say and that I could say 'No!' to [men]. And I think women here *don't* have that. When my girlfriends were visiting, we were talking about women here who don't even know they have the right to say 'No.' Is it abuse, or is it rape? Probably not, it's just *life* here."

While I did not ask specific questions about local women during interviews, I did ask research participants to describe themselves for me. And when they did, as some of their comments show, they almost always characterized themselves as "free" Western women who contrast favourably with local women. Marion thinks that "what [local women] envy about us is our independence, our ability to live alone and to make our own decisions, to make our own money. I point out to them that there can be *too much* independence and that people can become very lonely and very isolated, but they, of course, like everybody else, can only see good in what they don't have yet." As a notable exception, Anguita, who is not a development worker and did not go to Pakistan for putatively philanthropic reasons, tells a story that counters this notion that Western women live free of oppression. She does not "know what a bad experience is in Pakistan. I certainly had worse experiences in Europe. When I was young, I was raped in Yugoslavia because I was hitching. And I had a bad story once in Spain. If I bothered to look at it, I had more cases of abuse in the West than I've had in Pakistan."

While many Western women hope to enable the emancipation of Gilgiti women, Evelyn, in her usual pithy manner, contrasts herself with missionary NGO women who "convert" by example: "One of the things for these Christian women is to know that they could be playing this game for the rest of their lives. I'm going to leave, and I will probably hurt some people's feelings, but luckily they won't have to *see me around* [laughs]. I hope they can forget about me." Evelyn's effort to distance herself from other women's conversion activities destabilizes dominant beliefs about

Western women's superiority and shows that not all Western women agree about the best way to go about empowering Gilgiti women or making them anew. But most of my research participants see both their emancipated selves and their development work as sources of inspiration and redemption for Muslim Gilgiti women. For instance, Andy believes that "you can't solve the world's problems. You can't fight all the battles. And I prefer, in a way, to work at empowering local women to do it themselves. But I sometimes make a point of walking through the bazaar wearing a T-shirt and pants, because if I don't no [local woman] will ever be able to." Using an ethnocentric logic, Andy seems to assume that local women want to dress as Western women do but are prohibited.

The identity binary liberated/oppressed leads most of these Western women to overlook characteristics, events, and situations they have in common with local women. The freedom of Western women thus relies, in part, on demonstrating their cultural and racial superiority over local women. Andy, like some Western women in colonial India, did become acquainted with well-educated, wealthy local women who are fluent English speakers (Jolly 1993). But even her closest acquaintance of this type cannot satisfy her desire for intellectual conversations: "This is a horrible thing to say, but ... down-country Pakistani women, their education is so much less effective than the men's here that even the most educated women don't argue even on the same level as the men. They don't want to talk about the same things [I do]. Amina next door, she has her MBA from abroad and everything, but in terms of potential for challenging conversation — maybe about *clothes*."

Margaret stresses even more forcefully the lack of intellectual connections she has with local women. Her "friendships here [with local women] only go *so far*. Intellectually, people aren't stupid here, but we [Westerners] are light-years ahead [of them]. We're on a completely different planet ... You don't realize how *skilled* you are [until you], live and work here." Evelyn more subtly describes why she is reluctant to cultivate relationships with local women outside her workplace: "I see local women at work, but I don't see local women socially very much at all, and it's not because I don't like them. It's because I don't want to use my discretionary time that way to be truthful ... Language is not always a barrier. It's disposable time, and also feeling that a [visit] would be a very formal, lovely thing, but it wouldn't give me what it is I need in terms of intellectual connections." These quotations may suggest that my research participants feel discomforted by the prospect of being like local women. An unbearable likeness of being might undermine their sense of racial and cultural superiority, which is perpetuated as they draw on discourses of race to claim intellectual capacities, independence, and imperial authority.

While my research participants are ambivalently Orientalist at times, as Anguita's and Evelyn's comments show, they most often see local Muslim women as radically different from Western women. Thus, by viewing local women through an imperial lens as "oppressed," they can perceive themselves as "free" and autonomous. In this way, Gilgiti women are appropriated and codified through lingering, although ever-shifting, imperial discourses that are exercised and enabled in the contemporary world through international development processes. And in the process, discourses of Orientalism — particularly the notion that Western women, due to their autonomy, are superior to Muslim women (Mohanty 1984) — are perpetuated. Specific Orientalist practices also have troubling racist implications. For example, when Western women purposefully avoid interacting with Gilgiti women, presume they have nothing to learn from these "intellectually underdeveloped" women, and impose their cultural norms and practices on "ineffectual" locals, they reproduce oppressive discourses of race and the "Orient." These discourses in turn reinforce the notion that the two communities of women are radically different and hierarchically arranged.

Developing Community

Development work is understood by most Western women in Gilgit as philanthropic activity as well as a sign both of their freedom to travel as independent subjects and of their intellectual and cultural supremacy over Gilgiti women. Discourses of race that sustain the representation of Western women as liberated and advanced subjects in the world of work are once again employed by my research participants to differentiate themselves from local women. But once these discourses become enmeshed in "benevolent" practices of development meant to "improve" local people and socio-cultural systems, some of my research participants also (re-)enact imperial power relations.

Teaching abroad empowers Western women by increasing their knowledge, specialization, and experience, which can translate into professional advancement, work autonomy, and pay increases once they return to the West. Working overseas in educational development also allows them, like their colonial counterparts, to realize their intellectual potential, to find more fulfilling work immediately, to travel, and to garner some authority (Ware 1992). Most Western women in Gilgit are involved in the nurturing field of education, which also remains one of the few normatively appropriate professions for local women. But the gendered nature of their work is affected by the authority they gain by training mostly male teachers, by being Western educated, and by thinking of themselves — in contrast to local women — as independent and smart enough to do the work, and representing that work as an essential cultural "improvement" project.

Most of my research participants, like Julia, claim that they would not be in Gilgit, could not exist there, if it were not for satisfying development work: "Work is *so much* [of] your life here. There's no other reason to be here. So that's where people's focus is, why they come here, to get a certain *achievement* out of their job." Western women travel to Gilgit because of their development work, and the sense of achievement they experience through it helps them to develop a sense of themselves as confident, capable, and worthwhile people in various spheres of life. If Margaret "wasn't working, I don't think I'd stay, I'll be quite honest ... You're donating two years of your life, so you don't want to waste valuable work time." Rosemary works "because I believe in what I'm doing, and I need something to do ... You *need* to work for yourself, to keep you in action and elevate your mood ... It's a mental *survival* thing, it's not just financial ... I also want to contribute, especially with *women's* issues. But I would *never* not work." These quotations demonstrate that Western women in Gilgit understand their development work primarily as a means to gain a sense of themselves as capable, valuable women who earn money and make cultural improvements.

Rosemary also alludes to how work fulfills her philanthropic aspirations for local cultural change as well as her search for personal and professional development. Interweaving benevolent and professional facets of Self, Louise thinks that, "professionally, work's the most meaningful thing in life here. I do observations of teachers, and to look back at them it's lovely to see that they've actually changed because of something I've done." Janet is also satisfied to shape a legacy as a cultural benefactor: "This whole crowd of people I *know* have benefited from the service I have helped to provide. And there's this [local] colleague who's *grown* in stature and assurance and competence. That's not a bad legacy." While Christine downplays the personally satisfying aspects of work, she takes the "improvement" part of her job seriously: "I pointed out [to the teachers I train] that I was here to do a *job,* and the way we worked in the West was that you took your job *seriously*. I was here to do something, not just to drink tea with them and have a laugh all the time. Obviously, I tried to make training as light-hearted as I can, but, at the end of the day, they're to do a job, and I'm here to train them to do it better." By stressing her superior leadership, Christine contrasts herself — an independent, competent British woman with a good education and important work responsibilities — with local teachers who are represented as professionally uncommitted rather than as individuals who work according to a different set of values and a different understanding of an appropriate home/work balance.

Western educators feel driven to "develop" as many facets of local education as possible, bringing them in line with Western standards and methodologies. Conforming to an ethnocentric logic, they try to "improve" local teaching and learning styles, teachers' fluency in English, math, and science, the dominant work ethic, classroom discipline, school management and schedules, standards of hygiene at schools and in local homes, and the status of local women through educational initiatives to meet a "higher-quality" Western standard. They also strive to promote educational content that is cosmopolitan in perspective but still meets the needs of people whose culture, geographical location, and unwritten first languages are not addressed in government-issue textbooks.

Most of my research participants believe these changes are valuable and welcomed by local people. When they learn otherwise, the sense of autonomy they gain through development work may be unsettled. Jane, a forty-year-old teacher, reflects that "you have these ideas back in the UK that you're going to be able to do something and really make a difference to people's lives. And, yes, there has been a lot of that, but we hadn't realized that there'd be opposition from *within* communities. Who would guess ... people are not sure they really want our education and have misgivings about what it might do to the structure of society?" Ignoring the limited scope of many educational curricula in the West, Lyn also believes her teaching initiatives can improve local education and local culture by extension: "One of the *biggest* problems is this incredibly *narrow* education they have. Ask somebody where Canada is, and they won't have a clue. They have no concept of anything. And the biggest shock to me was that they don't *want* to know ... So better education comes first, and I think through education that would flow to the culture more generally. We *have* to free up the girls." Using the same ethnocentric logic that assumes locals do and know nothing, Rose, a fifty-four-year-old Dutch teacher trainer, finds the local work ethic "*unbelievable* ... It's nice [for teachers] to have this salary, but no one worries about work … About maths they know nothing. They even can't teach in Urdu … I can only show them how to do everything, giving demonstrations. Yeah, and basic things … like washing their hands and bringing a notebook … These teachers don't know how to do this … I hope my example will work." To summarize, the goal of educational development in Gilgit, according to most of the Western women who teach there, is personal, cultural, and societal advancement.

By drawing on this sense of themselves as improving philanthropists, which incorporates discourses of gender and race derived from imperialism, my research participants construct liberated and authoritative, yet nurturing, identities as they do their development work. The caring work of teaching becomes more fulfilling for Western women in this context as they enlist authoritative discourses of race and imperialism to temper the gendered nature of the work they do. Development work thus helps to constitute and confirm their identities as autonomous and superior metropolitan women. And the notion that local women are not allowed to do this work, or do it poorly, substantiates this construction of Self. For example, Joan told me that "there are only two or three professional women that I know here who have jobs that bring in money. And they say to their families, 'I have a full-time job, I'm having children. I'm prepared to peel potatoes, make the *chapatti,* but I will not maintain animals or go to the fields.' They're creating a different work role for themselves, … but these are very small beginnings." As I have shown, my research participants usually depict local women as economically dependent house servants with limited spatial mobility. Therefore, they believe that local women rarely obtain the education necessary to teach, the opportunity to land a job, and the time to do the work well, often despite what they see every day to the contrary.

In summary, what are the inferences that can be drawn from my research with these development workers in this setting? First, they forge a sense of community, personal autonomy, and professional empowerment through their social philanthropy. Second, and relatedly, "benevolent" development work serves to define and naturalize discursive differences between Gilgiti women who are ostensibly homebound, needy, and dull-witted and foreign women who are free to work abroad as capable benefactors. Discourses of gender and race derived from Orientalism intersect in the construction of these differences to reinforce an array of dominant binaries. Third, identity performances through "improving" work frequently enact imperial subjectivities and practices. Discourses of imperialism infuse their work: Western women often represent locals, in deeply patronizing ways, as unable to improve themselves. By denigrating most aspects of local education systems, they justify Western cultural intervention, especially in the lives of local women, as well as their "civilizing" mission. These dominant understandings have a long but fractured legacy in South Asia (Jolly 1993; Ramusack 1990; Spivak 1985), as do practices of social, cultural, and intellectual reform through white women's burden of education and health care (Ghose 1998; Jolly 1993; Ware 1992). While these authoritative practices and perceptions have always been contested by particular Westerners, and thus have shifted over time, they have been further unsettled by anti-racist discourses within contemporary feminist and multicultural movements that caution teachers against prejudiced, ethnocentric worldviews and activities, especially in the classroom. However, some Western women in Gilgit recuperate imperial practices of conversion when they try to mould local lives to fit a Western prototype and to impose metropolitan, yet ostensibly universally applicable, models, principles, behaviours, knowledge, and values through education — especially in the English language (Jayawardena 1995; Jayaweera 1990; Ramusack 1990).

Conclusion

My ethnographic case study of a transnational community of Western women development workers points to some of the contradictory impacts this community has on relations of power and autonomy in the local transcultural setting of Gilgit. These impacts occur as foreign women harness a range of global opportunities afforded by international development and the transnational cultural flows it facilitates to refashion lives and identities that secure greater degrees of self-determination. I propose that the discourse of autonomy organizes my research participants' desires for travel, their development work and philanthropic practices, and their constructions of Self and Other. They exercise intersecting discourses of autonomy and Orientalism in these instances to constitute themselves as free, independent, and authoritative individuals. These locally situated global processes usually enhance the autonomy of Western women development workers. But they also have negative and certainly unintended effects that compromise the contending autonomy of Muslim Gilgiti women in that these women are unable to realize an independent subjectivity in transcultural interactions with this community of Westerners due to imperial representations that suppress local women's heterogeneity, voices, and material realities.

My research participants' constructions of Self and Other seem not to be radically different from those exercised in the colonial era in South Asia as they recuperate racist, Orientalist, and imperial representations. In this instance, we can frame particular globalization and community-creating processes as disguised appropriations of identity that enable autonomy or, perhaps less subtly, as gendered and racialized forms of discursive violence. These contemporary processes are linked to past transcultural ventures in colonial South Asia but not as part of the pragmatic and diverse sets of practices used to establish and manage colonies abroad that we now call colonialism (Young 2001). Rather, they are elements of a lingering imperialism, a system of global social, economic, and cultural domination that operates from the metropolitan centre over ostensibly inferior subaltern populations without the agenda of political rule. Overt missionary conversion in the age of empire, for example, has a legacy in international development in that similar discourses organize their practices, but they are different global mechanisms with distinctive yet overlapping histories of global domination.

Considering this close articulation of globalization, community, and autonomy, I emphasize that community matters in globalization studies, especially in research that seeks to provide empirical evidence and analyses that can lead to the creation of more equitable global systems. As this chapter shows, community is a crucial discursive and material site for global struggles over cultural power and subjectivity. As I demonstrate, the effects of local community action in a global world cannot always be accurately predicted. Rather, the ambivalent and unintended consequences of Western women "performing" community, philanthropy, and self-determination in Gilgit show that globalization, as seen through the lens of contemporary development practice, can be risky for Othered communities and autonomies.

chapter 13   The Brotherhood of the
                    Rope: Commodification
                    and Contradiction in the
                    "Mountaineering Community"

Stephen Slemon

> *I have felt the rope between us. We are linked for life.*
> — Gaston Rébuffat, *Starlight and Storm*

ETYMOLOGICALLY, NOTES RAYMOND WILLIAMS, there is a fork in the
road to the concept of "community." One road — from the Latin *com-
munis,* meaning "fellowship, community of relations or feelings" *(Oxford
English Dictionary)* — leads to an intangible destination: "the quality of
holding something in common," "a sense of common identity and characteristics," as in a "community of interests" (Williams 1985, 75-6). The
other road — a faint one, Williams tells us, until the nineteenth century
— leads to something much more grounded: "the sense of immediacy or
locality," "a body of people organized into a political, municipal, or social unity" *(Oxford English Dictionary).* At some point, however, the second
road to "community" — the one that leads to a real group of individuals, cohabiting together, in one place and at one time — crosses over the
first. Inhabitants of a material, local community, Williams claims, are always
understood to be bound together by something "more immediate" than
the concept of "society." And so "community," notes Williams, comes to
occupy an unusual, indeed unique, location in the language of collectivist
nomenclature. "Unlike all other terms of social organization (*state, nation,
society,* etc.)," Williams observes, the concept of community "seems never
to be used unfavourably, and never to be given any positive opposing or
distinguishing terms" (ibid., 76). In the context of globalization and its

many contested autonomies, such an optimistic etymology appears to be positioned for some further elaboration.

My narrow interest in approaching the question of "community" via Williams' forking path is to provide a certain shaping to his provocative suggestion that community's two conceptual "tendencies" — "on the one hand the sense of direct common concern; on the other hand the materialization of various forms of common organization" (1985, 76) — necessarily result in a "difficult interaction." Williams' claim pertains to the definitional meaning of "community," but I hope to show that this "difficult interaction" must also be *lived* by community's inhabitants and that such interactions have genuine effects. At a broader level, my general purpose in this chapter is to suggest that this unquestioned positivity located within the concept of community requires substantial rethinking, at least in certain cases.

My test case here is a particular community — "the mountaineering community" — and my argument, in a nutshell, is that whatever else it may be doing, "community" — like "globalization," like "autonomy" — can also (to misquote Foucault) become "a violence we do to others." I suggest that the "difficult interaction" between (and these are not Williams' terms) the "grounded" and the "virtual" in the concept of community provides the seeding ground for this violence. I suggest that the notion of a grounded community affords a structure of unrealizable desire to the virtual community and that the virtual lends a structural alibi to the grounded. Mountaineering appears to be a radical expression of autonomy at the level of both the individual and the group. Such autonomy is achieved by a process of physical — and problematic — self-globalization. And so I proceed in this chapter on the assumption that "the mountaineering community," though in some obvious ways atypical of "community" as we commonly understand it, can nevertheless provide a useful locus for reading the problematic of globalization and autonomy in a more general sense. Like all instances of community in Williams' etymological sense, the mountaineering community inhabits a structure of constitutive contradiction. Mountaineering locates one of the ways in which powerful interests manage the contradictions of "community" in the interests of the profit motive and through the structural enablement of community's "opposing and distinguishing terms."

One can trace this structure of constitutive contradiction in the word *mountaineering* itself. The idea of "mountaineering" did not exist in Shakespeare's time, and neither did the word. Obviously, people did go up mountains for practical or spiritual reasons, and occasionally for the view,[1] but there is no record of any early human practice of climbing peaks by technically difficult routes for reasons of sport or style. The word *mountaineer,* however, was just coming into use in the early seventeenth century, and it is likely that Shakespeare coined it. The *Oxford English Dictionary* traces the first appearance of this word to *Cymbeline* (1609): a metropolitan dandy named Clotten calls Cymbeline's son Guiderius a "Rusticke Mountaineer," and the insult is thought sufficiently offensive to justify his beheading. The term *mountaineer* thus begins its linguistic life as a designation of both geographical distance and cultural difference between speaker and the designated individual. It is a term that characterizes someone who lives in the mountains — a location that is understood to be remote from the linguistic centre — and it comprises a form of identification that would not, unless ironically, be used as a designation of the Self. The mountaineer, at this moment of linguistic origin, is an Other.

The term begins its change in polarity — towards a form of self-identification — at the turn of the nineteenth century, when it is applied to those Romantics who "travel to mountains out of a spirit other than necessity" (Macfarlane 2003, 15). It achieves its rugged, self-heroizing meaning — the mountaineer as the epitome of the autonomous individual — in the middle of the nineteenth century, with "the invention of mountaineer*ing*" (Hansen 1995) as a specific form of organized and codified leisure activity. Though the original meaning of mountaineer — a designation of someone else, a "hillbilly" like Jed Clampett — will largely fade into obscurity, it remains, I think, a sedimentation in the conceptual apparatus of the contemporary mountaineer. This conceptual contradiction in the meaning of mountaineer — a "difficult interaction" between Self and Other — is an etymological allegory of what I now want to argue is the mountaineering community's structural dependence on something other than itself, a contingency on its autonomy, which continues to disturb.

"Mountaineering" as a form of self-identification, the name for "the action or sport of climbing mountains" *(Oxford English Dictionary),* is not only a relatively recent phenomenon — an "invention" by the British Victorians[2] — but also one that comprised itself within cultural, gendered, and class-specific limits. "Mountaineering" did not organize the way in which earlier scientific expeditions or Romantic travellers went into mountaineer regions. But in the 1850s, mountaineering became a distinct, coherent, and ultimately highly codified practice, and what made it so was the formation of a consolidated, organized, metropolitan, male-only, and middle-class community: the Alpine Club, formed in 1857, and centred in London, England. The Alpine Club was comprised primarily of "public school and Oxbridge educated" members, "academics, teachers and 'intellectuals'" (Robbins 1987, 585). Its declared objective was "to facilitate association among those who possess a similarity of taste, and to enable its members to make arrangements for meeting at some suitable locality whence they may in company undertake any of the more difficult mountain excursions ... The members will occasionally dine together" (Alpine Club 1857). The Alpine Club would not admit women until 1976.

It is hard to think of a more striking example of a grounded and localized "community of interest." The Alpine Club brought people together physically in one place in order to organize their individual and collective expeditions to the mountains and to foster a sense of mutuality and purpose in the men who practised mountaineering. The Alpine Club's first publication, a document entitled *Peaks, Passes, and Glaciers: A Series of Excursions by Members of the Alpine Club* (Ball 1859), speaks specifically of that "sense of common identity and characteristics" that Williams refers to as foundational to the concept of community, and it posits that sense of identity as arising from participation in a common kind of experience. "The community of taste and feeling," writes John Ball, the Alpine Club president, in his preface, "amongst those who in the life of the High Alps have shared the same enjoyments, the same labours, and the same dangers, constitutes a bond of sympathy stronger than many of those by which men are drawn into ... mutual feeling" (ibid., xi-xii).

The Alpine Club community was not only locally grounded but also self-globalizing. Expeditions to the Alps in the 1850s led to expeditions in the Caucasus Mountains in the 1860s (Hansen 1996) and thereafter to the Andes, the Rockies, and the Himalayas. Alpine Clubs were formed throughout Europe in the 1860s and 1870s; in New Zealand, the United States, and Canada in the 1890s and 1900s; in India and China in the 1930s and 1950s, respectively; and now exist in every place where money and interest conspire together. A discourse of shared experience, sentiment, and values, however, stays in the mountaineering community[3] long after mountaineering exceeds its singular association with the Alpine Club in London, and long after it goes global. At the funeral for George Mallory, the British mountaineer who perished on Mount Everest in 1926, the Bishop of Chester identified that discourse of sentiment as a brotherhood: "The lovers of the heights," he claimed, "are a brotherhood more intimate, more closely united, more affectionately disposed to one another than almost any other group of men" (Younghusband 1926, 244).

The picture that emerges from this assumption of intimate brotherhood is one of excessive group autonomy within a grounded community: the Alpine Club, and the ensuing mountaineering community that it will precipitate globally, are agential, self-knowing, full of purpose, and capable of extreme individual and team mobility. And yet the Alpine Club brotherhood was made possible by all kinds of contingencies, and they are important to my argument. One such contingency was a development in technology: "the extension of the railways through France to the Alps" (Robbins 1987, 586). This development, argues David Robbins, made it possible for British men in middle-class professions, men with relatively limited holiday time, to mountaineer in the Swiss or Austrian or Italian Alps and then to come promptly home — for mountaineering was an activity for amateurs with money.

Another contingency was the development of an Alps-based infrastructure for the management of tourists and travellers. Much of the documentation in the first three editions of *Peaks, Passes, and Glaciers,* and in the *Alpine Journal,* which followed from it, is given over to the discussion of the tariffs and per diems that ought to be given for Alpine, and later Himalayan, pack animals, porters, and guides. It hardly needs to be said that many of the heroic "first ascents," so proudly claimed in the *Alpine Journal* as evidence of mountaineering's onward advance, were in fact organized, enabled, and ultimately led by exactly those local inhabitants of mountainous areas — guides such as Michael Croz, who led Edmund Whymper to his famous first ascent of the Matterhorn — who in the earlier nomenclature would have been known as "rustic mountaineers."

A third contingency for the mountaineering community is a sociological one. Robbins notes that mountaineering came into existence as a distinct human practice in Victorian England at an uneasy point of intersection between "three different and potentially conflicting discourses or 'structures of feeling'": scientism (climbing for geographical and geological information, as was encouraged by the Royal Geographical Society), athleticism (mountaineering as a pure sport capable of affording "moral and physical improvements"), and Romanticism (mountaineering as "a means of penetrating to realities deeper than those encountered in everyday life") (1987, 587-93). There is an insuperably "difficult interaction" between these discourses: one cannot, for example, scientifically calculate altitude through boiling-point measurements for barometric pressure and at the same time experience Romantic awe in contemplation of the ineffable and mountainous Sublime. Mountaineering is therefore at some foundational level a deeply incoherent activity, but it is possible to see that the tension between these founding discourses also affords an enabling energy to mountaineering practice. Mountaineering could understand itself through all kinds of organizing motives, justify its activity through its affiliations with broader discursive movements, and define itself as a practice that took place at the nexus of debate between larger social forces.

A fourth structural contingency for mountaineering practice arises specifically from this structure of sociological overdetermination, and that is its overwhelming — indeed defining — dependency on the medium of print culture. As an activity within scientism, mountaineering needed a literature to sustain it: Robbins (1987, 586) argues that this is why the Alpine Club constituted itself as a learned society (like its sometimes rival, the Royal Geographical Society) and foregrounded scientific observation in the *Alpine Journal*. As a modality of sport — again, this is Robbins' finding — mountaineering became a competition acted out far from the playing field, with no immediate audience and no formalization of "the rules of the game": the *Alpine Journal* therefore did the work of providing the sport of mountaineering with its audience and its rules of engagement. It was the medium of publication, Robbins writes, that "established a climber's claim to a particular route" (ibid.). And as an exercise in Romantic feeling, mountaineering needed expression in a creative, poetic, and narrative literature. The preface to the second series of the Alpine Club's *Peaks, Passes, and Glaciers* shows just how thoroughly mountaineering derived its social force from readers "who had never been actors in adventures such as were narrated. The favour with which the First Series was received has encouraged the members of The Alpine Club again to endeavour to interest a wide circle of readers. The taste for these adventures is becoming more extended; the Club has doubled the number of its members" (Kennedy 1862, v).[4] From its beginnings, then, mountaineering constituted itself as foundationally — and these are Bruce Barcott's (1966, 65) words — "the most literary of all sports." The mountaineering community began as an excessively grounded and local community — a metropolitan club whose members travelled. But from the beginning, it was inseparably roped to a virtual community of readers.

A final set of contingencies arises from mountaineering's literary turn outward from its origins in male-only, club-based, white self-privilege. The literature of mountaineering draws consistently on military metaphors:

239

Charles Granville Bruce (1922) would title his book *The Assault on Mount Everest;* Sir John Hunt (1954) would call his *The Conquest of Everest;* Paul Bauer's (1937) is entitled *Himalayan Campaign: The German Attack on Kanchenjunga.* Mountaineering literature has retained and promulgated an inseparable association with nationalism. Lord Curzon once claimed that "the English being the first mountaineering race in the world, an Englishman ought to be the first on top of Kangchenjunga, and, if possible, of Everest also" (Hansen 1996, 62). James (Jan) Morris' book *Coronation Everest* (1958) is just one of the many literary documents that narrativizes mountaineering as a nationalist activity: it is a firsthand account of the intricate manipulations of timing and control of information that proved necessary to the coincident reporting of Hillary and Tenzing's "crowning glory" on Everest with the occasion of Queen Elizabaeth II's coronation as monarch of a resurgent British Empire (see Bayers 2003; Hansen 1996, 320; Slemon 1998). And mountaineering has consistently been narrativized as playing a socially symbolic role in the advancement of European imperialism. Hansen cites Victorian attempts to equate "the climbing spirit" with that "form of restless energy, that love of action for its own sake, of exploring the earth and subduing it, which has made England the colonizer of the world" (1995, 320). Walt Unsworth (1989, 141) reports this from the *Morning Post:* "The spirit which animated the attacks on Everest is the same as that which ... led to the formation of the Empire itself." No wonder that mountaineering has been one of the organizing themes in publications like the *Boy's Own Paper* (from 1879 onward) and continues to inform male self-fashioning in popular representations (think of Sylvester Stallone in *Cliffhanger* or Tom Cruise in *Mission Impossible II*).

It goes without saying that Victorian women climbed mountains by technical means and that women have climbed and continue to climb mountains at the highest levels of mountaineering attainment. PearlAnn Reichwein and Karen Fox (2001) have demonstrated that Alpine Club formation in Canada is actually dependent on the laboured participation of women, and this finding is just one of the many pieces of evidence that document mountaineering's foundational dependence on the participation of women from its earliest moments through its several globalizing turns. It also goes without saying that many, and possibly most, of the world's top climbers have come from the other side of the European colonial divide: the Nepalese high-altitude "sherpa," Apa Sherpa, for example, has "scaled Mount Everest a record of 16 times," this while carrying gear and oxygen for paying clients and guiding them to the top (*Taipei Times* 2006). But as a form of self-identification that takes its beginnings within cultural and gender-specific boundaries — European, middle-class, masculist, nationalist, imperialist — and as a social collective that seeks to disavow its structural contingency on technology, on discursive overdetermination, on print, on the presence and participation of a virtual audience of readers, and on the enabling labour of women and cultural Others, the mountaineering community has presented itself as something inherently resistant to inclusivity, to mutuality, and to outreach. It has manifested itself as a "brotherhood": something inherently difficult for Others — non-whites, women, readers — to fully identify with. My argument for this chapter, in a nutshell, is that this overdetermined structure of the mountaineering community as comprising both a grounded and a virtual constituency, and of mountaineering as a practice that is radically dependent on some Other that is innate to the community but necessarily disavowed, has real implications for the autonomy of individuals and communities across the spectrum of globalization's economic divide. Mountaineering's difficult interaction is ultimately a lived one, especially now in this contemporary moment of its communal globalization.

Signs of this "difficult interaction" are everywhere. The exemplary representative of this community — an amateur in Victorian times, like Virginia Woolf's bookish father Leslie Stephens — has morphed into a highly singularized, commercially sponsored, full-time professional climber whose accomplishments rise to a level of athleticism and risk that are light-years beyond the reach of almost all members of mountaineering's larger, virtual community. Mountaineering's various but integrated skill sets — large-group expedition activity, alpinism, ice climbing, mixed climbing, bouldering, rock climbing, ski touring, and so on — have fractured into professionalized, non-associational singularity, each now with its own separate literature and each with its own gear industry. A great deal of contemporary mountaineering activity now takes place far from actual mountains, much of it in that paradigmatic figure of contemporary alpine dissociation: the indoor climbing gym. Dependency on guiding services — always normative in mountaineering, though always disavowed — has become hyperactive and defining to climbing practice: the current rate for participation in a Mount Everest expedition, with a top-level professional guiding company, is US$60,000 (see Adventure Consultants website). The rise in gym climbing, and in "client" mountaineering, has effected a radical split between mountaineering's inner brotherhood and its virtual community inclusion seekers: "high alpinism has become tourism and show," claimed Reinhold Messner in 2004-5. "Mountaineering is over and alpinism is dead." This nostalgia for lost mountaineering presence within the brotherhood speaks in many voices: one of them is a radical disavowal of outward connectedness to, and contingency with, the virtual community of non-professional mountaineering participants. "Our climbing partnership, while it joined us and drew us nearer to others who had entered into similar brotherhoods," writes Mark Twight, "also separated us from climbers that did not resonate on the same plane. We brothers could only speak among ourselves" (2004, 55).

The professionalization of mountaineering's inner brotherhood has also intensified the representational distortion of mountaineering's masculist representational landscape, to use Susan Frohlick's metaphor and term, and rendered it fully "hypermasculine." Frohlick claims that mountaineering has always masculinized the terrain of "unmarked physicality" in climbing, so that all non-masculine participants and achievements (however they are conceived) need to be marked, and made separate, as feminine — for example, first "female ascent" (2000, 99-101). But in the contemporary global moment, mountaineering's masculism has become so excessive that even exemplary mountaineering individuals (such as Alison Hargreaves, the first climber to solo all six classic north faces of the Alps in a single season) are consistently represented as structurally egregious to the mountaineering brotherhood — when they are also women. "Our Brotherhood values courage over technique," continued Twight in his 2004 article, "because we believe that the risk of death is a necessary component of spiritual growth" (55). When Mallory, a father of three, died on Everest in 1926, his death was registered as a triumph of the human spirit, as well as a national tragedy. When Hargreaves died on K2 in 1995, her death provoked furious debate within the mountaineering community over her perceived "selfishness," her "self-serving" nature, and her temperamental irresponsibility, and this because she was a mother of two (see Rose and Douglas 1999).

"Mountaineering" in the global present can no longer coincide with "mountaineering" as a historical category of practice and self-identification. And mountaineering's virtual community — those who approach the brotherhood primarily through reading and viewing — can no longer coincide with the brotherhood of the rope. The idea of a unified mountaineering community still circulates widely in globalization's virtual present, but it circulates primarily as a *desire* for a coherence that is nevertheless understood to exist in no one place and to comprise no specific people. Run a phrase search in Google on "the mountaineering community" and you'll be taken to sites that explain how a particular climbing accident, or an environmental problem, or an ethics debate, or a climbing style controversy is being registered across a geographically dispersed collective. In almost every case, the mountaineering "community" will be understood as a projected "community of interests" whose locality is purely oppositional: it is not "the general public." One cannot join such a community except through virtual forms of upward mobility. One joins it through commodity fetishization — by literally buying in.

And the buy-in is ubiquitous. Mountaineering literature has become big business, with its own specialist publishers, shops, magazines, and festivals across Europe, Australasia, and North America. Recent television commercials have employed a mountaineering backdrop to sell beer, cars, home insurance, and acceptance into the US Marines. Schoolchildren regularly follow mountaineering expeditions through corporate-sponsored, Weblog hook-ups — Global SchoolNet's "KidsPeak," which followed expedition client Sandy Hill Pitman on Everest in 1996, was one of the first in this new pedagogical movement. Mountaineering now plays a cornerstone role in the growing industry of corporate "motivational presentations." Byron Smith, for example, draws on "parallels between his Everest 2000 Expedition and his proven business processes" to provide "an essential and universal strategy for setting and achieving goals" (see Byron Smith website). The University of Pennsylvania's Wharton Center for Leadership and Change Management organizes an annual Wharton Leadership Trek to Mount Everest to teach that "mountain climbers, like the mountains they climb, hold a central place in modern business and society." Mountaineers, claims the Wharton group website, comprise "a paradigm for how individuals striving for a goal can achieve what others label impossible." This global turn to the mountaineering buy-in also accounts, at least in part, for the extraordinary expansion of Canada's "largest supplier of quality outdoor equipment," Mountain Equipment Co-op (MEC): an idea "conceived in 1971 within the cozy confines of a storm-battered tent," according to the website, and now a "vibrant retail co-operative" with "stores across Canada" and "more than two million members in 192 countries." MEC positions itself as an entry point into the mountaineering community at every level of corporate self-representation. "We are a member-owned co-operative striving for social and environmental leadership," claims the website. "Mountain Equipment Co-op provides quality products and services for self-propelled wilderness-oriented recreation, such as hiking and mountaineering, at the lowest reasonable price." In doing background research for this chapter, I e-mailed the following question to an informed MEC staff member: "What percentage of MEC's total sales actually pertain to mountaineering?" The answer I received was this: "I feel it would be in the low single digits. We sell thousands more Trembant down jackets for people braving the ... winters than we do as an exclusive belay jacket. The amount of mountaineering boots we sell per winter can be counted on fingers and toes."[5]

And so the mountaineering community, once generally capable of disavowing its foundational contingencies, once thus imaginable as fully grounded and radically autonomous, has globalized itself into an amorphous zone of consumption. The mountaineering community has become a place where images, words, and goods circulate in unfulfillable fetishization of that commonality of sentiment, inclusion, and participatory belonging that gives community, in Williams' sense, its unopposed and unquestioned positivity. This transformation may appear to resemble the sociological understanding that energizes a certain kind of anti-globalization critique (though significantly not in this volume): the loss of "real" community autonomy under the forces of rampant globalization. My argument, however, has been that the mountaineering community's present configuration as "a fearful sphere, whose centre is everywhere and whose circumference is nowhere," to use Jorge Luis Borges' words (1962), is in fact a logical fulfillment of its foundational "difficult interaction" between grounded and virtual constituencies, one that is now being managed by the profit-taking motive, against the possibility of a community made whole.

The implications for autonomy are global ones. They pertain to the consumers of mountaineering fetishes — books, magazines, films, gear — who buy unstoppably into the virtual because they can never find a grounded entrance to the community that calls out. They pertain to those many mountaineers who climb for love of the activity but find the idea of a mountaineering "community" bewildering, and distant from themselves. They pertain to national control over "parks and wilderness" regions — under increased international and market pressure, for example, Nepal in 2001 "removed the necessity" for a liaison officer to accompany foreign expeditions on peaks below 6,500 metres (see Risk Online website). And they pertain to the environment. Everest, for example, despite recent cleanup attempts, remains "strewn with garbage" from Base Camp to summit (see World Tibet Network News website). And Gore-Tex, the soul of modern mountaineering clothing, is made from PFCs — "notorious, global chemical contaminants" that "contaminate human blood and wildlife the world over" (Environmental Working Group website). A distinguishing feature of PFCs — mountaineering's most persistent but invisible contingency at this contemporary moment of self-fashioning — is that they are completely resistant to biodegration. They circulate endlessly through our planet, and they never go away.[6]

chapter 14   **Why Community Matters**

Diana Brydon

Community is at the heart of many of the concerns and opportunities associated with globalizing processes. While traditional forms of community, especially those derived from a special relation to place and the physical proximity of neighbours, may seem to be threatened by global movements of peoples and the opportunities for developing virtual connections across distances afforded by the Internet, such changes also offer new ways of developing and expanding community. Place and face-to-face contact remain important components of community, but they no longer function exclusively in shaping trust and solidarity in the experience of increasing numbers of people. To what extent opportunities for proliferating membership in a range of communities enable individual and community autonomy remains in many instances an open question. Such enabling, however, is clearly what remains at stake in the formation of any viable community. Collectively, as well as individually, people require the power to define and represent themselves and determine their futures.

Communities are changing in response to globalizing pressures on the ways we live and work together and in response to the opportunities for expanded socializing and networking afforded by technological innovation. With a decline in the role of the social welfare state in wealthier countries and the continued unavailability of social policies in poorer ones, new demands are being placed on community at the very moment its traditional forms appear to be threatened. Will the evolving forms of renegotiated community be able to meet such demands? The jury is still out.

246

There is a clear need, however, to situate such questioning by paying full attention to the particular circumstances of each community. What works in one situation might not work in another. It is not possible to generalize about community in ways that might seem to be universally applicable or to define community without attending to the importance of emotive ties in sustaining and directing communal actions. Many disciplines within the humanities and social sciences see community as central to the mandates of their research while they frame their investigations quite differently. Literary studies is interested in how communities represent themselves and how they are represented through discursive and mediating systems. Anthropology investigates the intimate relations between community and culture; sociology, the dynamic linking of community to other social structures such as organizations, class, and family; political studies, the power structures linking community, nation, citizenship, and state; geography, the connections linking place, space, and community; and history, their changing manifestations over time. A full understanding of community requires each of these approaches but also a rethinking of the assumptions on which they have been based.

New interdisciplines such as postcolonial and cultural studies seek to integrate these perspectives with renewed attention to the dynamics of ethnicity, gender, sexual orientation, citizenship, and race. With globalization, these clearly delimited areas of responsibility are becoming blurred. Each discipline and interdiscipline now finds itself concerned with changing attitudes to the power of story, the nature of legitimation, and recastings of definitions of citizenship as a mode of belonging and exclusion. Knowledge itself becomes at once both more important for economic survival and more fragile as changing values and needs lead to renewed questioning of established modes of knowing and the assumptions on which they are based. Conventional divisions of responsibility across the disciplines are now being challenged from within each discipline as well as from without. Consequently, many disciplines are beginning to question their boundaries and to recognize the need for more concentrated interdisciplinary inquiry. This book is our response to such challenges.

Our approach to community seeks to integrate more closely attention to the pragmatic needs of community in particular situations with the various philosophical resources on which thinking through the relation of community and autonomy might rely. In this volume, we test Gayatri Chakravorty Spivak's belief that, "if the humanities and social sciences supplement each other, interrupt each other productively, then the

247

production of knowledge will not be such a 'been-there-done-that' game" (Chakravorty, Milevska, and Barlow 2006, 128). If knowledge as conventionally constituted has a tendency to seek certitude and reaffirm familiarity, then it can find itself ill equipped to deal with the genuinely new or unfamiliar. Understanding of community appears to have reached this point. Established definitions appear to be inadequate now, while evolving definitions are testing our knowledge-making resources.

As a result, this volume does not aspire to be the last word on the complex interrelations of globalization, autonomy, and community but a posting from Canada on what we see as the current stakes engaged in thinking through the ever-changing dynamic of the autonomy-community relation in global contexts. It represents our contribution to a growing global dialogue about what it means to be together in particular places, including the virtual, under intensifying transplanetary connections. Because we see community as a process that is always under construction through negotiation within specific contexts, we are unwilling to provide the usual kind of summation in which definitions of globalization, autonomy, and community might be fixed. At the same time, our title stresses renegotiation because globalizing processes are interrupting, if not breaking fully with, earlier patterns of community formation and renewal. While communities have always involved negotiations over boundaries and membership to a greater or lesser extent, the current situation, as described by Habermas, in which globalization "splits the world in two and at the same time forces it to act cooperatively as a community of shared risks" (cited in Cheah 2006, 46), seems in many ways unprecedented. Our trust in negotiation reflects our faith in autonomy as the value best suited to enable self-determination through self-conscious reflection and discussion across differences.

To claim autonomy as a value, however, is not necessarily to endorse its conventional associations with the primacy of the sovereign individual. Autonomy itself requires renegotiation in the current moment. Our use of autonomy here tends to follow Brian Jacobs' (2001, 145) assertions that, "insofar as it is constituted through social relations, autonomy has no meaning apart from its employment in communicative practice," and that, "insofar as it is a historical concept, autonomy is always contingent upon specific conditions." Hence our focus on a variety of case studies that demonstrate the different ways in which autonomy may be understood, valued, and practised within different situations. This approach enables us to examine how "autonomy and relatedness function as interrelated affective qualities, and how they are in tension with one another" (Fajans 2006, 109). These two dimensions of the autonomy/community relation vary from one group or one circumstance to another. Recognizing this variance enables us to move away from thinking of autonomy as purely a Western concept and from confusing it with notions of absolute separateness.

Our case studies reclaim the distinctive value of *community* as a term for describing particular sets of social relations from its overuse and idealization within a range of discourses, without idealizing community either as a past now lost to modernity or as a solution to national or global problems. We conclude this book with Jean-Luc Nancy's proposition that "to say that community has not yet been thought is to say that it tries our thinking, and that it is not an object for it. And perhaps it does not have to become one" (1991, 26). It is no accident that community is trying our thinking at this particular time in the West. The crisis of Enlightenment thinking brought to the fore by twentieth- and twenty-first-century geno- cides and decolonizations has been exacerbated by neoliberal justifications of globalization, leading to a sustained rethinking of every type of com- munity, including the ideals of cosmopolitanism and hopes for a global community. To say that "community has not yet been thought" is to chal- lenge the foundations and assumptions of Western forms of knowledge construction, which have up to now claimed for themselves a monopoly in this area. To say that community is not an object for thinking and may not have to become one, however, is a notion more difficult to grasp. It challenges much of the common sense about communities that is shared across ideological divisions by many. Nonetheless, this is an insight that we take seriously in this volume. Rather than conceiving of community as an object to be identified and defined, we focus here on community as a process under situated and constant renegotiation. Such rethinking has practical consequences. As Craig Proulx (2003, 155) notes, for example, re- ferring to Aboriginal peoples in Canada, it enables wresting definitions of Aboriginal community from the grip of the "reserve community" model. Such a step permits paying greater attention to urban Aboriginal com- munities and the "politics of control of identity" so crucial to community definition (ibid., 161).

At such moments, it is possible to see the ways in which current philo- sophical debates connect to the everyday politics of community renegotia- tion. Two special journal issues, one dedicated to Nancy's philosophy (*Journal for Cultural Research* 2005) and the other to his contributions to philosophical investigations of community (*Culture Machine* 2006), note the ways in which his work "offers the possibility for rethinking the ontological, ethical, and political after the deconstruction of the metaphysics of subjectivity" (Coward 2005, 323) and opens "the concept of community onto a broader politico-ethical and cultural — but perhaps also ontologically more fundamental — context" (Glowacka 2006, 1). It may be that it is exactly this ontological focus and the "powerful critique of traditional metaphysical regimes of value" that Nancy provides that make it especially difficult to derive "a political program from his philosophical thought" (Coward 2005, 328), necessary as such a task appears to be. While accepting the need to hold the notion of community in question, we have focused here on how various self-defining communities actually function and negotiate their autonomy rather than theorizing ideal forms of community yet to come (the focus of work by Agamben and Nancy). We find Stella Gaon's (2005, 397) observation that what is at stake in texts by Nancy and Blanchot is "not *a* politics but rather an interrogation of the political" very useful. That commitment to interrogation lies at the heart of contemporary theorizations of autonomy because, as Ernst Tugendhat notes, where philosophers and their societies once believed that they could specify what might constitute the truly good life, "we have lost that certainty today. But the loss can also be a gain." Thrown back upon the knowledge of our ignorance, he suggests, "we can learn to value the fact that we can *raise the question* of what is truly good" (1986, 323). For many philosophers, the questions of what is truly good and how best it may be determined are at the heart of autonomy debates. In this volume, we raise that question through an interrogation of the ways in which globalization, community, place, and autonomy may be thought together.

Working across disciplines to produce this book has "tried" our thinking, in the sense evoked by Nancy, and we hope that in this best sense it will continue to try yours, dear reader, whoever and wherever you might be. All writing in our current times can be expected to reach a variety of readers so that shared understandings and values cannot be assumed. Academic books, while addressed to a narrower segment of readers, are not immune to this rule. The community of readers drawn to this book may well derive different understandings from it. We ourselves have engaged respectfully with the conventions of each other's disciplines, teaching ourselves to read each other's work through intensive workshop sessions on our chapters. Nonetheless, it took us some time to understand the different assumptions that underlay our approaches to our four key working terms and how they might be deployed to understand the changes that we were observing in our fieldwork and our reading. Those efforts continue. Our venture with this book was to produce an interdisciplinary investigation, through which we hope to cross conventionally drawn academic borders between the humanities and the social sciences in order to pull together and reorient insights generated from these different but related scholarly traditions. The effort required considerable goodwill, trust, and compromise. The real work of communicating across conceptual divides proved rewarding for our thinking and for the collective achievement of this book. Each of us has had our certainties challenged and has seen our horizons broadened. The work continues. Together we have gained a greater sense of what is involved in the daily struggles of many people locally and across the world, and we have become convinced of the necessity of interdisciplinary scholarly study to comprehend what these struggles mean for achieving autonomy and solidarity in a changing world system.

Our refusal to assume that community is in any way given has led us to choose for study a range of communities, from those most commonly recognized as such to those whose constitutions challenge conventional assumptions about the limits of the term. In particular, we have been interested in testing the limits of community in two main ways: (1) by examining certain communities that would conventionally be recognized as paradigmatic to determine how they are changing and reconstituting themselves; (2) by studying various collectivities that might be seen as straining community's usual parameters. Our interest lies in locating community around the questions raised for collective and individual autonomy in times when new transplanetary connections are growing while the imagined societies of many nation-states and state-nations are coming into question. These are times too when the places in which communities are renegotiated are criss-crossed by those transplanetary relations. While working with actually existing communities in fieldwork or archival contexts, we have drawn on many different sources for making sense of community today.

What we have produced is in no way exhaustive. Many different kinds of communities, including those considered to be of major importance in globalization studies, are not considered here. In particular, we realize that given more space it could have been valuable to pay more attention to diasporic communities and multiple conditions of labour, including migrant labour, as well as to the changing power dynamics around classed, gendered, sexualized, and racialized tensions within a variety of emergent community contexts, such as new religious movements, transnational activist movements, indigenous peoples' reclamations, fan communities of various types, global queer communities, and the many types of emergent communities being facilitated by new technologies. More studies of current efforts to instrumentalize community, from the ways in which arts groups have seized on Richard Florida's (2002) ideas about "creative communities" to state-sponsored efforts at community building and mobilization, are also required.[1]

From the beginning, we have seen our Canadian-based perspective as a virtue. We wanted to begin from a perspective grounded in the globally less known. This place for our work has enabled us to approach certain universalizing theories with some skepticism. It has required us to pay particular attention to Canada's position as a settler-invader state-nation and in many ways a complicit partner in empires old and new. At the same time, it has limited our ability, beyond a few case studies, to present perspectives on the dynamic interrelations of community and autonomy as enacted within contexts elsewhere. Some of the other volumes within this series, especially the one generated by our Tunisian team (Essid and Coleman, forthcoming) and the one dedicated to indigenous studies (Blaser et al., forthcoming), go some way toward remedying this absence here. Nonetheless, much more work must be done before notions of the global can address with due respect and reciprocity the perspectives of many of the world's disenfranchised beings.

Throughout this book, we have insisted on the importance of the contingent and the particular. We do not share the belief, often attributed to Jürgen Habermas, that there can be an "ideal communication community" from which might be extrapolated a set of rational and universal principles (Kalyvas 2001, 4). Instead, we locate community in the contingent practices of everyday involvements in which reason and emotion are not so easily separated. Similarly, if Andreas Kalyvas is correct in arguing that "for Habermas political autonomy refers to the rational testing of the validity of social and political norms and not to their creation" (ibid., 6), then we share his discontent with such a limitation. While we understand the interest within certain fields, such as criminology, in studying how globalization affects the power of communal norms in regulating individual behaviour (see Keenan 2007), neither testing nor enforcing communal norms has engaged our interest here. We opt instead for a view of autonomy as potentially involving the creative and instituting dimensions of the imagination as theorized by a range of critics from Arjun Appadurai (2000, 2006b) to Cornelius Castoriadis (1991).

Many contemporary evocations of community are haunted by Donna Haraway's lament (1997, 264) that "I am sick to death of bonding through kinship and 'the family,' and I long for models of solidarity and human unity and difference rooted in friendship, work, partially shared purposes, intractable collective pain, inescapable mortality, and persistent hope." These alternative grounds on which human sociality might be built and extended in less violent and repressive ways have engaged us here and remain to be explored more fully, in practice and in theory. The extensive work currently devoted to alternative theories and practices of self-reflexivity and to constructions and presentations of the Self carry as yet undetermined implications for how autonomy might be reconfigured from its sources in a certain type of "possessive individualism" (Macpherson 1962) and its current neoliberal deformations. In this book, our focus has been primarily directed toward examples of communal autonomy, with much less attention paid to the category of the Self. One of the conclusions that has emerged for us from this work, however, is the necessity of paying more attention to the models of the person, the individual, and the subject that generate specific understandings of autonomy as well as communal practices and expectations. Theorizations of singularity carry major implications for the reorientation of how we understand autonomy and the kinds of communal structures that it can imagine and create. Similarly, theorizations of multitude and "forms of being-in-common that interrupt the myth of community" (Matteo 2005, 322) continue to "try" our thinking about communal autonomy and the many ways in which it confronts and creates globalization.

The pragmatically oriented research questions that first animated our project have led us to underplay explicit engagement with some of the more philosophical questions that concern postmodern theory, such as Nancy's meditations in *The Inoperative Community* (1991) and *The Creation of the World or Globalization* (2007) and Agamben's rethinking of the Nazi heritage in *Homo Sacer: Sovereign Power and Bare Life* (1998) and his cryptic study *The Coming Community* (1993). Nonetheless, our investigations confirm Nancy and Agamben's suspicion of what Nancy (1991, 10) terms "the retrospective consciousness of the lost community and its identity." This suspicion sharply distinguishes their work from the assumptions about individual and community that govern the thinking of critics such as Zygmunt Bauman (2001) and Anthony Giddens (2000) who see globalization as problematically destructive of traditional community. Our research reinforces suggestions by Nancy that the Christian and Fascist notions of a lost community characterized by fusion and communion must be contested if other ways of imagining "being in common" (1991, xxxvii) are to be elaborated. Although chapters on indigenous communities by Russell,

Mulrennan, and Preston may most explicitly reinforce this point, none of our chapters present globalization as uniformly destructive of communal values, nor do their authors associate community with lost or dying traditions from the past. Our view of modernity and its globalizing pressures finds more complex processes at work.

Agamben's (1998) analysis of the relations of sovereign power and "bare life" as they are exemplified in the phenomenon of the concentration camp and the notion of what he terms *homo sacer,* the life that can be killed without being sacrificed, carries profound implications for understanding such contemporary responses to global terror as extraordinary rendition, changing public tolerance for torture, and the proliferation of refugee camps and zones of exception such as Guantanamo Bay. These global developments force rethinking of the foundations of human and political communities and the scope for exercising autonomy within them. In *Homo Sacer* (1998, 8), Agamben relocates "the fundamental categorical pair of Western politics" from that of "friend/enemy" to "that of bare life/political existence, *zoë/bios,* exclusion/inclusion," arguing that "every attempt to ground political communities in something like a 'belonging' whether it be founded on popular, national, religious, or any other identity" (ibid., 181) must now be thrown into question.

The implications of theorizing political community through these renegotiated terms have yet to be fully worked through. While political community as such has not been our central focus here, we agree that belonging is a concept that requires further attention. For most people today, our research suggests, belonging remains a valued and necessary concept for negotiating the risks associated with daily life. Belonging is being reconfigured for many, finding its strongest manifestations at levels below and beyond that of the nation-state. For some, the challenges posed to belonging by the mix of proximate, whether local or transplanetary, social relations may lead to consolidation of older configurations of community and resistance to the new, while for others the loss of certainty is not a negative but an opportunity for increased autonomy. For some, such as Elspeth Probyn (1996, 22), Agamben's thinking moves the concept of belonging beyond "an ontology of belonging based in the individual possession of an intrinsic quality," enabling her to distinguish more finely between "specificity," which refers to "possible forms of belonging: being lesbian, being Welsh," and "singularity," which marks "the ways in which the general becomes realized by individuals as singular." Her *Outside Belongings* identifies a "wanting to belong" that is "fueled by yearning rather than the positing of identity as a stable state" (ibid., 19). As opportunities for communities of affiliation proliferate, belonging may lose some of its exclusive characteristics and more violent dimensions, moving "away from thinking and living difference and specificity as negative" and instead, as Probyn sees it, "conceiving specificity as the ground from where we move into the positivity of singularity" (ibid., 23).

We insist, with Probyn, that we must always remember that these opportunities are being taken up in particular places that shape the directions that they take. The interplay in Probyn's text between her theoretical engagements with these questions and her lived experience in Montreal, which for her "embodies a constant inbetweenness" (1996, 26), demonstrates what Probyn describes as her "engagement with where I live and how I wish to be able to live" (ibid., 153): "Where I live" is the place of community. "How I wish to be able to live" is the domain of autonomy. Such an interplay of engagements, while indebted to place, is not fixed by place. For Probyn, it is not ironic that a book intensely engaged with Montreal should end with her relocation to Sydney, Australia. Rather, she finds in her "transversal move" an indication of the "rhizomatic roots" that mark the matted "outside belongings" that strike her as characteristic of a period in which global and local engagements need not be seen as contradictory (ibid., 156).

For each of these thinkers, theories of the Self and the community are intertwined. Engaging with the work of Bataille, Nancy (1991, 23) suggests that, "for Bataille, as for us all, a thinking of the subject thwarts a thinking of community." As we have stressed throughout this volume, how autonomy is understood depends on how the person is theorized, whether that be as subject, self, individual, or singularity. To think of the subject in either liberal or neoliberal terms is to thwart the kind of thinking of community that Nancy desires. This notion of the subject is indebted to Foucault's description of "subjectification," picked up by Agamben (1998, 119), as those modern processes leading the individual to "objectify his own self, constituting himself as a subject and, at the same time, binding himself to a power of external control." Nancy identifies globalization, and the ecotechnology that he sees characterizing it, as revealing not only "a vanishing of the possibilities of forms of life and/or of common ground" (2007, 95) but also "the infinitely problematic character of any 'auto' in general" (ibid., 94). He writes that "politics is thus implicitly nothing other than the auto-management of ecotechnology, the only form of possible 'auto'-nomy that precisely no longer has recourse to any heretofore possible forms of a politics" (ibid., 94). To move from thinking the subject to thinking singularity, or to conceive "of politics without a subject" (ibid., 106), however abstract and ungraspable such notions may seem, remains an important project for renegotiating community beyond its conceptualization within the terms of modernity. Assumptions about the formation of "us all" are what is at stake in any attempt to theorize in universally applicable terms.

In wresting community from the realms of myth and common sense, Nancy suggests that "community means, consequently, that there is no singular being without another singular being, and that there is, therefore, what might be called, in a rather inappropriate idiom, an originary or ontological 'sociality' that in its principle extends far beyond the simple theme of man as a social being" (1991, 28). Modes of relationality based on theorizations of singularity attempt to bypass the divide that is often assumed to separate prioritizations of either individual or community (the terms of Shani Mootoo's [2001] "predicament of or," with which we began this book). In practice, however, the framework established by generations of thinking in terms of individual and community remains powerful and difficult to dislodge. While we recognize the importance of postmodern theoretical inquiry into the origins of community and the practices of the Self, our interest in this volume has been to understand communal efforts to exercise autonomy within particular places. Rather than asking what community is, we have asked where communities may be found today and how they are succeeding or failing to renegotiate their autonomy — including their right to self-define — under changing conditions, especially those created by increased structural relations of interdependence associated with globalization.

Agamben's and Nancy's focus on how language structures forms of belonging beyond identity, individuality, and universality has proved more useful, perhaps, to philosophers and literary critics than it has to social scientists. Given our interdisciplinary focus and the fieldwork methodology of most of our chapters, we have not emphasized these dimensions here. Kuisma Korhonen's eloquent meditation (2006, 2) on the "necessarily heterogeneous and asymmetrical," temporary yet sustaining, nature of textual communities demonstrates the productivity of thinking through these new paradigms. They stress the transformative potential of "shared experiences where singularities become a multitude" (ibid., 3). Echoing Nancy, Korhonen asks, "Is there still any form of community that would not lead us to the kind of 'identity rage' that created the Holocaust and the Gulag? That would still count as a 'community' and resist the war of everyone against everyone that governs the logic of neo-capitalism?" (ibid., 5). Our studies here suggest that such communities are indeed possible. Furthermore, we find that they are modelling community in productive ways within many difficult circumstances that test their cooperation and challenge their autonomy. Drawing out the implications of work by Nancy, Blanchot, and Derrida, Korhonen argues that "we need a new concept of community that is not based on the ideas of a shared time, space, or identity" (ibid., 15). While such a community may model an ideal for some, we find this claim too extreme. Many of the communities studied in this volume are reconfiguring relations that derived from ideas of a shared time, space, or identity without discarding them entirely, and they are creating sustaining relations with one another in the process. We take seriously Korhonen's warning that "no community can ever fulfil the visions of communication and recognition that the notion of community opens up to us" (ibid., 15). Reality will always fall short of the ideal. Our research shows, however, that many actually existing communities are indeed negotiating "new ways of being-together" (ibid., 15), including forms of community that continue to value their responsibility to place.

In short, the work of such philosophers and their literary-critical interpreters is suggestive in changing the terms through which questions of community and autonomy are usually posed. It is also important to remember that they sometimes have their counterparts in the pragmatic and instinctive decisions being taken by individuals and communities on the ground. The work of these philosophers constitutes a sustained engagement with the ethical challenges of globalization as they see it. Nancy (2007, 53) asks, "How do you engage the world?" He sees this task as "a struggle of the West against itself, of capital against itself," and he argues that "the 'thinking' of which we are speaking is necessarily involved both in the questioning of the 'sense of the world' and in immediate, political, economic, and symbolic acts." For Agamben (1998, 187), "every attempt to rethink the political space of the West must begin with the clear awareness that we no longer know anything of the classical distinction between *zoë* and *bios*, between private life and political existence, between man as a simple living being at home in the house and man's political existence in the city." Such philosophical attempts to deal with the challenges that globalization brings to understanding community and autonomy beyond currently dominant conceptualizations form one of the contexts for our case studies in this book. We are interested in determining the conditions in which sustaining forms of community arise and thrive and where they prove inadequate in meeting the challenges at a moment when trans-planetary connections are once again increasing and some of them are less constrained by territorial borders than in the past.

The implications of shifting the grounds of analysis away from what Seyla Benhabib (1996, 4) has termed "the inevitable dialectic of identity/differ-ence" toward Agamben's (1998, 131) examination of the "constant need" of modern biopolitics "to redefine the threshold in life that distinguishes and separates what is inside from what is outside" are profound. Agamben suggests that "the separation between humanitarianism and politics that we are experiencing today is the extreme phase of the separation of the rights of man from the rights of the citizen" (ibid., 133). For Agamben, "the refugee must be considered for what he is: nothing less than a limit concept that radically calls into question the fundamental categories of the nation-state, from the birth-nation to the man-citizen link" (ibid., 134). Nyers' chapter in this volume extends the implications of this argument for rethinking what is meant by community autonomy during this extreme phase. Throughout this study, we have focused on Benhabib's reminder that "the core of democratic self-governance is the ideal of public autonomy, namely, the principle that those who are subject to the law should also be its authors" (2004, 217). We have not pursued Agamben's other sugges-tion that "one of the essential characteristics of modern biopolitics" is "the integration of medicine and politics," creating an "ambiguous terrain in which the physician and the sovereign seem to exchange roles" (1998, 143). Nor have we engaged with his work as an example of current efforts "to rethink the ontological basis of politics" (Passavant 2007, 148). Such efforts, however problematic, spill over into current anxieties about the nature of community and desires for its realization, requiring more interdisciplinary interrogation than we could venture here.

In *Fear of Small Numbers: An Essay on the Geography of Anger,* Arjun Appadurai argues that, out of the many global contexts for violence, "ranging from the most intimate (such as rape, bodily mutilation, and dis-memberment) to the most abstract (such as forced migration and legal minoritization), the most difficult one is the worldwide assault against minorities of all kinds" (2006a, 40). Such assaults reveal the darker side of community. Our work here addresses this difficulty primarily through a focus on communities in which association is voluntary or at least ac-cepted. We spend less time on the very difficult question of negotiating exit rights for individuals from a cultural or religious community that claims them, although we value the work being done in this area (see Eisenberg and Spinner-Haley 2005). The balance in this book falls primarily on the challenges for negotiating community autonomy and only secondarily on questions related to individuals negotiating autonomy within their communal associations. At the same time, however, much of our work suggests that looking at community through the lens of autonomy enables an analysis that focuses on the interlocking character of the intimate and the global.

This book has investigated alternative models for community, which enable individual as well as community autonomy more scope, without casting them as necessarily in opposition to one another. As Bonnie Honig (2001) suggests, for example, alternative visionings of political communities based on the notion of foreigners as founders may enable new ways of constructing communities along more inclusive lines. We remain wary of state- and community-sponsored exercises in community building that rely on what Appadurai (citing Freud) terms the "fear of small numbers" (2006a). We choose instead to locate those places where people have demonstrated that together they can imagine different modes of cooperation and support beyond those modelled on primal scenes of violence. Honig (1996, 259) terms such spaces "dilemmatic spaces," defining them as places where a person's agency is constituted and sometimes enabled through making "daily dilemmatic choices and negotiations." These are the spaces of community autonomy on which our analyses have focused here.

Abbreviations

AAC	Annual Allowable Cut
AKRSP	Aga Khan Rural Support Program
AIM	American Indian Movement
ATSIC	Aboriginal and Torres Strait Islander Commission
CBC	community-based conservation
CEDAW	Convention on the Elimination of All Forms of Discrimination against Women
CMC	computer mediated communication
CONGO	Conference of NGOs in Consultative Relations with the United Nations
COSATU	Congress of South African Trade Unions
CRA	Cree Regional Authority
CUT	Unified Trade Union Federation of Brazil
DADT	don't ask, don't tell
DG	Directorate General
EAPN	European Anti-Poverty Network
EC	European Commission
ECOSOC	Economic and Social Council (of the United Nations)
EI	Electronic Intifada
ETUC	European Trade Unions Confederation
EU	European Union
HBC	Hudson's Bay Company

ICEM	International Federation of Chemical, Energy, Mine, and General Workers' Unions
ICFTU	International Confederation of Free Trade Unions
ICSW	International Council on Social Welfare
IFI	international financial institution
IGO	intergovernmental organization
IMF	International Monetary Fund
IODE	Imperial Order Daughters of the Empire
IPW	International Parliament of Writers
ITUC	International Trade Union Confederation
IWA	Industrial Wood and Allied Workers
IWRAW	International Women's Rights Action Watch
JBNQA	James Bay and Northern Quebec Agreement
KKH	Karakoram Highway
MEC	Mountain Equipment Co-op
NAFTA	North American Free Trade Agreement
NGO	non-governmental organization
Novib	Nederlandse Organisatie voor Internationale Bijstand
PA	Palestine Authority
PLO	Palestine Liberation Organization
PRRN	Palestinian Refugee Research Net
PSG PSOE	Partido dos Socialistas de Galicia-Partido Socialista Obrero Español (Socialist Party of Galicia-Spanish Socialist Workers' Party)
REI	Recreational Equipment, Inc.
SAP	structural adjustment program
SEWA	Self-Employed Women's Association
SIGTUR	Southern Initiative on Globalization and Trade Union Rights
TAGS	transnational advocacy group
TARI	Trans-Arab Research Institute
TFL	Tree Farm Licence
TNGO	transnational non-governmental organization
UN	United Nations
UNCLOS	United Nations Convention on the Law of the Sea
UNIFEM	United Nations Development Fund for Women
UNRWA	UN Refugee Works Agency
VSO	Volunteer Services Overseas
WCED	World Commission on Environment and Development

WCWC	Western Canada Wilderness Committee
WEDO	Women's Environment and Development Organization
WID	women in development
WSSD	World Summit on Social Development
YTS	Youbou TimberLess Society

Notes and Acknowledgments

Chapter 1: Globalization, Autonomy, and Community

1 The authors gratefully acknowledge Shani Mootoo's permission to reprint lines from her poem, "A Recognition," from her book, *The Predicament of Or.*
2 "Singularity," as used by these thinkers, is a complex alternative term for a mode of being that is differently conceived than that conveyed by terms such as the "subject" or the "individual." For an extended discussion of the different ways in which Derrida and Nancy employ this term, see Morin (2006).
3 We borrow our first two terms from Ernst Tugendhat's monumental analysis of these concepts, so central to theorizations of autonomy, translated into English as *Self-Consciousness and Self-Determination* (1986).

Chapter 2: Globalism, Primitive Accumulation, and Nishnawbe Aski Territory

1 The language/culture of the Mushkegowuk settlements on the west coast of James and Hudson Bays is also more typically referred to as "Cree." I have chosen to use the term "Ininew" for this chapter since it more commonly appears in public discourses about the communities in the region.
2 Since 1994, I have conducted research on community development and entrepreneurship in Fort Albany, and I am currently completing research on how recent neoliberal reforms are influencing daily life in the settlement.
3 This is a pseudonym used to protect the identity of other people noted in the summary of the interview given below.
4 Another slightly younger man made a similar distinction in an interview by identifying the settlement as a place where people clustered around the "veins" of services: water pipes, sewer lines, the store, telephone lines, and electricity. He contrasted these veins of services with the kin bonds that locate people in a hunting group in turn identified

with a hunting territory identified with that family. Not all land in the territory is strictly identified in these terms.

5   The pressure to accumulate resources is related in some discussions I have had with the increasing "value" of equipment required for harvesting (e.g., boats, motors, and skidoos) in that high-cost items cannot be readily shared with others for fear of damage or loss. Thus, owners of this technology can be seen as having accumulated the means for hunting that they deny to others.

6   In another of these 2005 interviews, a young man in his late thirties identifies the ministry's regulations as a pressure working against the reproduction of community because the regulations prevent "sharing" trapping territories, break up work units within families, and establish alliances between families who would otherwise share their territories in some years. Finally, this young man (who is a very successful and well-regarded harvester who hunts and fishes for food) argues that the system led to a decline in the beaver population, ultimately thwarting the conservation effort, in turn depriving the Ininew of the basis of their society — using the land and its resources.

7   It is important to note that women in Adam's mother's generation have a different view of this process of atomization of social roles and identify both the appeal of wage work and pressures to care for elderly relatives in the settlement as significant forces not felt by men.

Chapter 4: Reaffirming "Community" in the Context of Community-Based Conservation

1   The verb *articulate* is appropriate here, borrowed from Stuart Hall (1996, 141) to evoke a double meaning: "to speak" and "to link."
2   In this connection, I should note that "community" is not a preferred category for indigenous representatives in many domestic or UN settings. Indigenous leaders frequently seek recognition as distinctive "nations" within nation-states, and they seek recognition as "peoples" within international law. One implication of treating indigenous peoples as mere "communities" in the colloquial sense of highly localized entities with municipal powers at best is that their status in international law is restricted. For specific purposes, then, "community" must be understood in relation to various instances of collective existence — society, tribe, nation, people, et cetera.

Chapter 5: The Moral Economy of Global Forestry in Rural British Columbia

Thanks to Diana Brydon, William Coleman, and contributors to this volume for comments on an earlier draft. Thanks also to Emily Eaton, Debra Salazar, Geoff Mann, James McCarthy, and Michael Woods for comments on various drafts and this research more generally. A longer related discussion appears in Prudham (2008). Special thanks to the YTS for all the cooperation, support, and inspiration.

1   Specifically, in 1991, the mill processed 402,000 cubic metres, of which 318,000 cubic metres came from TFL 46. In 1993, the mill processed 240,000 cubic metres, of which 213,000 cubic metres came from TFL 46. Company characterizations of typical production data suggest that the mill processed on the order of 400,000 cubic metres, of which about 75 to 80 percent came from TFL 46. These specific data are quoted in a confidential memorandum of 12 December 1994 from Garry E. Mancell of Davis and Company

Legal Services to Bob Beard, Vice-President, South Island Region, TimberWest. In a BC Ministry of Forests internal memorandum of 18 July 2000 (file 19040/20/1050), the mill was characterized as processing 33 percent of the log volume coming from the TFL in 1998 and 1999, while the above figures suggest the mill processed closer to half the log volume coming from the TFL.

2   About 75 percent of the mill's output went to Japan in the mid-1990s. This figure comes from an e-mail message sent on 25 April 2000 by Jim Gowriluk, then the·manager of timber tenures with the BC Ministry of Forests. Obtained via a Freedom of Information request by the IWA Local 1-80.

3   For the version covering workers at the mill when it closed, see "Master Agreement 1997-2000 Forest Products Industries Coast Region British Columbia," signed by the International Woodworkers Association of Canada and Forest Industrial Relations Limited. In 2004, the IWA became part of the United Steelworkers union.

4   Reflecting the intent of appurtenance clauses as instruments to regulate capital's autonomy in relation to forest-dependent communities, the clause was originally inserted into the lease in 1991 by then forest.minister Dan Miller in response to pressure from the IWA and driven by concerns about job losses associated with industry restructuring and the transfer of the lease to TimberWest from Fletcher Challenge (Gelb 2001).

5   Letter from Gary Mancell of Davis and Company, Vancouver, to Don McMullan, Chief Forester, TimberWest, dated 10 October 1995. Obtained via the IWA.

6   Outlined in documents obtained via personal communication with the IWA.

7   The distinct features of this geography have been chronicled extensively, not least in the work of Trevor Barnes and Roger Hayter (see, e.g., Barnes and Hayter 1992; Barnes, Hayter, and Hay 2001; Hayter 2000; Hayter and Barnes 1990), who have themselves employed the idea of a structured coherence.

8   For a historical discussion of the origins of this exploitation axis, see Prudham (2007).

9   In fact, Burda and Gale (1998) estimate that about 90 percent of British Columbia's harvest was exported in the mid-1990s.

10 There are parallels here to the global articulation and integration of Canadian resource extraction and processing more generally (see Drache 1982; Hayter and Barnes 1990, 2001; Innis 1956).

11 Specifically, in a letter of 28 February 2001 from Paul McElligott, President and CEO, TimberWest, to Carmen Rocco, Vice-President, IWA Local 1-80, the company required the union to work out all its planning and the details of its proposal by 23 March 2001, or the company would refuse to further consider the matter and proceed with its decommissioning plans.

12 This is broadly referred to as community natural resource management (see, e.g., Agrawal 2001; Agrawal and Gibson 1999; Baker and Kusel 2003; Berkes and IUCNNR 1989; Gauld 2000; Gebremedhin, Pender, and Tesfaye 2003; Gibson, McKean, and Ostrom 2000; Halseth 1996; Kellert et al. 2000; Klooster 1999, 2000; Klooster and Masera 2000; Kull 2002; Leach, Mearns, and Scoones 1999; Nagendra 2002).

13 Letter from Banister and Company, Barristers and Solicitors, to IWA-Canada Local 1-80, 25 April 2003, 5.

14 YTS members campaigned actively and successfully in support of Doug Routley, the NDP candidate for the provincial riding of Cowichan-Ladysmith, helping to displace an incumbent member of the provincial cabinet, Liberal Graham Bruce, who had been the sitting minister of skills development and labour.

15 On the politics of sustained yield in British Columbia, see Prudham (2007) and my chapter in Coleman and Weaver (forthcoming).

Chapter 6: From Servitude to Dignity?

1   Galicia is located in northwestern Spain and is divided into four provinces (A Coruña, Lugo, Ourense, and Pontevedra), which are home to about 2.7 million inhabitants. The area is ethnically, linguistically, and culturally distinct from other regions in the Spanish state. I conducted fieldwork there for my dissertation from September 2002 to August 2003 and from November to December 2003. During that time, I lived in the capital city of Lugo in the interior province of Lugo with two Galician university students. My research is based on the combination of several methodologies, including participation in the social movement that I describe in this chapter, open-ended interviews with both Galicians who partook in the movement and with some others who did not, and archival research. I also systematically collected newspaper articles in two regional newspapers as another way to obtain information on public discourse and debate about the sinking of the *Prestige* and on issues pertaining to place and identity. All translations from Galego, the Galician language, and Castilian Spanish to English are my own unless indicated otherwise. All names in this chapter are pseudonyms.

2   For an overview of the history of the regional government in Galicia since the end of the dictatorship, see Lagares Díez (2003). After twenty-five years of majority rule, in the regional elections in 2005, Fraga's party lost to the Galician socialist party, the Partido dos Socialistas de Galicia-Partido Socialista Obrero Español (Socialist Party of Galicia-Spanish Socialist Workers' Party or PSG PSOE).

3   Also see Arias Veira (2003); Catalán Deus (2003); Gómez and Ordaz (2003) for discussions on the response of the government to the sinking of the *Prestige*.

4   I thank Dr. William Coleman for making this point.

5   For information on the composition of the social movement (Nunca Máis), including the number of registered associations, see Aguilar Fernández and Ballesteros Peña (2004). The core of the social movement is not homogeneous. Some activists in the movement are from union and labour parties; others are from cultural associations and political parties opposed to the governing Partido Popular. Some activists have previously participated in social movements, while others have not. The spokespeople are from an educated circle of Galician entertainers and well-known writers. The movement attracted a variety of Galicians, from students to stay-at-home mothers to fisherwomen and -men. In this chapter, I focus on the dominant reading of the critical event and the dominant definition of regional community that emerged from the social movement.

6   I examine the dominant portrayal of the Galician region. However, I am not suggesting that the Galician region is homogeneous. As noted above, Galicia comprises four provinces and is rich in diversity and linguistic variation.

7   This interpretation was furthered following the first elections after the sinking of the *Prestige,* the municipal elections in May 2003, when the Partido Popular government was again voted in with an absolute majority in the coastal areas most affected by the oil slick, nicknamed "ground zero" along the Costa da Morte.

8   More recently, Étienne Balibar (2004) has examined this tension through an analysis of the term "border," which he argues is undergoing a change in meaning.

9   I thank Dr. William Coleman for helping to formulate this point.

10 See, for example, Núñez (2002). Also see Falcón (2002) for a view from the perspective of the region's president, Manuel Fraga.

Chapter 7: Community without Status

1 Unless otherwise noted, quotations for this chapter are drawn from extensive focus group discussions and individual qualitative interviews with non-status immigrants, refugees and migrant rights activists, community agency workers, lawyers, and academics. These interviews were conducted in June-August 2004 and June-August 2005 in Toronto and Montreal. The non-status immigrants interviewed for this study represent a diverse group and include members from the Algerian, Argentinean, Bangladeshi, Brazilian, Caribbean, Colombian, Iranian, Palestinian, and Philippine non-status communities in Toronto and Montreal. I would like to thank Carolina Berinstein, Heather Johnson, Erika Khandor, Jean McDonald, Natasha Pravaz, Cynthia Wright, and Sima Zerehi for their work in organizing, facilitating, and transcribing the focus group discussions and interviews.

2 For a discussion of these demands, see the Solidarity Across Borders website at http://solidarityacrossborders.org.

3 While the Canadian government has been reluctant to introduce such a measure, various Canadian governments have implemented several regularization programs since 1960. Some of the largest have included the Chinese Adjustment Statement Program, which regularized 12,000 Chinese "paper sons" between 1960 and 1972; the Adjustment of Status Program of 1973, which regularized about 39,000 people from over 150 countries in a two-month period; and the Deferred Removal Orders Class, which regularized about 3,000 failed refugee claimants between 1994 and 1998. Many of these regularization programs were implemented as a direct result of effective political advocacy by directly affected communities of non-status immigrants. The "Special Regularization Programs" for Haitians (1981) and Algerians (2002) residing in Quebec are two good examples.

Chapter 8: Transnational Women's Groups and Social Policy Activists around the UN and the EU

Patricia Young would like to thank the University of Victoria European Union Initiative for financial support for interviews conducted in Europe. The following organizations were interviewed.

In Brussels: European Anti-Poverty Network (EAPN); European Women's Lobby (EWL); The Platform of European Social NGOs (Social Platform); European Trade Union Confederation (ETUC)

In Budapest: Women's Rights Association (NANE); Foundation for the Women of Hungary (MONA); Alliance of Social Professionals

In Bucharest: Romanian Society for Feminist Analyses (ANA); Partners for Change; Romanian Community Development Association; "Brotherhood" National Confederation of Free Trade Unions (CNSRL — Fratia); National Trade Union Block (BNS)

1 These norms include a commitment to descriptive representation and to representation of disadvantaged groups as well as a commitment to achieving consensus in the presence of institutionalized dissent (Weldon 2006).

2 Labour has traditionally been the group that addresses social policy.

3 Maxine Molyneux, the proponent of this distinction, later dissociated herself from the tendency, in the literature, to consider strategic gender interests as superior to practical interests (Rowbotham and Linkogle 2001, 9).

4 Keck and Sikkink (1998) present a thorough account of the emergence of the violence against women framework, with more details on the role of individual agency.

5 See the debate on the importance of women's movement autonomy from the state summarized in Ray and Korteweg (1999).

6 Trade unions are considered here in their role as social policy actors. For another look at international labour organizing, see the chapter by O'Brien in this volume.

7 These interviews were conducted on a confidential basis with representatives of NGOs and NGO networks in Belgium, Hungary, and Romania.

8 The power of keywords attractive to donors in shaping how eastern European NGOs define themselves (at least toward outsiders) is also noted in ethnographic accounts of Russian civil society (Hemment 2004).

9 A national umbrella organization has been created in Hungary despite this conflict, but women's groups in Romania have not yet agreed on how they should be represented at the European level.

10 Both Romanian confederations interviewed said they have closer ties with the International Confederation of Free Trade Unions than with ETUC.

Chapter 10: Transnational Transformation

I would like to thank Joe Farag and Meagan Heath for their research assistance and Melina Baum-Singer, Diana Brydon, Will Coleman, Jim Novak, and an anonymous reviewer for their helpful comments. Funding for this project was provided by the SSHRC-MCRI grant for the Globalization and Autonomy Project, McMaster University.

1 One of many bumper stickers and T-shirt slogans seen on 20 April 2002 in Washington, DC, where "tens of thousands of protestors joined forces to ... demonstrate against everything from US policy in the Mideast to globalization and corporate greed" (Fernandez 2002).

2 This project was initially conceived as a contribution to theory development and to the ethnographic literature on the practices of TAGs. Its aim was to contribute to a better understanding of the political and cultural contexts of transnational activists in action. In addition to conducting open-ended, semi-structured individual interviews with activists, I wanted to observe how their organizations worked, for example, how members negotiated the production of their newsletters, e-mail postings, action alerts, and events. That is, I was interested in the "everyday life" of the organization and the goals that activists set for themselves (their "mission" for lack of a better word); the relationships they developed with governmental and non-governmental institutions as well as with other TAGs; and their self-assessments of their practices. The events of September 11 and the PATRIOT Act intervened, and I was forced to drop the conventional placed-based ethnography and limit my study to a Web-based analysis.

3 E-mail communication with one of TARI's founders, Dr. Elaine C. Hagopian, August 2006.

4 To be fair, Nagel and Staeheli do note that "Palestinians do not have a state to call their own ... a condition that has to shape the kinds of transnationalism that they may experience" (2004, 20).

5 In making his case that the rise of the word and claim to *indigeneity* emerged, in part, as a result of indigenous organizing on the Internet, Ronald Niezen (2005) fails to account for a long history of association prior to the rise of these technologies. Neglecting to historicize the relationship between and among indigenous communities and Palestinian organizing, he writes that "the connection between indigenous identity and Palestinian nationalism is not something that would have arisen naturally through face-to-face dialogue or through the epiphany of encounter at international meetings. High-ranking Palestinians and indigenous representatives simply do not mingle in the same circles" (545). Missing here is any reference to the relationships and alliances that existed between the American Indian Movement (AIM) and the Palestine Liberation Organization (PLO) through the 1960s and 1970s.

6 "In the last few years, the use of CMC [computer mediated communication] has been crucial in the organizational phases of very large, transnational demonstrations, that have been staged with a frequency and number of participants previously unheard of. CMC makes transnational mobilization easier whether in the form of a series of demonstrations going on at the same time in different countries, as happened in the hundreds of demonstrations against the war against Iraq on 15 February 2003, or protest events in one place with the participation of activists from different states and continents, as was the case of the World Social Forum" (Della Porta and Mosca 2005, 170). Langman writes that, "on February 15, [2002], the largest demonstration in history took place as more than 10 million people in 350 cities across the world marched in protest. The rapid mobilization, coordination, and size of these protests was a direct result of the Internet and the existence of a large number of global justice movements" (2005, 66).

7 Cammaerts and Van Audenhove write, "when looking at unbounded notions of citizenship, civil society plays an even bigger role than within the classical definition of nation state citizenship ... The lack of formal democratic control at the international level of governance means that many issues linked to unbounded citizenship — such as ecology, global social justice, or debt relief for developing countries — require solution[s] that transcend the national context" (2005, 183).

Chapter 11: The Tensions of Global Imperial Community

Research for this chapter was completed with the generous support of a SSHRC Doctoral Fellowship, the Mary Routledge Fellowship provided by the Faculty of Arts at the University of Western Ontario, an International Council for Canadian Studies (ICCS) Graduate Student Scholarship, a Research Assistantship funded through the Globalization and Autonomy SSHRC-funded MCRI, and a stipend funded through Diana Brydon's Standard Research Grant. I presented a much earlier and considerably shorter version of this chapter as "Reconsidering Empire: Rereading the IODE's Globality" at the Congress of the Humanities and Social Sciences in 2004. Thanks to the other authors in this volume who took part in workshops in May and September 2005 for their comments on the earlier work in progress.

1 Margaret Polson Murray, "A League of 'Daughters of the Empire,'" Library and Archives Canada (hereafter LAC), Imperial Order Daughters of the Empire (hereafter IODE) Fonds, MG 28 I 17, vol. 18, file 3 (Constitution), 7. Murray refers to the South African War (1899-1902), which is sometimes still called the (Anglo-)Boer War in Canada.

2 This imagining was one of the forces stimulating a counterimagining of an independent, non-imperial Canada by nationalists in Quebec, including "French Canadian" women.

3   *The Federation of the Daughters of the British Empire and the Children of the Empire* (Montreal: N.p., 1900), 4-5, LAC, IODE Fonds, MG 28 I 17, vol. 18, file 3 (Constitution).

4   LAC, IODE Fonds, MG 28 I 17, vol. 18, file 4 (Constitution and Statutes of IODE, 1901).

5   Mrs. R.E.A. Land to S.M. Burrows, Esq., 16 February 1904, LAC, IODE Fonds, MG 28 I 17, vol. 25, file 1 ("Essays on Canada" Competition).

6   *Constitution and Statutes of the Imperial Order of the Daughters of the Empire and the Children of the Empire (Junior Branch),* 5-6, LAC, IODE Fonds, MG 28 I 17, vol. 18, file 4 (Constitution and Statutes of the IODE, 1901).

7   Mrs. Stowton [to National Chapter, IODE], 5 February [1905], LAC, IODE Fonds, MG 28 I 17, vol. 20, file 1 (Miscellaneous Correspondence, 1901-5).

8   Muriel Talbot to Mrs. Nordheimer, 21 March 1905, LAC, IODE Fonds, MG 28 I 17, vol. 20, file 1 (Miscellaneous Correspondence, 1905-6). The calling card for Miss Fawns is in LAC, IODE Fonds, MG 28 I 17, vol. 20, file 1 (Miscellaneous Correspondence, 1905-6).

9   Mrs. R.E.A. Land to Lady Hopetoun, 12 January 1902, LAC, IODE Fonds, MG 28 I 17, vol. 20, file 3 (Miscellaneous Correspondence, 1902-3).

10 Ibid.

11 Mrs. Gertrude van Koughnet to "Dear Madam," 3 May 1903, LAC, IODE Fonds, MG 28 I 17, vol. 20, file 5 (Miscellaneous Correspondence #5, 1903).

12 Mary Mosely to Mrs. Land, n.d., LAC, IODE Fonds, MG 28 I 17, vol. 20, file 3 (Miscellaneous Correspondence, 1902-3).

13 Mrs. R.E.A. Land to Lady Hopetoun, 12 January 1902, LAC, IODE Fonds, MG 28 I 17, vol. 20, file 3 (Miscellaneous Correspondence, 1902-3).

14 Florence Cameron to Mrs. Land, 10 March 1902, LAC, IODE Fonds, MG 28 I 17, vol. 20, file 3 (Miscellaneous Correspondence, 1902).

15 Henry Knisley to Constance R. Boulton, 16 April 1902, LAC, IODE Fonds, MG 28 I 17, vol. 21, file 3 (Miscellaneous Correspondence, 1902).

16 James Evans to Constance R. Boulton, 16 April 1902, LAC, IODE Fonds, MG 28 I 17, vol. 21, file 3 (Miscellaneous Correspondence, 1902).

17 Honorary Secretary, Canadian South Africa Memorial Association, to President of the Loyal Guild of Women of South Africa, 18 April 1902, LAC, IODE Fonds, MG 28 I 17, vol. 28, file 8 (Guild of Loyal Women of South Africa).

Chapter 13: The Brotherhood of the Rope

"The Brotherhood of the Rope: Techniques and Tools" is the title of the last chapter in Rébuffat's *Starlight and Storm* (1954), to which I owe the title of this chapter.

1   Chris Bonington (1992) notes that Emperor Hadrian climbed to the summit of Mount Etna in the second century AD in order to see the sunrise.

2   David Robbins writes that "mountaineering was invented by the British in the middle decades of the nineteenth century. Prior to this it is not possible to draw a distinction between mountaineering and other activities, science and tourism, of which it was an aspect. The earliest ascents of the highest peaks of the European Alps had been undertaken for purposes of scientific research and cartography and it subsequently became fashionable for adventurous tourists to include an ascent of Mont Blanc or some other notable viewpoint in the itinerary of their European or Alpine tour. In the 1850s, however, the practice of visiting the Alps specifically to climb the peaks and cross the passes was for the first time recognized by participants as a distinctive form of activity" (1987, 583-4).

3   I now drop the invasive quotation marks around this term, but I hope they persist conceptually — a silent citation to a prior hypothesis and representation — as the chapter proceeds.

4   Peter Hansen (1995) argues that one of the earliest forces behind the popularization of mountaineering was the London music hall. Albert Smith's virtual representation, at the Egyptian Hall in Piccadilly, of the first ascent of Mont Blanc connected strongly with a rising middle class in search of leisure and sports symbols that were not associated with the gentry and helped to transform British mountaineering into a defining symbol of the nation.

5   My thanks to the anonymous reader who pointed out that this specific argument could also have been grounded to REI (Recreational Equipment, Inc.), a major consumer cooperative for mountaineering equipment in the United States. I agree with this claim: after all, REI was founded by mountaineers thirty-three years before MEC and now has over eighty stores, most of them in urban centres located far from climbing. I work with MEC rather than REI in part because it is close at hand: here I have access to something akin to an inside voice. But beyond that, my strategy here is to practise what Gayatri Spivak preaches: and that is to generalize from the local — the subordinate term — and not always from the salient and the dominant.

6   I owe this final point to climber and scholar Zac Robinson, extraordinary historian of mountaineering activity in the Canadian Rockies, who also worked as my research assistant through the Globalization and Autonomy collective. My thanks extend through Zac to a wide range of active participants in many climbing communities throughout Alberta and British Columbia and at the Alpine Club in London who have shared their knowledge and thoughts with me and have taught me mutually to think and to climb. Dave Cockle has long been the leader on this rope. I write this chapter in a spirit of unflagging admiration for what I have come to understand as climbing's most urgent desire for an ethical, environmentally committed way of being in the world. My own participation in "the brother-/sisterhood of the rope" is structurally inseparable, despite my critique, from Rébuffat's undying and egregious claim about friendship. This chapter could not have been written had it not been for the guiding hand of that community of scholars brought together by Will Coleman, Diana Brydon, and many others. May we all climb on.

Chapter 14: Why Community Matters

1   We note the interesting discussion by David Bray (2006, 350) charting "the growing prominence of the idea of 'community' within public discourse in the People's Republic of China (PRC)" after its disappearance in the early 1950s and his discussion of whether or not it is appropriate to translate the Chinese term *zizhi* as "autonomy" (543).

Works Cited

Adler, Glen, and Eddie Webster. 1995. Challenging transition theory: The labour movement, radical reform, and transition to democracy in South Africa. *Politics and Society* 23 (1): 75-106.

Adventure Consultants. http://www.adventureconsultants.co.nz/AdventureInternational/Everest/.

Agamben, Giorgio. 1993. *The coming community.* Trans. Michael Hardt. Minneapolis: University of Minnesota Press.

—. 1998. *Homo sacer: Sovereign power and bare life.* Trans. Daniel Heller-Roazen. Stanford: Stanford University Press.

Agrawal, A. 2001. State formation in community spaces? Decentralization of control over forests in the Kumaon Himalaya, India. *Journal of Asian Studies* 60 (1): 9-40.

Agrawal, A., and C.C. Gibson. 1999. Enchantment and disenchantment: The role of community in natural resource conservation. *World Development* 27 (4): 629-49.

Aguilar Fernández, Susana, and Ana Ballesteros Peña. 2004. Debating the concept of political opportunities in relation to the Galician social movement "Nunca Máis." *South European Society and Politics* 9 (3): 28-53.

Akram, Susan. 2001. Reinterpreting Palestinian refugee rights under international law. In *Palestinian refugees: The right of return,* ed. N. Aruri, 165-94. Sterling, VA: Stylus.

Al-Awda: The Palestine Right to Return Group (Canada). http://www.al-awda.ca.

Al-Awda: The Palestine Right of Return Coalition (US). http://www.al-awda.org.

Al-Awda: The Palestine Right of Return Coalition (UK). http://www.al-awda.org.uk.

Alpine Club. 1857. *First circular concerning the Alpine Club, 1857.* http://www.alpine-club.org.uk/alpineclub/objectives.htm.

Alvarez, Sonia. 2000. Translating the global effects of transnational organizing on local feminist discourses and practices in Latin America. *Meridians: Feminism, Race, Transnationalism* 1 (1): 29-67.

Aly, Abdel Monem Said, Rashid I. Khalidi, Ian S. Lustick, Camille Mansour, Moshe Ma'oz, Anthony Parsons, William B. Quandt, Eric Rouleau, Ghassan Salame, and Khalil Shikaki.

1996. Reflections on the peace process and a durable settlement: A roundup of views. *Journal of Palestine Studies* 26 (1): 5-26.

Anderson, Benedict. 1983. *Imagined communities: Reflections on the origin and spread of nationalism.* London: Verso.

—. 1991. *Imagined communities: Reflections on the origin and spread of nationalism.* Rev. ed. London: Verso.

Anderson, James, Liam O'Dowd, and Thomas M. Wilson, eds. 2003. Introduction: Culture and cooperation in Europe's borderlands. *European Studies: An Interdisciplinary Series in European Culture, History, and Politics* 19: 13-29.

Anderson, Jon W. 1997. Cybernauts of the Arab diaspora: Electronic mediation in transnational cultural identities. Paper prepared for the Couch-Stone symposium Postmodern Culture, Global Capitalism, and Democratic Action, 10-12 April, University of Maryland, http://www.bsos.umd.edu/CSS97/papers/anderson.html.

Appadurai, Arjun. 1996. *Modernity at large: Cultural dimensions of globalization.* Minneapolis: University of Minnesota Press.

—. 2000. Grassroots globalization and the research imagination. *Public Culture* 12 (1): 1-19.

—. 2006a. *Fear of small numbers: An essay on the geography of anger.* Durham, NC: Duke University Press.

—. 2006b. The right to research. *Globalisation, Societies, and Education* 4 (2): 167-77.

Appiah, Kwame Anthony. 2005. *The ethics of identity.* Princeton: Princeton University Press.

Arendt, Hannah. 1968. *Imperialism: Part Two of the origins of totalitarianism.* New York: Harvest.

Aretxaga, Begoña. 2003. Maddening states. *Annual Review of Anthropology* 32: 393-410.

Arias Veira, Pedro. 2003. *Prestige: El barco de los locos.* Madrid: Espasa.

Artz, Donna. 1996. *Refugees into citizens: Palestinians and the end of the Arab-Israeli conflict.* New York: Council of Foreign Relations Press.

Baehr, Peter. 2005. Social extremity, communities of fate, and the sociology of SARS. *European Journal of Sociology* 46 (2): 179-211.

Bairoch, Paul. 2000. The constituent economic principles of globalization in historical perspective: Myths and realities. *International Sociology* 15 (2): 197-214.

Baker, M., and J. Kusel. 2003. *Community forestry in the United States: Learning from the past, crafting the future.* Washington, DC: Island Press.

Balibar, Étienne. 2000. What we owe to the *sans-papiers.* In *Social insecurity: Alphabet City, no. 7,* ed. L. Guenther and C. Heesters, 42-3. Toronto: Anansi.

—. 2002. *Politics and the other scene.* New York: Verso.

—. 2004. *We, the people of Europe? Reflections on transnational citizenship.* Princeton: Princeton University Press.

Ball, John, ed. 1859. *Peaks, passes, and glaciers: A series of excursions by members of the Alpine Club.* 3rd ed. London: Longman, Green, Longman, and Roberts.

Barclay, Linda. 2000. Autonomy and the social self. In *Relational autonomy: Feminist perspectives on autonomy, agency, and the social self,* ed. Catriona Mackenzie and Natalie Stoljar, 52-71. New York: Oxford University Press.

Barcott, Bruce. 1966. Cliffhangers: The fatal descent of the mountain-climbing memoir. *Harper's Magazine* August: 64-8.

Barker, Joanne. 2005. For whom sovereignty matters. In *Sovereignty matters: Locations of contestation and possibility in indigenous struggles for self-determination,* ed. Joanne Barker Lincoln, 1-31. Lincoln: University of Nebraska Press.

Barnes, T.J., and R. Hayter. 1992. The little town that did: Flexible accumulation and community response in Chemainus, British Columbia. *Regional Studies* 26 (7): 647-63.

Barnes, T.J., R. Hayter, and E. Hay. 2001. Stormy weather: Cyclones, Harold Innis, and Port Alberni, BC. *Environment and Planning A* 33: 2127-47.

Barsh, R.L. 1999. Taking indigenous science seriously. In *Biodiversity in Canada: Ecology, ideas, and action,* ed. S. Bocking, 153-73. Peterborough, ON: Broadview Press.

Basu, Amrita. 1995. Introduction. In *The challenge of local feminisms: Women's movements in global perspective,* ed. Amrita Basu, 1-21. Boulder: Westview Press.

Battiste, Marie. 2000. Unfolding the lessons of colonization. In *Reclaiming indigenous voice and vision,* ed. Marie Battiste, xvi-xxx. Vancouver: UBC Press.

Bauer, Paul. 1937. *Himalayan campaign: The German attack on Kanchenjunga.* Trans. Sumner Austin. Oxford: Blackwell.

Bauer, Rainer. 1987. Inheritance and inequality in a Spanish Galician community, 1840-1935. *Ethnohistory* 34 (2): 171-93.

—. 1992. Changing representations of place, community, and character in the Spanish Sierra del Caurel. *American Ethnologist* 19 (3): 571-88.

Bauman, Zygmunt. 2001. *Community: Seeking safety in an insecure world.* Cambridge, UK: Polity.

Bayers, Peter. 2003. *Imperial ascent: Mountaineering, masculinity, and empire.* Boulder: University of Colorado Press.

Beauchamp, Tom L. 2005. Who deserves autonomy, and whose autonomy deserves respect? In *Personal autonomy: New essays on personal autonomy and its role in contemporary moral philosophy,* ed. James Stacey Taylor, 310-29. Cambridge, UK: Cambridge University Press.

Beck, Julie. 2000. (Re)negotiating selfhood and citizenship in the postcommunist Czech Republic: Five women activists speak about transition and feminism. In *Gender and global restructuring: Sightings, sights, and resistances,* ed. Marianne Marchand and Anne Sisson Runyan, 176-93. London: Routledge.

Beckett, J. 1987. *Torres Strait Islanders: Custom and colonialism.* Cambridge, UK: Cambridge University Press.

Beiras, Ricardo. 2003. A catástrofe do *Prestige*: Unha oportunidade para a transformación da sociedade galega. *Grial: Revista galega de cultura* 157: 15-26.

Beiras, Xosé Manuel. 1997 [1972]. *O atraso económico da Galiza: Santiago de Compostela.* Galicia: Edicións Laiovento.

Bengston, D. 1994. Changing forest values and ecosystem management. *Society and Natural Resources* 7 (6): 515-33.

Benhabib, Seyla. 1992. *Situating the self: Gender, community, and postmodernism in contemporary ethics.* New York: Routledge.

—. 1996. The democratic moment and the problem of difference. In *Democracy and difference: Contesting the boundaries of the political,* ed. Seyla Benhabib, 3-18. Princeton: Princeton University Press.

—. 2004. *The rights of others: Aliens, residents, and citizens.* Cambridge, UK: Cambridge University Press.

Berdahl, Daphne. 1999. *Where the world ended: Re-unification and identity in the German borderland.* Berkeley: University of California Press.

Berkes, F. 2003. Alternatives for conventional management: Lessons from small-scale fisheries. *Environments* 31 (1): 5-20.

—. 2004. Rethinking community-based conservation. *Conservation Biology* 18 (3): 621-30.

Berkes, F., N. Bankes, M. Marschke, D. Armitage, and D. Clark. 2005. Cross-scale institutions and building resilience in the Canadian North. In *Breaking ice: Renewable resource and ocean management in the Canadian North,* ed. F. Berkes, R. Huebert, H. Fast, M. Manseau, and A. Diduck, 225-48. Calgary: University of Calgary Press.

Berkes, F., and IUCNNR (International Union for Conservation of Nature and Natural Resources). 1989. *Common property resources: Ecology and community-based sustainable development.* London: Belhaven Press.

Bernal, G., S. Bissell, and A. Cortes. 1999. Effects of globalization on the efforts to decriminalize abortion in Mexico. *Development* 42 (4): 130-4.

Bernstein, Steven F., and William D. Coleman. Forthcoming. *Unsettled legitimacy: Political community, power, and authority in a global era.* Vancouver: UBC Press.

Bielasiak, Jack, and Barbara Hicks. 1990. Solidarity's self-organization: The crisis of rationality and legitimacy in Poland, 1980-81. *East European Politics and Societies* 4 (3): 489-512.

Blaikie, P., and H. Brookfield. 1987. *Land degradation and society.* London: Methuen.

Blanchot, Maurice. 1988. *The unavowable community.* Trans. Pierre Joris. Barrytown, NY: Station Hill Press.

Blaser, Mario E., Ravindra de Costa, Deborah McGregor, and William D. Coleman, eds. Forthcoming. *Indigenous peoples and autonomy: Insights for a global age.* Vancouver: UBC Press.

Block, F. 2003. Karl Polanyi and the writing of the *Great Transformation. Theory and Society* 32 (3): 275-306.

Block, F., and M.R. Somers. 1984. Beyond the economistic fallacy: The holistic social science of Karl Polanyi. In *Vision and method in historical sociology,* ed. T. Skocpol, 47-84. Cambridge, UK: Cambridge University Press.

Blowfield, Mick. 1999. Ethical trade: A review of developments and issues. *Third World Quarterly* 20 (4): 753-70.

Bonington, Chris. 1992. *The climbers: A history of mountaineering.* London: Hodder and Stoughton.

Booth, W.J. 1994. On the idea of the moral economy. *American Political Science Review* 88 (3): 653-67.

Bordo, Michael D., Barry Eichengreen, and Douglas A. Irwin. 1999. Is globalization today really different than globalization one hundred years ago? Working Paper 7195. Washington, DC: National Bureau of Economic Research.

Borges, Jorge Luis. 1962. The fearful sphere of Pascal. In *Labyrinths: Selected stories and other writings,* ed. J.E. Irby and D.A. Yates. New York: New Directions.

Borneman, John, and Nick Fowler. 1997. Europeanization. *Annual Review of Anthropology* 26: 487-514.

Borrini-Feyerabend, G., A. Kothari, and G. Oviedo. 2004. *Indigenous and local communities and protected areas: Towards equity and enhanced conservation.* Gland, Switzerland: IUCN.

Botkin, D.B. 1990. *Discordant harmonies: A new ecology for the twenty-first century.* New York: Oxford University Press.

Bradshaw, B. 2003. Questioning the credibility and capacity of community-based resource management. *Canadian Geographer* 47 (2): 137-50.

Brainard, Lori A., and Jennifer M. Brinkerhoff. 2004. Lost in cyberspace: Shedding light on the dark matter of grassroots organizations. *Nonprofit and Voluntary Sector Quarterly,* Supplement 35 (3): S32-S53.

Braun, B. 2002. *The intemperate rainforest: Nature, culture, and power on Canada's West Coast.* Minneapolis: University of Minnesota Press.

Bray, David. 2006. Building "community": New strategies of governance in urban China. *Economy and Society* 35 (4): 530-49.

Brenner, N. 1999. Beyond state centrism? Space, territoriality, and geographical scale in globalization studies. *Theory and Society* 28 (1): 39-78.

Bronfenbrenner, Kate, Sheldon Friedman, Richard W. Hurd, Rudolph A. Oswald, and Ronald L. Seeber, eds. 1998. *Organizing to win: New research on union strategies.* Ithaca: Cornell University Press.

Brosius, J.P., and D. Russell. 2003. Conservation from above: An anthropological perspective on transboundary protected areas and eco-regional planning. *Journal of Sustainable Forestry* 17 (1-2): 39-65.

Brosius, J.P., A. Tsing, and C. Zerner. 1998. Representing communities: Histories and politics of community-based natural resource management. *Society and Natural Resources* 11 (2): 157-68.

Brown, K. 2002. Innovations for conservation and development. *Geographical Journal* 168 (1): 6-17.

Bruce, Charles Granville. 1922. *The assault on Mount Everest.* London: Longmans, Green.

Burawoy, M. 2000. Introduction: Reaching for the global. In *Global ethnography: Forces, connections, imaginations in a postmodern world,* ed. M. Burawoy et al., 1-40. Berkeley: University of California Press.

—. 2003. For a sociological Marxism: The complementary convergence of Antonio Gramsci and Karl Polanyi. *Politics and Society* 31 (2): 193-261.

Burda, C., and F. Gale. 1998. Trading in the future: British Columbia's forest products compromise. *Society and Natural Resources* 11 (6): 555-68.

Burda, C., F. Gale, and M. M'Gonigle. 1998. Eco-forestry versus the status quo: Or why innovative forestry is neither contemplated or permitted within the state structure of British Columbia. *BC Studies* 119: 45-72.

Burnett, Jon. 2007. Review of *Community cohesion: A new framework for race and diversity,* by Ted Cantle. *Race and Class* 48 (4): 115-18.

Burton, Antoinette. 1990. The white woman's burden: British feminists and the Indian woman, 1865-1915. *Women's Studies International Forum* 13 (4): 295-308.

Bush, Julia. 2000. *Edwardian ladies and imperial power.* London: Leicester University Press.

Buzard, James. 1993. *The beaten track: European tourism, literature, and the ways to "culture," 1800-1918.* Oxford: Clarendon Press.

Cammaerts, Bart, and Leo Van Audenhove. 2005. Online political debate, unbounded citizenship, and the problematic nature of a transnational public sphere. *Political Communication* 22 (2): 179-96.

Campbell, L.M., and A. Vainio-Mattila. 2003. Participatory development and community-based conservation: Opportunities missed or lessons learned? *Human Ecology* 31 (3): 417-37.

Cantle, Ted. 2005. *Community cohesion: A new framework for race and diversity.* Basingstoke: Palgrave Macmillan.

Carroll, William K., and Robert A. Hackett. 2006. Democratic media activism through the lens of social movement theory. *Media, Culture, and Society* 28 (1): 83-104.

Castelao, Alfonso Daniel Rodríguez. 1977 [1944]. *Sempre en Galiza.* Madrid: Akal Editor.

Castells, Manuel. 1996. *The rise of the network society.* Oxford: Blackwell.

—. 1997. *The power of identity.* Vol. 2 of *The information age: Economy, society, and culture.* Oxford: Blackwell.

Castoriadis, Cornelius. 1991. *Philosophy, politics, autonomy,* ed. David Ames Curtis. New York: Oxford University Press.

Catalán Deus, Gustavo. 2003. *Desprestige: El ocaso del PP ante la mayor catástrofe ambiental en España.* Madrid: La Esfera.

Cerny, Philip. 2000. Political globalization and the competition state. In *Political economy and the changing global order*, ed. R. Stubbs and G. Underhill, 300-9. Toronto: Oxford University Press.

Chakravorty, Swapan, Suzana Milevska, and Tani E. Barlow. 2006. *Conversations with Gayatri Chakravorty Spivak*. London: Seagull.

Chan, Anita. 2001. *China's workers under assault: The exploitation of labor in a globalizing economy*. Hong Kong: Asia Resource Monitor Centre.

Chang, Grace. 2000. *Disposable domestics: Immigrant women workers in the global economy*. Boston: South End Press.

Chapin, M. 2004. A challenge to conservationists. *World Watch* 17 (6): 17-32.

Cheah, Pheng. 2006. *Inhuman conditions: On cosmopolitanism and human rights*. Cambridge, MA: Harvard University Press.

Chesters, Graeme, and Ian Welsh. 2005. Complexity and social movement(s): Process and emergence in planetary action systems. *Theory, Culture, and Society* 22 (5): 187-211.

Christiansen, Thomas. 1996. Reconstructing European space: From territorial politics to multilevel governance. EUI Working Paper RSC. No. 96/53. Florence: European University Institute.

CNSRL Fratia (The "Brotherhood" National Confederation of Romanian Free Unions). 2004. Miscarea sindicala din Romania: Ghid introductiv [The union movement in Romania: An introductory guide]. Unpublished manuscript.

Code, Lorraine. 2000. The perversion of autonomy and the subjection of women: Discourses of social advocacy at century's end. In *Relational autonomy: Feminist perspectives on autonomy, agency, and the social self*, ed. Catriona Mackenzie and Natalie Stoljar, 181-209. New York: Oxford University Press.

Coleman, William D. and John C. Weaver. Forthcoming. *Property rights: Struggles over autonomy in a global age*. Vancouver: UBC Press.

Colley, Linda. 2003. What is imperial history now? In *What is history now?* ed. David Cannadine, 132-47. New York: Palgrave Macmillan.

Cook, Nancy. Forthcoming. *Gender, identity, and development in northern Pakistan*. New York: Palgrave Macmillan.

Coutin, Susan B. 2000. *Legalizing moves: Salvadoran immigrants' struggle for U.S. residency*. Ann Arbor: University of Michigan Press.

Coward, Martin. 2005. Editor's introduction. *Journal for Cultural Research* 9 (4): 323-9.

CRC Torres Strait. http://www.crctorres.com/postgrad/student.htm.

Dallmayr, F. 1994. Culture and global development. *Journal of Contemporary Thought* 4: 99-111.

Das, Veena. 1995. *Critical events: An anthropological perspective on contemporary India*. Delhi: Oxford University Press.

DeFilippis, James, Robert Fisher, and Eric Shragge. 2006. Neither romance nor regulation: Re-evaluating community. *International Journal of Urban and Regional Research* 30 (3): 673-89.

De Genova, Nicholas P. 2002. Migrant "illegality" and deportability in everyday life. *Annual Review of Anthropology* 31: 419-47.

Delanty, Gerard. 2003. *Community*. London: Routledge.

Della Porta, Donatella, and Lorenzo Mosca. 2005. Global-net for global movements? A network of networks for a movement of movements. *Journal of Public Policy* 25 (1): 165-90.

Della Porta, Donatella, and Sidney Tarrow. 2005. Transnational processes and social activism: An introduction. In *Transnational protest and global activism*, ed. Donatella Della Porta and Sidney Tarrow, 1-17. Lantham: Rowman and Littlefield.

Dellert, L.H. 1998. Sustained yield: Why has it failed to achieve sustainability? In *The wealth of forests: Markets, regulation, and sustainable forestry*, ed. C. Tollefson, 255-77. Vancouver: UBC Press.

Demeritt, D. 2001. Scientific forest conservation and the statistical picturing of nature's limits in the Progressive-Era United States. *Environment and Planning* 19 (4): 431-59.

Derrida, Jacques. 2001. *On cosmopolitanism and forgiveness*. New York: Routledge.

de Sousa Santos, Boaventura, and Joao Arriscado Nunes. 2004. Introduction: Democracy, participation, and grassroots movements in contemporary Portugal. *South European Society and Politics* 9 (2): 1-15.

de Toro, Suso. 2002. *Nunca Máis: Galiza á intemperie*. Vigo: Edicións Xerais.

Deyo, Fredric C. 1989. *Beneath the miracle: Labor subordination in the new Asian industrialism*. Berkeley: University of California Press.

Dirlik, Arif. 2000. Globalization as the end and the beginning of history: The contradictory implications of a new paradigm. Working Paper Series, Institute on Globalization and the Human Condition, McMaster University, Hamilton.

—. 2001. Place-based imagination: Globalism and the politics of place. In *Places and politics in an age of globalization*, ed. Roxann Prazniak and A. Dirlik, 15-52. Lanham: Rowman and Littlefield.

—. 2003. Modernity in question? Culture and religion in an age of global modernity. *Diaspora* 12 (2): 147-68.

Disney, Julian. 2000. Civil society, the Copenhagen Summit, and international governance. In *Civil Society, NGOs, and Global Governance*, ed. Bob Deacon, 9-22. GASPP Occasional Papers 7. Helsinki: Globalism and Social Policy Programme.

Doyal, Len, and Ian Gough. 1991. *A theory of human need*. New York: Guilford Press.

Drache, Daniel. 1982. Harold Innis and Canadian capitalist development. *Canadian Journal of Political and Social Theory* 6 (1-2): 35-60.

Dunn, John. 2003. Autonomy's sources and the impact of globalization. In *Virtues of independence and dependence on virtues*, ed. Ludvig Beckman and Emil Uddhammar, 47-62. New Brunswick, NJ: Transaction.

Earth Negotiations Bulletin. Various issues. Vol. 10: *A daily report on the World Summit for Social Development*. http://www.iisd.ca/wssd95.html.

Edelman, Marc. 2001. Social movements: Changing paradigms and forms of politics. *Annual Review of Anthropology* 30: 285-317.

Eder, Mine. 1997. Shop floor politics and labor movements: Democratization in Brazil and South Korea. *Critical Sociology* 23 (2): 3-31.

Eisenberg, Avigail, and Jeff Spinner-Haley, eds. 2005. *Minorities within minorities: Equality, rights, and diversity*. Cambridge, UK: Cambridge University Press.

Electronic Intifada. http://electronicintifada.net/new.shtml.

Enloe, Cynthia. 2004. *The curious feminist: Searching for women in a new age of empire*. Berkeley: University of California Press.

Environmental Working Group. PFC's, a family of chemicals that contaminate the planet. www.ewg.org/reports/pfcworld/.

Escobar, Arturo. 2001a. Culture sits in places: Reflections on globalism and subaltern strategies of localization. *Political Geography* 20 (2): 139-74.

—. 2001b. Place, economy, and culture in a postdevelopment era. In *Places and politics in an age of globalization,* ed. Roxann Prazniak and A. Dirlik, 193-218. New York: Rowman and Littlefield .

Essid, Yassine, and William D. Coleman, eds. Forthcoming. Deux Méditerranées: Les voies de la mondialisation et de l'autonomie. Vancouver: UBC Press.

Ester, Peter, and Henk Vinken. 2003. Debating civil society: On the fear for civic decline and hope for the Internet alternative. *International Sociology* 18 (4): 659-80.

ETUC (European Trade Union Confederation). 2003. *Make Europe work for the people: Action programme.* Brussels: ETUC.

Etzioni, Amatai. 1995. *The spirit of community.* London: Fontana.

—. 1996. *The new golden rule: Community and morality in a democratic society.* New York: Basic.

Fairbrother, Peter, and Charlotte Yates, eds. 2002. *Trade unions in renewal: A comparative study.* London: Routledge.

Fajans, Jane. 2006. Autonomy and relatedness: Emotions and the tension between individuality and sociality. *Critique of Anthropology* 26 (1): 103-19.

Falcón, Pilar. 2002. *Fraga y Galicia.* Barcelona: Editorial Ronsel.

Fernandez, James. 1997. The North-South axis in European popular cosmologies and the dynamic of the categorical. Provocations of European ethnology, special issue, *American Anthropologist* 99 (4): 725-8.

Fernandez, Manny. 2002. Demonstrators rally to Palestinian cause. *Washington Post,* 21 April. http://www.commondreams.org/headlines02/0421-02.htm.

Fernández de Rota Monter, José Antonio. 1998. Difference from the people's point of view. In *Democracy and ethnography,* ed. Carol J. Greenhouse, 124-42. New York: SUNY Press. http://europa.eu.int/comm/regional_policy/intro.

Fernback, Jan. 2007. Beyond the diluted community concept: A symbolic interactionist perspective on online social relations. *New Media and Society* 9 (1): 49-69.

Fineman, Martha Albertson. 2004. *The autonomy myth: A theory of dependency.* New York: New Press.

Fischbach, Michael R. 2002. The United Nations and Palestinian refugee property compensation. *Journal of Palestine Studies* 31 (2): 34-50.

Florida, Richard. 2002. *The rise of the creative class: And how it's transforming work, leisure, community, and everyday life.* New York: Basic.

Foucault, Michel. 1977. *Discipline and punish: The birth of the prison.* Trans. A. Sheridan. New York: Vintage Books.

—. 1978. *The history of sexuality.* Vol. 1. Trans. R. Hurley. New York: Vintage Books.

—. 1980. *Power/knowledge: Selected interviews and other writings.* Trans. C. Gordon, L. Marshall, J. Mepham, and K. Soper. Brighton: Harvester.

Friedman, Adina. 2003. Unraveling the right of return. *Refuge* 21 (2): 62-9.

Friedman, Elisabeth Jay, Kathryn Hochstetler, and Ann Marie Clark. 2005. *Sovereignty, democracy, and global civil society: State-society relations at UN World Conferences.* Albany: SUNY Press.

Frohlick, Susan. 2000. The hyper-masculine landscape of high-altitude mountaineering. *Michigan Feminist Studies* 14: 81-104.

Gaon, Stella. 2005. Communities in question: Sociality and solidarity in Nancy and Blanchot. *Journal for Cultural Research* 9 (4): 387-403.

Gauld, R. 2000. Maintaining centralized control in community-based forestry: Policy construction in the Philippines. *Development and Change* 31 (1): 229-54.

Gebremedhin, B., J. Pender, and G. Tesfaye. 2003. Community natural resource management: The case of woodlots in northern Ethiopia. *Environment and Development Economics* 8 (1): 129-48.

Gelb, D.D.M. 2001. *Independent review of TFL 46: Report on material reviewed to date, May 31, 2001.* Victoria: MacIsaac and Company.

George, Rosemary. 1994. Homes in the empire, empires in the home. *Cultural Critique* 26: 95-127.

Geske, Mary, and Susan Bourque. 2001. Grassroots organizations and women's human rights: Meeting the challenge of the global-local link. In *Women, gender, and human rights,* ed. Marjorie Agosin, 246-64. New Brunswick, NJ: Rutgers University Press.

Ghose, Indira. 1998. *Women travellers in colonial India: The power of the female gaze.* Delhi: Oxford University Press.

Gibson, C.C., M.A. McKean, and E. Ostrom. 2000. *People and forests: Communities, institutions, and governance.* Cambridge, MA: MIT Press.

Gibson-Graham, J.K. 1996. *The end of capitalism (as we knew it): A feminist critique of political economy.* Cambridge, MA: Blackwell Publishers.

Giddens, Anthony. 2000. *Runaway world: How globalization is reshaping our lives.* New York: Routledge.

Gill, Stephen. 2000. "Towards a postmodern prince? The Battle in Seattle as a moment in the new politics of globalization. *Millennium: Journal of International Studies* 29 (1): 131-40.

Gills, Barry, Joel Rocamora, and Richard Wilson, eds. 1993. *Low intensity democracy: Political power in the new world order.* London: Pluto Press.

Gilroy, Paul. 1993. *Black Atlantic: Modernity and double consciousness.* Cambridge, MA: Harvard University Press.

Gindin, Sam. 2004. The auto industry: Concretizing working class solidarity: Internationalism beyond slogans. Socialist Interventions Pamphlet Series. Socialist Project. http://www.socialistproject.ca/documents/.

Glowacka, Dorota. 2006. Community: Comme-un? *Culture Machine* 8. http://culturemachine.tees.ac.uk/Cmach/Backissues/j008/Articles/editorial.htm.

Gómez, Luis, and Pablo Ordaz. 2003. *Crónica negra del Prestige.* Madrid: Ediciones El Pais.

Graham, Ian. 2003. It pays to be union, US figures show. *Labour Education* 128: 13-16. http://ilo.law.cornell.edu/public/english/dialogue/actrav/publ/128/.

Green, T.L. 2000. Confusing liquidation with income in BC's forests: Economic analysis and the BC forest industry. *Ecological Economics* 34 (1): 33-46.

Greenfield, Gerald. 1998. The ICFTU and the politics of compromise. In *Rising from the ashes: Labour in the era of global capitalism,* ed. Ellen Wood, 180-9. New York: Monthly Review.

Greenhouse, Carol J., and Davydd J. Greenwood. 1998. Introduction: The ethnography of democracy and difference. In *Democracy and ethnography,* ed. Carol J. Greenhouse, 1-24. New York: SUNY Press.

Gregory, Derek. 1995. Imaginative geographies. *Progress in Human Geography* 19 (4): 447-85.

Grunberg, Laura. 2000. Women's NGOs in Romania. In *Reproducing gender: Politics, publics, and everyday life after socialism,* ed. Susan Gal and Gail Kligman, 307-36. Princeton: Princeton University Press.

Gulevich, Tanya. 1995. Gender, class, and rural urban distinctions in a Spanish city. PhD diss., University of Michigan.

Hall, Catherine. 2000. Introduction: Thinking the postcolonial, thinking the empire. In *Cultures of empire: Colonizers in Britain and the Empire in the nineteenth and twentieth centuries,* ed. Catherine Hall, 1-33. New York: Routledge.

Hall, Gary. 2007. The politics of secrecy: Cultural studies and Derrida in the age of empire. *Cultural Studies* 21 (1): 59-81.

Hall, S. 1996. On postmodernism and articulation: An interview with Stuart Hall. In *Stuart Hall: Critical dialogues in cultural studies,* ed. D. Morley and K. Chen, 131-50. London: Routledge.

Halseth, G. 1996. "Community" and land-use planning debate: An example from rural British Columbia. *Environment and Planning A* 28 (7): 1279-98.

—. 1999a. Resource town employment: Perceptions in small town British Columbia. *Tijdschrift voor Economische en Sociale Geografie* 90 (2): 196-210.

—. 1999b. "We came for the work": Situating employment migration in BC's small, resource-based, communities. *Canadian Geographer/Geographe canadien* 43 (4): 363-81.

Hanieh, Akram. 2001. The Camp David papers. *Journal of Palestine Studies* 30 (2): 75-97.

Hansen, Peter H. 1995. Albert Smith, the Alpine Club, and the invention of mountaineering in mid-Victorian Britain. *Journal of British Studies* 34 (3): 300-24.

—. 1996.Vertical boundaries, national identities: British mountaineering on the frontiers of Europe and the Empire, 1868-1914. *Journal of Imperial and Commonwealth History* 24 (1): 48-71.

Haraway, Donna J. 1988. Situated knowledges: The science question in feminism and the privilege of partial perspective. *Feminist Studies* 14 (3): 575-99.

—. 1997. *Modest_witness@second_millennium. FemaleMan©_meets_OncoMouse™: Feminism and technoscience.* London: Routledge.

Harcourt, Wendy. 2001. Rethinking difference and equality: Women and the politics of place. In *Places and politics in an age of globalization,* ed. Roxann Prazniak and A. Dirlik, 299-322. Lanham: Rowman and Littlefield.

Hardt, Michael, and Antonio Negri. 2000. *Empire.* Cambridge, MA: Harvard University Press.

—. 2004. *Multitude: War and democracy in the age of empire.* Harmondsworth: Penguin.

Harrod, Jeffrey. 1987. *Power, production, and the unprotected worker.* New York: Columbia University Press.

—. 1992. *Labour and Third World debt.* Brussels: International Federation of Chemical, Energy, and General Workers Unions.

Hart, G. 2002. *Disabling globalization: Places of power in post-apartheid South Africa.* Berkeley: University of California Press.

—. 2004. Denaturalizing dispossession: Critical ethnography in the age of resurgent imperialism. Paper prepared for the conference Creative Destruction: Area Knowledge and New Geographies of Empire, Center for Place, Culture, and Politics, CUNY Graduate Center, 15-17 April, New York.

Harvey, D. 1982. *The limits to capital.* Oxford: Blackwell.

—. 1985. *The urbanization of capital: Studies in the history and theory of capitalist urbanization.* Baltimore: Johns Hopkins University Press.

Hayter, R. 1997. High-performance organizations and employment flexibility: A case study of in situ change at the Powell River paper mill, 1980-1994. *Canadian Geographer/Géographe canadien* 41 (1): 26-40.

—. 2000. *Flexible crossroads: The restructuring of British Columbia's forest economy.* Vancouver: UBC Press.

—. 2003. The war in the woods: Post-Fordist restructuring, globalization, and the contested remapping of British Columbia's forest economy. *Annals of the Association of American Geographers* 93 (3): 706-29.

Hayter, Roger, and Trevor Barnes. 1990. Innis' staples theory, exports, and recession: British Columbia, 1981-86. *Economic Geography* 66 (2): 156-73.

—. 1997. Troubles in the rainforest: British Columbia's forest economy in transition. In *Troubles in the rainforest: British Columbia's forest economy in transition,* ed. T. Barnes and R. Hayter, 1-11. Victoria: Western Geographical Press.

—. 2001. Canada's resource economy. *Canadian Geographer* 45 (1): 36-41.

Held, David. 1995. *Democracy and the global order.* Stanford: Stanford University Press.

Held, David, Anthony McGrew, David Goldblatt, and Jonathan Perraton. 1999. *Global transformations.* Palo Alto: Stanford University Press.

Hemment, Julie. 2004. The riddle of the third sector: Civil society, international aid, and NGOs in Russia. *Anthropological Quarterly* 77 (2): 215-41.

Henderson, James (Sákéj) Youngblood. 2000. *Ayukpachi:* Empowering Aboriginal thought. In *Reclaiming indigenous voice and vision,* ed. Marie Battiste, 248-78. Vancouver: UBC Press.

Henderson, Jennifer. 2003. *Settler feminism and race making in Canada.* Toronto: University of Toronto Press.

Herz, Judith Scherer. 2004. Individual. *English Studies in Canada* 30 (4): 33-7.

Highway, Tomson. 1989. *Dry Lips oughta move to Kapuskasing.* Saskatoon: Fifth House.

Hirst, Paul, and Graham Thompson. 1999. *Globalization in question.* 2nd ed. Cambridge, UK: Polity Press.

Hobbs, Holly. 1994. *City hall goes abroad: The foreign policy of local politics.* Thousand Oaks, CA: Sage.

Honig, Bonnie. 1996. Difference, dilemmas, and the politics of home. In *Democracy and difference: Contesting the boundaries of the political,* ed. Seyla Benhabib, 257-77. Princeton: Princeton University Press.

—. 2001. *Democracy and the foreigner.* Princeton: Princeton University Press.

Hulme, D., and M. Murphree. 1999. Communities, wildlife, and the "new conservation" in Africa. *Journal of International Development* 11 (2): 277-85.

Hunt, Sir John. 1954. *The conquest of Everest.* New York: Dutton.

Hyde, Lewis. 1998. *Trickster makes this world.* New York: Farrar, Straus, and Giroux.

Icken Safa, Irene. 1995. Women's social movements in Latin America. In *Women in the Latin American development process,* ed. Christine Bose and Edna Acosta-Belen, 227-41. Philadelphia: Temple University Press.

Ignatieff, Michael. 2000. *Rights revolution.* Toronto: Anansi.

Imig, Doug, and Sidney Tarrow. 2001. *Contentious Europeans: Protest and politics in an emerging polity.* New York: Rowman and Littlefield.

Innis, Harold Adams. 1956. *Essays in Canadian economic history.* Toronto: University of Toronto Press.

Instituto Galego de Estatística. http://www.xunta.es/auto/ige/Datos/Gal-98/c03/3-04.htm.

Isin, Engin F. 2002. *Being political: Genealogies of citizenship.* Minneapolis: University of Minnesota Press.

Jacobs, Brian. 2001. Dialogical rationality and the critique of absolute autonomy. In *Critical theory: Current state and future prospects,* ed. Peter Uwe Hohendahl and Jaimey Fisher, 139-53. New York: Berghahn.

Jameson, Fredric. 1994. *Postmodernism: Or, the cultural logic of late capitalism.* Durham: Duke University Press.

Jayawardena, Kumari. 1995. *The white women's other burden: Western women and South Asia during British rule.* London: Routledge.

Jayaweera, Swarna. 1990. European women educators under the British colonial administration in Sri Lanka. *Women's Studies International Forum* 13 (4): 323-31.

Jessop, Bob. 1993. Towards a Schumpeterian workfare state? Preliminary remarks on post-Fordist political economy. *Studies in Political Economy* 40: 7-40.

—. 2001. Regulationist and autopoieticist reflections on Polanyi's account of market economies and the market society. *New Political Economy* 6 (2): 213-32.

—. 2004. On the limits of the *Limits to Capital*. *Antipode* 36 (3): 480-96.

Johannes, R.E. 2002. The renaissance of community-based marine resource management in Oceania. *Annual Review of Ecological Systems* 33: 317-40.

Jolly, Margaret. 1993. The maternal body and empire. In *Feminism and the politics of difference*, ed. S. Gunew and A. Yeatman, 103-27. Halifax: Fernwood Publishing.

Joseph, Miranda. 2002. *Against the romance of community*. Minneapolis : University of Minnesota Press.

Kalyvas, Andreas. 2001. The politics of autonomy and the challenge of deliberation: Castoriadis contra Habermas. *Thesis Eleven* 64: 1-19.

Kaplan, E. Ann. 1997. *Looking for the other: Feminism, film, and the imperial gaze*. London: Routledge.

Karam, Azza. 2000. Feminisms and Islamisms in Egypt: Between globalization and post-modernism. In *Gender and global restructuring: Sightings, sights, and resistances*, ed. Marianne Marchand and Anne Sisson Runyan, 194-208. London: Routledge.

Kavanagh, Andrea, John M. Carroll, Mary Beth Rosson, Debbie D. Reese, and Than T. Zin. 2005. Participating in civil society: The case of networked communities. *Interacting with Computers* 17 (1): 9-33.

Keck, Margaret, and Kathryn Sikkink. 1998. *Activists beyond borders: Advocacy networks in international politics*. Ithaca: Cornell University Press.

Keenan, Patrick J. 2007. Do norms still matter? The corrosive effects of globalization on the vitality of norms. University of Illinois College of Law, Law and Economics Working Papers 73. http://law.bepress.com/uiuclwps/papers/art73.

Kellert, S.R., J.N. Mehta, S.A. Ebbin, and L.L. Lichenfeld. 2000. Community natural resource management: Promise, rhetoric, and reality. *Society and Natural Resources* 13 (8): 705-15.

Kelley, Heidi. 1994. The myth of matriarchy: Symbols of womanhood in Galician regional identity. *Anthropological Quarterly* 67 (2): 71-80.

Kennedy, Edward Shirley, ed. 1862. *Peaks, passes and glaciers: Being excursions by members of the Alpine Club*. Second Series. London: Longman, Green, Longman, and Roberts.

Kerr, Johanna. 2002. From "WID" to "GAD" to women's rights: The first twenty years of AWID. Association for Women's Rights in Development, Occasional Paper 9. http://www.awid.org/go.php?cid=28.

Keung, Nicholas. 2004. Women face dilemma: Abuse or deportation? *Toronto Star,* 3 August.

Khalidi, Rashid. 1992. Observations on the right of return. *Journal of Palestine Studies* 21 (2): 29-40.

—. 1998. *Palestinian identity: The construction of modern consciousness*. New York: Columbia University Press.

Klein, Naomi. 2001. Reclaiming the commons. *New Left Review* 9: 81-9.

Klooster, D. 1999. Community-based forestry in Mexico: Can it reverse processes of degradation? *Land Degradation and Development* 10 (4): 365-81.

—. 2000. Community forestry and tree theft in Mexico: Resistance or complicity in conservation? *Development and Change* 31 (1): 281-305.

Klooster, D., and O. Masera. 2000. Community forest management in Mexico: Carbon mitigation and biodiversity conservation through rural development. *Global Environmental Change — Human and Policy Dimensions* 10 (4): 259-72.

Knapman, Claudia. 1986. *White women in Fiji, 1835-1930.* London: Allen and Unwin.

Kooses, D. 2004. Are diamonds a Cree's best friend? *Globe and Mail,* April 5.

Korhonen, Kuisma. 2006. Textual communities: Nancy, Blanchot, Derrida. *Culture Machine* 8. http://culturemachine.tees.ac.uk/Articles/Korhonen.htm.

Kull, C.A. 2002. Empowering pyromaniacs in Madagascar: Ideology and legitimacy in community-based natural resource management. *Development and Change* 33 (1): 57-78.

Laclau, E. 2005. Populism: What's in a name? http://www.essex.ac.uk/centres/TheoStud/onlinepapers.asp.

Lagares Díez, Nieves. 2003. O Partido Popular de Galicia. In *Os partidos políticos en Galicia,* ed. Xosé Manuel Rivera Otero, 19-98. Vigo, Galicia: Edicións Xerais de Galicia.

Lambert, Rob, and Eddie Webster. 2001. Southern unionism and the New Labour Internationalism. *Antipode* 33 (3): 337-62.

—. 2003. Transnational union strategies for civilizing labor standards. In *Civilizing globalization: A survival guide,* ed. R. Sandbrook, 221-36. Albany: SUNY Press.

Langdon, S.J. 2002. "Construing conservation": An examination of conceptual construction and application to Yup'Ik cultural practice. Paper presented at the Ninth International Conference on Hunting and Gathering Societies, 9-13 September, Edinburgh.

Langman, Lauren. 2005. From virtual public spheres to global justice: A critical theory of internetworked social movements. *Sociological Theory* 23 (1): 42-74.

La Plataforma Cidadá Nunca Máis. www.plataformanuncamais.org.

La voz de Galicia. 2003. La voz dedicó más de cinco mil páginas a seguir la catastrophe. *La voz de Galicia,* 13 November.

Leach, M., R. Mearns, and I. Scoones. 1999. Environmental entitlements: Dynamics and institutions in community-based natural resource management. *World Development* 27 (2): 225-47.

Lester, Alan. 2002. Constructing colonial discourse: Britain, South Africa, and the Empire in the nineteenth century. In *Postcolonial Geographies,* ed. Alison Blunt and Cheryl McEwan, 29-45. London: Continuum.

Lind, Amy. 2000. Negotiating boundaries: Women's organizations and the politics of restructuring in Ecuador. In *Gender and global restructuring: Sightings, sights, and resistances,* ed. Marianne Marchand and Anne Sisson Runyan, 161-75. London: Routledge.

Linkogle, Stephanie. 2001. Nicaraguan women in the age of globalization. In *Women resist globalization: Mobilizing for livelihood and rights,* ed. Sheila Rowbotham and Stephanie Linkogle, 118-33. London: Zed Books.

Lobato, Xurxo. 2003. *No país do Nunca Máis.* Vigo, Galicia: Editorial Galaxia.

Lowry, Michelle, and Peter Nyers. 2003. "No One Is Illegal": The fight for refugee and migrant rights in Canada. *Refuge: Canada's Periodical on Refugees* 21 (3): 66-72.

Lui, Getano, Jr., 1995. Torres Strait self-government and the Australian nation state. In *Becoming visible: Indigenous politics and self-government,* ed. Terje Brantenberg, Janne Hansen, and Henry Minde, 62-75. Tromsø, Norway: Centre for Sámi Studies, University of Tromsø. http://www.uit.no/ssweb/dok/series/no2/en/211luig.htm.

Lynd, Staughton, Sam Bahour, and Alice Lynd, eds. 1994. *Homeland: Oral histories of Palestinians.* New York: Olive Branch Press.

Macfarlane, Robert. 2003. *Mountains of the mind: Adventures in reaching the summit.* New York: Random House.

Mackenzie, Catriona, and Natalie Stoljar, eds. 2000. *Relational autonomy: Feminist perspectives on autonomy, agency, and the social self.* New York: Oxford University Press.

Macpherson, C.B. 1962. *The political theory of possessive individualism: Hobbes to Locke.* Oxford: Oxford University Press.

Magnusson, W., and K. Shaw. 2003. *A political space: Reading the global through Clayoquot Sound.* Minneapolis: University of Minnesota Press.

Marchak, M.P. 1983. *Green gold: The forest industry in British Columbia.* Vancouver: UBC Press.

Marchak, M.P., S.L. Aycock, and D. Herbert. 1999. *Falldown: Forest policy in British Columbia.* Vancouver: David Suzuki Foundation; Ecotrust Canada.

Marchand, Marianne, and Anne Sisson Runyan. 2000. Introduction. In *Gender and global restructuring: Sightings, sights, and resistances,* ed. Marianne Marchand and Anne Sisson Runyan, 1-22. London: Routledge.

Marshall, T.H. 1950. *Citizenship and social class.* Cambridge, UK: Cambridge University Press.

Matteo, Perin. 2005. The sense of freedom, the surprise of being-in-common. *Law and Critique* 16: 315-38.

Mazzarella, William. 2004. Culture, globalization, mediation. *Annual Review of Anthropology* 33: 345-67.

McCarthy, J. 2002. First World political ecology: Lessons from the wise use movement. *Environment and Planning A* 34: 1281-1302.

McCay, B.J., and S. Jentoft. 1996. From the bottom up: Participatory issues in fisheries management. *Society and Natural Resources* 9: 237-50.

McManus, P. 2002. The potential and limits of progressive neo-pluralism: A comparative study of forest politics in coastal British Columbia and south east New South Wales during the 1990s. *Environment and Planning A* 34: 845-65.

McMichael, Philip. 1997. Rethinking globalization: The agrarian question revisited. *Review of International Political Economy* 4 (4): 630-62.

Melman, Billie. 1992. *Women's Orients: English women and the Middle East, 1718-1918.* Ann Arbor: University of Michigan Press.

Messner, Reinhold. 2004-5. Messner says alpinism is dead. *Gripped: The Climbing Magazine* 6 (6): 14.

Mezzadra, Sandro. 2004. The right to escape. *Ephemera* 4 (3): 267-75.

Mezzadra, Sandro, and Brett Neilson. 2003. Né qui, né altrove: Migration, detention, desertion. A dialogue. *Borderlands E-Journal* 2 (1), http://www.borderlandsejournal.adelaide. edu.au/vol2no1_2003/mezzadra_neilson.html.

Miller, J. Hillis. 2004. Community. *English Studies in Canada* 30 (4): 11-15.

Minde, H., R. Nilsen, and S. Jentoft, eds. 2003. *Indigenous peoples: Resource management and global rights.* Delft, Netherlands: Eburon.

Mishra, Ramesh. 1999. *Globalization and the welfare state.* Cheltenham: Edward Elgar.

Mohanty, Chandra. 1984. Under Western eyes: Feminist scholarship and colonial discourses. *Boundary 2* 12 (3): 333-8.

Mootoo, Shani. 2001. *The predicament of or.* Vancouver: Polestar.

Morantz, Toby. 2002. *The white man's gonna getcha: The colonial challenge to the Crees in Quebec.* Montreal and Kingston: McGill-Queen's University Press.

Morin, Marie-Eve. 2006. Putting community under erasure: Derrida and Nancy on the plurality of singularities. *Culture Machine* 8. http://culturemachine.tees.ac.uk?Articles/morin.htm.

Morris, J. 1958. *Coronation Everest.* London: Faber and Faber.

Mountain Equipment Co-op. http://www.mec.ca.

Mulrennan, M.E., and C.H. Scott. 2000. *Mare nullius:* Indigenous rights in saltwater environments. *Development and Change* 31 (3): 681-708.

—. 2005. Co-management: An attainable partnership? Two cases from James Bay and Torres Strait. *Anthropologica* 47 (2): 197-214.

Mye, George. 1992. Address by Mr. George Mye, MBE, ATSIC commissioner for Torres Strait, to the United Nations Working Group on Indigenous Populations, Geneva, July. http://www.cwis.org/fwdp/Oceania/atsic.txt.

Nacher, D.C., and C.G. Hickey. 2002. Putting the community back into community-based resource management: A criteria and indicators approach to sustainability. *Human Organization* 61 (4): 350-63.

Nagel, Caroline R., and Lynn Staeheli. 2004. Citizenship, identity, and transnational migration: Arab immigrants to the United States. *Space and Polity* 8 (1): 3-23.

Nagendra, H. 2002. Tenure and forest conditions: Community forestry in the Nepal Terai. *Environmental Conservation* 29 (4): 530-9.

Nancy, Jean-Luc. 1991. *The inoperative community.* Ed. Peter Connor. Trans. Peter Connor, Lisa Garbus, Michael Holland, and Simona Sawheny. Minneapolis: University of Minnesota Press.

—. 2000. *Being singular plural.* Trans. Robert D. Richardson and Anne E. O'Byrne. Stanford: Stanford University Press.

—. 2007. *The creation of the world or globalization.* Trans. François Raffoul and David Pettigrew. Albany: SUNY Press.

Navaro-Yashin, Yael. 2002. *Faces of the state: Secularism and public life in Turkey.* Princeton: Princeton University Press.

Nazzal, Nafez. 1978. *The Palestinian exodus from Galilee 1948.* Beirut: Institute for Palestine Studies.

NGO Forum. 1995. The Copenhagen Alternative Declaration. 8 March. http://www.un.org/documents/ga/conf166/ngo/950310124616.htm.

Niezen, Ronald. 2005. Digital identity: The construction of virtual selfhood in the indigenous peoples' movement. *Comparative Studies in Society and History* 47 (3): 532-51.

Núñez, Xosé Manoel. 2002. History and collective memories of migration in a land of migrants: The case of Iberian Galicia. *History and Memory* 14 (1-2): 5-12.

Nyers, Peter. 2003. Abject cosmopolitanism: The politics of protection in the anti-deportation movement. *Third World Quarterly* 24 (6): 1069-93.

—. 2006. *Rethinking refugees: Beyond states of emergency.* New York: Routledge.

Oates, J.F. 1999. *Myth and reality in the rainforest: How conservation strategies are failing in West Africa.* Berkeley: University of California Press.

O'Brien, Robert. 2002. Workers and world order: The tentative transformation of the international union movement. *Review of International Studies* 26 (4): 533-55.

O'Brien, Susie, and Imre Szeman. 2001. Introduction: The fiction of globalization/the globalization of fiction. *South Atlantic Quarterly* 100 (3): 601-24.

Olesen, Thomas. 2005. Transnational publics: New spaces of social movement activism and the problem of global long-sightedness. *Current Sociology* 53 (3): 419-40.

O'Riain, S., and F. Block. 2003. Introduction. *Politics and Society* 32: 187-91.

Ostrom, E. 1998. Scales, polycentricity, and incentives: Designing complexity to govern complexity. In *Protection of global biodiversity: Converging strategies,* ed. L.D. Guruswamy and J.A. McNeely, 149-67. Durham: Duke University Press.

Ostry, A. 1999. The links between industrial, community, and ecological sustainability: A forestry case study. *Ecosystem Health* 5 (3): 193-203.

Padgham, Oona. 2005. Drawing detention: A conversation with No One Is Illegal. *Fuse Magazine: Art, Media, Politics* 28 (2): 15-18.

Palestine Remembered. http://www.palestineremembered.com.

Palestinian Center for Policy and Survey Research (PSR). http://www.pcpsr.org.

Palestinian Refugee Research Net. http://www.arts.mcgill.ca/mepp/new_prrn/.

Pasha, Mustapha Kamal, and David Blaney. 1998. Elusive paradise: The promise and peril of global civil society. *Alternatives* 23: 417-50.

Passavant, Paul A. 2007. The contradictory state of Giorgio Agamben. *Political Theory* 35 (1): 147-74.

Pauly, Louis W., and William D. Coleman. 2008. *Global ordering: Institutions and autonomy in a changing world.* Vancouver: UBC Press.

Paz, Xavier, and Alba Vázquez Carpentier, eds. 2003. *Nunca Máis: A voz da cidadanía.* A Coruña, Galicia: Difusora de Letras, Artes e Ideas.

Peck, J. 2002. Political economics of scale: Fast policy, interscalar relations, and neoliberal workfare. *Economic Geography* 78 (3): 331-60.

Perelman, Michael. 2000. *The invention of capitalism: Classical political economy and the secret history of primitive accumulation.* Durham: Duke University Press.

Peterson, V. Spike, and Anne Sisson Runyan. 1993. *Global gender issues.* Boulder: Westview Press.

Pickles, Katie. 2000. Exhibiting Canada: Empire, migration, and the 1928 English schoolgirl tour. *Gender, Place, and Culture* 7 (1): 81-96.

—. 2002. *Female imperialism and national identity: Imperial Order Daughters of the Empire.* New York: Manchester University Press.

Pishchikova, Kateryna. 2006. The promise of transnational NGO dialogue: The argument and the challenges. *Cambridge Review of International Affairs* 19 (1): 49-61.

Polanyi, K. 1944. *The great transformation.* Boston: Beacon Press.

Pratt, Anna. 2005. *Securing borders: Detention and deportation in Canada.* Vancouver: UBC Press.

Pratt, Mary Louise. 2001. Modernity and periphery: Toward a global and relational analysis. In *Beyond dichotomies: Histories, identities, cultures, and the challenge of globalization,* ed. Elisabeth Mudimbe-Boyi, 21-48. New York: SUNY Press.

Preston, Jennifer C. 1990. Tomson Highway: Dancing to the tune of the Trickster. MA thesis, University of Guelph.

Preston, Richard J. 1975. Eastern Cree community in relation to fur trade post in the 1830s: The background of the "posting" process. In *Proceedings of the 6th Algonquian Conference,* vol. 7, ed. W. Cowan, 324-35. Ottawa: National Museum of Man.

—. 1980. Eastern Cree notions of social grouping. In *Papers of the 11th Algonquian Conference,* vol. 11, ed. W. Cowan, 40-8. Ottawa: Carleton University.

—. 1982. The politics of community relocation: An Eastern Cree example. Special issue. *Culture* 11 (3): 37-49.

—. 1986. Twentieth century transformations of the West Coast Cree. In *Proceedings of the 17th Algonquian Conference,* vol. 17, ed. W. Cowan, 239-51. Ottawa: Carleton University.

—. 1999. Reflections on culture, history, and authenticity. In *Theorizing the Americanist tradition,* ed. L. Valentine and R. Darnell, 150-62. Toronto: University of Toronto Press.

—. 2001. James Bay Cree culture, malnutrition, infectious and degenerative diseases. In *Papers of the 29th Conference on Algonquian Studies*, vol. 32, ed. J.D. Nichols, 374-84. Winnipeg: University of Manitoba.

—. 2004. Cumulative cultural change in the Moose and Rupert river basins: Local cultural sites affected by global influences. In *Globalization and community: Canadian perspectives*, ed. J.L. Chodkiewicz and R.E. Wiest, 87-98. Winnipeg: University of Manitoba.

—. Forthcoming. Appendix. In *The autobiography of Henry Connolly, Métis fur trader*, ed. Richard J. Preston and James Morrison. Winnipeg: Rupert's Land Research Centre.

Preston, Richard J., and John S. Long. 1998. Apportioning responsibility for cumulative change: A Cree community in northeastern Ontario. In *Papers of the 32nd Conference on Algonquian Studies*, vol. 29, ed. J.D. Nichols, 264-75. Winnipeg: University of Manitoba.

Preston, Sarah C. 1982. Competent social behaviour within the context of childbirth: A Cree example. In *Papers of the 13th Algonquian Conference*, vol. 13, ed. W. Cowan, 211-17. Ottawa: Carleton University.

—. 1986. *Let the past go: A life history narrated by Alice Jacob*. Ottawa: National Museums of Canada.

Prieto de Pedro, Jesús. 1998. Democracy and cultural difference in the Spanish Constitution of 1978. In *Democracy and Ethnography*, ed. Carol J. Greenhouse, 61-80. New York: SUNY Press.

Probyn, Elspeth. 1996. *Outside belongings*. New York: Routledge.

Proulx, Craig. 2003. *Reclaiming Aboriginal justice, identity, and community*. Saskatoon: Purich Publishing.

Prudham, S. 2007. Sustaining sustained yield: Class, politics, and post-war forest regulation in British Columbia. *Environment and Planning D: Society and Space* 25 (2): 258-83.

—. 2008. Tall among the trees: Organizing against globalist forestry in rural British Columbia. *Journal of Rural Studies* 24 (2): 182-96.

Prudham, S., and R. Penfold. 2005. *Fractured lives: Results of the 2003 survey of Youbou sawmill workers*. Victoria: Youbou TimberLess Society; Vancouver Island Public Interest Research Group.

Ramusack, Barbara. 1990. Cultural missionaries, maternal imperialists, feminist allies: British women activists in India, 1865-1945. *Women's Studies International Forum* 13 (4): 309-21.

Rancière, Jacques. 1999. *Dis-agreement: Politics and philosophy*. Minneapolis: University of Minnesota Press.

Rankin, K. 2003. Anthropologies and geographies of globalization. *Progress in Human Geography* 27 (6): 708-34.

Ray, R., and A.C. Korteweg. 1999. Women's movements in the Third World: Identity, mobilization, and autonomy. *Annual Review of Sociology* 25: 47-71.

Rayner, J. 1996. Implementing sustainability in West Coast forests: CORE and FEMAT as experiments in process. *Journal of Canadian Studies* 31 (1): 82-101.

Rayner, J., M. Howlett, J. Wilson, B. Cashore, and G. Hoberg. 2001. Privileging the subsector: Critical subsectors and sectoral relationships in forest policy-making. *Forest Policy and Economics* 2 (3-4): 319-32.

Rébuffat, Gaston. 1954. The brotherhood of the rope: Tools and techniques. In *Starlight and storm: The conquest of the great north faces of the Alps*. Trans. Wilfrid Noyce and Sir John Hunt. New York: Modern Library.

Redclift, M. 1987. *Sustainable development: Exploring the contradictions*. London: Methuen.

Redford, K.H., K. Brandon, and S.E. Sanderson. 1998. Holding ground. In *Parks in peril: People, politics, and protected areas,* ed. K. Brandon, K.H. Redford, and S.E. Sanderson, 455-63. Washington, DC: Island Press.

Redford, K.H., and S.E. Sanderson. 2000. Extracting humans from nature. *Conservation Biology* 14 (5): 1362-4.

Reed, M.G. 1999. "Jobs talk": Retreating from the social sustainability of forestry communities. *Forestry Chronicle* 75 (5): 755-63.

Reichwein, PearlAnn, and Karen Fox. 2001. Margaret Fleming and the Alpine Club of Canada: A woman's place in mountain leisure and literature, 1932-1952. *Journal of Canadian Studies* 36 (3): 35-60.

Rempel, Terry. 1999. The Ottawa process: Workshop on compensation and Palestinian refugees. *Journal of Palestine Studies* 29 (1): 36-49.

—, ed. 2000. *Palestinian refugees in exile: Country profiles.* Campaign for the Defense of Palestinian Refugee Rights. BADIL Resource Center for Palestinian Residency and Refugee Rights, Bethlehem, Palestine.

Riedi, Eliza. 2005. Teaching empire: British and dominions women teachers in the South African War concentration camps. *English Historical Review* 120 (489): 1316-47.

Risk Online. http://www.risk.ru/mount/events/Nepal/index.html.

Robbins, David. 1987. Sport, hegemony, and the middle class: The Victorian mountaineers. *Theory, Culture, and Society* 4 (3): 579-601.

Robertson, Roland. 1992. *Globalization: Social theory and global culture.* London: Sage.

Robinson, Andrew, and Simon Tormey. 2005. A ticklish subject: Žižek and the future of left radicalism. *Thesis Eleven* 80 (1): 94-107.

Roe, D., J. Mayers, M. Grieg-Gran, C. Kothari, C. Fabricius, and R. Hughes. 2000. *Evaluating Eden: Exploring the myths and realities of community-based wildlife management: Series overview.* London: International Institute for Environment and Development.

Rose, David, and Ed Douglas. 1999. *Regions of the heart: The triumph and tragedy of Alison Hargreaves.* London: Penguin.

Roseman, Sharon. 1993. Santiago de Carreira: Stories of labour in a community of Galician worker-peasants. PhD diss., McMaster University.

—. 1995. "Falamos como Falamos": Linguistic revitalization and the maintenance of local vernaculars in Galicia. *Journal of Linguistic Anthropology* 5 (1): 3-32.

—. 1999. "Fixo Ben" (she did the right thing): Women and social disruption in rural Galicia. In *Feminist fields: Ethnographic insights,* ed. Rae Bridgman, Sally Cole, and Heather Howard-Bobiwash, 212-28. Peterborough, ON: Broadview Press.

—. 2003. Poniendo la artesanía gallega y el turismo rural gallego en el mapa global: Políticas administrativas y propuestas locales. In *Las expresiones locales de la globalización: México y España,* ed. Carmen Bueno and Encarnación Aguilar, 381-404. Mexico: Universidad Iberoamericana.

—. 2004. Bioregulation and *Comida Caseira* in rural Galicia, Spain. *Identities: Global Studies in Culture and Power* 11 (1): 9-37.

Roseman, Sharon, and Heidi Kelley. 1999. Introduction: Anthropological analyses of gender in northwestern Iberia. *Anthropologica* 41 (2): 89-101.

Roudometof, Victor. 2005. Transnationalism, cosmopolitanism, and glocalization. *Current Sociology* 53 (1): 113-35.

Rowbotham, Sheila, and Stephanie Linkogle, eds. 2001. *Women resist globalization: Mobilizing for livelihood and rights.* London: Zed Books.

Rupert, Mark. 1995. (Re)politicizing the global economy: Liberal common sense and ideological struggle in the US NAFTA debate. *Review of International Political Economy* 2 (4): 658-92.

Sabel, Robbie. 2003. The Palestinian refugees, international law, and the peace process. *Refuge* 21 (2): 52-61.

Said, Edward. 1978. *Orientalism: Western representations of the Orient.* New York: Vintage Books.

—. 1986. *After the last sky: Palestinian lives.* New York: Pantheon Books.

—. 1993. The morning after. *London Review of Books,* 21 October. http://www.lrb.co.uk/v15/n20/said01_.html.

—. 1994. *The politics of dispossession: The struggle for Palestinian self-determination, 1969-1994.* New York: Pantheon Books.

—. 1996. *Peace and its discontents: Essays on Palestine in the Middle East peace process.* New York: Vintage Books.

Said, Wadie E. 2003. Palestinian refugees: Host countries, legal status, and the right of return. *Refuge* 21 (2): 89-95.

Salazar, D.J., and D.K. Alper. 1996. Perceptions of power and the management of environmental conflict: Forest politics in British Columbia. *Social Science Journal* 33 (4): 381-99.

Salon.com. http://www.salon.com.

Samaddar, Ranabir. 2004. *The politics of dialogue: Living under the geopolitical histories of war and peace.* Aldershot: Ashgate.

Sassen, Saskia. 2002. Towards a sociology of information technology. *Current Sociology* 50 (3): 365-88.

—. 2004. Local actors in global politics. *Current Sociology* 52 (4): 649-70.

—. 2006a. When national territory is home to the global: Old borders to novel borderings. In *Key debates in new political economy,* ed. Anthony Payne, 106-27. London: Routledge.

—. 2006b. *Territory, authority, rights: From medieval to global assemblages.* Princeton: Princeton University Press.

Satterfield, T. 2002. *Anatomy of a conflict: Identity, knowledge, and emotion in old-growth forests.* Vancouver: UBC Press.

Saunders, Doug. 2003. Raids on Wal-Mart expose dark side of US economy. *Globe and Mail,* 24 October, A1.

Sayigh, Rosemary. 1979. *Palestinians: From peasants to revolutionaries: A people's history.* London: Zed Books.

Schirmer, J.G. 1989. Those who die for life cannot be called dead: Women in human rights protest in Latin America. *Feminist Review* 32: 3-29.

Schneider, Jane, and Peter Schneider. 2003. *Reversible destiny: Mafia, antimafia, and the struggle for Palermo.* Berkeley: University of California Press.

Scholte, Jan Aart. 2000. *Globalization: A critical introduction.* New York: St. Martin's Press.

—. 2003. What is globalization? The definitional issue again. IGHC Working Paper 03/4, Institute on Globalization and the Human Condition, McMaster University, Hamilton.

—. 2005. *Globalization: A critical introduction.* 2nd ed. London: Palgrave.

Scoones, I. 1999. New ecology and the social sciences: What prospects for a fruitful engagement? *Annual Review of Anthropology* 28 (1): 479-507.

Scott, C.H. 2001. On autonomy and development. In *Aboriginal autonomy and development in northern Quebec and Labrador,* ed. Colin H. Scott, 3-20. Vancouver: UBC Press.

—. 2004. Our feet are on the land, but our hands are in the sea: Knowing and caring for marine territory at Erub, Torres Strait. In *Woven histories, dancing lives: Torres Strait Islander identity, culture, and history*, ed. R. Davis, 259-70. Canberra: Aboriginal Studies Press.

—. 2005. Co-management and the politics of Aboriginal consent to resource development: The Agreement Concerning a New Relationship between le Gouvernement du Québec and the Crees of Quebec (2002). In *Canada: The state of the federation, 2003*, ed. Michael Murphy, 133-63. Montreal and Kingston: McGill-Queen's University Press.

Scott, C.H., and M.E. Mulrennan. 1999. Land and sea tenure at Erub, Torres Strait: Property, sovereignty, and the adjudication of cultural continuity. *Oceania* 70 (22): 146-76.

Scott, J.C. 1976. *The moral economy of the peasant: Subsistence and rebellion in Southeast Asia*. New Haven: Yale University Press.

Sharpe, Jenny. 1993. *Allegories of empire: The figure of woman in the colonial text*. Minneapolis: University of Minnesota Press.

Shore, C. 1993. Community. In *The Blackwell dictionary of twentieth-century social thought*, ed. W. Outhwaite and T. Bottomore, 98-9. Oxford: Blackwell.

SIGTUR. 2001. The origins and development of SIGTUR: New vulnerabilities, new space, and initiative for struggle. Briefing document. SIGTUR: Seoul Conference.

Slemon, Stephen. 1998. Climbing Mount Everest: Postcolonialism in the culture of ascent. *Canadian Literature* 158: 15-41.

Slyomovics, Susan. 1998. *The object of memory: Arab and Jew narrate the Palestinian village*. Philadelphia: University of Pennsylvania Press.

Smith, Byron. N.d. See you at the top: Exploring the leader from within. http://www.byron-smith.ca/motivational/index.html.

Smith, N. 1992. Contours of a spatialized politics: Homeless vehicles and the production of geographic scales. *Social Text* 33: 54-81.

Snyder, Margaret. 1995. The politics of women and development. In *Women, politics, and the UN*, ed. Anne Winslow, 95-116. Westport, CT: Greenwood Press.

Sørensen, Georg. 2004. Nationhood and identity: Community beyond the state. In *The transformation of the state*, ed. Georg Sørensen, 83-102. New York: Palgrave Macmillan.

Spivak, Gayatri. 1985. Three women's texts and a critique of imperialism. *Critical Inquiry* 12 (1): 243-61.

—. 1988. Can the subaltern speak? Speculations on widow sacrifice. In *Marxism and the interpretation of culture*, ed. C. Nelson and L. Grossberg, 271-313. London: Macmillan.

Staeheli, Lynn A., Valerie Ledwith, Meghann Ormond, Katie Reed, Amy Sumpter, and Daniel Trudeau. 2002. Immigration, the Internet, and spaces of politics. *Political Geography* 21 (8): 989-1012.

Steyn, Melissa. 2005. "White talk": White South Africans and management of diasporic whiteness. In *Postcolonial whiteness: A critical reader on race and empire*, ed. Alfred J. López, 119-35. Albany: SUNY Press.

Stienstra, Deborah. 2000. Dancing resistance from Rio to Beijing: Transnational women's organizing and United Nations conferences, 1992-6. In *Gender and global restructuring: Sightings, sights, and resistances*, ed. Marianne Marchand and Anne Sisson Runyan, 209-24. London: Routledge.

Sutcliffe, B. 1999. The place of development in theories of imperialism and globalization. In *Critical development theory*, ed. R. Munck and D. O'Hearn, 135-54. London: Zed Books.

Swedenburg, Ted. 1995. *Memories of revolt: The 1936-1939 Rebellion and the Palestinian national past*. Fayetteville: University of Arkansas Press.

Swyngedouw, E. 1997. Neither global nor local: "Glocalization" and the politics of scale. In *Spaces of globalization: Reasserting the power of the local,* ed. K.R. Cox, 137-66. New York: Guilford Press.

Swyngedouw, E., and N.C. Heynen. 2003. Urban political ecology, justice, and the politics of scale. *Antipode* 35 (5): 898-918.

Sylvester, Christine. 1992. Feminists and realists view autonomy and obligation in international relations. In *Gendered states: Feminist (re)visions of international relations theory,* ed. V. Spike Peterson, 155-77. Boulder: Lynne Rienner Publishers.

Tamale, Sylvia. 2001. Between a rock and a hard place: Women's self-mobilization to overcome poverty in Uganda. In *Women resist globalization: Mobilizing for livelihood and rights,* ed. Marianne Marchand and Anne Sisson Runyan, 70-85. London: Zed Books.

Tamari, Salim. 1999. Palestinian refugees and the Palestinian-Israeli negotiation. *Journal of Palestine Studies* 29 (1): 81-9.

Taipei Times. 2006. King of the Sherpas. *Taipei Times,* 16 June, 15. http://www.taipeitimes.com/News/feat/archives/2006/06/17/2003314145.

Tarrow, Sydney. 1998. *Power in movement: Social movements and contentious politics.* 2nd ed. Cambridge, UK: Cambridge University Press.

—. 2005. *The new transnational activism.* Cambridge, UK: Cambridge University Press.

Taylor, Charles. 2004. *Modern social imaginaries.* Durham: Duke University Press.

Taylor, James Stacey. 2005. *Personal autonomy: New essays on personal autonomy and its role in contemporary moral philosophy.* Cambridge, UK: Cambridge University Press.

Terborgh, J. 1999. *Requiem for nature.* Washington, DC: Island Press.

Thompson, E.P. 1968. *The making of the English working class.* Harmondsworth: Penguin.

—. 1975. *Whigs and hunters: The origin of the Black Act.* New York: Pantheon.

Tollefson, C. 1998. Introduction. In *The wealth of forests: Markets, regulation, and sustainable forestry,* ed. C. Tollefson, 3-15. Vancouver: UBC Press.

Tomlinson, John. 1999. *Globalization and culture.* Chicago: University of Chicago Press.

Tönnies, Ferdinand. 1957 [1887]. *Community and society: Gemeinschaft und Gesellschaft.* Trans. Charles P. Loomis. Ann Arbor: Michigan State University Press.

Trouillot, Michel-Rolph. 2001. The perspective of the world: Globalization then and now. In *Beyond dichotomies: Histories, identities, cultures, and the challenge of globalization,* ed. Elisabeth Mudimbe-Boyd, 3-20. New York: SUNY Press.

Tsing, Anna Lowenhaupt. 2005. *Friction: An ethnography of global connection.* Princeton: Princeton University Press.

Tugendhat, Ernst. 1986. *Self-consciousness and self-determination.* Trans. Paul Stern. Cambridge, MA: MIT Press.

Twight, Mark. 2004. Barbarians at the gate: The gospel of the pure church and a case for a climbing jihad. *Rock and Ice* 138: 54-6.

UNRWA. http://www.un.org/unrwa/index.htm.

Unsworth, Walt. 1989. *Everest.* London: Grafton.

van Reisen, Mirjam. 2001. The "prehistory" of Social Watch: The transformation of NGO networking in ongoing international negotiations. Report prepared for Social Watch. http://www.socialwatch.org/en/acercaDe/dientesDelLeon.htm.

Villares, Ramón. 1980. Idade contemporanea. In *Historia de Galiza,* ed. X.C. Bermejo, M.C. Pallares, X.M. Pérez, E. Portela, X.M. Vázquez, and R. Villares, 221-91. Madrid: Editorial Alhambra, SA.

—. 1998 [1984]. *A historia.* Vigo, Galicia: Editorial Galaxia.

Vosko, Leah F. 2000. *Temporary work: The gendered rise of a precarious employment relationship.* Toronto: University of Toronto Press.

Vreeland, James Raymond. 2001. The effect of IMF programs on labor. *World Development* 30 (1): 121-39.

Wagner, Roy. 1986. *Symbols that stand for themselves.* Chicago: University of Chicago Press.

Wakim, Wakim. 2001. The "internally displaced" seeking return within one's own land: An interview. *Journal of Palestine Studies* 31 (1): 32-8.

Walker, R.B.J. 2000. Both globalization and sovereignty: Re-imagining the political. In *Principled world politics: The challenge of normative international relations,* ed. Paul Wapner and Lester Edwin J. Ruiz, 23-34. Lanham, MD: Rowman and Littlefield.

—. 2004. Sovereignty, exceptions, worlds. In *Sovereign lives: Power in global politics,* ed. J. Edkins, V. Pin-Fat, and M.J. Shapiro, 367-82. New York: Routledge.

Wapachee, George, and Lawrence Jimiken. 1977. Nemaska background documents.

Ware, Vron. 1992. *Beyond the pale: White women, racism, and history.* London: Verso.

Watts, M. 2000. Contested communities, malignant markets, and gilded governance: Justice, resource extraction, and conservation in the tropics. In *People, plants, and justice: The politics of nature conservation,* ed. C. Zerner, 21-51. New York: Columbia University Press.

—. 2004. The antinomies of community. *Transactions of the Institute of British Geographers* 29(2): 195-216.

WCED (World Commission on Environment and Development). 1987. *Our common future.* Oxford: Oxford University Press.

Weaver, J.C. 2003. *History, globalization, globality: Preliminary thoughts.* Institute on Globalization and the Human Condition, McMaster University, Hamilton.

Weldon, Laurel. 2006. Inclusion, solidarity, and social movements: The global movement against gender violence. *Perspectives on Politics* 4 (1): 55-74.

Wells, M., and K. Brandon. 1992. *People and parks: Linking protected area management with local communities.* Washington, DC: World Bank; World Wildlife Fund; US Agency for International Development.

Wharton Center for Leadership and Change Management. http://leadership.wharton.upenn.edu/everest/index.html.

Williams, J.S. 2001. Exporting BC's future. Wilderness Committee Mediawire.

Williams, Raymond. 1976. *Keywords.* New York: Oxford University Press.

—. 1985. *Keywords: A vocabulary of culture and society.* New York: Oxford University Press.

Wilshusen, C.L., S.R. Brechin, P.R. Fortwangler, and P.C. West, eds. 2003. *Contested nature: Promoting international biodiversity with social justice in the twenty-first century.* Albany: SUNY Press.

Wilson, G.A., and R.L. Bryant. 1997. *Environmental management: New directions for the twenty-first century.* London: University College London Press.

Wilson, J. 1998. *Talk and log: Wilderness politics in British Columbia, 1965-96.* Vancouver: UBC Press.

Wilton, Shauna. 2000. Manitoba women nurturing the nation: The Manitoba IODE and maternal nationalism, 1913-1920. *Journal of Canadian Studies/Revue d'études canadiennes* 35 (2): 149-204.

Witte, Griff. 2004. As income gap widens uncertainty spreads. *Washington Post,* 20 September, A1.

Wolff, Janet. 1993. On the road again: Metaphors of travel in cultural criticism. *Cultural Studies* 7 (1): 224-39.

World Tibet Network News. http://www.tibet.ca/en/wtnarchive/2004/12/13_9.html.

Wright, Cynthia. 2003. Moments of emergence: Organizing by and with undocumented non-citizen people in Canada after September 11. *Refuge: Canada's Periodical on Refugees* 21 (3): 5-15.

Yardley, Jim. 2004. In a tidal wave, China's masses pour from farm to city. *New York Times,* 12 September, 6.

Young, Iris Marion. 1990. The ideal of community and the politics of difference. In *Feminism/postmodernism,* ed. Linda J. Nicholson, 300-23. New York: Routledge.

Young, Robert. 2001. *Postcolonialism: An historical introduction.* Oxford: Blackwell Publishing.

Younghusband, Sir Francis. 1926. *The epic of Mount Everest.* Reprint. London: Pan.

Zerner, C. 1999. *Justice and conservation: Insights from people, plants, and justice: The politics of nature conservation.* New York: Rainforest Alliance.

—. 2000. *People, plants, and justice: The politics of nature conservation.* New York: Columbia University Press.

Zochrot. http://www.nakbainhebrew.org/index.php?lang=english.

Zureik, Elia. 1994. Palestinian refugees and peace. *Journal of Palestine Studies* 24 (1): 5-17.

Contributors

Diana Brydon is Canada Research Chair in Globalization and Cultural Studies at the University of Manitoba, where she directs the Centre for Globalization and Cultural Studies and teaches postcolonial literature and theory. Her current research investigates global imaginaries and critical literacies in the context of discourses of home.

William D. Coleman is a Canada Research Chair on Global Governance and Public Policy. He is also founder and director of the Institute on Globalization and the Human Condition and professor of political science at McMaster University. His research interests include theories of globalization, global dimensions of public policy, and the politics of agriculture and food.

Nancy Cook is an assistant professor of sociology and core faculty member of the graduate program in Social Justice and Equity Studies at Brock University. Her research interests include gendered processes of globalization and imperialism and transcultural interactions in Pakistan.

Jasmin Habib is an associate professor in history and global studies at Wilfrid Laurier University. Recent publications include *Israel, Diaspora and the National Routes of Belonging*, "Memorialising the Holocaust: Diasporic Encounters" in *Anthropologica*, and "Both Sides Now: Reflections on the Israel-Palestine Conflict" in *Human Rights Quarterly*.

Monica Mulrennan is an associate professor in the Department of Geography, Planning, and Environment at Concordia University, Montreal. She has worked closely with Torres Strait Islanders in northern Australia and James Bay Crees in northern Quebec for more than fifteen years. Her research interests focus on the politics and knowledge of environmental protection in these indigenous settings.

Peter Nyers is an assistant professor in the Department of Political Science, McMaster University. He is the author of *Rethinking Refugees: Beyond States of Emergency* and the co-editor (with Engin Isin and Bryan Turner) of *Citizenship between Past and Future.*

Robert O'Brien is the LIUNA Mancinelli Professor of Global Labour Issues and chair of the Political Science Department, McMaster University. He is also co-editor of *Global Social Policy.*

Richard J. "Dick" Preston is professor emeritus of anthropology at McMaster University and continues a career-long interest in James Bay Cree culture and the oral tradition that expresses the spiritual basis of the culture. Throughout his career he has been guided and inspired by the programmatic ideas of Edward Sapir.

Scott Prudham is an associate professor in the Department of Geography and the Centre for Environment at the University of Toronto. He is the author of *Knock on Wood: Nature as Commodity in Douglas-fir Country*, co-editor of *Neoliberal Environments: False Promises and Unnatural Consequences*, and an editor of the journal *Geoforum*. His research concerns the relationships among capitalism, environmental change, and environmental politics.

Wendy Russell is an assistant professor at the Centre for Global Studies at Huron University College in London, Ontario. Her current research explores the impacts of neoliberal reforms on daily life in the Nishnawbe Aski region of northern Ontario, Canada.

Jessica Schagerl is a SSHRC post-doctoral fellow in the Department of English and Cultural Studies at McMaster University. She is currently completing a critical edition of the letters of Julia Grace Wales, a Canadian peace activist, written between 1915 and 1917.

Stephen Slemon is a professor in the Department of English and Film Studies at the University of Alberta and a student of imperial and post-colonial representations. His current research focuses on how social understandings of "criminality" circulated in British India from the mid-nineteenth century onwards and on the literature of mountaineering.

Michael Webb is an associate professor of political science at the University of Victoria. He is author of *The Political Economy of Policy Coordination*. His recent publications on the Organisation for Economic Co-operation and Development and global tax governance examine the impact of non-state actors and norms on the revenue-raising side of social welfare policy.

Amanda White teaches courses in gender relations, development and globalization, and applied anthropology in the Department of Sociology and Anthropology at the University of Ottawa. She completed her PhD in anthropology at McMaster University in 2007. Her current research investigates the cultural formation of "the state" in connection to desires for nationhood and social justice in an age of globalization.

Patricia T. Young is a PhD candidate in comparative politics at Rutgers University in New Brunswick, New Jersey. She holds a master's degree in economics from the University of Victoria and is a graduate of the 2007 Arizona winter school of the Institute for Qualitative Research Methods.

Index

Aborigines (Australia), 76

Action Committee of Non-Status Algerians, 126, 128, 132

Action Committee of Pakistani Refugees, 132

activist communities. *See* cyberactivism; transnational activist groups (TAGs); transnational non-governmental organizations (TNGOs)

After the Last Sky: Palestinian Lives (Said), 183

Aga Khan Foundation, 217, 220

Aga Khan Rural Support Program (AKRSP), 220

Agamben, Giorgio: on community and autonomy, 254; on Foucault's "subjectification," 255; on ideology and community, 13, 14; on lack of distinction between private and political, 257; on language and belonging, 256; on the refugee and the nation-state, 258; works by, 253

Agenda 21, 67, 78

agriculture: liberalization of, 171, 172; subsistence, transformation into commercially based agriculture, 172

Air Creebec, 39

al Nakba Oral History project (website), 191

al-Aqsa Intifada, 187

Al-Awda Coalition for the Right of Return (website): activities, 188-9; as alternative

view to US media's pro-Israel standpoint, 189; goals, 188; as transnational Palestinian-centred cyberactivist site, 185

All China Federation of Trade Unions, 171

Alpine Club, 237, 238. *See also* mountaineering

Anderson, Benedict, 7

Anderson, John, 200

Appadurai, Arjun: on assaults against minorities, 258; "culturalism," definition, 48; on imagination and social practice, 9; on imagination, global applications of, 3; on means of communication and sense of belonging, 11; on negative aspects of community, 14

Appiah, Kwame Anthony: on autonomy, 12; on individual rights and community, 15

Aretxaga, Begoña, 110

Association of Women in Development, 146-7

Attawapiskat (Ontario), 37

authority, of Torres Strait Islanders over resources, 75

autocthony: definition, 17; territorial, as insufficient for describing community, 17

autonomy: challenged by deterritorialization of globalization, 141; collective, 28, 120, 212, 213; under colonialism, travel as exercise in autonomy, 225; communal, 5-6, 109-11, 253; and community, 3-4, 14-16,

to social justice organization, 102; original goal of continued mill operation, 90; political role and values, 97-8; protest of unprocessed log exports, 90-1; shifting view of community, as less territorial and more globally political, 93-4, 95. *See also* Cowichan sawmill (Youbou, BC)

Young, Iris Marion, 14

Zapatistas, 34

Zirnhelt, David, 93

Zochrot (website): Israeli site supportive of Palestinian right of return, 191; sponsorship of March of Return in Tel Aviv (2004), 192; as transnational Palestinian-centred cyberactivist site, 185

PRINTED AND BOUND IN CANADA BY FRIESENS
SET IN BEMBO BY GEORGE KIRKPATRICK

Text design: GEORGE KIRKPATRICK
Copy editor: DALLAS HARRISON
Proofreader: LESLEY ERICKSON
Indexer: ANNETTE LOREK